EVALUATING SOCIAL SCIENCE RESEARCH

EVALUATING SOCIAL SCIENCE RESEARCH

Second Edition

Paul C. Stern

National Research Council

Linda Kalof

State University of New York, Plattsburgh

New York   Oxford

OXFORD UNIVERSITY PRESS

1996

Oxford University Press

Oxford   New York
Athens   Auckland   Bangkok   Bombay
Calcutta   Cape Town   Dar es Salaam   Delhi
Florence   Hong Kong   Istanbul   Karachi
Kuala Lumpur   Madras   Madrid   Melbourne
Mexico City   Nairobi   Paris   Singapore
Taipei   Tokyo   Toronto

and associated companies in
Berlin   Ibadan

Library of Congress Cataloging-in-Publication Data
Stern, Paul C., 1944–
Evaluating social science research / Paul C. Stern, Linda Kalof.—
2nd ed.
p. cm.
Includes bibliographical references and index.
ISBN 0–19–507969–8 (alk. paper).—ISBN 0–19–507970–1 (pbk. :
alk. paper)
1. Social sciences—research. 2. Social sciences—methodology.
I. Kalof, Linda.   II. Title.
H62.S7545   1996
300′.72—dc20   95-17528

Printing (last digit): 9 8 7 6 5 4 3 2 1

Printed in the United States of America
on acid-free paper

To Sue Stern and Mary Elizabeth Henry,
with love and appreciation

Preface

When *Evaluating Social Science Research* was written in the mid-1970s, it filled no standard niche in undergraduate curricula of that time. Research methods courses generally were intended only for the training of researchers, so they put strong emphasis on statistical techniques and the technical language of research methodologists, and assumed implicitly that students who learned these things would become good judges of the quality of their own research and that of others. A few psychology professors at Elmira College found this approach inadequate for our students, who could benefit from learning how to be good judges of research but were not likely ever to actually do social science research and had no particular need to learn the technical jargon. We invented a course for research consumers that made concepts and skills the center of attention. This book was one result.

Since the first edition appeared in 1979, much has happened that seems to justify its approach to research methods. The book's basic goals seem, if anything, more important now than they were then. One goal was to train students to be intelligent consumers of social science research. Although few of our liberal arts students would become active social science researchers, they all read research in college and needed to develop a critical understanding of it. The consumer-oriented approach of the book fit well with the "critical thinking" movement that arose in education during the 1980s, and the appearance of several texts with a similar approach to research methods suggests that our perspective was widely shared.

The book also had an educational purpose that was more general, and we think ultimately much more important, than teaching college students how to read critically in the academic journals. Knowing how to make critical, independent judgments of scientific claims is an important skill of living in a world in which scientific claims are increasingly used to influence personal and political behavior. Advertising, for example, is full of supposedly scientific claims, and hardly a day goes by without a major news story trumpeting new scientific findings: about the health effects of indirect exposure to tobacco smoke, the effectiveness of a new treatment for AIDS, the extent of public support for the president's foreign policy, the changing rate of teenage pregnancy, damage to the earth's ozone layer, the effect of coffee drinking on cancer, the effect of capital punishment on murder rates, and many other important issues. The claims are often controversial, and they often contradict previous claims based on scientific evidence. And for each of us, some of the claims make a real personal difference. We are often in a position where we would take action based on the science, if only we knew what to believe. So, to make many important choices in our lives, we need ways to judge the validity of these claims.

Often, we decide what to believe and what to doubt by using an informal rule of thumb, such as "believe the source you trust." There are problems with such guidelines, however. For example, sometimes proponents of both sides of a controversy seem expert and trustworthy. And sometimes, a decision is so important that we want to make our own judgment rather than relying on a simple rule. Should I choose surgery or chemical treatment for breast cancer? Should I cancel a vacation trip to Miami because of reports of crime there? Should I stop drinking coffee because it may increase my risk of a kind of cancer that runs in my family? Should I buy a home in a neighborhood where they are considering placing a solid-waste incinerator? How should I vote in the upcoming referendum on privatizing my children's schools?

This book remains timely because it addresses the perennial need of students and all citizens to develop critical thinking skills. But as science changes, the skills of judging it also undergo change. The changes in the second edition reflect developments in the last 15 years of social science research, both in methods and perspective.

We have added some sections to the book to discuss methods that have become much more prevalent in the social science journals over the past 15 years and issues of validity that are more clearly understood now. Thus, there is explicit discussion of quasi-experimental research design, including an added distinction between equivalent-group and nonequivalent-group experiments. We have also added explanations of the logic of multiple regression analysis, causal modeling, and meta-analysis. In our discussions of these methods and concepts, we have maintained the first edition's strategy of emphasizing the underlying ideas and their implications for the validity of research conclusions, while leaving the mathematics and most of the technical terminology for other texts.

Social science has also changed in a more fundamental way. There is increasing debate and skepticism about the adequacy of the positivistic model of empirical research that provided the philosophical grounding for the first edition of this book and for the rules it offered for evaluating knowledge claims. The debate focuses on several issues. One is the idea that there are valid forms of knowledge and ways of knowing that cannot be judged by the rules we present in this book. We accept that such knowledge exists. The rules and concepts we offer for evaluating knowledge claims in both editions of this book are not the only possible ones, and may not be the only valid ones, but they are powerful ones, valuable for reaching conclusions about a very wide range of conditions in the world. We believe they are indispensable for critical thinking. Still, conclusions reached by following the rules presented here sometimes conflict with conclusions that may result from other ways of knowing. In such situations, it is beyond the scope of this book to adjudicate between the competing claims.

A second focus of debate is the idea that all observations are colored by the observer's theoretical perspective, historical grounding, and social-structural position—that what anyone sees and records is shaped by his or her cultural tradition, disciplinary training, race, gender, social class, economic standing, and so forth. The idea is that some of the world is invisible to certain kinds of observers, or that certain kinds of observers see things in a distorted way, so that they cannot make valid observations themselves or judge the validity of the observations of others. Some critics claim that no amount of training in scientific method can free a researcher from his or her blinders or tendencies to distort reality. This claim implies that all observations are biased. It suggests that valid scientific observation is impossible, and seems further to imply that valid knowledge cannot be attained.

Despite the fundamental nature of these critiques of positivism, some of the arguments of the critics are consistent with our basic understanding of how to develop and evaluate knowledge. In our view, they demonstrate that there is a wider range of threats to the validity of research than were discussed in the first edition. For instance, it has been noted that women, or members of cultural or racial minority groups, may be sensitive to phenomena that men or majority-group members overlook or assume out of existence. If this is the case, it should be possible by using standard scientific methods for those who can make the observations to demonstrate to those who previously could not that the phenomena in question in fact exist. Even distorted perceptions may be correctable by standard scientific methods: if, for example, male and female observers see different things in a marital disagreement, it should be possible, by examining the situation in detail and by looking at the observers' accounts, to determine the source of the differences in perception. The result of this effort may be to uncover new knowledge both about marital disagreements and about sources of bias in scientific observation. We discuss these sorts of issues in a much-expanded section of Chapter 3 devoted to observational methods, in which we identify numerous sources of omission and distortion in observations, discuss the threats they pose to validity, and present ways to address these threats.

Some claims have been made about the effect of the observer's position that raise issues that cannot be resolved by the rules for developing valid knowledge we present in this book. For example, some writers claim that there is some knowledge that men (or white Americans, or some other group) can never grasp, or some insights that certain individuals cannot reach because of their "false consciousness" or psychological defense mechanisms, or that there are such different criteria for developing and validating knowledge in different cultures that a common definition of knowledge for all human beings is impossible. If these claims are literally true, using the analytic methods of this book will not lead to agreement on what is known.

Our response to the debates about positivist methods in social science is, ultimately, to retain the basic thrust of the book. We have made changes to reflect the significant problems of inference raised by the critics of positivism, but we have attempted to move on with the task of evaluating knowledge claims in recognition that the task is more difficult than appears from the first edition. We remain persuaded of the great usefulness of empirical methods that pursue knowledge systematically, that value the effort to separate observations from the preconceptions of the observer, and that assume the possibility of interobserver agreement. We believe that much can be learned about conditions in the world by reducing general propositions to hypotheses testable by specific observations, making the observations, and checking the observations and conclusions by other observers and other methods. Of course, not all disagreements about states of the world can be resolved this way, and the individuals and intellectual communities that use empirical methods will continue to have their own blind spots and prejudices. Nevertheless, rules based on what is often called "scientific method" still have great value. For us, the critiques of positivism are a reminder to remain humble about how much certainty can be attained by empirical research and to be increasingly vigilant for threats to validity.

As researchers or as critical readers of research, we all have our blind spots and our tendencies to distort. We believe that the best strategy for approaching truth in a world of imperfect observers involves a dialogue among researchers and their critics, including the critical readers of research this book is written to train. We hope this book will teach students how to participate in this dialogue by being competent and self-critical practitioners of a very powerful method for judging truth.

The text of the second edition retains language from the first edition that comes from the positivist tradition—in particular, the centrally important terms "statement of fact" and "scientific evidence." We define "statement of fact" narrowly as something that can be confirmed by sensory observation or sensing technology. By adopting this definition, we bypass questions such as whether there can be moral facts, whether knowledge rooted in personal experience (sometimes called "subjective") can be factual, and in what sense the idea of culturally specific facts is a meaningful one. We see such questions as legitimate, but the concept of "statement of fact" as we narrowly define it remains useful regardless of whether or not these other kinds of "facts" are worthy of the term.

Like the concept of "statement of fact," our concept of scientific evidence is useful for addressing a wide variety of observations even though questions remain about the scientific utility of certain kinds of observations. We define "scientific evidence" narrowly to refer to claims that meet two criteria: their abstractions are concretized (usually with operational definitions), and the relevant observations are reliable in the sense of being repeatable or confirmable by other observers. This narrow definition leaves out a variety of evidence that may be valuable for scientific purposes—for example, observations of unique historical events, and observations admittedly colored by the observer's personal involvement with the phenomena being observed, and so not offered for possible replication. The narrow definition puts an extra burden on observations that cannot be independently confirmed, but we see this as appropriate. As already suggested, it is reasonable to presume that all observations are colored in some way; this is argument enough for caution in interpreting any evidence that cannot be confirmed by other observers.

Thus, although we recognize the limitations of the positivist epistemology, we believe that empirical methods based in positivism, but using a process of cross-checking observations and interpretations, remain essential tools for developing knowledge. The recent debates about the validity of positivist science do not, in our opinion, diminish the value of the methods and concepts presented in this book. They do, however, have important implications for the use of those methods and concepts. First, they warn against arrogance: although the methods we present remain valuable, even indispensable, for advancing knowledge, one should never presume that they offer complete or ultimate knowledge. The history of science is too full of widely shared misconceptions to place absolute trust in conclusions, even if they have been repeatedly checked by the members of a research community. The critiques of positivism remind us that knowledge is always tentative.

Second, the recent debates have identified ways of knowing that can supplement the usual scientific methods and provide useful perspectives, added insights, and checks against premature claims of certainty. An example is the insights about gender relations that emerged from feminist consciousness-raising groups in the 1970s. Although these did not come from standard scientific methods, they revealed blind spots and distortions in previous research and generated new hypotheses that could later be confirmed by standard methods.

Third, and perhaps most relevant for this book, the recent questioning of positivist methods underlines the importance of the process of evaluating research. For if it is the case that all observers are inherently biased and that no scientific report can be trusted to be free of unacknowledged but significant assumptions, the best way for knowledge to proceed is by using one set of biases to check the errors of another. A process of dialogue between scientific observers, particularly observers with different perspectives and presumptions, is then essential to the progress of knowledge. Such a dialogue cannot be found in individual research reports, but only in the comparison of these reports, and particularly in the comparison of reports that appear to be inconsistent with each other. The individual who evaluates a body of research literature, such as the student using this book, is thus in a privileged position for advancing knowledge beyond what is known by the scientists whose work he or she reads because he or she can orchestrate the dialogue between perspectives—use each scientific report to critique the others—and potentially arrive at a level of knowledge that makes sense of both scientific consensus and scientific dispute. The recent critiques of positivism thus demonstrate that the activity of evaluating research is not one of mere summarization, but can be a creative activity of advancing knowledge. We always thought we were teaching something important.

In addition to all the people who influenced the first edition of this book, we wish to thank Joan Bossert, our editor at Oxford University Press who elicited this second edition from us. Linda Kalof's work on this book was supported by a Drescher Award from the State University of New York, Plattsburgh. We are grateful to the faculty and students in the Department of Sociology at SUNY, Plattsburgh, for their expressions of support and enthusiasm for this project. We give special thanks to the students in Linda's methods courses (Logic of Sociological Inquiry and Social Research Methods) who helped refine much of her contributions to this edition through their comments and criticisms. For Linda, the book would not have been possible without the encouragement of Tom Dietz, Alexandra and Adam Kalof, and of course Darwin, the golden retriever who lay at her feet from start to finish. Paul Stern expresses his special gratitude to Sue and Sarah Stern, who provided support, encouragement, and education. Their sensitivity to developments in feminist methodology and epistemology and related fields, and their willingness to engage with the positivist assumptions of the first edition of this book, helped lead us to a revision that benefits from the insights of feminist and other critics of positivism. These insights have been sources of intellectual progress for us, and we hope they will help our readers become more careful and critical evaluators of social science research.

Ritchie, Maryland   (P. C. S.)
Grand Isle, Vermont   (L. K.)
January 1995

Preface to the First Edition

This book is the result of a concern shared by several people who have been on the psychology faculty at Elmira College. We felt that our students were insufficiently prepared to devise research or even, in many cases, to read critically in the professional journals. We decided to design a course explicitly for training students in the skills of critically evaluating empirical research. First titled "Advanced General Psychology," the course was used as a prerequisite for Experimental Psychology and other upper-level courses. As interest in the course spread to faculty and students outside psychology, the course broadened into "Evaluating Social Science Research."

This course has been useful to students in several disciplines because its primary focus is on the development of cognitive skills that are appropriate for analyzing any empirical research. These skills, combined with some knowledge of the relevant content areas, give students a good background for critical reading of empirical research in a number of fields.

In the course and in this book, the emphasis is on evaluation of research instead of acquisition of a new methodological vocabulary. Although terms common in methodology textbooks are used, the main interest is in getting students to apply the concepts; I am less concerned about whether they learn to define the terms. This emphasis is reflected in heavy reliance on exercises and problems—students develop critical capacities by practicing them and by getting feedback on their progress.

This book was developed for a particular twelve-week course, yet the rationale behind it is equally valid in other educational contexts. Most likely, it will be used by instructors who, like myself, find themselves teaching research methods to students who do not yet know how to review a body of empirical literature. For such instructors, it will supplement books that emphasize conducting research, handling statistics, and writing research reports, but do not deal with the first step in the research process: the evaluation of existing knowledge about a possible research question.

My hope is that the book will also be used outside of curricula aimed at training people to do competent empirical research. Most undergraduate students will never conduct empirical research, yet the skills taught here are valuable for them too. In fact, the most gratifying outcomes of teaching "Evaluating Social Science Research" are the changes in students who have seen the value of their critical skills in their nonacademic lives. These students report that they now question the poorly supported claims of "experts" whose word they once would have taken on faith. Some put it more strongly: they feel an increased sense of personal control and power because they are able to make important judgments for themselves and need not be dependent on what they hear or read in the popular media. Such reports point to the greatest value of explicit training in critical thinking skills, and they confirm that—at least sometimes—material that has a place in a curriculum can also help people to gain an education.

This work is the result of my interaction with students over a period of five years, and it has benefited greatly from constant revision. But the book owes its very existence to a person I have never met. Dr. James E. Bell preceded me at Elmira College and left behind the idea of teaching a course such as the one eventually created. He also left behind some of his teaching materials. I owe to him the concept of teaching critical thinking through examples and problems, and also some of the terminology used, especially in the first chapter. Dr. Bell continues to teach critical thinking in a more accepting educational atmosphere at Howard Community College in Maryland.

Jim Bell's ideas came to me through Dr. Richard Ek, my colleague at Elmira until 1976, who has provided continual moral and intellectual support for the preparation of these materials. His support and encouragement have been invaluable. Rick continues his educational work at Corning Community College in New York.

I also wish to thank all the students who served as Teaching Fellows over the last five years and who helped teach this material. Special thanks are due to Kathy Parsons, Jan Guild, Eileen Kirkpatrick, Jerry Bortz, Bob Dietrich, Gary Millspaugh, George Greger, Marsha Kokinda, Beth Dalton, Laurel Tormey, Linda Maceda, and Penny Chick, each of whom, in one way or another, is responsible for some of what is in this book. Comments and criticism from other Teaching Fellows and students have also been of great value.

In the typing and preparation of this volume, I have been greatly assisted by the work of Sue Stern, Kim Sykes, Phyllis Peters, Melissa Williams, Linda Maceda, and especially Chris Hummer, who has always managed to find the time to help when it was needed most. Finally, I want to thank Sue and Sarah Stern, who somehow put up with endless hours of my writing and typing in attic, basement, and elsewhere over the years, postponing other things we could have done.

New Haven   P. C. S.
September 1978

Contents

EVALUATING SOCIAL SCIENCE RESEARCH

INTRODUCTION

This book is designed to help you answer two important questions:

1. How can I find out about something I want to know more about?
2. When I do find out, how will I know what to believe?

These two questions cover a huge area, and you may wonder how this book can claim to do so much. Our goals are actually narrower than this. The material here will be most useful if the things you want to know about have certain characteristics.

1. The focus is on questions of *fact*, rather than questions of *value*. Values are relevant to this book only when they raise questions of fact. If you want to know, for example, whether racial integration is good for children, this book will not be of any direct help. Such a value question cannot be decided until you are clear about what you mean by "good." But if you value integration, you may believe in it because it increases understanding between people. This belief raises a question of fact: Do people raised in integrated environments understand others better than comparable people raised in segregated surroundings? Whether or not they do is a factual question, and this book deals with such questions.

A question of fact is one that we try to answer by making observations with our senses of the things we want to understand, and checking the accuracy of these observations against the observations of others. By making observations that can be confirmed by others, we take a step beyond our individual feelings and impressions toward knowledge that can be shared.

Because this book emphasizes knowledge based on observations—what we call "factual knowledge"—there are several important kinds of knowledge that we do not discuss except as they relate to observational knowledge. One of these is self-knowledge. Although its importance has been recognized at least since the ancient Greeks, we do not concern ourselves with it here because it is *private*. If you know something about yourself, other people may not be able to observe what gave you that knowledge—your emotions, physical sensations, desires, and so forth. Self-knowledge is real, but because it is private, we leave it out of the book.

We also leave out knowledge gained by doing (experiential knowledge). You can know how to ride a bicycle, paint a landscape, diagnose a disease from a brief physical examination, or shape a loaf of Italian bread, but these are not kinds of knowledge you can gain by observation alone.

We omit the kinds of knowledge you can gain from interacting with other people. For example, you may know your friends well enough to decide which ones can be brought together to make a successful social gathering. This is sometimes called "second-person knowledge" (Code, 1991)—knowledge that comes from personal relationships between "me" and "you," as opposed to the kind of knowledge described in this book, which may be called third-person knowledge because it comes when "I" observe "it."

We also omit moral knowledge from the book. People may learn to know right from wrong by reading religious and philosophical texts, discussing moral issues with others, and considering their actions in light of their basic values. This knowledge may also be real, but the rules for distinguishing moral knowledge from error are very different from the rules for distinguishing observational knowledge from error.

2. The focus is on questions of fact, not questions of *theory*. Theory is important for factual knowledge both because theory is often based on observation and because inferences from theory raise questions of fact. But the focus in this book is not on how to build theory, or make inferences from it. Our concern is with how to check the inferences through observations.

For example, Freud's theory of the unconscious proposed that dreams have an important psychological function. It follows from the theory that people who are deprived of the opportunity to dream will dream more than usual after dream deprivation. Whether or not this occurs is a question of fact that can be answered by observation (for example, of brain waves during sleep), and the answer to the question is evidence for or against Freud's theory. Theories are tested by making them generate factual statements and appealing to the observational evidence to confirm or disconfirm those statements.

Although this book does not attempt to show you how to make predictions from theories, it does teach you how to pass judgment on the accuracy of predictions. You will not learn how to derive such predictions as "Dream time increases after dream deprivation," but you will learn skills needed to judge the truth of this statement. You will also learn ways to judge how far to generalize from the existing observational knowledge—a skill that is crucial for developing theories.

3. The focus is on questions about people, their institutions, their interactions, and their behavior. We will also look at some questions concerning the behavior of nonhuman animals. These questions fall within the traditional disciplines of psychology, sociology, anthropology, economics, education, political science, psychotherapy, and so on. We focus on these questions because the research methods used to study them are fairly similar, as are the difficulties of getting acceptable answers. Thus, what you learn about evaluating research on a problem related to education will be useful in evaluating research on a sociological problem.

4. The focus is on *evaluating* research someone else has already done. If there are no reported observations pertaining to your question, this book won't help much; it is not a guide for gathering actual evidence. However, if you become good at evaluating other people's research, you will have acquired a skill necessary for doing good research of your own.

With all these restrictions, many different kinds of questions still "qualify." Here are some examples:

Are women more conforming than men?
Is there really a "Hispanic vote" in presidential elections?
Can a teacher's expectation influence a pupil's IQ?
Do anti-abortion laws increase the birth rate?
Does marijuana use impair memory?
What is the effect of a ½% increase in the prime interest rate on the money supply?
Is it true that schools inculcate "middle-class values"?
Is schizophrenia an inherited disease?
Are sex-role differentiations related to the means of subsistence of a culture?
Do people learn better when they are a little anxious?

Of course, it's impossible to "cover" all these topics in one place, and this is not our purpose. This book aims to provide the tools you need to arrive at the best possible answer to your own question, whatever it is. We are assuming that you already have two things when you begin. First: *a subject area you want to find out about.* You are in good shape if you have an interest you can phrase as a question, such as, "What causes juvenile delinquency?" or "Is marijuana psychologically harmful?" If your interest cannot yet be put in question form, consult the Appendix, which is devoted to showing how to turn a general interest into a question answerable by what we define in Chapter 1 as scientific evidence. Second: *at least an elementary knowledge of the language people use in talking about your kind of question.* If you have in mind a sociological question, you should have the equivalent of a sociology course's worth of knowledge of sociological language (or else a strong determination to learn). We are not assuming prior knowledge of statistics, although such knowledge will certainly help you to understand scientific articles. We explain the most essential statistical concepts as they become necessary.

As you start to pursue your question, you will learn new and more specialized language that is meaningful to researchers working on your question. You will also gain exposure to the current theories and methods used in research about your subject. The less you know about the question you are asking, the more you should expect to learn.

In working through this book, you will be learning:

To ask questions so that they are answerable
To use bibliographic resources to find existing research about your question
To use standards of evidence employed by social scientists in judging statements of fact

Although it is possible to learn each of these skills separately, it makes more sense to present them together. If you have a genuine interest in a topic or question, it will be beneficial to learn how to use library resources so that you can frame an answerable question and find the information you need to try to answer that question.

Because this book cannot be written exclusively for your own personal interest area, you should be doing two things as you progress through it: improving the skills you need by using examples in the book for practice, and practicing your skills in your own area of interest by reading scientific material on that subject.

The book is divided into five chapters and an Appendix:

Chapter 1: *Scientific and nonscientific statements of fact*
Chapter 2: *Methods of gathering scientific evidence*
Chapter 3: *Evaluating scientific evidence: What conclusions follow from the evidence?*
Chapter 4: *Evaluating scientific evidence in the published literature*
Chapter 5: *Reviewing a body of literature: The problem of generalization*
Appendix: *Asking answerable questions and finding scientific evidence*

The chapters are presented in a logical order, with the material in each building on what was presented earlier. The Appendix is intended as a reference whenever you begin to search for bibliography and can, therefore, be used at various points in the chapter sequence. The language in the Appendix assumes mastery of the first two chapters.

Each chapter is devoted to a limited number of related skills. Your goal as a student should not be to memorize terms and definitions, but to learn to *use concepts* when evaluating scientific writing. Exercises and problems are included to allow you to practice until the skills are well established, and additional problems may be used for further practice. When you finish the book, you should be able to define a question and find and critically evaluate the available scientific evidence relevant to that question. Thus, you will be better able to know what to believe.

1

SCIENTIFIC AND NONSCIENTIFIC STATEMENTS OF FACT

We define a "statement of fact" as *any statement that you can try to confirm or disconfirm by looking at the evidence of the senses (or sensing technology).* This includes statements that are true, those that are false, and statements about which truth or falsity is undetermined. Thus, both the statement "Smoking causes cancer" and the statement "Smoking is unrelated to cancer" are statements of fact by this definition. Whatever one believes about the truth or falsity of these statements, we can agree that to confirm or disconfirm them, one must appeal to the senses of doctors (who can, with the help of technology, diagnose cancer), and to the senses of anyone at all, who can determine whether someone is a smoker. Although there may be some disagreement about the relationship between smoking and cancer, and while at least one of the statements must be false, both statements are factual in the present sense.

Some statements are not factual in this sense. Consider the statement "Socialism is the best form of government." This is not a statement of fact because of the strong judgmental element in the word "best." One cannot reasonably hope to decide on what is best by making observations, because people differ so much in their criteria for "best." But you could hope to confirm or disconfirm the statement if you knew what its author meant by "best." Thus, before trying to confirm or disconfirm, you would appeal to the author for a definition. Note that definitions are *not* statements of fact. Suppose the author of the statement about socialism said, "By 'best,' I mean 'provides the highest possible standard of living.' " This is the author's definition, and you wouldn't try to confirm or disconfirm it at all. (You could, of course, agree or disagree with it.) If you combine the statement about socialism and the definition that is given to the observationally troublesome word "best," you now have a factual statement: "Socialism gives its people a higher standard of living than any other form of government." This statement is factual in that you would look for evidence to confirm or disconfirm it. It may not be possible to find the evidence that would lead to a clear-cut confirmation or disconfirmation, but this does not change the way you would go about confirming or disconfirming.

We should emphasize that the process of confirming a statement of fact does not necessarily lead to definitive knowledge of "facts." The example of standards of living under socialism provides an illustration. After the Soviet Union collapsed in

7

1991, it became clear that almost all previous estimates of the standard of living there had been too high. Both Soviet officials and economic analysts in the U.S. intelligence community had, perhaps for their own political reasons, overestimated the output of the Soviet economy. The new, revised "facts" made Soviet socialism look worse in economic terms than it had before. This may seem like an extreme example, but even very simple factual statements can be far less than definitive "facts." Consider the "fact" that the population of New York City was 7,071,639 on April 1, 1980. This was the official count of the U.S. Bureau of the Census, but because of illegal immigrants hiding from the census takers, homeless people living in subway tunnels, and others whom the census may not have counted, the official figure is probably too low. The population of New York is factual in the sense that it is countable in principle, but we put the term "fact" in quotation marks because we have no way in practice of knowing exactly what the population is.

Some statements in theoretical discussions are also not factual statements. These include statements that relate parts of a theory to each other, such as "A neurotic symptom both conceals and expresses a repressed wish." While such a statement seems to refer to something in the world, we do not know where or how to look for confirmation until we know more about what the author means by "neurotic symptom," "conceals," "expresses," and "repressed wish." If the abstractions contained in the statement are related to actual people and events so that we know what exactly the author is referring to, the statement can be turned into a statement of fact.

In short, the distinction between statements of fact and other statements is in the way you go about confirming them (and whether you even try to confirm them; you don't, with definitions). If you want to make observations to answer a question, it is probably factual. If it seems that no amount of evidence would matter, it is nonfactual.

The main point of this chapter is to make clear the minimum requirements for what we call "scientific statements." A discussion of statements of fact will make these requirements stand out. Here are some interesting statements of fact:

"Properly spaced children from small families are brighter."

"In a normal two-person conversation more than 65 percent of the social meaning is carried by nonverbal messages."

"Today the war of national liberation . . . has become a favorable breeding-ground for mental disorders."

"A child learns its native language by patient and persistent experiment."

"In large cities, crime rates are higher in disadvantaged Negro areas than anywhere else."

These statements are taken from books and periodicals that attempt to give authoritative information. But are these statements believable? As they stand, none is supported by any evidence. That is, the authors have not, as far as we know now, presented any firsthand knowledge of what they are talking about. They are making assertions of fact, but they have not (yet) reported any personal experience, observations, or data to support their assertions. Such bare statements of fact, with no supporting evidence, are called *unsupported assertions*.[1]

---

1. The term "unsupported assertion," and many ideas throughout this book, are owed either directly or indirectly to Dr. James F. Bell (Bell, 1974). Citations of references in this book use the style of the American Psychological Association: articles are cited by author and date, and the references will be

UNSUPPORTED ASSERTIONS

Unsupported assertions are commonly found in such popular sources as television ads: "Bufferin enters the bloodstream twice as fast as aspirin," political speeches: "violent crime is at its highest rate in U.S. history," and magazines, especially of the sensational type: "New sex therapy saves thousands of marriages." Such statements sound interesting, but it is wise to ask: Is there any evidence? In the case of TV ads, enough people share this reaction that many ads have been compelled to cite their evidence: "According to EPA tests, Chevette delivers 40 miles per gallon on the highway, 24 in the city," or whatever. We expect any reputable source to cite the evidence for its statements of fact.

All the statements of fact quoted at the beginning of this section are supported by something more than just words. We are right to call them all unsupported assertions as they stand, but let us also see what kind of support the authors offer for their statements.

APPEALS TO AUTHORITY

The statement about small families being brighter came from the publication *Intercom* (Small Families are Smarter, 1976), which said it was based on "an intriguingly simple theory posed by Psychologist Robert Zajonc of the University of Michigan." So, small families have brighter children because Zajonc's theory says so. If you can trust Zajonc, or if you believe in the reputations of psychologists at the University of Michigan, you can believe that small families have brighter children. *Intercom* seems to be *appealing to authority*. A statement is supported by appeal to authority if the best evidence offered is that someone else (besides the author) says it is so. The problem with appeals to authority is that there is no factual support for the authority's statement of fact. In a sense, the author has appealed to someone else's unsupported assertion. You may say that a psychologist at the University of Michigan wouldn't make an unsupported assertion, but it is not safe to take anyone's statements on faith. Certainly another psychologist would not accept Zajonc's statement without supporting evidence, even though he is respected in the field.

The statement about nonverbal communication also turns out to be an appeal to authority. The statement comes from a book by David W. Johnson (1973), and is supported by a reference to another source (McCroskey, Larson, & Knapp, 1971). Because we have no idea whether McCroskey et al. have factual evidence to support their statement, we have to conclude that Johnson is making his statement merely on the other writers' authority. If we are unsatisfied with this as evidence, as we should be, we must go to the McCroskey book to see if their statement is supported by evidence.

We can distinguish *appeal to authority* from mere *unsupported assertion* by the fact that in an appeal to authority someone besides the author believes the statement. This is the essential difference. Although it sometimes matters to us who is cited as

found, alphabetically by author, at the end of the book. Our style of citing sources may serve as a model for students in disciplines commonly using this style (e.g., psychology, education, speech and hearing). Students in other disciplines may consult their respective professional journals for stylistic models.

an authority, and while it is reassuring to have a recognized authority on one's side, with scientific questions it is the evidence, not its source, that matters. Some authorities may in fact be better than others, but the best way to get believable facts is by looking for the evidence on which the authorities based their conclusion. It is safer to err by being too skeptical.

Both appeals to authority and unsupported assertions are distinguished by the fact that they offer no *observable evidence*. The only support offered for the statement is verbal. To be believed, statements of fact must be based on observations. When we encounter an assertion, even by a psychologist at the University of Michigan, it is best to consider it unsupported until we find the observations that support it. Once we know what was observed, we can make our own judgments.

STATEMENTS SUPPORTED BY OBSERVATIONS

This last statement is central to understanding what constitutes acceptable scientific evidence: *Once we know what was observed, we can make our own judgments.* Not all observations are scientifically useful. The most basic criterion for scientifically acceptable evidence is that everyone knows what was observed. Some examples will make this clearer.

Consider the statement "Today the war of national liberation . . . has become a favorable breeding-ground for mental disorders." The author of this statement was Frantz Fanon (1966), a black Algerian psychiatrist writing about the war for Algerian independence. The statement is followed by forty pages of evidence in the form of Fanon's observations of patients he interviewed while working in Algeria during this protracted guerilla war. Fanon presents brief case descriptions of people with "mental disorders," including cases of impotence, psychosis, homicidal impulsions, and the murder by 13- and 14-year-old Algerian boys of their European playmate. If we are to decide whether we agree with Fanon that the war of national liberation breeds mental disorders, we must know what he observed, then decide whether these observations justify the conclusion.

Fanon says he has observed "the war of national liberation" and the "mental disorders" he says were "bred" by the war. Wars of national liberation and mental disorders are not things you can observe in the same way you can observe trees, trucks, 14-year-old boys, and other concrete objects. It is usually easy to get observers to agree about which things are trees (in spite of a few disagreements about large bushes) or trucks, or 14-year-old boys (again, in spite of disagreements in some questionable cases), but it is not nearly as easy to get observers to agree about which events are "wars of national liberation" and which people are suffering from "mental disorders." The key terms in Fanon's statement are *abstractions,* and to know what was observed, we must have a concrete understanding of the abstractions. We must know exactly what events Fanon refers to by the terms "the war of national liberation" and "mental disorders." *For observations to be scientifically useful, their abstractions must be concretized.*[2] This is the only way we can know exactly what the author is talking about.

2. The terms "concretized abstraction" and "unconcretized abstraction" are drawn from *Clear Thinking for Composition,* by Ray Kytle (Kytle, 1969).

Concretizing Abstractions

There are two ways to concretize an abstraction. The first is by pointing to every instance. This is practical when there are few instances. For example, when Fanon talks of "the war of national liberation," he makes it clear that he is referring only to the war that was going on in Algeria from 1954 until his book was written in 1961. He does not intend to make a statement about all "wars of national liberation," although what he observed may also occur outside Algeria. For Fanon's purposes, "war of national liberation" has been concretized. However, we may be more interested in the *kinds* of conditions that breed mental disorders than the fact that one particular war may have had this effect. We may also be more interested in the effects of wars of national liberation in general than in the effects of the Algerian war. We may want to know what to expect in the future. Scientists like to draw general conclusions and, where possible, to make predictions. If we are interested in the effect of wars of national liberation, in general, on mental health, we must concretize "war of national liberation" in some way that allows us to know one when we see one. The same is true if we want to make a statement about 14-year-old boys in general, or about such abstractions as prejudice, anxiety, competition, power, intelligence, alienation, or learning.

If we cannot enumerate all instances of an abstraction, or if we want the abstraction to be useful when new instances occur, we must have rules for using the abstraction. Consider Fanon's abstraction "mental disorders." If we want to know how to identify a mental disorder, we need some rules for proceeding. Here are some possible rules:

1. When dealing with hospitalized patients, we can classify people by the most current diagnosis in the medical record. We can specify those diagnoses we consider to be "mental disorders."
2. We can empanel three psychiatrists to examine people in the way they see fit, ask them to decide whether the person has a "mental disorder" or not, and classify people as having mental disorders only when all three psychiatrists agree they do.
3. We could employ a standard psychological test, such as the MMPI (Minnesota Multiphasic Personality Inventory), and state that all people scoring above X value on certain specified scales of the test will be classified as having mental disorders.
4. We could interview people, asking them about their thoughts, feelings, physical complaints, and so on, and decide to classify anyone with more than X number out of a specified list of symptoms as having a "mental disorder."

It should be obvious that many other rules for proceeding can be devised. All the above rules have certain things in common. First, the abstractions in the rules are much more concrete than the original abstraction. It is easier to agree on who is a psychiatrist, what a patient's current recorded diagnosis is, or what the score on a personality test or symptom checklist is than it is to agree on whether a person has a "mental disorder." Second, the rules are stated so that you must, to find out who has a mental disorder, perform a series of *operations* either on the person or the person's records. Because the term "mental disorder" is defined by a series of operations, the four sets of rules stated above are called *operational definitions*. Operational definition is the predominant method of concretizing abstractions in science; it is unusual for an abstraction to be concretized by enumerating instances.

Reliability

The first requirement for observations to have scientific value is that *abstractions be concretized*. This is generally done by using *operational definitions* for each abstraction. It is necessary to concretize abstractions so that we know just what was observed. Unless we can agree on what Fanon means by "mental disorders," it makes no sense to debate whether the war of national liberation bred them. The test of whether an abstraction is adequately concretized is whether independent observers use it in the same way. Operational definitions are used to make it easier for observers to agree, but we should not accept an operational definition as adequate on faith. Consider, for example, rule 4. The symptoms a person complains of might depend on who is doing the interviewing. Thus, the same person may be classified as having mental disorders if the interviewer is female, or a medical doctor, or a fellow Algerian, but not if the interviewer is male, or a nonmedical person, or a European. The fact that operations have been defined for using an abstraction does not guarantee that different observers would use the abstraction in the same way. The same problem exists with the panel of psychiatrists: Unanimous agreement will depend on which psychiatrists are included in the panel. The use of a test such as the MMPI would eliminate much of this problem, because there is no room for interpreting the answers; however, other psychological tests, such as the Rorschach, are evaluated differently by different observers. In short, for observations to have scientific value, there must be assurance that different observers of the same people or events would use the abstractions in the same way. The technical term for this is *reliability*.

Reliability is the second requirement for observations to have scientific value. Independent observers must use the same abstractions in the same way. If psychiatrists are almost always in agreement about who has a "mental disorder," there is high *interjudge reliability*. If a person reports the same history of symptoms from one week to the next, there is high *test retest reliability* (the same questions get the same responses). If someone's score on the odd-numbered items on the MMPI is very close to his/her score on even-numbered items, the test has high *split-half reliability*. Regardless of the technical terms referring to types of reliability, the notion of reliability is that to the extent something looks the same every time it is measured, the measurement technique is reliable. Reliable measurement is a requirement for scientifically acceptable observations.

One might quarrel with some of the operational definitions suggested for "mental disorders." Even if they successfully concretize the abstraction, and even if they can be made to give reliable observations, they may not measure what Fanon was talking about. Can you really evaluate the mental status of an Algerian peasant in wartime with a test developed using peacetime Americans (the MMPI)? Is there a symptom checklist that adequately reflects the types of mental disorders suffered by people who have witnessed their families being tortured, or who have survived a mass murder? Fanon is talking about bizarre and frightening circumstances, and it is hard to believe that any standard set of operations can accurately measure or describe the effects of such events on people's mental state.

The question being raised here is one of the *validity* of the operational definitions. Do they in fact measure what they set out to measure? Obviously, this question is crucial to the evaluation of scientific evidence, and it is the first question to ask about an operational definition after determining that it is reliable. We postpone discussion of validity for two reasons: It is too complex to discuss adequately without further background and, more important, observations can be scientifically useful even though their validity is questioned. If we have reliably measured *something* about Algerians in the war of national liberation, we have usable information, even if what we have measured is not "mental disorder." We may have a measure of psychiatrists' prejudice, or cultural differences in response to standard test materials, or something yet undefined. If an invalid measure of mental disorder is used, it will be useless for the study of mental disorder, but if the measure is reliable, it may become scientifically useful for some other purpose. Thus, for observations to have scientific value, they must *reliably concretize abstractions.* Whether the operational definitions are *valid* is an important question that is discussed in Chapter 3, where we deal with the problem of evaluating scientific evidence.

In summary, for observations to have scientific value, they must satisfy two conditions: All abstractions must be concretized (this is usually done by providing operational definitions), and the observations must be reliable. If we have assurance that independent observers use the abstractions in the same way, we know that given the same events or people, we could reproduce what the author did. Given the same Algerians, and a reliable operational definition of mental disorder, anyone would agree pretty well about which Algerians suffered from mental disorders. These are the basic requirements for scientifically acceptable observations.

When observable evidence does not meet these criteria, we call it *casual observation.* The term "casual" suggests the absence of the care and precision required to ensure that one's observations could be repeated by another observer. If the criteria of concretized abstractions and reliability are met, we will call the observations *scientific evidence.*

Before proceeding, we should clarify what is and is not implied by the distinction between scientific evidence and what we call nonscientific statements of fact. The distinction is simply this: scientific statements are those that can be checked, using methods we describe later in the book, by making observations independent of those of the statement's author. The possibility of independent checking is central to the process of agreeing on what is true about the world, and science provides powerful rules for independent checking. We do *not,* however, imply that scientific statements are more likely to be true than nonscientific ones. The statements of fact that meet our definition of "scientific" can be either true or false, and so can the statements of fact that fail our tests of concretized abstractions and reliability. The difference lies in the ways we have to determine the truth of factual statements. Scientific statements meet criteria that allow us to use certain methods to confirm or disconfirm them by observation. For nonscientific statements, we cannot use those methods, so we have a more difficult time arriving at judgments about truth or falsity that can be cross-checked by other observers.

Let us look briefly at some of the examples of factual statements to see which qualify as scientific evidence.

Fanon said, "the war of national liberation . . . has become a favorable breeding-ground for mental disorders." This statement, in itself, is an unsupported assertion until Fanon provides some evidence to support it. His evidence is in the form of case descriptions of people he met in his work as a psychiatrist. In short, Fanon has made observations. Our problem is to decide whether the evidence is or is not scientific. First, are the abstractions concretized? As we have already said, Fanon makes clear that by "the war of national liberation" he refers to a particular war in Algeria. This is concrete, and does not need an operational definition. But what about "favorable breeding-ground" and "mental disorders"?

Nowhere does Fanon define "favorable breeding-ground," yet it seems fairly clear what he means. He must mean that mental disorders begin more easily, or more frequently, in a war of national liberation than in other situations. He may also mean that the war of national liberation led to types of mental disorder that are not observed under other conditions. "Favorable breeding-ground" implies a comparison between a war of national liberation and something else, some "normal" situation. Fanon's statement can be translated into a statement about the relative frequency of "mental disorders," such as, "The proportion of people suffering mental disorders in a nation increases during a war of national liberation." Thus, we know what is meant by "favorable breeding-ground" once we are clear about what constitutes a "mental disorder."

But "mental disorders" remains unconcretized. Fanon presents cases, but do we know how he decided that the people had mental disorders? Here is what Fanon says: "We shall mention here some Algerian cases which have been attended by us and who seem to us to be particularly eloquent. We need hardly say that we are not concerned with producing a scientific work. We avoid all arguments over semiology, nosology, or therapeutics. The few technical terms serve merely as references" (Fanon, 1966, p. 204). Fanon gives it away by disclaiming interest in producing a scientific work—he knows his observations do not qualify as scientific evidence. The reason why they are nonscientific should be clear. He has selected cases "who seem to us to be particularly eloquent." In other words, the criterion for selection was the subjective judgment of Fanon and, possibly, his co-workers. Further, he avoids "all arguments over . . . nosology." That is, he does not wish to discuss diagnosis. But we cannot agree on who has a mental disorder without setting up a procedure for reliable diagnosis. In other words, Fanon has selected cases that potently promote his point, and has avoided all the essential steps toward producing scientifically acceptable evidence. The advantage of Fanon's work over what sometimes appears in print is that he knows what he has done and admits it. His justification for this procedure seems to be that some of the cases he reports are so bizarre and unusual that these particular mental states could only have been bred in total war. The examples are intended to speak for themselves. Still, the evidence is weak; it does not meet acceptable scientific criteria; it is *casual observation*.

By classifying Fanon's observations as casual, we do not mean to imply that his conclusions are false—only that they are not given with enough concreteness to be checked reliably by other observers. Fanon was a careful observer, and there may be much of value in his conclusions even though they are nonscientific. The case of

murder by adolescents, for example, was apparently so far outside the range of observed behavior in Algeria at the time that the case description alone was enough to
convince many readers of the truth of Fanon's claim. Fanon's work is also valuable
because it may have been the best method of observation available for studying the
mental health of a civilian population during a revolution. After all, a wartime situation makes science difficult; in such a situation, casual observation may be the best
available method for finding truth. Scientific procedures may be nearly impossible to
follow in other situations as well. But we should emphasize nevertheless that one
cannot have as much confidence in the truth of statements based on casual observation as we might like to have, or as we could have if scientific evidence were
available.

Earlier in the chapter, we quoted the statement "Properly spaced children from
small families are smarter," which was published in *Intercom* and attributed to the
psychologist Robert Zajonc. The quoted statement is unsupported; when attributed to
Zajonc, it is an appeal to authority. But does Zajonc have observations to support his
assertion? The article in *Intercom* says that Zajonc's theory is supported by "earlier
large-scale studies in Scotland, France, and The Netherlands." If there was a study,
one can assume that observations were made. But is the evidence scientifically acceptable? We must look at the original assertion to see if the abstractions are concretized. Abstractions: "properly spaced children," "small families," "smarter." *Intercom*
describes the studies as having found that "first-born children from small families did
better on intelligence tests than later-borns and children from large families, regardless of race, class, or income level." This is all the information *Intercom* gives on
these studies. It is hard to be sure whether the evidence is scientific. What is a "small
family"? If the studies define "small family" and "large family" by the number of
children present, and show that the more children, the lower the average intelligence
test score of each, we know what is meant: It is usually easy to agree on how many
children are in a family. We can hope this is what the studies did, but we are not
certain. The term "smarter" seems to be operationally defined as intelligence test
scores. If the same intelligence test was used for all the children in a study, and
"smarter" is operationally defined as the score on the test (higher scores being
"smarter"), again we know what was done. Given the name of the test, we could
repeat the study. But what about "properly spaced"? While these studies *may* give
scientific evidence about the assertion "children from small families are smarter,"
they seem to say nothing about the companion assertion "properly spaced children
are smarter." The latter assertion at this point is based on no more than Zajonc's
authority. To be certain whether the assertion about children from small families is
supported by scientific evidence or mere casual observation, one must look at the
studies themselves. However, since "small families" is so easily concretized and
since "smarter" seems to refer to doing "better on intelligence tests," we can at least
expect that the evidence will prove to be scientific. Still, it is best to be skeptical,
and say the statement is based on *at least* casual observation.

More examples will follow shortly, for you to work on individually. When you
begin reading about subjects of interest, you will have to constantly evaluate whether
or not statements of fact are based on evidence, and whether the evidence is or is
not scientifically acceptable. The best way to improve this skill is to practice.

In this and the other chapters of this book, there are exercises, followed by suggested answers to the questions. These are followed by more problems, for which we have not provided discussion. Constant practice and discussion of the points on which you are unclear are the best ways of gaining the confidence necessary for evaluating scientific writing.

The exercises for this chapter test your ability to use the following key terms:

Unsupported assertion (defined on p. 8–9)
Appeal to authority (p. 9)
Casual observation (p. 13)
Scientific evidence (pp. 10–11)
Concretized abstraction (pp. 12–13)
Unconcretized abstraction (pp. 12–13)
Operational definition (pp. 11–12)
Reliability (p. 12)

A diagram summarizing the distinctions among the four types of statements of fact appears in Figure 1.1. You may find it helpful in making the distinctions and in mastering the exercises.

EXERCISES

These exercises are designed to give you practice in using the key terms on new material.

For each statement of fact, classify it as either an unsupported assertion, an appeal to authority, a casual observation, or scientific evidence. For casual observations, identify an unconcretized abstraction. For scientific evidence, identify a concretized abstraction, and the operational definition stated or implied for this abstraction.

Sometimes the statement you are given is divided into parts. When working these exercises, evaluate the first part on the basis of what is present in that statement. When working subsequent parts, you may refer back to the previous statements to

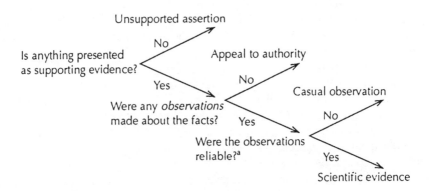

[a]Observations can't be reliable unless the relevant abstractions are concretized.

Figure 1.1 Decision-making procedure for distinguishing among four types of statements of fact.

judge what is said in context. Thus, if an abstraction is unconcretized at first, but is concretized in a later part of the statement, only the later part can be judged as scientific evidence.

Write your answers in the spaces provided. If you have any doubts about the answer, write them down too. You can use your notes to clarify the points you are uncertain about.

1. Everyone knows that alcohol in moderation has therapeutic effects.

2. I've never met a man I didn't like.

3. (a) Cigarette smoking *is* dangerous to health. (b) The Surgeon General's Committee *unanimously* decided to apply the word "cause" to the smoking–mortality relationship.
   (a)

   (b)

4. (a) Tryon (1940) selectively bred strains of maze-dull and maze-bright rats. (b) By the eighth generation, the maze-bright rats made an average of 25 errors in their first 19 trials in a standard maze, while the maze-dull rats made an average of 120 errors in their first 19 trials in the same maze.
   (a)

   (b)

5. According to Rogers (1970) leaderless groups can be as effective as other encounter groups with trained leaders.

6. (a) Dr. Stanley Schachter has reported that effects of a drug depend on the subject's expectations of what the drug will do. (b) Subjects injected with epinephrine and given no information about its effects were more strongly influenced in their reports of their mood by the experimenter's confederates (stooges) than were subjects who had been accurately informed that the drug was a stimulant.

(a)

(b)

7. (a) According to research by Dr. J. P. Jones, women who tolerate stress well have less difficulty from menstrual cramping than women who have difficulty tolerating stress. (b) Jones conducted detailed interviews with 100 consecutive female patients admitted to Sanford Memorial Hospital, and found that those women she classified as high in tolerance to stress were less likely to report a history of painful menstrual cramping than the women classified as low in stress tolerance.
(a)

(b)

8. (a) Early experience with weaning has profound effects on personality. (b) A long-term study of children found that those who were weaned at six months were more possessive than a comparable group of children in the same study who were weaned at one year. (c) The two groups did not differ, however, in their scores on the MMPI (a personality test) given when they reached age 20.
(a)

(b)

(c)

ANSWERS TO EXERCISES

1. Unsupported assertion. No evidence is given.
2. Casual observation. The generalization is based on personal experiences. "Liking" is not concretized.
3. (a) Unsupported assertion.
   (b) Appeal to authority. We do not know the basis for the committee's decision. Although we'd like to believe that such a committee would only act on evidence, we can only take their conclusion on authority, given what we know. (Note that

the statement is an unsupported assertion about the Surgeon General's Committee, but in the context, read it as a statement about the effects of smoking.)

4. (a) Unsupported assertion about Tryon. Taken as a statement about the rats, it is an appeal to Tryon's authority. If you had the reference, you could decide whether Tryon has scientific evidence that he created these two different strains.

(b) This statement is the evidence for the assertion that the rats were, in fact, maze-dull and maze-bright. The abstractions "bright" and "dull" are concretized in terms of *number of errors in 19 trials of running a maze* (the operational definition of dullness or brightness). Call this scientific evidence.

5. The statement about leaderless groups is an appeal to authority. It is not clear whether Rogers' statement is based on any observations of groups. (If you read Rogers, you will find that it is, and you will be able to evaluate the quality of the observations.)

6. (a) Appeal to authority. This is essentially the same as 5.

(b) This is Schachter's evidence. It can be called scientific if all abstractions are concretized. "Epinephrine" is fairly concrete; it is operationalized as administration by injection (since the dosage and time of injection are unspecified, epinephrine is incompletely concretized; the operational definition is incomplete). "Given information" is also concretized; it is operationally defined as being "informed that the drug was a stimulant," as opposed to being told nothing about the drug's effects. "Mood" is made somewhat concrete; it is operationalized as the people's *reports* of their mood. Since we don't know if they merely described their mood, or used a more reliable form of reporting, such as a questionnaire or checklist, the operational definition is incomplete. "Influenced" seems to refer merely to the fact that the mood reports differed for the two groups; this is concrete. In spite of reservations, especially about the abstraction "mood," this statement can be said to be based on scientific evidence.

7. (a) There is no scientific evidence in this statement, although it does make reference to "research." If we can assume that "research" always involves some kind of observation, this must be casual observation, because "tolerating stress well" and "difficulty from menstrual cramping" are unconcretized. However, if Jones' "research" was done in the library, Jones made no relevant observations, and the statement is an appeal to authority.

(b) Here is Jones' evidence, and she *did* make observations. Her evidence is scientific if the abstractions are concretized so that reliable observations can be made. "Women" is concretized. "Menstrual cramping" is also concretized: women either report a history of painful cramps or they don't. "Tolerance for stress," however, isn't clearly concretized. The doctor classified the women on her own, providing no set of rules that another observer could use to measure stress tolerance. We have no way of knowing whether another doctor would have classified the women the same way Jones did. Call this a casual observation.

8. (a) Unsupported assertion.

(b) "A long-term study" presumes that there were observations made. "Weaning" is now concretized as "weaned at six months" versus "weaned at one year." While we might ask if these are the ages when weaning began or when it ended, this is still fairly concrete. "Personality" (the term in statement 8a) is here narrowed to "possessiveness" (presumably a part of personality), but there is no attempt made to concretize "possessiveness." Casual observation.

(c) "Weaning" is used the same way as in 8b—fairly concrete. "Personality" is here operationally defined as scores on a particular test, given at a particular time. Though the MMPI may not cover all of personality, the language is concrete and the observations here are reliable. Scientific evidence. Note, though, that the only scientific evidence in this example fails to support the assertion in 8a.

PROBLEMS

Try your skills on these problems. Answers are not provided. For each statement of fact, classify it as an unsupported assertion, an appeal to authority, a casual observation, or scientific evidence. For casual observations, identify an unconcretized abstraction. For scientific evidence, identify a concretized abstraction and give the operational definition that is stated or implied for the abstraction. If you have any doubts, explain your answer.

1. Reward is most effective when given immediately after a response.

2. Dr. X found that when patients with senile psychoses are given a chance to play a normal role, their symptoms of senility and psychosis diminish.

3. (a) Dr. Y has produced evidence that exposure to televised violence increases children's aggressive behavior. (b) Children in this study watched either a violent TV film (a gunfight from an old Western) or a nonviolent film that also involved physical activity (a cowboy chasing a runaway stagecoach, from the same Western). After the film, each child was observed individually through a one-way mirror during a ten-minute free play period in a room with toys. The number of aggressive acts performed by children who watched the violent film was more than double the number of aggressive acts of children who watched the nonviolent film.
(a)

(b)

4. (a) The available evidence on privacy indicates that people confined together in pairs are less anxious and perform better when privacy is not provided. (b) Taylor, Wheeler, and Altman (1968) found that subjects confined in pairs for eight days in a single room reported themselves less anxious than similar subjects confined in two adjoining rooms (where they could have complete privacy) for the same length of time. (c) In another study, Altman, Taylor, and Wheeler (1971) reported that groups

allowed privacy performed less well on group tasks than nonprivacy groups. (Studies cited above are taken from Freedman, 1973.)

(a)

(b)

(c)

5. Research by Kornhauser (1962, cited by Watson & Johnson, 1972) concluded that 57% of skilled factory workers had good mental health, as compared to 37% of semi-skilled workers and 12% of those doing repetitive work.

6. (a) Oakes (1970) reports significant effects of the steroids in birth control pills on users' feelings of aggression, hostility, nurturance, and affiliation. (b) Women whose pills were high in estrogen concentration scored higher on self-reported aggression and hostility than women taking pills high in progestin. (c) Women taking high-progestin pills scored higher in their reports of nurturance and affiliation. (Cited by Bardwick, 1973.)

(a)

(b)

(c)

7. (a) Social maturity depends partly on intelligence. (b) The most socially mature kids in my second-grade class are also the most intelligent.

(a)

(b)

2

METHODS OF GATHERING SCIENTIFIC EVIDENCE

Chapter 1 set forth the basic requirements for scientifically useful observations. The purpose of this chapter is to introduce you to the major methods social scientists use to gather evidence. You will see that the method a scientist uses is dictated by the kinds of questions he/she can ask, by the amount of knowledge or theory at the scientist's disposal, and by the amount of control the scientist has over events. Although there are many useful distinctions among the methods of gathering scientific evidence, it is convenient to divide these methods into seven categories:

Naturalistic observation
Retrospective case study
Sample study
Correlational study
Within-subjects experiment
Between-subjects experiment, nonequivalent group design
Between-subjects experiment, equivalent group design

In the course of learning to distinguish these seven methods, you will learn some other language useful for evaluating evidence. You will also begin to see how each method has its particular advantages and disadvantages. This knowledge will become increasingly useful when you begin to judge scientific reports.

We introduce the seven methods in the context of an interest you may share with us. We have all heard of the "population explosion" and many of us are concerned about the effects that a vastly increased population might have on individuals and on society. Let us suppose that we are following up our concern by looking for scientific evidence on the effects of crowding, or dense populations, on individuals, their behavior, and their feelings. We are starting out with a general question something like this: "What effects does crowding have on people?" Our goal is to find a scientifically acceptable answer.

Our question contains a key abstraction: "crowding." For evidence to be scientifically acceptable, this abstraction must be concretized in some way. We might choose to make up an operational definition, but most scientists, when they know as little as we do now, would choose the other method of concretizing—they would enumerate a situation (one that intuitively involves "crowding") and observe what happens in that situation. The observations could still be scientifically acceptable, since the situation has been concretely specified. For example, a scientist could observe behavior on a New York subway in rush hour. If the number and location of the people were recorded, we would know concretely what was observed, even though crowding has not been operationally defined. For observations of this type to be useful, they must be carefully *recorded in concrete language*. This method of gathering evidence is called naturalistic observation, and it has some definite rules.

NATURALISTIC OBSERVATION

Naturalistic observation is a method of gathering evidence that strives for complete and accurate recording of relevant events, as they occur, with minimal interference with the events. (Naturalistic observation is usually used when a scientist begins with a general question, such as "What effects does crowding have on people," or other questions of the type "What is the nature of *X* situation?")

> *Complete and accurate recording.* This is necessary for the data to be scientifically useful. We presume in this definition that it is fairly easy to separate the events relevant to a research question (the ones to be recorded completely) from irrelevant events. This is often the case, but not always. Scientists try to record the relevant events completely in order to reduce biases that show up when they record only events that seem important as well as relevant. Once the observer makes any arbitrary selection from what is relevant, we do not see the whole event, but rather the event as the observer saw it. Accuracy is necessary for reliability: The events must be recorded in *concrete language* because this is the only language that independent observers would be likely to agree on.
>
> *Events as they occur.* The most complete records are those made on the spot. Memories are faulty and tend to be selective. When events are filtered through an observer's memory, the observer's report is bound to emphasize one person's idea of what is important and to deemphasize everything else.
>
> *Minimal interference.* It is impossible to make a complete record of events without being noticed (barring hidden cameras), and it is therefore next to impossible to make a record without interfering with events. But, to be "naturalistic," it is important to make an attempt to be relatively unobtrusive, and to avoid any deliberate tampering with naturally occurring events.

Naturalistic observations can sometimes be found in a secretary's notes for the minutes of a meeting. Scientific examples include Jane van Lawick-Goodall's observations of chimpanzee society (1971), and some of Jean Piaget's early work on cognitive development in children. These works tend to be filled with highly detailed accounts of behavior (without inferring motives or thoughts), with any conclusions clearly separate from the evidence on which they are based. Thus, another scientist could agree with the observations of the author but disagree about conclusions.

An example of naturalistic observation of the effects of crowding can be found in Konrad Lorenz's work, *On Aggression* (Lorenz, 1966).[1] Lorenz noted in his observations of the Beau Gregory, a tropical fish, that the fish would attack other members of its species when they intruded into the area occupied by the original fish. Beau Gregories do not similarly attack members of other species, and the "intruding" fish, even though larger, generally retreats from such attacks. It seems as if Beau Gregories have a territory, possibly a "hunting ground," that they defend from encroachment. In the Beau Gregory, one response to being crowded seems to be aggressive attack.

Lorenz's observations of the Beau Gregory can clearly be separated from his conclusions (which appear in the last two sentences of the preceding paragraph). It is possible to agree with the observations but reject the conclusions. But the observations are at least consistent with the conclusions, and they were valuable to Lorenz in that they suggested a general theory that goes beyond the observations. From such observations, with several species of animals, Lorenz theorized that there is a territorial instinct: Animals in general need territory, and respond to invasions of their territory with aggression. It is often true of naturalistic observations that they help suggest theory. They also raise questions that lead to further research. We now know, for example, that crowding is, in at least some species and situations, related to *aggression*. To ask the question "How are crowding and aggression related?" is to suggest a direction for research on crowding.

Before looking at other types of research, some limitations of naturalistic observation can be mentioned briefly. Although the behavior of the Beau Gregory suggested the theory of a territorial instinct, the same observations may be consistent with other theories. For example, the aggressive behavior may reflect a competition for food rather than for territory. Aggression may result from scarcity of life-sustaining resources, and territory thus is not the central issue. Naturalistic observations may yield information that is consistent with a theory, yet it is not always possible to rule out other explanations. To find out whether Beau Gregories are instinctively territorial or merely compete for food, we would have to observe them in a setting where there was unlimited food. Since this does not occur in the natural environment, other methods are needed.

Naturalistic observation has suggested that crowding may cause aggression. One way to test this possibility would be to look at situations in which aggression has taken place, and try to determine whether crowding was a contributing factor. We would then look for a naturally occurring instance of aggression and go *back in time* to see if crowding was an antecedent condition. We might, for example, talk to people right after a fight and ask them to recall the causes. We would then try to evaluate whether feelings of being crowded or being intruded upon were among the causes mentioned. In this method of gathering evidence, it is again unnecessary to operationally define such terms as "aggression" and "crowding," so long as we faithfully record a description of the fight and the statements of the participants. From this concrete information, we can draw tentative conclusions. This method is similar to naturalistic observation in that it avoids interference with events (because the events are in the past, it is successful at noninterference), but it is different in three

---

1. This and other examples of research on crowding used in this chapter were suggested by the discussion in Jonathan Freedman's book, *Crowding and Behavior* (Freedman, 1975).

ways: (1) events are not observed as they occur, (2) because of this, records cannot be complete, and (3) instead of making direct observations, the researcher must rely on the observations and memories of the participants, after the fact. We call this method *retrospective case study*.

RETROSPECTIVE CASE STUDY

Retrospective case study attempts to answer a fairly general question (of the type "Why did X happen?") by gathering evidence after the fact. This evidence might come from talking to people involved, or from looking at records of the events in newspapers, medical records, artifacts, and so forth. A question such as "What factors led to the disintegration of the Soviet Union in 1991?" lends itself to this method. A retrospective case study may study an individual ("Why did he commit suicide?"), or a social system ("Why did the baby-sitting cooperative collapse?"). The hope is usually that a detailed knowledge of what happened in a particular case will lead to principles by which to understand other, similar cases.

Let's look at an example of a retrospective case study that is relevant to the question of whether crowding causes aggression. During the 1960s, a number of riots occurred in crowded African-American neighborhoods in many American cities. It would be interesting to us to find out whether the crowded conditions contributed to the violence. We can look for data in the report of the National Advisory Commission on Civil Disorders (1968). This Commission, chaired by Otto Kerner, then Governor of Illinois, gathered retrospective data on riots and near-riots that occurred in the United States during 1967, in an attempt to find out why the riots happened.

The Kerner Commission researchers used a variety of methods characteristic of the retrospective case study. They interviewed city officials to obtain their accounts of events, and they interviewed rioters, police, nonparticipant members of the community, and others who had firsthand information about events. They conducted surveys of attitudes of blacks and whites in the affected cities. They consulted census data to create profiles of the socioeconomic conditions of blacks and whites in each of the cities studied, both in the neighborhood of the riot and elsewhere in the city. Information was gathered on income, unemployment, age distribution of the population, and many other factors. Weather conditions preceding and during the riot were also recorded. In short, a vast amount of information was gathered in an attempt to find a pattern to the riots: What did cities with riots have in common?

Regarding the effects of crowding, the Commission found that "the final incident before the outbreak of disorder, and the initial violence itself, generally took place in the evening or at night at a place in which it was normal for many people to be on the streets" (National Advisory Commission, 1968, p. 6). The Commission concluded that "crowded ghetto living conditions" were one of the factors that recurred in the 1967 disturbances. However, crowding was not considered one of the basic causes. The basic causes of the rioting, according to the Commission, were white racism, discrimination, frustrated hopes of blacks, a social climate encouraging violence as a form of protest, increased racial pride among blacks, and the actions of the police, who symbolize white power. Crowding was seen as a less important factor, and one that in turn depended on segregation in housing and on patterns of migration of blacks into, and whites out of, the cities. Crowding seems to contribute to violence, but not because of an innate territoriality. The Commission's conclusions suggest that crowding served only to make an unpleasant situation more intolerable.

The report of the Kerner Commission is a good example of a retrospective case study. It asks the question "Why did the riots happen?" and attempts to answer it by gathering information about the past. An advantage of this approach is that there is no other practical way to study mass violence except retrospectively. We cannot make naturalistic observations because we cannot accurately predict when riots will occur. Even if we could, we might feel ethically bound to try to stop the violence; nor can we ethically incite a riot in order to study it. Thus, retrospective study is sometimes the only possible method. At other times, the retrospective method is much more practical than the alternatives. To find a relationship between childhood experiences and later delinquency, or neurosis, or personality development, it is easier to begin with the recollections of the people being studied than it is to observe children and await their development.

The retrospective method also has its limitations. People tend to remember what makes sense to them. Memories of what preceded a riot are colored by a person's ideas about the causes of riots, and memories of childhood are influenced by a person's present feelings about parents and siblings. Thus, memories are distorted by prejudice and preconceptions, and it is often difficult to find other witnesses who can either confirm or question someone's recollections. Furthermore, the results of a study depend on the questions that are (or aren't) asked. The cause of the 1967 riots may have been something that was completely neglected by the Kerner Commission's investigators. Problems like these are discussed in more detail in Chapter 3.

Both naturalistic observations and retrospective case studies are valuable because they provide concrete observations, relatively uncluttered by anyone's theories and conclusions. From such observations, it is possible to produce theories to try to explain the events. We can then look to new events to test the theories. Lorenz's observations suggested the theory of an innate territorial instinct, and this theory implies that crowding will always produce aggression. The Kerner Commission report led to a theory of the causes of urban riots, which in turn suggested that when certain specified social conditions exist, crowding can contribute to riots. In short, both naturalistic observation and retrospective case study are particularly useful for turning a relatively vague question into a theoretical analysis. The theory, in turn, suggests *hypotheses* for future research.

Hypotheses and Variables

A *hypothesis* is a statement of possible fact, usually focusing on one or more abstractions. Here are some examples:

"Animals *respond aggressively* to *crowding*."
"Most Americans *think they are not making enough money*."
"People with *premarital sexual experience* have more *stable marriages*."
"*Intelligence* does not depend on *race*."
"*Education* makes people more *tolerant of other beliefs*."
"The effect of a *deterrent strategy* on the *opponent's response* increases as the *risk of war* increases."

The phrases in italics are the abstractions central to each hypothesis. The prominence of abstractions in these statements suggests the possibility of operationalizing the abstractions and making observations to test the truth of these hypotheses. This is the strategy that is used in the remaining methods of gathering scientific evidence.

It will make sense at this point to look more closely at the process of operationalizing. An operational definition is a *procedure* for classifying, ordering, or measuring something. In the case of "crowding," an operational definition would give us rules for either

Classifying situations (as crowded or not crowded)

Ordering situations (as uncrowded, mildly crowded, moderately crowded, and severely crowded, for example)

Quantifying crowdedness (in a city, we could measure it in terms of the average number of residents per square mile)

When we operationalize "crowding," we are seeing it as a property ("crowdedness") that is measurable by its presence or absence, or else by the amount of it that is present. The concept "crowding" has become the measurable *variable* "crowdedness."

A *variable* is any property of a person, thing, event, setting, and so on that is not fixed. Variables may be properties that are different in different places (crowding in Manhattan vs. central Wyoming) or different times (crowding in a city before and after a large influx of refugees) or different people (some people feel crowded while others in the same place do not). Variables may be relatively concrete concepts such as height, number of people, annual income, and so forth, or abstractions, such as intelligence, alienation, anxiety, stress, political power, and urbanization. It is possible to conceive of variables that are either concrete or abstract. However, since scientific observation requires that variables be measured, all research on variables begins by concretizing them. By operationalizing abstractions like those italicized in the hypotheses above, we turn them into variables. We begin to think of more quantitative questions: "How crowded must an animal be to aggress?" "What percentage of Americans think they are not making enough money?" "Is tolerance greater among college students than among high school students?" Such questions require other methods of observation.

We have seen Lorenz's findings on aggression in animals, and the results of the Kerner Commission report. Each of these sources suggested directions for more research, and both suggested a relationship between crowding and aggression. To learn more, we might next want to ask, "How frequent are different types of aggression when people are crowded?" We could look for an answer by studying a situation generally recognized as crowded (if we concretely describe the situation, we do not have to operationalize "crowded"), and count the instances of aggression. To do this, we must operationalize "aggression." If the crowded situation of interest is "living on Manhattan Island," we might define "aggression" as having been convicted of homicide, aggravated assault, or rape while living in Manhattan. If the crowded situation is the stands at the Super Bowl, "aggression" might be defined as participating in a fistfight or shouting such aggressive slogans as "Kill 'em!"

These operational definitions are fine in theory, but it will be very difficult to get the criminal records of everyone in Manhattan, and it might be even more difficult to accurately determine the number of people in fistfights at the Super Bowl. The difficulties include getting information on everyone (you can't see the whole crowd at once), avoiding mistakes (it is sometimes hard to tell participants from bystanders in a fistfight), and getting *complete* information on anyone. It becomes necessary to draw conclusions from only some of the people in a crowded situation.

Populations and Samples

A *population* is any defined group of people, things, or events. Some examples are "registered Republicans living in Nebraska," "six-year-olds," "revolutions," "Christian church congregations," "city governments," "sixth grade reading texts," and "spectators at the 1995 Super Bowl."

A *sample* is a group of some members of a population. Thus, the Republicans of Scottsbluff are a sample of Nebraska Republicans, the congregations in Los Angeles are a sample of all congregations, and so on. Note that to sample from a population, the population must be concretely defined. To take a sample of revolutions, for example, there must be a concrete definition of "revolution" so that you know whether the events sampled are actually members of the population of revolutions.

It is generally true that when one asks a question such as "How frequent are different types of aggression when people are crowded?" or any similar question of how much or how many, information cannot easily be obtained on the whole population about which the question is asked. It is necessary to draw conclusions about the population from a sample. The discipline of *statistics* has developed ways to describe and draw conclusions about populations using information about samples. You will see statistics at work when you read research in the social sciences; now it is sufficient to present some of the barest principles so that you can understand the nature of the scientific methods that rely on statistics.

To find out how frequent various types of aggression are under crowded conditions, you might enter a crowded situation and observe a sample of people for aggressive behavior, or interview a sample of people looking for evidence of aggressive feelings. You could then attempt to generalize from the sample to the whole population. We use a hypothetical piece of research as an example, for reasons that will soon become clear. In this hypothetical research, a sample of 500 adults living in Manhattan was obtained. Each person was interviewed and asked a number of questions, including some about the person's experiences with aggressive acts during the past year. Fourteen percent reported having been robbed or "mugged" during the past year (only one-third of these reported the event to the police), 20% said they had had their apartments burglarized, and 8% reported a series of annoying or obscene phone calls. A whopping 57% had "felt like physically attacking someone" during the past year (88% of males; 26% of females). (Remember, these percentages are all hypothetical!) We might conclude from these findings that the same percentages hold for all people living in Manhattan. If we draw this conclusion, we might say that the data from Manhattan are consistent with the theory that crowding increases aggression, since there seems to be a lot of aggression in crowded Manhattan. The hypothetical research described here is called a sample study.

SAMPLE STUDY

A sample study is one in which some of the people, groups, or events are sampled from a population of interest, and an attempt is made to draw conclusions about the whole population. These studies usually begin with a question about how much, or how often, or how common something is. Researchers attempt to get an answer by carefully choosing a sample from the population, making observations, and using statistical methods to make inferences about the whole population.

The most common form of sample study involves a survey, using a questionnaire or an interview schedule as in the made-up example. There are other ways of sampling, though. It is possible, for example, to measure the amount of aggressive behavior in a classroom by *observing* the behavior of a sample of the children, during a sample of the school days. The crucial thing about a sample study is that its goal is to *determine the frequency* of something by looking at a selected sample. You will see that in other methods of gathering evidence, samples are also drawn from populations, but the term *sample study* is used here in a restricted sense. By *sample study,* we mean only the pure case, a study whose only purpose is to determine the frequency of some variable (or variables) in a population.

The sample study has an advantage over naturalistic and retrospective methods in that it provides a useful alternative to trying to describe events completely. Scientists who rely on observations quickly find that too much is happening to describe completely, so some selection must be made. Even in a very simple setting, such as a conversation between two people, much more is going on than it is practical to record. There are not only words, but gestures, facial expressions, intonations, interruptions, meaningful silences, and more. Most of this can be captured electronically, as on videotape, but a videotape still contains too much information to put into a report of the observation, and the scientist must select. Since arbitrary choices are likely to reflect the observer's judgments and biases about what is and is not important, and the goal is a set of observations that can be repeated by others, simplifying the setting by some systematic and impersonal means—sampling—is an attractive scientific method.

Another advantage of the sample study is that it is quantitative. In the example of crowding and aggression, sample studies can show not only that there is *some* aggression under crowded conditions, but they can give an idea of how much of a particular kind. Only quantitative methods can clearly point out the magnitude of a phenomenon.

The information we get from a sample study is limited in two major ways, however. First, we must be sure that the sample used is *representative* of the population. To draw conclusions about the population, we must be sure that the people or events sampled do not differ in any important way from the people or events left out of the sample. A look at the problem of sampling the adults living in Manhattan will suggest the difficulty of getting a representative sample. We could list all the million-plus adults and choose randomly (by drawing their names from a giant hat, for example), but we are unlikely to get an up-to-date list. We could obtain a list of all the street addresses and sample those, but which residents do you interview in a multifamily dwelling? Even if you could decide this, you might make several trips before finding the person at home, and the other information may then be out of date. If you took an easy way out and concentrated only on certain neighborhoods, you would have to be sure that the level of violence and crowding in these neighborhoods was representative of violence and crowding all over Manhattan. These sampling problems are discussed in more detail in Chapter 3.

A second problem exists with sample studies, even if you are confident that the sample is representative. Social scientists usually want to understand the relationships between events. If 57% of Manhattanites "felt like physically attacking someone," what does this tell us? It certainly does *not* tell us that Manhattanites are unusually aggressive. Maybe 57% of suburbanites in Scarsdale have the same feelings. And even if we knew that 57% was unusually high, we could not conclude that this aggressiveness was related to crowding. The aggressiveness may be due to other important features of living in Manhattan: the noise level, the air pollution, the ethnic mix of the population, the types of work people do, and so on. (In fact, violent crime has increased in Manhattan over the past few decades while the population has declined.) Sample studies give information, but they do not help clarify the relationships between events.

It is because sample studies do not give satisfying answers to questions about the relationship between crowding and aggression that we found it necessary to invent a sample study to illustrate the method. Sample studies are useful for gathering information about one variable at a time, but social scientists generally want to study the effects of variables on one another. For this reason, sampling methods are usually used as part of more complex methods of gathering evidence. To study the relationship between crowding and aggression, for example, a researcher might take a series of questions about aggressive feelings and give them to samples of people living in cities of varying population density. If people in less crowded cities tended to give fewer aggressive answers, one might conclude that aggressiveness is related to population density (crowding). This research method is called the *correlational study*.

CORRELATIONAL STUDY

The following is an example of a correlational study of the effects of crowding. Mitchell (1971) was interested in the effects of high-density housing on people's physical and mental health and happiness. He operationally defined crowding in terms of the amount of space available per person in the housing units people lived in (more space = less crowding). In the city of Hong Kong, he found people living in the same city under vastly different conditions of crowding (anywhere between 20 square feet and hundreds of square feet per person in the housing units). Mitchell interviewed thousands of people, recording the density of their living space and their answers to questions about their health, their feelings, and their happiness. He also recorded information about income level (since crowding is related to low income, it is important to have this information; we do not want to blame the effects of poverty on crowding). Mitchell sampled the people of Hong Kong, but he was mainly interested in comparing parts of the sample with each other. He had a subsample of people living in very crowded conditions that he could compare with a subsample living in relatively uncrowded conditions in the same city. He was also able to compare people with similar incomes living at higher and lower densities. Thus, he could not only tell whether many people living in crowded conditions complained of nervousness (for example), but he could also tell whether these people were more likely to have the complaint than a comparable group of people (same city, similar income) living in less crowded conditions. Mitchell reported that with comparable groups of people, health, happiness, and mental health were the same in crowded and less crowded conditions.

Mitchell's method was the correlational study. A *correlational study* is one that measures two or more variables and attempts to assess the relationship between them, without manipulating any variable.

Correlational studies begin with an implicit or explicit question: *"Is there a relationship between X and Y?"* In Mitchell's study there were several parallel questions: "Is there a relationship between crowding and health? happiness? mental health?" The term "relationship" can be stated in another way. Mitchell is asking whether knowledge of the density of a person's living space tells anything about health, happiness, or mental health. If we know someone lives in a tiny apartment, can we make a better prediction about his/her happiness, say, than we could without this piece of knowledge? If Mitchell could establish, even for Hong Kong, that people in small apartments are generally less happy than people in large houses, this would mean that knowledge about density was useful for predicting happiness (at least in Hong Kong). The greater the density, the less the happiness. (Mitchell did not find this relationship.)

Notice that a relationship like this gives information in both directions. If you know that "the greater the density, the less the happiness," you can predict that a person in a large apartment is probably happy, and also that a happy person probably has a large apartment. (You *cannot* conclude that the person is happy *because* of the large apartment.)

Relationships between variables often can be translated into simple statements such as "The more of X, the more of Y," or "The more of X, the less of Y." There are also more complicated relationships, such as *"X is greatest at moderate levels of Y, and there is less X with very low or very high amounts of Y."* All these statements have in common the ability to predict either of the variables based on knowledge of the other.

Correlational studies are distinguished from sample studies by the fact that more than one variable is measured, and information is collected about whether the variables are related. If Mitchell had determined that 20% of the people in Hong Kong had less than 40 square feet of living space, and that 22% rated themselves as "unhappy" or "very unhappy," he would have been doing a sample study that measured two variables. Only when he provides information that allows us to tell whether the unhappy people are the same people who are crowded does he give information about the *relationship* between crowding and happiness. Because he has provided this information, his study is correlational.

Correlational studies are distinguished by the fact that they *do not manipulate variables*. A correlational study of crowding and aggression observes and measures these two variables, but it does not either create or modify the crowding or the aggression. If you studied the effects of crowding on aggression by putting people in a crowded room and observing their responses, you would be manipulating crowding, and the study would not be correlational.

The correlational study is a very commonly used method in the social sciences, and it takes many forms, some of which do not, at first, bear much resemblance to Mitchell's study. Here are some examples:

(a) Baby girls (6 to 12 months) who vocalized frequently in a testing situation had higher IQs as adults than girls who did not vocalize (Cameron, Livson, & Bayley, 1967). Note that this study compares two variables (vocalization in infancy and IQ in adulthood) within a single group of subjects.

(b) In towns undergoing political change, political conflicts are much more likely to be rancorous ("dirty" tactics used on both sides) than in politically stable towns (Gamson, 1966). Here there are two groups, politically stable towns and politically unstable towns, and the frequency of the variable "rancorous conflict" is compared.

(c) It has been said that first-borns are prone to seek company when anxious. Therefore, Zucker, Manosevitz, and Lanyon (1968) predicted that first-borns caught in the great electrical blackout in 1965 would be more likely than later-borns to seek the company of others. This study also relates two variables: seeking company (did vs. didn't) and birth order (first vs. later). The study is correlational because it relates the variables (by comparing the frequency of company-seeking in first-borns and later-borns) without manipulating either variable. (The prediction was not strongly supported by the evidence.)

(d) College women waiting to be subjects in an experiment in which they were to receive electric shocks were given the choice of waiting alone or in a group of others. First-borns were more likely to choose waiting in a group (Schachter, 1959). This study is much like (c), in that both studies compare first-borns and later-borns in their affiliative responses to anxiety. The major difference is that the researcher in this study did not wait for the anxiety to be produced naturally. He created a standard anxiety-producing situation to which he exposed his subjects. Thus, Schachter manipulated the situation. He did not, however, manipulate the *variables* he was studying (birth order and affiliation). Schachter *did* manipulate anxiety, but since everyone was in the same anxiety-producing situation, anxiety was presumed to be a constant (not a variable) in the study. Schachter could have manipulated anxiety. For example, he might have told half the subjects that they would be judging the lengths of lines, mentioning nothing about shock. We could assume that these subjects were less anxious than the others. Had the study run this way, Schachter would have been treating anxiety as a variable and he would have been manipulating it. He would have been conducting an *experiment*.

Correlational studies generally *test a hypothesis* about two variables *by observing and measuring the variables* to see if they are related. Correlational studies may bring subjects into a lab and have them do something there, as in example (d), *as long as they do not manipulate the variables involved in the hypothesis*. (When a variable is manipulated, the study is classified as an experiment.) Here's another example of the difference between a correlational study and one that manipulates variables. Hypothesis: Married couples who communicate well with each other are happier because of it. A correlational study to test this hypothesis might have couples play a game like the old TV game "Password," in which one partner gives cue words and the other guesses a target word (Goodman & Ofshe, 1968). The number of cue words needed to elicit the correct answer could measure communication efficiency. The couples could be questioned independently about their married life, and an index of marital happiness, derived from their responses, could be correlated with communication efficiency. If couples who play the game well score high in happiness, the data are consistent with the hypothesis. The same hypothesis could be tested by manipulating the variable of communication. The researcher might take a sample of couples applying for marriage counseling (and therefore presumed to be relatively unhappy as couples) and give half the couples a training program in interpersonal communications skills while putting the other half on a waiting list. If the trained group scores higher on the index of marital happiness there is evidence to support the hypothesis. The couples are happier, presumably because they have learned communications skills. This study differs from the correlational method in that it has manipulated the variable of communication.

An advantage of the correlational study over the other methods discussed above is that it can establish a *relationship* between variables. This can be done only when each of the variables is measured in each individual being studied. Another advantage of the correlational study is that it can be used to evaluate the contribution of third variables. In Mitchell's study, for example, the relationship between crowding and happiness could be studied with income removed as a factor. This was possible because all three variables were measured, and people could be matched on income for purposes of comparison.

A limitation of correlational studies is that they cannot give strong evidence about the causes of the relationship between variables. Reconsider the two studies about whether good communication between marriage partners makes them happier. In the correlational study we find out that people who play "Password" well (i.e., communicate efficiently) are happy, but we don't know if good communication made them happy, or if happiness made them communicate better, or if their common interests were responsible for both their happiness and their success at communication. All we know from this study is that the couples who are happy tend to be the same ones who communicate well.

It is possible for correlational research to produce somewhat more definitive information about causation. Suppose that a number of couples was followed from the time they became engaged for the next five years. Some of the couples break up before marriage, some marry then get divorced, and others are still married after five years, with varying degrees of happiness. If the couples who communicated well at the beginning of the five-year period tended to be those who got married, stayed married, and were happily married after five years, we could at least conclude that good communication was a useful *predictor* of marital happiness. Since we know that efficient communication *preceded* marital happiness, happiness could not have been the primary cause of success at communication. Still, it may be that some couples are more happily *engaged* than others, and that smooth sailing during the engagement period may cause both efficient communication and happy marriages. Other explanations of the communication-happiness relationship are also still possible—for example, common interests could be the cause of both efficient communication and happy marriages. There are even more complex and sophisticated forms of correlational research, which can further increase our confidence about causes. Still, *we cannot make conclusive statements about causes and effects on the basis of correlational studies.*

The study in which people are given training in communication skills provides more certain information about causes than one can usually get from correlational research. We can be reasonably sure that communication training was responsible for increased happiness, because couples who weren't trained did not get any happier.

This study, which manipulates one variable to assess its effect on another variable, is an *experiment*.

EXPERIMENTS: WITHIN SUBJECTS AND BETWEEN SUBJECTS

An experiment is a study in which the effect of one variable on another is measured by manipulating the first variable and observing the second.

The hypothesis in any experiment assumes a cause-effect relationship between variables. In the example about communication skills and marital happiness, communication is assumed to be a cause of happiness. (One could hypothesize the reverse, that happiness improves communication, but that would be the hypothesis of a different experiment.) It is possible to think of an experimental hypothesis as an if . . . then statement: "*If* the communications skills of a married couple are improved, *then* their marital happiness will improve." In general, experiments test hypotheses of the form "*If* you manipulate variable *I*, *then* you will observe a change in variable *D*." [2] That is, the "if" variable is the one manipulated in an experiment. This "variable *I*" is called the *independent variable*. The "then" variable is the one observed; it (variable *D*) is called the *dependent variable*. It is important to note that some hypotheses have independent and dependent variables and others don't. Let's reproduce some of the hypotheses listed on page **26**, and try to translate them into if . . . then form to get a clearer understanding.

"Animals respond aggressively to crowding." This translates as: *If* an animal is crowded, *then* it will respond aggressively. This is a *causal hypothesis*, since it presumes that one variable causes another. In this case, crowding causes aggression, rather than the other way around. This hypothesis (or any causal hypothesis) can be the hypothesis for an experiment. The experiment would get an animal, crowd it, and observe the aggressiveness of its response.

"Most Americans think they are not making enough money." This hypothesis has only one variable, so it cannot be causal. It cannot be stated in if . . . then form, and it cannot be the hypothesis of an experiment.

"People with premarital sexual experience have more stable marriages." This hypothesis asserts a relationship between two variables, but it does *not* imply that one variable causes another. It is very different from the similar-sounding hypothesis "Premarital sexual experience makes for more stable marriages." Although both hypotheses relate the same variables, only the second hypothesis implies that they are causally related. The second hypothesis has independent and dependent variables; it asserts that marital stability is *dependent* on premarital sexual experience. The first hypothesis contains no such implication. It is quite possible that people with premarital sexual experience have more stable marriages, and yet that sexual experience has no effect on marital stability. Both of these variables may depend on age at marriage. People who marry older have had more time to engage in premarital sex; they may

2. Some writers make a distinction between a hypothesis and an "expected finding," reserving the term "hypothesis" for a relationship between the terms of a theory, and referring "expected finding" to what would be expected in a particular study if the hypothesis is true. When we talk about the hypothesis in an experiment, we are referring to the prediction the experiment was designed to test—whether it is a "hypothesis" in the theoretical sense or only an "expected finding."

also be more able to make a mature judgment about whom to marry. If this is in fact the nature of the relationship between premarital sex and marital stability, the first hypothesis would be true and the second false. The hypothesis "People with premarital sexual experience have more stable marriages" is *noncausal;* it does not identify either variable as dependent on the other. It would be inappropriate to test this noncausal hypothesis by manipulating a variable, even if one could be ethically manipulated. A hypothesis like this can be appropriately tested with a correlational study.

"Intelligence does not depend on race." The word "depend" suggests that the hypothesis is causal: race, somehow, is supposed to cause a difference in intelligence. Intelligence is supposed to be *dependent* on race. The independent variable is race, and intelligence is the dependent variable. In theory, this hypothesis could be tested by an experiment. In practice, of course, race cannot be manipulated. Since an experiment is impossible, we must settle for correlational studies, and correlational studies never definitively test causal hypotheses. The reason for this will become clearer in Chapter 3.

"Education makes people more tolerant of other beliefs." This is causal— "makes" gives it away. Tolerance is *dependent* on education; it is the dependent variable. The independent variable is education. An experiment could be done to test this hypothesis.

Several points are embedded in the above paragraphs.

An *experiment* has been defined as a study in which the effect of one variable on another is assessed by manipulating the first variable and observing the second.

In an experiment, the first (manipulated) variable is called *independent*, the second (observed) *dependent*.

The hypothesis in any experiment is causal, and can be written as: "If you manipulate variable I (independent), you will observe a change in variable D (dependent)."

Any causal hypothesis can, in principle, be tested by experiment.

The hypothesis of a correlational study may or may not be causal.

A correlational study can definitively confirm a noncausal hypothesis; it is less than definitive in supporting causal hypotheses.

There are many ways to conduct experiments, but two major types stand out. The following studies in the area of crowding and behavior exemplify these types and the essential differences between them.

McAfee (1987) observed 19 moderately retarded 12–15-year-olds who had been divided into two classes, recording the frequency of their aggressive behavior. Each class was placed in crowded and uncrowded conditions by alternately closing and opening a movable partition that crossed its classroom. Aggressive acts, defined as hostile or threatening verbal behaviors (such as making threats or calling names) or hostile conduct (such as hitting, pushing, or pinching), were observed more frequently in both classes under crowded conditions.

In the other experiment, Freedman, Levy, Buchanan, and Price (1972) randomly assigned groups of adults to meet in either large (about 300 square feet) or small (about 100 square feet) rooms to hear mock jury trials. The cases were designed to sound realistic, and to be weighted somewhat in favor of conviction. Aggressiveness was operationally defined as the severity of sentences given to the defendants. (The researchers found that there was no overall effect of crowding, but that all male groups were more aggressive in the crowded room, while all female groups were less aggressive.)

There are many differences between these studies, including the type of people studied, the way aggression was measured, and the nature of the aggression (physical vs. symbolic). However, both studies manipulated crowding and measured the effects on aggression. There is an important difference in the way crowding was manipulated. McAfee observed the same groups twice, once in the divided room and once in the undivided room. He compared subjects' aggressiveness in the small space with the aggressiveness *of the same individuals* in the large room. An experiment that measures an effect by comparing the same subjects' behavior under different conditions of the independent variable is a *within-subjects experiment,* or within-subjects design.

The study by Freedman et al. had each jury convene only once. Juries met in the large room *or* the small room, but not both. Thus, the effect of crowding was measured by comparing people who met in the large room with *other people* who met in the small room. This study is called a *between-subjects experiment,* or a between-subjects design, because it measures an effect by comparing the performance of *different people* under crowded and uncrowded conditions.

Between-subjects experiments provide very strong evidence about causal hypotheses because researchers can assume that the subjects who experienced an experimental set of conditions were comparable in all other ways to the subjects who did not. If this comparability is in fact achieved, the manipulated variable must have caused whatever differences are observed between subjects at the end of the experiment. But in fact, two different individuals or groups are never identical in all ways. So it is important for evaluating between-subjects experiments to distinguish the ways they try to make subjects comparable.

The jury experiment by Freedman and his colleagues is called a *between-subjects experiment, equivalent-group design* because it achieved comparability between groups by *randomly assigning* the subjects to either the small room (crowded condition) or the large room (uncrowded condition). A between-subjects experiment, equivalent group design tests a hypothesis about variables by manipulating at least one variable, using two or more groups of subjects that are made comparable by randomly assigning each one to a condition of the experiment. Random assignment, or *randomization,* deals with the fact that no two subjects are alike by giving every one an equal chance of being exposed to each condition of the experiment. In this way, the subjects in each group are comparable on the average—although they are not identical, they are equivalent. We explain in Chapter 3 why randomization gives a strong assurance that groups are comparable and why other methods of assigning subjects to groups do not.

Random assignment implies the use of a systematic procedure to give everyone an equal chance of being assigned to each group. Drawing names from a hat, flipping a fair coin, or using random numbers are some acceptable procedures. In the jury experiment, groups of jurors were randomly assigned to either an experimental group that convened in a small room (the crowded condition) or to a control group that convened in a large room (the uncrowded condition). Groups in the two conditions were treated identically except for the size of the rooms in which they met (the operational definition of crowding). Freedman and his colleagues found that groups meeting in large and small rooms did not give sentences of different severity; the authors concluded that aggressiveness was not attributable to crowding alone.

The assumption that the subjects in the treatment and control groups are comparable is necessary in all between-subjects experiments. It would be difficult to compare groups if they differed from each other in important ways besides the independent variable. But there are many instances in which randomization is not possible nor desirable. Between-group experiments that do not employ randomization are common in social science research. These experiments are called *between-subjects experiments, nonequivalent-groups design*.

A between-subjects experiment, nonequivalent-groups design tests hypotheses about variables by manipulating an independent variable and comparing two or more groups that have not been created by randomization. We call such groups nonequivalent because when groups are not formed by randomization, we have no assurance of their comparability. Such groups are only *presumed* to be similar, but they may be different in ways that affect the dependent variable. Baum and Valins (1977) conducted a study of crowding that used a nonequivalent-groups experimental design. Dormitory residents who shared a common area with 33 other students were compared with residents of a dormitory who shared a common area with only 5 other students. Although the two dormitories had comparable densities and amounts of space, students in the larger residential grouping felt more crowded and had less involvement in dormitory social situations. After controlling important background variables to reduce variability in subjects (for example, using only first-year dormitory residents in the analysis), the researchers concluded that the student populations of the two dormitories were basically similar and "that the groups would have been equivalent had it not been for the architectural treatment" (Epstein & Baum, 1978, p. 152). Thus, they attributed observed differences between the groups, such as in involvement in the dormitory's social life, to differences in crowding. But the students had not been assigned to the dormitories at random, so it may still be the case that the students assigned to the two dormitories differed in some way that the researchers did not examine and that would have affected their behavior even if the architecture had been identical. For example, if the students had any choice about which dormitory to live in, this may have influenced the results. Students who like to participate in groups may have preferred the dormitory in which they shared space with a small group, while students who prefer to spend time alone might have chosen the other dormitory, expecting to spend their time mainly in their own rooms. Such a preference would have made the groups nonequivalent, and could explain the study's findings even if crowding has no effect at all.

The second major type of experimental design uses one group only. A one-group or *within-subjects experiment* tests a hypothesis about variables by manipulating at least one variable, and drawing inferences by comparing the subjects' performances under the influence of that variable with their assumed or known performances under other conditions. As in all experiments, the manipulated variable is the independent variable, and changes in the subject's behavior are attributed to the independent variable. In McAfee's study, groups were observed in both large and small spaces.

Changes in their aggressiveness from one setting to the other were attributed to the difference in density between the spaces. Comparable groups are not needed because each person is being compared to him/herself.

In a within-subjects experiment, the effect of a manipulated variable is assessed by looking at the changes it produces in a single subject, or in a series of subjects who are all exposed to the variable. This type of experiment occurs when doctors, having failed with all standard treatments, try out a new medicine on a hopeless case to see if it helps. Any effect is measured by comparing the patient's survival with what would have been expected without the treatment. If the treatment appears successful, it is tried with another patient and another, until it has been used with a series of patients. Each treatment is a within-subjects experiment, and the group of treatments together can be considered a within-subjects experiment.

The within-subjects method of experimentation has been used extensively by followers of B. F. Skinner, who have demonstrated relationships between behavior and its consequences (rewards and punishments) by intensive within-subjects study of single cases. Frequently these studies use *repeated* manipulation of the same variable to demonstrate that behavior changes back and forth depending on whether the variable is present or absent. For example, a child cries every night at bedtime. The parents decide to ignore the crying, rather than give the child any attention (talking to it, punishing it, etc.) Each night, the number of minutes of crying is noted, and within a week, the crying has stopped. (This is the end of one experiment.) At this point, the parents respond to one isolated instance of crying, and to another, and the crying increases in length. (This is the end of a second, if unintended, experiment.) The parents then systematically ignore the crying again, and after a week or two, it stops (a third experiment). If you consider the three parts together as one within-subject experiment, you can see how this method can provide very good evidence of the relationship between two variables (in this case, between attention and crying at bedtime).

The between-subjects experiment with equivalent-groups design is the classical model of experimentation in social science. It both manipulates variables and uses randomization to control for the effects of variables not included in the hypothesis. Experiments that do not employ random assignment of subjects are sometimes referred to as *quasi-experimental designs* because they are experimental in some ways (manipulation of variables) but not others (randomization). As we discuss in detail in Chapter 3, when treatments are not randomly assigned, a study is open to a variety of criticisms on the basis of variables other than the independent variable that might affect the dependent variable. But quasi-experiments are very common in social science research, particularly when randomization is not possible, desirable, or ethical, and also when it is simply difficult to achieve. For example, in the study of dormitory crowding, it would have been difficult to change the university's procedures for assigning students to dormitories just for the sake of an experiment on crowding. But useful data can be obtained by using "natural laboratories" and naturally occurring situations that provide good opportunities for control (Campbell & Stanley, 1963). Even though students were not assigned to dormitories at random, the situations in these two dormitories controlled for a number of variables relevant to crowding, such as overall density, and thus made it useful to collect data on the natural experiment of assigning students to dorms.

Experiments, in general, have an advantage over correlational studies because they can directly test causal hypotheses. With an experiment, it is possible to look for causes by manipulating a variable hypothesized to be causal and observing whether the predicted effect occurs. Between- and within-subjects experiments have their relative advantages and disadvantages. In a within-subjects experiment, it is not necessary to assume that different people are the same for the purposes of the study. One can use people who *are* the same. Unfortunately, people change after being in an experiment. In McAfee's experiment on crowding and behavior, for example, the effects of being in a small space may have carried over to the large space, since the same individuals were involved. McAfee tried to reduce the effect of carryover by alternating between the large- and small-space conditions. Another solution to this kind of carryover problem is to use a between-subjects design, as Baum and Valins did in their experiment. However, the study of dormitory crowding could not randomly assign students to crowded conditions, and there is always the possibility that an uninvestigated variable is causing students to feel crowded, and participate less in social activities. Perhaps students in the larger residential grouping felt more crowded and were less social because they had grown up in smaller families. A solution to this problem is to use a between-subjects, equivalent-groups design, as Freedman and his associates did in their experiment.

After reading about research such as that by McAfee, Freedman, Baum and Valins, and others, you may be wondering what happened to the question we started this chapter with: "What effects does crowding have on people?" It has been transformed in the process of trying to get scientific answers. It may be clear by now that the original question was much too broad to obtain a scientific answer. Naturalistic observations and retrospective case studies can examine broad questions, but they are most often used to *suggest hypotheses* and to *identify variables* that may be worth studying further. The other methods all require operational definitions of variables, and this requires them to deal more in details. By the time you heard about Freedman's research, "effects . . . on people" had been transformed into "aggression," and then into "severity of sentences handed out to defendants." "Crowding" had become a jury meeting in a small room rather than a large one. In the Baum and Valins (1977) study, the effects of dormitory crowding was measured in part by the degree of student involvement in social situations. There are obviously many "effects on people" and many types of crowding that these research studies did not even attempt to investigate.

The process of scientific research is such that it is considered more valuable to have information on the effects of a small jury room on the severity of sentences than it is to have information on the effects of "crowding" in general. This is so because only with operationally defined variables can we be clear about what has been observed, and only with the more sophisticated methods of gathering evidence (correlational studies and, especially, experiments) can we define the relationships between variables and the influences variables have on each other.

When you begin to look for the scientific evidence on a question you are interested in, be prepared to find that the best studies available deal with only a small part of your topic. (The Appendix gives useful hints for refining a general question and for locating detailed studies relevant to your narrowed question.) To make meaningful generalizations, you will have to work backwards from particular, closely related pieces of research on what may seem like a minute part of the problem to research on related subjects of more general interest. Freedman's study of the mock juries, for example, was part of his attempt to determine some of the effects of crowding. His work included a number of experiments and correlational studies conducted in his laboratory, as well as detailed reading and evaluation of the theories and research produced by other people. Freedman's conclusions about the effects of crowding and their implications for life in cities are summarized in his very readable book *Crowding and Behavior* (1975). His general conclusion is that crowding of itself has no specific effect on behavior; it only intensifies the effects of the feelings and social interactions that are already there. Although this conclusion seems reasonable, and is consistent with all the evidence Freedman presents, the book does not resolve the issue of crowding and aggression or the larger question of what effects crowding has on people.

The exercises at the end of this chapter provide practice in identifying hypotheses and variables and classifying reports of research according to the method used to gather the evidence. They specifically test your ability to use these key terms:

Naturalistic observation (defined on p. 23)
Retrospective case study (p. 25)
Sample study (p. 29)
Correlational study (p. 31)
Within-subjects experiment (p. 37)
Between-subjects experiment, nonequivalent-groups design (p. 36)
Between-subjects experiment, equivalent-groups design (p. 36)
Random assignment (p. 36)
Hypothesis (p. 26)
Causal and noncausal hypotheses (pp. 34–35)
Variable (p. 27)
Independent variable (p. 34)
Dependent variable (p. 34)

Before working the exercises, you may want to consult Table 2.1 and Figure 2.1. The figure gives a decision-making procedure for classifying scientific research according to which method was used to gather evidence.

EXERCISES

For each report of research described below:

(a) Classify it as a naturalistic observation, retrospective case study, sample study, correlational study, within-subjects experiment, between-subjects experiment with equivalent-groups design, or between-subjects experiment with nonequivalent-groups design.

(b) If there is a hypothesis, state it, identifying it as causal or noncausal.

(c) Name all variables in the hypothesis, identifying the independent and dependent variables if the hypothesis is causal.

Write your answers in the spaces provided, and also write down any doubts or questions you may have about your answers.

Table 2.1. Seven Methods of Gathering Scientific Evidence

Method	Question Asked	Hypothesis	Variables	Comparison Group	Random Assignment
Naturalistic observation	What happens? (open-ended)	None	None	No	No
Retrospective case study	Why did event (E) occur?	None	None; sometimes one	No	No
Sample study	How often does X (variable) occur? What is its average value?	Sometimes (noncausal)	One	No	No
Correlational study	Are X and Y (variables) related?	Yes (causal or noncausal)	Two or more; none manipulated	Sometimes	No
Within-subjects experiment	Does X (independent variable) have an effect on Y? (dependent variable)?	Yes (causal)	Two or more; one manipulated	No (subjects compared with themselves)	No
Between-subjects experiment, nonequivalent-groups design	Does X (independent variable) have an effect on Y? (dependent variable)?	Yes (causal)	Two or more; one manipulated	Yes	No
Between-subjects experiment, equivalent-groups design	Does X (independent variable) have an effect on Y? (dependent variable)?	Yes (causal)	Two or more; one manipulated	Yes	Yes

1. A Head Start program in Midwest City was used to test the effectiveness of Head Start. A group of disadvantaged preschoolers in Midwest City was chosen to enter the program. IQ tests were given during the first week of the program and again at the end of the school year. There was an average gain of seven IQ points. It was concluded that Head Start can increase children's IQ scores.
   (a)

   (b)

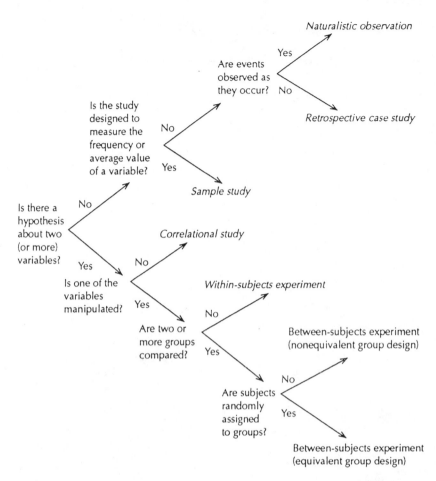

Figure 2.1 Decision-making procedure for distinguishing among seven methods of gathering scientific evidence.

(c)

2. Head Start increases IQ scores. A sample of preschoolers in Midwest City was given IQ tests at the start of a school year, and was then divided into two groups: for each pair of children with the same scores, one child was randomly assigned to the Head Start class, and the other was sent to a traditional day care program. At the end of the year, the Head Start children scored seven points higher on IQ than the paired children in traditional day care.

(a)

(b)

(c)

3. Head Start increases children's IQ scores. Children in Head Start in a ghetto neighborhood of Midwest City scored seven points higher on an IQ test than a group of children from the same neighborhood who went to traditional day care programs.

(a)

(b)

(c)

4. Head Start increases children's IQ scores. Two of the teachers in a large pre-school in Midwest City volunteered to receive Head Start training, and their classrooms were given a full Head Start program for a year. Children in two other classrooms were given their normal program with their normal teachers. At the end of the year, the average IQ score in the Head Start classrooms was seven points higher than the average in the classrooms given the normal pre-school program.

(a)

(b)

(c)

5. Students at Moreland University have an average SAT Verbal score of 520. This was the average score reported by a randomly selected group of 40 Moreland U. students.

(a)

(b)

(c)

6. People who sit at the head of the table tend to become leaders in groups of people who have not met before. In a study using mock juries (Strodtbeck & Hook, 1961) subjects took seats at a table for twelve which had single seats at each end and five seats on each side. When subjects rated each other on the amount each had contributed to the group's final decision, subjects seated at the ends of the table got higher ratings than subjects seated at any other position. It was concluded that people turn to those at the head of the table for leadership.

   (a)

   (b)

   (c)

7. Research indicates that misperception of friendliness as sexual interest occurs commonly in natural settings. Abbey (1987) asked college undergraduates to describe incidents during which their friendliness toward someone of the other gender had been mistakenly perceived as a sexual invitation. The results indicated that misperception is most likely to occur at a party while talking with a casual friend who eventually makes an unwanted move toward intimacy, such as touching or kissing. While most of the incidents were quickly resolved without problems, some incidents involved forced sexual activity, leaving the individual angry, humiliated, and depressed.

   (a)

   (b)

   (c)

8. "A number of years ago I was given a female lamb taken from its mother at birth. My wife and I raised it on the bottle for the first ten days of life and then placed it out in the pasture with a small flock of domestic sheep. As might have been expected from folklore, the lamb became attached to people and followed the persons who fed it. More surprisingly, the lamb remained independent of the flock when we returned it to pasture. Three years later it was still following an independent grazing pattern" (Scott, 1945).

   (a)

   (b)

   (c)

9. Guagnano, Stern, and Dietz (1995) hypothesized that proenvironmental attitudes would have different effects on behavior, depending on the difficulty of the behavior. They conducted a survey in a large suburban area during a period in which the local government was instituting a curbside recycling program, one neighborhood at a time. At the time of the survey, one quarter of the area had curbside pickup of recyclable trash, and people living in those areas had been given blue bins to use to leave their recyclables at the curb. The researchers found that people who had been given blue bins were much more likely to report that they recycled glass, aluminum, and plastic. They also found that proenvironmental attitudes made a difference in the reported behavior of people who did not yet have blue bins, but no difference among people who had been given the bins. They concluded that proenvironmental attitudes make a difference in behavior that is moderately difficult to perform, but that when a behavior is made easy enough (with curbside pickup), differences in attitude no longer matter because nearly everyone's attitude is strong enough to result in recycling.

   (a)

   (b)

   (c)

10. A study compared 25 community leaders in a small Southern city with a group of randomly selected citizens matched with them for sex and age. All subjects

were interviewed, and asked a series of questions about their background, to find differences that might explain community leadership. It was discovered that 17 of the leaders had been members of the YMCA as children, compared with only six of the randomly selected group.

(a)

(b)

(c)

11. Subtle rewards can influence verbal behavior. Subjects were reinforced with a head nod whenever they said plural nouns during an interview. The frequency of plural nouns was higher in the last five minutes of the interview than in the first.

(a)

(b)

(c)

12. In the male South European Emerald Lizard, aggressive behavior is elicited by the colors of the rival male. The inhibition against biting females depends on smell. When Lorenz (1966) colored a female lizard in male colors with crayons and put her in an enclosure with a male, the male attacked with open jaws. On reaching the female, he stopped abruptly and somersaulted over her. He then examined her carefully with his tongue and took no more notice of the male colors. For a long time afterward, "this chivalrous lizard examined real males with his tongue, that is to say he checked upon their smell before attacking them. Apparently it had affected him deeply that he had once nearly bitten a lady!" (Lorenz, 1966, pp. 118–119).

(a)

(b)

(c)

13. Based on data from a representative sample of 3,862 university students, Koss (1985) concluded that 38 percent of college women had experienced sexual victimizations that met the legal definition of rape or attempted rape.

(a)

(b)

(c)

14. To test a prediction that racial isolation led blacks to violence, Ransford (1968) conducted a study of blacks in the Watts section of Los Angeles after the 1965 riot. Ransford asked subjects if they had "ever done anything social" with white people they had contact with on jobs, in their neighborhood, and so on, "like going to the movies together or visiting in each other's homes." Subjects who had had such social contact with whites were less likely than other subjects to say they were "willing to use violence to get Negro rights."

(a)

(b)

(c)

15. Wolfenstein (1951) attempted to outline changing conceptions of child-rearing in the United States over the period from 1914 to the date of her article. She used as data the bulletin *Infant Care,* published by the U.S. Department of Labor Children's Bureau in 1914, 1921, 1929, 1938, 1942, and 1945. Wolfenstein reported that the child in 1914 was seen as having many dangerous impulses

(e.g., masturbation, thumb-sucking) that must be forcibly restrained (e.g., by tying feet to the crib to prevent self-stimulation from rubbing legs together). By 1945, impulses toward self-stimulation are seen as innocuous and less important. Infants were seen as being interested in exploring the world, rather than their bodies. Wolfenstein interprets the data as indicating that a "fun morality," more accepting of play, was emerging in American culture during this period.

(a)

(b)

(c)

16. Schein (1960) interviewed released POWs from Chinese prison camps during the Korean War. He concluded that the key to Chinese success in eliciting false confessions and in persuading prisoners was a procedure that involved destroying social solidarity and interpersonal communication among the prisoners. The conclusion was based on evaluation of many prisoners' accounts.

(a)

(b)

(c)

17. Zimbardo and his colleagues (1974) attempted to show (among other things) how a social structure can bring out brutality in presumably "normal" people. He randomly assigned student volunteers to be either prisoners or guards in a simulated prison. The "prisoners" were arrested by real police, booked, finger-printed, and brought to a "jail" where their care, feeding, and basic privileges were totally controlled by the "guards." In less than a week, some of the guards had become so sadistic and some of the prisoners so hateful that the simulation was canceled for fear it would permanently harm the participants.

(a)

(b)

(c)

18. Muehlenhard (1988) hypothesized that attitudes toward date rape depend on dating scenarios. College students (272 women and 268 men) read brief descriptions of dating situations that manipulated who initiated the date (he asked, she hinted, or she asked), where the couple went (religious function, movie, or his apartment to talk), and who paid the dating expenses (the man paid or they split expenses). Participants then rated how much they thought the woman wanted sex (sex-willingness rating) and how justified the man would be in having sex with her against her wishes (rape-justifiability rating). Ratings on sex willingness and rape justifiability were highest when the woman asked for the date, when the man paid for the date, and when they went to the man's apartment. The sex-willingness and rape-justifiability ratings given by the college women were lower than the ratings given by the men, indicating that a man may misinterpret a date's interest in sex and that he may later feel that he had been led on.
(a)

(b)

(c)

ANSWERS TO EXERCISES

1. (a) Within-subjects experiment.
(b) Hypothesis: Head Start can raise IQ scores of disadvantaged preschoolers. (Because everyone in the study is a disadvantaged preschooler, economic and social situation and age are not variables in this study.) The hypothesis is causal.
(c) Independent variable: Head Start
    Dependent variable: IQ
This is an experiment because the children have been *assigned* to Head Start; the independent variable is manipulated. It is within-subjects because the effect on IQ is measured by looking within each child. When something's "effectiveness" is tested, a causal hypothesis is implied.
2. (a) Between-subjects experiment, equivalent-groups design.

(b) Hypothesis: Head Start increases children's IQ scores. (Essentially, this is the same hypothesis tested in example 1.)

(c) Variables are the same as in example 1.

Again, attendance at Head Start is manipulated, so this is an experiment. Here, however, the effect of Head Start is assessed by comparing the outcome of Head Start with the outcome of a comparison program (traditional day care). Thus, we have a comparison group (between-subjects) design. The groups are equivalent because students were randomly assigned to Head Start or traditional day care. Note that pairing the students by IQ scores is not sufficient to make the groups equivalent. Two children with the same IQ scores may differ in many other ways that could affect their scores at the end of the year—for example, racial or ethnic group membership and parental support for learning. Random assignment gives all the children an equal chance of being included in each program.

3. (a) Correlational study.

(b) Hypothesis: Head Start increases children's IQ scores.

(c) Variables are the same as in examples 1 and 2. The researcher has stated a causal hypothesis, even though these correlational data cannot establish cause and effect. The study is correlational because the children were already in Head Start when the study began. This is an important difference between this study and studies 1 and 2. It may be that children enrolled in Head Start differ from their neighbors in many ways related to IQ. Possibly, children with the most intelligent, or most literate, parents are the only ones who get enrolled, because only these parents have the information that a Head Start school is open. It may also be that Head Start enrolls mainly the kids on the same block as the school, and the block may be in an especially well-off or run-down part of the neighborhood. In other words, differences in IQ found in this study may be due to many factors related to home life, and unrelated to the Head Start program itself.

4. (a) Between-subjects experiment, nonequivalent-groups design. The independent variable, Head Start, was manipulated because two classrooms were selected to get the Head Start Program, and results were compared with two classrooms selected not to get the treatment. Thus, it is a between-subjects experiment. The groups are not equivalent because they were not randomly assigned to treatments. Even if they were randomly assigned to classrooms, the classrooms were assigned to Head Start according to the preferences of the teachers. It may be that the teachers who volunteered for Head Start training were more professionally ambitious than the other teachers, and could be expected to work harder at increasing the abilities of the children in their classrooms. Because of this possibility and others, we cannot be sure the groups were equivalent in all important respects except Head Start.

(b) Head Start increases children's IQ scores.

(c) Variables are the same as in examples 1, 2, and 3.

5. (a) Sample study. The only purpose is to generalize from a sample to the whole population of Moreland U. students.

(b) There is no hypothesis. The study was apparently done to answer an open-ended question: "What is the average SAT Verbal score of students at Moreland U.?"

(c) There *is* a variable (SAT Verbal scores), but with only one variable in the study, it cannot be called either independent or dependent.

6. (a) Correlational study.

(b) Hypothesis: People who sit at the head of a table tend to become leaders in groups of people who have not met before. Noncausal.

(c) Variables: sitting at the head of the table, leadership.

If you look closely, you will see that the variable of seating position at the table was *not* manipulated. Subjects were allowed to choose their own seats, rather than being arbitrarily assigned to seats. Thus, subjects—not the experimenter—were responsible for seating positions. This implies that differences in leadership *cannot* safely be attributed to seating position. It may be that the most assertive subjects chose the end seats, because they wanted attention from the group, or because they were prone to become leaders. Both leadership and seating position might have been determined by subjects' personalities.

The hypothesis is a bit ambiguous as to causality. It asserts that people who sit at the head of the table become leaders, but it does not assert that they become leaders *because* of where they sit. Hence, the hypothesis does not assert a causal relationship between the variables.

7. (a) Retrospective case study. The research was undertaken to collect descriptive information about how misperceptions of friendliness as sexual interest occurs in actual interactions between women and men.

(b) There is no hypothesis.

(c) There are no variables explicitly defined in the study. The college students were expected to render their own interpretations to the meaning of "misperceptions of friendliness as sexual interest" and to describe their experiences on an open-ended format.

8. (a) Naturalistic observation. (You might object that taking a lamb from its mother is manipulative, rather than naturalistic, and you would have a point. We call this a naturalistic observation, because from the time the Scotts got the lamb they proceeded to make fairly complete and concrete observations of its admittedly unusual situation, without manipulating variables, yet minimizing interference with the lamb's life.)

(b) There is no hypothesis.

(c) There are no variables explicitly being studied.

9. (a) This is both a correlational study and a between-subjects experiment, nonequivalent-groups design. The relationship between proenvironmental attitudes and behavior is studied correlationally: neither variable is manipulated. But the effect of the curbside recycling program on behavior is studied experimentally: some people had been given blue bins for curbside pickup and others did not yet have the curbside program. The report does not tell how individuals were assigned to get blue bins, but "one neighborhood at a time" does not appear to be a random method of assignment, so we cannot be certain that the households that had blue bins were comparable to the other households in all ways that might affect their recycling behavior. The researchers took advantage of a "natural experiment," an ongoing process in which a variable of interest was manipulated (though not by them), to gather data on a dependent variable in a quasi-experimental manner.

(b) Hypothesis: Proenvironmental attitudes have different effects on behavior, depending on the difficulty of the behavior.

(c) Variables: This hypothesis contains two independent variables (proenvironmental attitudes, and difficulty of behavior), and one dependent variable (proenvironmental behavior, operationally defined as self-reported recycling). One independent variable, difficulty of behavior, is manipulated (by providing blue bins and curbside pickup), and the other, proenvironmental attitudes, is not. The hypothesis is tested in a study that is partly correlational and partly a quasi-experiment. The study illustrates why quasi-experimental designs are common in research on public policy. It might be possible to assign each household in the area at random to receive curbside pickup either early or late, but it is much easier and less expensive to assign households to start curbside pickup by neighborhoods because that allows the haulers of recyclables to stop at every home in some neighborhoods and drive by the others, rather than going everywhere in the area and stopping at a scattering of houses.

10. (a) We call this a *retrospective case study* on the grounds that the study seems to have proceeded from a fairly general question "What background produces leaders in this city?" Although researchers identified one variable, leadership, they did not clearly specify other variables with which they believe leadership correlates.

The researchers did, however, choose to look into the subjects' "background" for answers, and it can be assumed that they were asking for only selected background information. Since the study did relate leadership to a finite (and probably preselected) number of other variables, it seems also to be a *correlational study*. One could say that the researchers began with the idea that leadership depends on a person's background—a vague sort of hypothesis. The conclusion that YMCA membership is related to leadership is clearly correlational. Either answer, if adequate justification were given, seems appropriate.

(b) No hypothesis; if this is a retrospective case study. If you see it as correlational, you must assume an implicit hypothesis, such as "a person's background *determines* that person's leadership." This hypothesis is causal. The implicit hypothesis may also be noncausal: "People from different backgrounds are not equally likely to become leaders."

(c) In a retrospective case study, there are no variables "in the hypothesis." Leadership is apparently conceptualized as a dependent variable for which independent variables are being sought. If this is seen as a correlational study, the dependent variable is leadership, and the independent variable is "background" or some similar abstraction.

11. (a) Within-subjects experiment.

(b) Subtle rewards can influence verbal behavior. Causal.

(c) Independent variable: subtle rewards
    Dependent variable: verbal behavior

Another, possibly more precise way to state this hypothesis would be: "Nonverbal reinforcement of a verbal response increases the frequency of that response." This is more precise because the nature of the dependent variable is much clearer when it is identified as the *frequency* of the response. This tells us exactly what kind of variability is being measured.

There is no comparison group in this study, so it is a within-subjects experiment. Since behavior is measured both before and after subtle rewards are given, the subjects are being compared with themselves.

12. (a) Within-subject experiment. (This reads like a naturalistic observation, and it is, in the sense that more-or-less naturally occurring events are carefully described in concrete language. However, by coloring the female lizard, Lorenz has manipulated a crucial variable.)

(b) Hypothesis: "In the male South European Emerald Lizard, aggressive behavior is elicited by the colors of the rival male. The inhibition against biting females depends on smell." Both color and smell are involved in the hypothesis, but only color is manipulated. You could actually say that this is an experiment (within-subject) on the effects of color, and a naturalistic observation of the effects of smell. Thus, the hypothesis *of the experiment* is that "aggressive behavior is elicited by the colors of the rival male." The hypothesis is causal.

(c) Independent variable: colors of the male lizard

Dependent variable: aggressive behavior

13. (a) Sample study. The study was designed to determine the frequency of rape among college women.

(b) There is no hypothesis.

(c) There is one variable studied, rape.

14. (a) Correlational study. Although a survey method was used, and a sample was taken, the purpose was more than one of generalizing from a sample. From the start, the study was investigating the relationship between two variables. For this reason, it is not a sample study. It is not a retrospective case study, even though retrospective methods were used, because retrospective case studies do not have hypotheses in advance.

(b) Hypothesis: Racial isolation is a contributing cause of black violence. Causal.

(c) Independent variable: racial isolation

Dependent variable: black violence

Because neither variable is manipulated, the study is correlational. Given Ransford's results, it is possible that willingness to use violence may produce racial isolation, rather than the other way around. It is plausible that blacks who are willing to voice approval of violence to a researcher might also turn off white acquaintances enough to qualify as "isolated." Thus, this correlational study cannot strongly support its causal hypothesis.

15. (a) Retrospective case study.

(b) There seems to be no hypothesis. The study appears to have been conducted to answer a general question: "How have conceptions of child-rearing in the U.S. changed from 1914 to the 1950s?"

(c) Since there is no hypothesis, there are no variables in the hypothesis. The abstraction "conceptions of child-rearing" is really too vague to qualify as a variable (we don't even know along which dimensions these conceptions may vary), but other abstractions coming out of the study (such as "dangerous impulses" attributed to children, interest in exploring the outer world–vs.–own body, etc.) would qualify as variables. Since these variables were not anticipated by the author, I have classified the study as retrospective, rather than correlational.

16. (a) Retrospective case study.

(b) No hypothesis. Schein seems to have been trying to explain how the Chinese were so successful, but he does not have a hypothesis beforehand.

(c) No variables "in the hypothesis." One could say that the variable "success in persuading" is being studied as a dependent variable, with the independent variable(s) to be determined. The interviews led Schein to suggest that social solidarity and interpersonal communication may have been potent independent variables.

This "case study" of a social structure was built up from interviews with a large number of the participants. Because the interviewees may have been in several different prison camps, it is not a case study in the technical sense of studying one particular time and location. Retrospective case study is the most appropriate category.

17. (a) Between-subjects experiment.

(b) Hypothesis: Social structures (the social structure of a prison, to be more specific) can bring out brutality in "normal" people. The hypothesis is causal.

(c) Independent variable: social structure (of a prison)

Dependent variable: brutality

This is clearly an experiment, because the social structure was manipulated, and people were put into it. We call it a between-subjects experiment because the people who became brutal (presumably the "guards") can be compared to the other subjects ("prisoners"), who were exposed to different—you might say opposite—social pressures. It is an equivalent-groups design because students were randomly assigned to be "prisoners" or "guards." Zimbardo's experiment as described could be called a within-subjects experiment, the striking feature of which was the *increasing* brutalization of the subjects. As time went on, people changed in comparison to themselves. The direction of causality in the hypothesis is clear. Zimbardo's point is that prison makes people brutal rather than brutality causing people to become prisoners or guards, as is often argued.

18. (a) With respect to the hypothesis stated in the first sentence of the description, this is a within-subjects experiment. Each participant received all the experimental stimuli (they each read all the dating scenarios). Thus, to determine how attitudes toward date rape depend on dating scenarios, the subjects are being compared to themselves. The researchers also drew a conclusion about the particular tendencies of college men to misinterpret a date's interest in sex. This conclusion was based on a comparison between men's and women's responses to the same experimental stimuli, rather than within individuals. The analysis tested the implicit hypothesis that "a man may misinterpret a date's interest in sex," and as far as this analysis goes, the study is correlational because neither variable, gender nor sex willingness, was manipulated.

(b) The hypothesis of the within-subjects experiment is "attitudes toward date rape depend on dating scenarios." It is causal. The hypothesis of the correlational study, "a man may misinterpret a date's interest in sex," seems to be causal also. The misinterpretation is presumably caused by something about being a man, possibly something in the experience of socialization about dating. The findings, of course, establish only a relationship, not causation.

(c) In the within-subjects experiment, the independent variable is dating scenarios (more specifically, there are three variables—who asked for the date, where the date took place, and who paid the expenses). The dependent variable is attitudes toward date rape (more specifically, perceived sex willingness of the woman and perceived justifiability of rape).

In the correlational study, the independent variable is gender and the dependent variable is "misinterpreting a date's interest in sex." In fact, the two dependent variables measured are the same as in the within-subjects experiment, but Muehlenhard interprets a discrepancy between men's and women's responses as a misinterpretation by the men, presumably on the assumption that on the average, women's responses in the experiment accurately reflect what women would feel in the situations described in the scenarios.

PROBLEMS

Try your skills at these problems; answers are not provided. For each report of research described below:

(a) Classify it as a naturalistic observation, retrospective case study, sample study, correlational study, within-subjects experiment, between-subjects experiment, nonequivalent-groups design, or between-subjects experiment, equivalent-groups design.

(b) If there is a hypothesis, state it, identifying it as causal or noncausal.

(c) Name all variables in the hypothesis, identifying the independent and dependent variables if the hypothesis is causal. Write down any doubts you have about your answers.

1. Rabin (1965) studied men's and women's motives for having children by asking them to complete sentences such as "Men want children because . . . ," "Women want children because . . . ," and so on. Two judges classified all responses under categories of motivation such as altruistic, narcissistic, and so forth. Almost half of the men's motives were narcissistic, involving proof of virility, perpetuation of self, and so on, while only nine percent of the female respondents mentioned "proof of femininity" as a motive for having children.

(a)

(b)

(c)

2. A researcher attempted to decrease the aggressive behavior of a preschooler via a program of rewards for nonaggressive behavior. The child was given praise

whenever he was able to interact with another child without any physically aggressive acts. At first, praise was given at the first sign of acceptable behavior, but as such behavior became more frequent, the reward was made contingent on longer and longer intervals of nonaggressive interaction. During this period, the frequency of the child's aggressive outbursts consistently decreased until it was almost zero.

(a)

(b)

(c)

3. An investigator observing seating patterns in a bus station waiting room observed that people almost always sit at opposite ends of benches less than eight feet long, except when both ends of the benches are already occupied. He suggested that the management might be able to seat more people comfortably if they replaced the benches with separate chairs.

(a)

(b)

(c)

4. On the basis of interviews with 112 commuting students at Suburban Community College, a researcher reported that only 8% were currently coming to school in car pools. Of those who were not pooling, 63% had considered the idea but had rejected it. The most commonly stated reasons for not pooling were inconvenience of schedule (31%), lack of information about who was available to pool with (22%), and the feeling of a loss of independence (19%).

(a)

(b)

(c)

5. To test the effectiveness of written requests—what behavioral psychologists call "prompts"—on proenvironmental behavior, Geller, Wylie, and Farris (1971) handed out one-page fliers to shoppers entering a convenience store encouraging them to purchase their soft drinks in returnable bottles. The researchers then observed customers' purchases when they were and were not distributing the fliers. The percentage of customers purchasing most of their soft drinks in returnable bottles increased by 32% when the fliers were being given out.

(a)

(b)

(c)

6. A group of people who had used LSD twenty times or more was given a battery of psychological tests. Compared to the norms for these tests for the general population, the LSD group differed significantly in one respect: LSD users scored higher than the general population on a test measuring social introversion. It was concluded that the use of LSD tends to make people withdraw from social contacts.

(a)

(b)

(c)

(d) Why is the conclusion unacceptable on the basis of the evidence given? (This study was not really done.)

7. Rose and Frieze (1989) investigated whether or not there are gender differences in behavioral expectations on a first date. Participants were asked to list 20

expected actions involved in a first date for a woman and for a man. The lists of exceptions for women emphasized the private sphere (concern about appearance, conversation, and controlling sexuality); the lists of exceptions for men focused on control of the public domain (planning, paying for, and orchestrating the date). The results indicate that young adults' interpersonal "scripts" for dating maintain the traditional gender-power relationship.

(a)

(b)

(c)

8. Janis and Mann (1965) tested the effectiveness of role-playing techniques in an attempt to change cigarette smoking behavior. Smokers were randomly assigned either to play the role of someone who has just been informed she has lung cancer or to listen to a recording of such a role-playing session. Two weeks later, the number of cigarettes smoked daily had declined in the role-playing group compared to the subjects who only listened to role-playing.

(a)

(b)

(c)

9. Antunes and Gaitz (1975) hypothesized that members of disadvantaged ethnic groups would "compensate" by having higher levels of social and political participation than persons of the same social class who are members of the dominant social group. They found that while blacks generally do participate more than whites of the same social class, Mexican-Americans tend to participate less than whites.

(a)

(b)

(c)

10. The effects of sexually violent music on males' attitudes toward women and acceptance of violence against women were studied by St. Lawrence and Joyner (1991). Undergraduate men were randomly assigned to listen to one of three types of music: sexually violent heavy-metal rock, Christian heavy-metal rock, or easy-listening classical. One month before and again immediately after the exposure to music, participants were administered the Attitudes toward Women Scale, and four subscales measuring rape-supportive beliefs. The results indicated that exposure to either kind of heavy-metal rock music, regardless of lyrics, increased males' sex-role stereotyping and negative attitudes toward women.

(a)

(b)

(c)

11. In a study to determine the effect of anxiety on response to perceptual cues, people who scored either high or low on the Taylor Manifest Anxiety Scale were asked to observe two simultaneous events. Subjects faced a screen on which groups of dots appeared at irregular intervals. At each presentation, subjects were asked to report the number of dots. Subjects were also asked to press a key whenever they saw a light flash at the edge of the screen. The number of errors in counting dots and in failure to respond to lights were measures of responsiveness. On both measures, the low-anxiety group scored better (fewer errors).

(a)

(b)

(c)

12. Eder and Parker (1987) conducted an ethnographic study of adolescents' peer activities in middle school. The researchers found that extracurricular activities

shaped student behavior along the lines of traditional gender roles. Males received status and recognition through athletic activities that emphasized competition, achievement, and aggression. But female athletes did not have high status among their peers. Instead, females acquired status through cheerleading activities that emphasized appearance, attractiveness, smiling, and "bubbly personalities."

(a)

(b)

(c)

3

EVALUATING SCIENTIFIC EVIDENCE: WHAT CONCLUSIONS FOLLOW FROM THE EVIDENCE?

You are now ready to begin evaluating scientific evidence. You have learned how to distinguish scientific evidence from nonscientific statements (Chapter 1) and how to discriminate among the major methods of gathering scientific evidence (Chapter 2). You may also have attempted to formulate a question that is answerable by scientific evidence and to find some of the evidence relevant to your question (using the strategy outlined in the Appendix). If so, this evidence may now be before you. The rest of this book is devoted to teaching the skills that will allow you, once you have found the evidence, to decide for yourself what conclusions to draw from it.

To get an idea of the dimensions of this task, consider a piece of research. Glock, Ringer, and Babbie (1967) theorized that the function of churches in our secular society is to compensate people for their social deprivations. This theory suggested the hypothesis that the more socially deprived people are, the more involved they will be in church activities. To test this hypothesis, the authors evaluated social deprivation and church involvement in a sample of Episcopalians from 234 congregations. Social deprivation was measured on a zero to eight point scale with people being given points for being female (two points), over 30 (one point), over 50 (one more point), unmarried (one point), childless (one point), and middle class (one point) or lower class (two points). The total points assigned to a person was the social deprivation score. Church involvement was measured on the basis of subjects' responses to questions about their participation in specific church activities. The researchers found that the higher a person's social deprivation score, the higher the index of church involvement. The results supported the hypothesis, and were taken as evidence for Glock's theory of the function of churches. (Glock and his colleagues presented more evidence than this, but this summary is enough for our purposes.)

The authors' conclusion is clear, but we should not accept these conclusions without first checking them ourselves. It is proper to ask two kinds of questions about a study before we accept its conclusions:

1. Do the data support the authors' conclusions with respect to the population studied? (In this study, we ask whether social deprivation influenced church involvement among U.S. Episcopalians in 1952, the year the data were collected.)

2. If the conclusions are sound, do they generalize beyond the population sampled and the setting studied? (We must ask whether Glock's results generalize to other churches and to other years. Remember, Glock theorized about *all* churches, but studied only one religious denomination.)

The first question involves what Campbell and Stanley (1963) have called *internal validity*. A study has internal validity to the extent that the data support conclusions about the hypothesis in the specific instance studied. We make judgments about internal validity by examining the details of the study itself and the reasoning that the author used to draw conclusions from the evidence. For instance, we examine the procedural details of the study to decide whether the procedures used to measure and manipulate variables faithfully represented those variables. The Glock study has no internal validity unless the social deprivation scores actually measure social deprivation. For example, if the assumption that people over 30 are more socially deprived than people under 30 is false, the operational definition of social deprivation is not measuring social deprivation, and it follows that conclusions about social deprivation cannot be drawn. The same kind of problem exists with the measure of church involvement. When people are asked about their participation in church activities, they sometimes say what they feel they should have participated in, rather than what they actually did. If this happens to any great extent, the "index of involvement" may be more an index of guilt about church activities, and conclusions about church involvement cannot be drawn. These illustrations should suggest that procedural details can make a difference in what a study is actually measuring. It is difficult to judge the internal validity of a piece of research.

A careful look at the conclusions the author drew from the evidence can sometimes reveal errors of reasoning that undermine the conclusions that seem to follow from the study. Suppose that the Glock study does not have measurement problems—that the scales actually measure what the authors claim. If so, the study would show that socially deprived Episcopalians are more strongly involved in church activities than are others of their faith. But it does not show that social deprivation was a *cause* of their church involvement. And even if the Glock study, combined with other evidence, convinced you that social deprivation did cause these people's church involvement, knowing this would not be enough to support Glock's hypothesis, even for Episcopalians, that "the function of churches . . . is to compensate people for their social deprivations." If we somehow knew that social deprivation caused people to become more involved in church, we could only conclude that compensating for deprivation is *one* of the functions that church involvement has for socially deprived people. We would have learned nothing about what other functions church might have for them, or for other people, or about why people who are not socially deprived join churches.

Glock's study illustrates that even when research produces just the results the researcher expected, the study may not mean what it seems. It is particularly easy to jump to the conclusion that if a study is consistent with its hypothesis, the hypothesis must be correct. In reading research reports, look out for such errors in reasoning. It is especially important to be alert when the research results support your own preconceived ideas, because that is when we are least critical of our own reasoning or someone else's.

The purpose of this chapter is to teach you which questions to ask about the procedures and observations used in a study so that you can make your own judgment of a study's internal validity. Although we do not emphasize the kinds of reasoning problems just mentioned, you will learn how to scrutinize research and uncover many kinds of flaws in imperfect research (and if you look closely enough, almost all research is imperfect). By looking carefully at the pitfalls in research you will increase your ability to make independent judgments about the factual claims that researchers make, and also gain an appreciation of well-conducted research when it can be found. In the exercises and problems, we give you summarized research reports to analyze and evaluate in terms of the concepts presented here. (Chapter 4 provides practice in using the same skills to evaluate actual reports from professional journals.)

The second question mentioned above concerns whether the findings of a study can be generalized to other populations and settings. This involves *external validity,* and it only has meaning once the internal validity of a study has been established. A study has external validity to the extent that its results can be generalized to other situations in which the same variables operate. Thus, Glock's findings have external validity if they hold for other churches in other times, and for other types of social deprivation besides those Glock measured. As this example may suggest, external validity is best determined by comparing the findings of different pieces of research about the same variables. The evaluation of external validity is discussed in Chapter 5.

According to the working definition presented above, a study has *internal validity* when it is possible to draw conclusions about the hypothesis from the data. Internal validity depends on the link from concrete observations to the abstractions they are supposed to be related to; from operational definitions to their corresponding variables. For example, Glock's study has no internal validity unless people's *reports* of their church activities reflect their actual involvement in the church. If these reports actually reflect a desire to look like a good Christian, or to please the interviewer, or to conform to behavioral standards in the community, the authors have measured not church involvement, but some *extraneous variable.*

An *extraneous variable* is a variable capable of explaining the findings of a study without invoking the hypothesis. In other words, the presence of an extraneous variable allows for *alternative explanations* of a set of observations: either the observed relationships are due to the variables in the hypothesis, *or* they result at least in part from an extraneous variable.

A researcher's central problem in demonstrating the internal validity of a piece of research is to achieve control over extraneous variables—there must be a way to rule out alternative explanations of the findings. For example, here is an alternative explanation of Glock's results: women in our society are supposed to be a religious influence in the family, so they may claim more church involvement than they actually have. Because the operational definition of deprivation gives women higher scores than men, this explains why people who score high on deprivation also score high on church involvement. This alternative can be ruled out if high social deprivation scores are related to high involvement scores when only women (or only men) are compared. In such groups, the relationship of social deprivation scores to church involvement scores cannot be due to gender differences.

The task of judging internal validity is the task of interpreting evidence. In Chapter 1, it was noted that "for observations to have scientific value, they must reliably concretize abstractions." Thus, useful evidence must be in concrete language. But there can be many ways that evidence may relate to the abstract variables we are really interested in. So the logical jump from concrete evidence to abstract variables is crucial to the scientific process. To evaluate a scientist's report of research, one must identify the scientist's conclusion from the evidence (the hypothesized explanation), and compare it with other possible conclusions (alternative explanations). Internal validity increases as these alternative explanations can be ruled out.

This chapter provides a guide for finding alternative explanations for social scientists' findings. It introduces some common extraneous variables and gives information about where to expect them and how they may be controlled. You will come across many new terms. Keep in mind that your purpose is not to memorize the terms but to get a feeling for the extraneous variables that exist in various types of research, so that you can suggest alternative explanations for research findings you read. Your primary goal is to learn to analyze and evaluate research reports.

This guide is organized around the seven methods of gathering evidence presented in Chapter 2. Because each of these methods has its own procedures, each has its own characteristic extraneous variables. Consequently, your search for alternative explanations of the evidence will take different directions depending on the method used to gather the evidence. Some extraneous variables are almost universal problems in scientific research, while others cause difficulty primarily with particular research methods. The most basic research method (naturalistic observation) tends to raise the most universal problems, while the most refined method (experiment) has its own particular difficulties.

NATURALISTIC OBSERVATION: PROBLEMS OF OBSERVER INTERFERENCE AND IMPERFECT RECORDING

Observation is the most basic method of gathering scientific evidence, and it raises the most basic questions about validity—questions that arise in all methods of empirical research. We can see these questions by looking closely at the definition of naturalistic observation, which has two main requirements:

1. Complete and accurate recording of the relevant events
2. Minimal interference with the events

In practice, neither of these requirements can be completely met: researchers can only strive to approach them as ideals. The ways they fall short of the ideals open the possibility for alternative interpretations of observations. Let's look first at the ideal of minimal interference with events.

Problems Caused by the Presence of an Observer

Naturalistic observation strives to introduce "minimal interference with events," but there is no way to know for certain how much the observer's presence has changed things. To find out, we would have to observe the events both with and without the observer, and see how much difference there is. This is, of course, a logical impossibility and therefore we can never be sure how much the research process has changed the people and events being studied. The methods of naturalistic observation have raised this issue, yet it is obviously crucial to all methods of social science research.

The presence of an observer can affect observations in many ways. We divide them into two categories. When people behave differently because of a desire to create some kind of impression on the observer, we refer to these temporary changes as "on stage effects" (Agnew & Pyke, 1969) to suggest that people are acting for the benefit of an audience. Observers can also cause more persistent changes in the people and events they are observing that may continue even when the observer leaves the scene. We discuss these types of observer-produced effects separately.

"On Stage" Effects Experience has taught social scientists to identify situations in which the research process is most likely to interfere with events. One type of effect an observer can produce by merely being present has been called the *"on stage effect"* (Agnew & Pyke, 1969). This theatrical metaphor suggests that people may begin to "act" when they are aware there is an "audience." The problem of "putting on an act" can be expected to become more serious the more aware people are that there is an audience, the better they know what about them is being observed, and the more the subject of observation is personal or controversial. That is, the more difference it makes to people what impression they make, the more likely they are to act for the researcher. Below are some classic types of "on stage effects" and some methods used to control them.

Social desirability. People sometimes tell an observer what they think they "should" say. When people are asked about their values, many tend to report culturally acceptable values, even when they do not hold them. Such people's responses are influenced by their perceptions of social desirability. When people's adherence to a social norm is observed, it is reasonable to assume that the observer's presence may increase *apparent* conformity.

Evaluation apprehension. Sometimes people believe the observer to be somehow judging their personal adequacy or mental health. This belief, called evaluation apprehension (Rosenberg, 1965, 1969) obviously becomes stronger when the observer is labeled "psychologist." The effects of evaluation apprehension depend on the subject's perception of what mentally healthy people are supposed to do in the situation being studied.

Looking bad. Subjects of research occasionally try to make themselves look bad. This is perhaps due to a desire to sabotage the research or because the person feels something can be gained by looking bad. Some mental patients have been seen to do this when they fear being released from a comfortable hospital stay (Braginsky & Braginsky, 1967).

Demand characteristics. People sometimes try to please a researcher by doing what they think she/he wants them to do. Someone who means to please may become attuned to subtle cues in the interaction, called demand characteristics (Orne, 1962), that give a clue to what the researcher is looking for. Orne originally argued that subjects could be expected to accept these cues and would try to do whatever they thought the researcher wanted. However, subjects might also use these cues to "sabotage" the study, or to outwit the researcher. There is evidence that this is a common attitude among people coerced into being research subjects, such as students who become subjects to fulfill a course requirement (Cox & Supprelle, 1971).

These examples suggest only a few of many types of on stage effects. People's behavior may alter in many different ways, depending on their beliefs about a researcher's identity or purposes. Ethnographers who study small communities may find that their hosts believe they are present to solve the community's problems, to critique the community, as government spies, as police informers, or in other roles that may have no relation to the researcher's actual purposes but that may lead the people being observed to behave in unusual ways because of the impression they want to create on the researcher. Martyn Hammersley and Paul Atkinson (1983) describe numerous examples from community studies, including this extreme case reported by Den Hollander (1967):

> In a town in southern Georgia [in 1932] it was rumoured after a few days that I was a scout for a rayon concern and might help to get a rayon industry established in the town. My denial reinforced the rumour, everyone tried to convince me of the excellent qualities of the town and its population—the observer had turned inito a fairy godmother and serious work was no longer possible. Departure was the only solution.

Such "on stage effects" are called *artifacts* of research, because they are created by the researcher and are not normally part of the phenomenon the researcher wants to study. Thus, to the extent that people are acting differently because they are "on stage," any observations of variables in their behavior are also measuring extraneous variables. These extraneous variables—the desire to look "healthy," to please or outwit the experimenter, to say the acceptable thing, and so on—provide possible alternative explanations for observed behavior whenever there is reason to suspect that people are "acting."

The on stage type of artifact is produced when people are aware that they are being observed, and when they desire to make some sort of impression on the observer. This is most likely to occur under these conditions:

When there is little purpose for the researcher's presence other than to observe the subject—that is, when the observer is *obtrusive*. This is frequently the case in survey research, where subjects not only know they are being observed, but usually know what about them is being observed because the questions are straightforward.

When the researcher holds higher status than the subject. If the researcher holds higher status this should increase the subject's desire to influence the impression he/she makes. The problem is most serious when the researcher can control important events in the subject's life, such as when a teacher or professor studies a student, or a psychiatrist or psychologist observes a mental patient, or a corrections staff member studies a prison inmate.

Observers are obtrusive whenever they are strikingly different from the people being observed and therefore particularly difficult for them to ignore. For example, in many anthropological and sociological studies the observer comes from a culture or subculture alien to those being observed, is markedly different in language, ethnicity, or social background, and does not know the norms of behavior in the group.

It is easy to imagine people in the presence of such a complete outsider trying to impress, or confuse, or play tricks on the observer. And it is easy to imagine the outsider not realizing what is happening, and failing to recognize that he or she is observing people on stage. So the possibility that people are "acting" provides a wealth of possible explanations of any behavior in the presence of an outside observer.

This possibility is a major threat to validity in research conducted by outside observers. Yet it is virtually impossible to conduct observations of some groups without bringing in complete outsiders. For example, it is almost always outsiders who want to conduct research on indigenous peoples of the Amazon, the workings of organized crime, and the play of small children. And with many other groups and activities, the researchers are frequently outsiders. So addressing on-stage effects is fundamental to the methods of ethnography and participant observation that are common in anthropology and sociology.

METHODS OF CONTROL

Here are some methods social researchers use to handle "on stage" effects.

Unobtrusive measures. Webb, Campbell, Schwartz, and Sechrest (1966) wrote a book on ways to measure subjects' behavior without their knowing it is being measured. These unobtrusive measures may or may not involve invasions of individual privacy. Consider these examples: to compare the popularity of various exhibits at a museum, the carpets in each gallery are examined for wear. To measure the effect of social status as an inhibitor of aggression, Doob and Gross (1968) had either a late-model Chrysler or an old, inexpensive car model stop at a light and stay stopped when the light turned green. The length of time it took the car behind to honk measured the inhibition of aggression. To measure racial prejudice, two people claimed to be identifiable by voice as black and white, dialed telephone numbers (ostensibly wrong numbers). The callers explained they were calling from a pay phone on the parkway, where their car had broken down. They were trying to reach a garage and had run out of coins. The people answering the phone were asked to please call the garage with the message. The number given was that of a researcher, who simply tabulated results (Gaertner & Bickman, 1972).

Deception. These last-mentioned unobtrusive measures also involve deception. On stage effects can be controlled by deceiving the subjects concerning the purpose, or even the presence, of the researcher. Thus, any attempt to respond to the researcher's purpose is nullified. Holdaway (1982) was a police officer who, after studying sociology, wanted to do observational research on the police. He decided to conduct the research covertly because he believed that if he had asked permission, the officers in charge would have denied permission or obstructed the research. Festinger, Riecken, and Schachter (1956) did a classic observational study of an apocalyptic religious group in which they wanted to test their hypotheses about how the group members would respond when the world did not end when they expected it to. They joined the group and did not reveal themselves as researchers, because to do so would have invalidated their observations or gotten them thrown out of the group. Researchers sometimes conceal part of their purpose or misinform their subjects deliberately in order to get more honest answers to questions.

Of course, there are some serious problems with deception as a strategy. For one thing, its ethics are questionable. There is a serious debate, especially among psychologists, about when deception is ever justified in research, and some guidelines have been developed (American Psychological Association, 1982). It is generally agreed, at the very least, that deception should be avoided whenever it is possible to get acceptable data by any other strategy. Many also feel that it is better to give up on some research questions rather than deceive participants in the research. A second major problem with deception is a practical one. Since it is known that social researchers, particularly psychologists, use deception, potential subjects are sometimes suspicious even of research that involves no deception. Thus, subjects' expectations to be deceived may influence their behavior.

Demand characteristics control group. One way to control any artifact in research is to manipulate it experimentally, using a comparison group design. One group gets whatever demand characteristics are in the experiment as planned, and another group gets a different demand, intentionally produced. For example, in a study on persuasion, it is desirable to be sure that any effects result from the persuasive communication used in the study, not the subject's desire to please the speaker, or some other extraneous variable. To control for this possibility, an investigator might run one group in which the persuader is introduced in the usual way, and another group in which subjects are also told that the experimenter disagrees with the point of view about to be presented. In this second group (control group), demand characteristics are *added,* to counter the persuasion attempt. Comparing this group with the experimental group will help determine whether demand characteristics influence persuasion in the experiment. An *evaluation apprehension control group* can be set up along similar lines to control for this extraneous variable.

Special controls for social desirability. In research that collects data by interview or questionnaire techniques, it is possible to control for the social desirability effect by the use of carefully worded questions. If, for example, people are asked to choose between alternatives that have been previously rated as equal in social desirability, their choice must be based on the content of the questions, rather than on the social desirability of the answers.

Inside observers. Observations by insiders—members of the group being observed—can be freer of on stage effects because the people being observed do not change their behavior for the benefit of the observer. This is one reason ethnographers often rely on informants—members of the group being studied who report to the researcher about what goes on in the group. The use of informants is not a form of naturalistic observation because it cannot hope to achieve complete and accurate recording of events as they occur. It is therefore vulnerable to other problems, such as biased observation or reporting by the informants and the possibility that the informant sees only a slice of life in his or her group and therefore gives the researcher a mistaken view. To get around these problems, social scientists sometimes train insiders in observational techniques. This procedure can help eliminate on stage effects without sacrificing completeness of observation. But it is not necessarily the case that insiders' observations are more valid than outsiders'. Insiders have an advantage in that they are more likely to know what is meaningful in a group, but they may also be so immersed in the group's culture as not to notice important aspects of life in the group that quickly strike an outsider.

Extended periods of observation. Anthropological and sociological field research-ers, as well as ethologists who observe animal behavior in natural settings, typically spend long periods in observation before they produce a final report of their observa-tions. They do this in part to control on stage effects by letting them dissipate over time: it is unlikely that the people or animals they are watching can maintain the same "act" for months or years.

Cross-checking observations. Another advantage of extended observation is that when the observer has seen a variety of behavior over time, it becomes possible to check the validity of the observations by comparing earlier observations with later ones, checking observations of some people against observations of others, and com-paring different methods of observation (for example, comparing informants' reports with the researcher's own observations). These sorts of comparisons allow a re-searcher to distinguish behavior "on stage" from other behavior.

Many of the above methods of control assume that behavior "on stage" is some-how less valid than other behavior. But there is another way to think about social performances. Some social scientists believe with Erving Goffman (1959) and Shake-speare that all the world's a stage and that everyday life is like a play, in which people normally perform social roles for each other. From that point of view, it is possible to separate the roles people play for the researcher's benefit from the roles they play for the other people in their social settings. An observer might choose to record only the behavior he or she considers to represent the "natural" behavior of the observed, but it might be better to record both the behavior judged to be natural and the behavior judged to be "on stage," along with the reasons for making those judgments. This allows others to decide whether or not to accept the observer's judg-ment. And, if life is in fact best interpreted as a series of performances, then observa-tions of people's performances in different situations is the best way to gain under-standing, and performances for the researcher are as valid a slice of life as performances for others.

More Persistent Changes Caused by Research

While on stage effects are serious problems for social research, the presence of a researcher can create more subtle and pervasive changes in the people being studied. This presence can, in some situations, cause people to change in ways that are more than just acting—that is, changes may occur that persist even when the subject is "off stage." Here are some classic ex-amples.

Hawthorne effect. A famous set of experiments on worker productivity in an industrial plant in Hawthorne, Illinois, called attention to one possible on stage ef-fect. The researchers (Roethlisberger & Dickson, 1939) reported that productivity increased every time the workers were shifted to new, experimental conditions, but soon leveled off, only to increase as soon as they were shifted again—even if they were shifted to conditions in which they had produced more slowly before. This behavioral pattern of improved performance because of the researcher's presence, which came to be known as the Hawthorne effect, has been attributed to the subjects' awareness that they were in an experiment, or that they were being given special treatment. Some have questioned the existence of the Hawthorne effect. Subsequent researchers have reexamined the data from the Hawthorne experiments and claimed that the Hawthorne effect never occurred there (Adair, 1984; Jones, 1992); questions have also been raised on the basis of a number of studies about whether Hawthorne effects occur in educational settings (Adair, Sharpe, & Huynh, 1989). Nevertheless, it still seems plausible that Hawthorne-type effects may occur in some settings, such as when research subjects are suffering from boredom or lack social contacts (e.g., chronic mental patients, residents of nursing homes or schools for the retarded, and possibly even assembly-line workers like those in the original experiments).

Placebo effect. When a person expects a treatment or experience to change her/ him, the person often changes, even when the "treatment" is known to be an inert or ineffective one. This effect is best known in research on drugs, in which the effect of the drug must be carefully separated from the effect of the fact that the patient is being given a prescription by a competent doctor. The "bedside manner" or the "power of suggestion" can heal too. This placebo effect has been offered as an explanation or partial explanation of voodoo death, religious healing, and psychotherapeutic cures.

Researcher expectancy effect. Robert Rosenthal (1966) had people look at photographs and judge how successful the people in the photos appeared to be. The experimenters in Rosenthal's studies were told either that the mean rating of success would be about +5 or about −5 on a scale of −10 to +10. The experimenters who were given the positive expectancy obtained more positive ratings from their subjects than the experimenters given the negative expectancy. Rosenthal suggested that the researcher's expectancy may somehow change her/his behavior toward subjects, and that subjects may respond to these subtle cues, creating a self-fulfilling prophecy: the researcher's actions cause subjects to behave as expected.

The most famous example of this effect comes from experiments in which grade-school teachers are told that certain of their pupils (randomly selected) have been tested and found to be "late bloomers" who can be expected to show great improvements in performance during the coming school year. At the end of the year, those students had in fact blossomed, as measured by such indicators as increased IQ scores, compared with pupils who had not been labeled late bloomers. Following the famous story of the street urchin who was taught to become a lady, this effect of a positive expectancy has come to be known as the *Pygmalion effect* (Rosenthal & Jacobson, 1968/1989).

There is some evidence that one way a researcher can communicate an expectancy is through the tone of voice in which instructions are given (Duncan & Rosenthal, 1968; Duncan, Rosenberg, & Finkelstein, 1969). In Rosenthal's study, experimenters with positive expectancies tended, for example, to emphasize "plus ten" more than "minus ten" when reading the instructions that described the rating scale.

Personal relationship effect. Sidney Jourard (1971) demonstrated that time spent in mutual self-disclosure of personal material by subject and experimenter could affect the rate of learning of meaningless material by subjects. It seems that subjects' performance may be affected by their emotional reaction to an experimenter as a person. Jourard suggests further that in typical laboratory experiments, in which the experimenter attempts to be impersonal (to "control" emotional reactions), subjects may act in an atypical manner. If so, people's behavior under these conditions may be, in part, a response to the extraneous variable of a "cold" researcher. This source of distortion can be called a personal relationship effect.

Personal relationship effects become increasingly difficult to avoid the longer a researcher spends making observations. They pose especially difficult problems in anthropological and sociological field research because over a long period of presence in a social group, many personal relationships are bound to develop and some of them are likely to change some of the individuals being observed, or possibly the entire group. In fact, the ability of an outsider to observe for any extended period depends on some sort of a personal relationship between the observer and at least one member of the group, who provides access to the group and is available to explain to other group members why the researcher is present. Decisions about which observations to record often depend on personal relationships, too. Imagine an anthropologist visiting a small, remote tribe of people previously unknown to Western societies. It may be impossible for such an observer even to tell which behavior is worth recording without learning the group's language and establishing personal relationships with several group members who can help explain the meanings of the group's activities. These "informants" are likely to want to learn about the observer, too—but that part of the personal relationship introduces group members to the mind of an outsider and inevitably introduces a new element into the group's life. The group may be changed permanently by its contact with the observer. Even when the observer and the observed are not so extremely different, these sorts of interactions still occur. It is impossible to remain in extended contact with other human beings without establishing relationships with them: the attempt to avoid relationships would be so bizarre as to be a relationship of its own kind, possibly one that is highly disruptive to what is being observed. For this reason, the possibility that the observer has, by the mere act of observation, changed what is being observed is an ever-present issue in observational research.

All these persistent changes that might be caused by the researcher's presence, like those that happen only when those being observed are "on stage," result from some extraneous variable unintentionally introduced into the research—the element of novelty, a person's expectation of change, the researcher's expectation about the behavior of the observed, or the quality of the relationship between the researcher and the people being observed. Each of these variables, whenever it may be operating, suggests an alternative explanation of behavior. It should be clear from the examples that these extraneous variables can affect any kind of observation—not just naturalistic.

METHODS OF CONTROL

Here are some methods used to achieve some control over these threats to validity caused by the fact of observation:

Blind measurement. To address the possibility that a researcher may affect the behavior of someone being observed by conveying subtle cues that communicate the researcher's expectancy, techniques of blind measurement can be used. There are two types of blind measurement. In one, the person being studied is kept "blind" to the researcher's presence—for example, by recording responses on paper or electronic media. In the other, the researcher is kept "blind" by having some other member of the research team, who is not told what to expect, interact with the person being observed and make the observations.

Double-blind technique. This is an extension of the blind measurement technique.

In a double-blind experiment, both the researcher *and* the subject are blind to the treatment (i.e., they do not know what treatment the subject is getting). This method was developed for drug research, but it also has applications in social science. In a drug study, one experimenter assigns subjects to treatment conditions, and prepares the medication for all subjects. All preparations look, smell, and taste alike, although the contents are different. A second experimenter then administers the drugs to all subjects, without knowing who is getting what. This procedure controls for self-fulfilling prophecies by giving the researcher in contact with the subject the same expectancy for all subjects. It controls for the placebo effect by giving all subjects the same expectations of help. The effect of personal relationship is probably about the same for both treatment groups.

Placebo control group. This methodology was also developed for drug research, and it too has social science applications. A placebo control group is treated exactly as an experimental group, except that instead of the experimental drug, a substitute is used that is physiologically inert (has no physical effects) but is indistinguishable from the drug by sight, smell, or taste. The purpose of the placebo is to separate the effect of the drug from the effect of expecting to be cured, talking to the doctor, and other aspects of the treatment situation that might help the patient, but do not depend on the specific medication given. Thus, any improvement in the drug treatment group above and beyond what is observed in the placebo group can be attributed to the drug. This procedure controls for the Hawthorne effect and the self-fulfilling prophecy, which both depend on the situation surrounding administration of treatment, rather than the specific treatment itself.

The principle of the placebo control procedure can be used in a variety of settings. In research on psychotherapeutic techniques, teaching methods, and treatment programs for juvenile delinquents, drug addicts, and so on, there is probably no completely inert treatment. In such research, various comparison groups have been used—people who want psychotherapy but are on the waiting list at the clinic, people getting an established, nonexperimental form of treatment, people meeting in a discussion group not designed as treatment, and so forth. While people in all these comparison groups might undergo change as a result of their treatment, no group is, strictly speaking, a placebo group. However, these comparison groups have the same function as a placebo group because they represent treatments that either are presumed to be relatively inert, or at least do not have the specific effects expected from the experimental treatment.

Warm-up period. One way to minimize the Hawthorne effect is for the researcher to spend some time with the person or group being observed to diminish the novelty of the interaction, which is believed to be a cause of the effect. A warm-up period might also control for personal relationship effects caused by researchers trying to be impersonal. However, it might be that the researcher forms strong relationships with some of the people being observed and not others, introducing an extraneous variable. This possibility suggests another control tactic.

The "canned" researcher. This is an invented name for a commonly used method of controlling demand characteristics and personal relationship effects. Unlike "blind" observers, who interact with the people being observed in ignorance of the researcher's expectation, "canned" observers are automated. This control technique deals with difficulties in the researcher-subject relationship by eliminating it. Any instructions to be given to the research subject might be written out or presented in prerecorded form. (Note that while this procedure holds the researcher-subject relationship constant, it does not meet Jourard's (1971) criticism that "cold" experiments bring out atypical behavior in subjects.) If the subject never meets the experimenter personally, it is very difficult for the researcher to communicate expectancies by means of subtle nonverbal cues. Thus, the effects of self-fulfilling prophecy and demand characteristics are lessened. Also, it is certain that all subjects have received the same instructions, even down to tone of voice.

MAKING VALID OBSERVATIONS WHEN CONTROL TECHNIQUES CANNOT BE USED

The above techniques for controlling the research situation are intended to prevent the research act from changing what is being studied. But using such methods of control is not always possible in social science research. The difficulties are most obvious for field researchers who spend long periods in foreign cultures or other unfamiliar social settings. All the above techniques with the exception of the warm-up period are impossible to implement in such settings. Good field researchers are sensitive to the fact that whatever they do has the potential to permanently alter the setting they are studying. Even laboratory researchers must deal with this fact: if subjects respond differently to a canned researcher and a real researcher, how is one to know for certain which response (if either) corresponds with what they would have done in the researcher's absence?

Ethnographers have given considerable thought to the problem they call *reflexivity:* that social researchers are part of the world they study so that to some degree their observations are always observations of themselves and their effects on their surroundings. A good detailed account of the implications of reflexivity for the practice of field research is given in Hammersley and Atkinson's (1983) book, *Ethnography: Principles in Practice.* Reflexivity implies that there is no way "in principle . . . to isolate a body of data uncontaminated by the researcher" (Hammersley & Atkinson, 1983, p. 14). Reflexivity further implies that no observation is free of threats to its validity and that the only way to reach valid conclusions from observation is ultimately to study (rather than try to eliminate) the researcher's effects on what is being observed. In this view, observer effects, rather than being "artifacts" to be eliminated by control, are data to analyze. The strategy of *cross-checking observations,* already mentioned as a way to address on stage effects, is the best way to understand permanent changes caused by the researcher's actions. Even if no observation is fully valid, useful knowledge can come from examining how different kinds of observations distort reality in different ways. By comparing different kinds of observations, it is possible to learn what is invariant in the face of different kinds of interventions from outside (the researcher's activities) and also how the people being studied respond differently to different kinds of interventions. Both of these are important information on whatever is being studied.

This is not to say that whatever a researcher does in the field provides equally valuable information. Ethnographers carefully consider what impression they want to give to the people they are observing to increase their chances of getting useful information. We have already mentioned situations in which researchers have had to conceal their identities as social scientists because being open would have made it impossible to make valid observations. Field researchers may carefully choose their clothing so as not to stand out too much from the people they are studying. Sometimes they are very careful how they present their own beliefs and attitudes: sociologists who study deviant groups find that group members often want reassurance that the researcher does not disapprove of them. Such choices about self-presentation may well affect the quality of a researcher's observations; certainly, experienced ethnographers claim that they do.

Keeping distant or getting close? Some researchers prefer to present themselves very much as outsiders, maintaining a strong degree of social detachment and reserve from the people they are observing and justifying this stance on the ground that social distance is needed to maintain objectivity. Others prefer to establish close personal relationships with members of the group being observed and justify this stance on the ground that deeper understanding is possible when emotions are allowed to enter the social interaction. A good case can be made for either approach, but a researcher must choose some position on the continuum from pure observer to pure participant, understanding that each position affects the observations. A common piece of advice is for the field researcher to cultivate the role of an "acceptable incompetent" (Lofland and Lofland, 1984), someone who will not be rejected by the group, and who may also benefit from instruction by group members in the way the group works. But certainly, people behave differently around incompetents in their culture than around sophisticates, so even the acceptable incompetent's position affects what is observed.

The question of what stance to take in making observations highlights a dilemma that is very stark in long-term field research but that exists to some degree with observations generally. Each stance holds the researcher's attitude constant, so it is a kind of control, but each one also affects what is observed, so it is also a kind of extraneous variable. To make progress despite this dilemma, in which every control is a source of bias in the observations, good field researchers often try different ways of interacting in the field setting as a way to cross-check their findings. They also are explicit about how they presented themselves to the people they studied, so that others can make their own judgments about whether the researcher's behavior gives reasons to question the researcher's findings.

Comparing observers. One problem can never be solved by a researcher observing for a long time or cross-checking his or her own observations. Every researcher is a particular individual with a particular social background, style of interaction, set of preconceptions, and so forth, so all the interactions of that individual with the people being studied may be colored by the characteristics of that individual. Gender differences provide a good example. Hammersley and Atkinson (1983) point out that "in male-dominated settings, for instance, women may come up against the male 'fraternity,' from which they are excluded; women may also find themselves the object of 'hustling' from male hosts . . . [but] female researchers may find advantageous trade-offs. The 'hustling' informant who is trying to impress the researcher may prove particularly forthcoming to her . . ." (p. 85). We are not advocating the use of sexuality as a research tool, only warning that sex and gender may affect research observations in various ways. Male researchers, of course, may also affect the behavior of the people they study merely because of their gender, and equally significant effects can result from the researcher characteristics other than gender.

Ultimately, the best way to find out whether the researcher's individuality made a difference is to compare the reports of different observers. It may be especially useful, depending on the situation, to compare the observations of researchers who differ in cultural background, gender, race, religion, social status, and in their strategy of distancing themselves from, or interacting closely with, the people they study.

To summarize a long discussion: Researchers can produce two types of unwanted effects on what they are observing by their mere presence: on stage effects and the more persistent "real" changes in people that can result from the research process. These unwanted effects exist because researchers unintentionally introduce extraneous variables when they observe events. Table 3.1 presents the material in this section in condensed form.

This discussion and the tables in this chapter are intended to help you to raise questions when you read scientific literature. If you have a good sense of how the research process can change people and events, you will be in a position to offer plausible alternative explanations for the findings of some of the research reports you read. Only when all reasonable explanations are collected can you make an educated judgment about how strongly a set of research results justifies an author's conclusions.

Table 3.1. Extraneous Variables Due to the Presence of an Observer

Extraneous Variables	Alternative Explanations	When a Problem	Methods of Control
On-Stage Effects			
Social desirability	Subject may be saying what he/she "should" believe	Survey research, controversial topics	Careful construction of questions; unobtrusive measurement; extended observation
Evaluation apprehension	Subject may be trying to impress someone juding "mental health," IQ, etc.	Survey research; when researcher has high status	Deception; unobtrusive measurement; extended observation; insider observers; comparing observers
Faking bad	Subject may be trying to sabotage research	High status researcher; coerced subjects	Deception; unobtrusive measurement; extended observation; insider observers; comparing observers
Demand characteristics	Subject may be doing what he/she thinks researcher wants	High status researcher; volunteer subjects	Decpetion; unobtrusive measurement; special control group; extended observation; "canned" researcher; insider observers; comparing observers

(*continued*)

Table 3.1. (*continued*)

Extraneous Variables	Alternative Explanations	When a Problem	Methods of Control
More Persistent Changes Caused by Research			
Hawthorne effect	Performance improves merely because of change in routine	Subjects lack social contacts	Comparison group with different treatment; warm-up period
Placebo effect	Subject may be changing because he/she expected to	"Therapy" settings where people expect to change	Warm-up periods; placebo control group; double-blind technique; "canned" researcher
Researcher expectancy (self-fulfilling prophecy)	Researcher may subtly communicate an expectancy that subject acts to fulfill	Researcher and subject in close contact	Bllind measurement; double-blind technique; placebo control group; "canned" researcher; deception about expectancy
Personal relationship effect	Subjects may perform differently because of nature of relationship with researcher	A general problem	Warm-up period; "canned" researcher; comparison group with different relationship; comparing observers
Reflexivity problems	Responses may be due to researcher's personal characteristics or behavior with subjects	General; becomes more serious with more researcher presence	Comparing observers; cross-checking results

Problems of Incomplete or Inaccurate Recording

By our definition, naturalistic observation requires "complete and accurate recording of the relevant events." Like noninterference with events, this is an ideal rather than a realistic possibility in social research. One problem is that observers may be excluded from observing certain events that are essential for understanding the people being observed. Even when access is unlimited, a researcher cannot be sure about the selection of relevant events and the rejection of irrelevant ones. Complete recording is typically a practical impossibility because too much may be going on, even in a simple social situation, and some further selection may have to be made. And it is always possible for a researcher to record inaccurately without realizing it.

Selection and potential inaccuracy are always a part of naturalistic observation, as with all scientific methods. They pose a difficult question for an observer: How can I know that nothing important was left out or distorted in my record of observations? And they pose a doubly difficult question for readers of research: If the observer omitted important events or distorted the observations—and may not even realize it—how can I tell?

Incomplete Access Observers often have difficulty gaining access to the phenomena they want to observe. Hammersley and Atkinson (1983) discuss two illustrative examples. Chambliss (1975) reports his difficulties trying to study organized crime in Seattle. First, dressed like a truck driver, he visited a skid-row cafe and learned about an illegal poker game in the back room. Over some months, he played poker, visited pornography shops, and engaged in conversations with gamblers, bartenders, and all sorts of low-status participants in organized crime, but never gained any understanding of how the criminal enterprises were organized. Finally, after revealing himself to the manager of the cardroom as a sociology professor with a "purely scientific" interest in the operation, he began to receive calls from others at higher levels in organized crime who were willing to talk with him. He became able to see, if only at second hand, things he could never have seen without the assistance of others.

Hansen (1977), in studying rural village life in Catalonia, politely asked villagers for interviews, and learned very little. By chance he interviewed one of the few noblemen in the area, who told him that as a person whose looks and education marked him as superior to most villagers, he should command people to give interviews. The count then accompanied Hansen to visit landholders and ordered them to give Hansen all the information he wanted. After that, it became fashionable to be interviewed, and Hansen reported a flood of volunteers.

In both these examples, researchers got assistance from helpful insiders who gave them access to observations and other information they could not otherwise have obtained. Their reports would have been much different, and probably much less insightful, without this enhanced access. It is of course possible that the researchers were still misled somehow by their informants, but because they had greater access, they were put in a position that allowed them to compare what they learned from different informants and thus offer a more accurate picture of what they were observing than they could hope to write with more limited access.

It is always wise to ask of observational studies whether the researcher had access to all the important aspects of the phenomenon being observed. Some of the same researcher characteristics that lead to on stage effects may also lead people to conceal important information from researchers. Most social groups have secrets, and even conceal some social phenomena from some individuals within the group (children, for example). They often conceal the same information from researchers, especially when their scientific role is obvious or when they are strikingly different from the people being studied in gender, race, social status, or other important characteristics. An observer with incomplete access cannot record all the relevant events, and the selection of events created by incomplete access will usually tend to mislead the researcher in some way and to bias the researcher's interpretation of what was observed. This sort of bias comes from the effort of those being studied to conceal or deceive.

Researcher Selectivity Researchers can also introduce biases of their own into their observations. This can happen when a researcher begins with a theory (often implicit) that directs the questions that will be asked and the phenomena that will be observed. It can also happen when factors in the researcher's background or some aspect of the way the observer enters the situation leads to increased attention to parts of a phenomenon, which are selected as relevant, and a failure even to notice other parts. Consider the following three examples:

Suppose an education professor studies parent participation in education by observing an elementary school in a middle-class African-American suburb where most of the students are performing well below grade level. The professor notices that parent visits to teachers and the principal are very infrequent, and interprets this observation as evidence of parent disinterest in the children's education. Such a conclusion would fit well with "cultural deficit" theories about the causes of poor school performance among African-Americans and with concepts and theories that emphasize parent interest and involvement as an important factor in pupils' performance. But a study emanating from the experiences and perspective of African-American parents in one such school told a different story. African-American parents' attempts to participate had been systematically discouraged by school officials, who refused to make appointments, broke appointments without reason, and treated interested parents dismissively and with disrespect (S. Stern, 1994). What looks like parent disinterest from a dominant perspective, such as that of most white, middle-class researchers or of school officials, looks like a quite different phenomenon—parent push-out—when observed from the parents' position in the system. As the parents see it, they stay away not out of disinterest, but because they are unwelcome and because their visits accomplish nothing positive for their children. What is significant here is not just that an observer can reach the wrong conclusion about what is going on, but that the observation itself may be biased: the observer fails entirely to observe an important part of the process (the part the parents see), and does not realize it.

Several best-selling guidebooks purport to offer applicants to American colleges all the important information they need to choose a college. Their authors collect data on the colleges, and some even send observers to describe the quality of life on campus. The guides report all sorts of information, from the number of books in the library to the availability of vegetarian dining to the quality of the college newspaper, but they do not report on many things of interest to African-American college applicants, such as the graduation rate for African-Americans, the number of black professors, the availability of programs for students who need remedial work, and the climate of race relations on campus. To fill the gap, *The Black Students' Guide to Colleges* (Beckham, 1984) has been published and updated. The success of this volume suggests that the best-sellers are really *white* students' guides, without saying so. They report a great variety of information, but their observations of the colleges are incomplete because they omit information that is essential to many potential students. Some of what they omit is important for *all* races of students, such as the information about race relations and remedial programs. Although the best-sellers claim to be based on observations of everything important about a college, they are not, and again, the authors do not realize it.

Some feminist authors (Dalmiya & Alcoff, 1993; Ehrenreich & English, 1973) claim that when physicians displaced midwives as the main practitioners of obstetrics, much knowledge was lost because the physicians (who were almost exclusively male) did not fully observe, and therefore did not fully understand, childbirth. Physicians usually attended women only at delivery, whereas midwives attended them throughout labor, and physicians considered only physical matters of childbirth (and then, only part of the body), whereas midwives also concerned themselves with psychological aspects. And because physicians were almost exclusively male and midwives female, there were stark differences in their abilities to understand childbirth empathically and to be sensitive to subtle changes in the condition of a woman in labor. The feminists claim that physicians, because they lacked the perspective and knowledge that midwives had, were inferior observers of their patients and inferior practitioners. One example given in this literature is that physicians innovated the practice of giving birth from a supine position, which allowed the obstetrician greater control but had no advantage for the mothers' or babies' well-being and, as midwives knew, made delivery more difficult for the mothers than it was from a sitting position.

In each of these examples, well-meaning observers who want their observations to be complete and accurate fail to see all of what they are trying to observe and, as a result, the knowledge they develop is faulty. Selective observation may have many causes. It may come from theory or other implicit presuppositions, such as that schools are equally open to parental involvement of African-American and white parents, or that African-American parents are culturally uninterested in their children's education. It may come from failure to recognize that not everyone shares one's social position and attendant concerns—the failure to discuss the climate of race relations in college guides may be an example. It may come from the professionalization of the observer—for example, the physicians whose training and experience led them to focus only on physical aspects of birthing and more on delivery than on labor. It may come from lack of empathy rooted in differences between the observer and the observed: white observers of black parents and male observers of the birth process may fail to observe what someone with greater empathy would quickly see.

Whatever the cause, the effect of selective observation is not only that things are left out, but that they are left out systematically. As a result, the entire observation is biased or distorted, as well as incomplete.

Systematic neglect of certain information is almost a universal problem in social research, because all methods of observation involve choices about which data to observe and which to ignore. The difficulty with making selections is that we do not know whether every possible fact has an equal chance of being observed. With human observers, it is safe to assume that the facts do *not* have an equal chance of being observed, because people have theories, or at least mental sets to look for certain kinds of facts, and because observation is affected by the observer's position in relation to what is being observed. Often we, as observers, are not aware of the classes of information we are ignoring, and this is as true of scientists as it is of everyone else. When a researcher selects information to look at, the reader generally gets a *biased sample of information*.

METHODS OF CONTROL

One way to control this is not to try to eliminate the bias (how can one know when it is gone?) but to be explicit about it. Researchers do this when they identify variables and define them operationally. The reader then knows exactly which information was observed (information about the variables mentioned) and which was left out (everything else). The selectivity is still there, but the bases for the selection are known to all. In short, the way to handle the inevitable bias resulting from a researcher's selection of events is to use a research method that selects variables and defines them operationally. For this reason, naturalistic observations and retrospective case studies tend to be done early in the research history of a subject, before enough is known to decide which variables to study in depth. Later in the research history, when *theories* are developed, it is easier to make the researcher's bias explicit. Theory dictates which events should be studied and which neglected; not all events are equally likely to be studied. Thus, a theory simplifies a researcher's job by defining some facts as irrelevant. A researcher with a theory need not observe everything, and can therefore be more careful about measuring what is considered most important. Theory is also valuable in that it makes explicit the bias that is inevitable whenever an observer chooses not to record everything. All this is in addition to the major values of theory: to advance understanding and give direction to research.

Another way to address the problem of researcher selectivity is to use one observer's biases to reveal another's. The African-American parents could see things the observer of the school could not; black observers of colleges saw things white observers overlooked; and midwives could see important aspects of childbirth that male physicians overlooked. This does not necessarily mean that African-Americans and midwives were the best observers—they may have overlooked important things, too. But comparing observers, and particularly comparing observers who can be expected to have different points of view on a phenomenon, can reveal each researcher's selectivities and biases, and thus lead to a more complete and accurate picture than any one observer is likely to produce, no matter how carefully that observer records events.

Although the above examples focus on observational methods, the same problems arise with other research methods as well. One reason is that all research methods involve observation, and whenever there is room for judgment in making or recording observations, biases can enter. Moreover, faulty observations lead to faulty hypotheses for other research methods. Consequently, researchers using other methods may head off in the wrong direction by paying attention to irrelevant variables or failing to study important ones.

Researcher Distortion The same factors that can affect what an observer notices can influence the researcher's interpretation of events. Researcher distortion is a serious problem, especially where strongly held values are at stake and where a researcher has a stake in a particular hypothesis or theory. The evidence of research on attitudes suggests that anyone who spends many years of effort working on a theory is likely to come to believe in it, and this may affect what he or she sees. Consider an example: A psychologist who does group psychotherapy professionally wants to assess the effectiveness of her therapy. She believes that a diversity of personalities among the therapy group is counterproductive. She evaluates the progress of a diverse group of patients seen together and another diverse group of patients she is seeing in individual psychotherapy (control group). At the end of therapy, she reviews her notes, and rates patients "much improved," "somewhat improved," "no change," "somewhat worse," or "much worse," compared with when therapy began. Since she knows who was seen individually and who was seen in group, and she has a stake in the outcome, we might not want to trust her ratings as a measure of patient improvement. Suppose her observations were that the group patients did not improve (just as she expected). The psychologist might conclude that diversity in therapy groups is counterproductive, but we could offer an alternative explanation: Because of her bias, the psychologist did not see evidence of improvement in the group-treated patients and exaggerated the improvement of those in individual therapy. This distortion is most serious when the reliability of observations is questionable. However, even when variables are carefully operationalized, distortion is possible.

An observer's social position can also cause observations to become distorted. The example of parent participation in schools suggests how this can happen. A social scientist who comes from a privileged majority-group background may have a basic belief, rooted in personal experience, that social institutions are generally responsive to the needs of individuals. Such a researcher would probably conclude that when parents are failing to intervene in a school where their children are performing poorly, the cause must lie in the parents rather than the school. As a result, the researcher might do two things: fail to look closely at the parents' behavior and experience (selective observation), and misinterpret the lack of parental contact with the school as parental unconcern (distortion). A social scientist whose personal experience had included disdainful treatment by official representatives of social institutions might be less likely to engage in the same distortion.

METHODS OF CONTROL

If the psychologist conducting the study of group therapy is a conscientious scientist, she does not trust her own judgment, but brings in someone else to evaluate the patients. She would control the possible effects of her distortion by using blind measurement. With the judgment of a competent colleague who does not know her hypothesis, she can obtain more accurate information about each patient's progress. The judge would review a transcript of the therapist's notes, edited to remove information on whether the patient is being seen individually or in a group, and would make the same ratings the therapist might make. Whatever bias the colleague may have would not influence the results because this judge doesn't know which patients were seen individually and which in group, or that a difference between individual and group therapy is expected.

Control could go a step further. The researcher could *misinform* the judge about the hypothesis, or about her bias, or about the patients' progress (e.g., she could tell the judge that none of the patients seemed to be responding to treatment), and let the judge evaluate each patient. This procedure might be an improvement because it would counter any subtle communication of the researcher's bias that might prejudice the judge.

Distortions caused by social position can most easily be discovered and corrected by observers with a different social position. In research on racism, the observations of researchers of different racial backgrounds might complement each other. Differences between the observations could then be interpreted as possible omissions or distortions on the part of either observer, or both. Similarly, where gender is an issue in what is being observed, having male and female observers can help correct distortions. When power is an issue, it can help to have observers who can take the point of view of those with power and of those without it.

To summarize this discussion of incomplete or inaccurate recording, observational data are often open to alternative explanations because of incomplete access, researcher selectivity, and distorted observation. Table 3.2 briefly summarizes the ways this can happen and some methods for controlling, or at least revealing and understanding, the limitations of observational research.

RETROSPECTIVE CASE STUDY: PROBLEMS OF MEMORY

Retrospective case studies share many of the limitations of observational research, particularly problems of access, selectivity, and distortion. In addition, they have one essential characteristic that allows for alternative explanations for their findings. Because they collect data from the past, retrospective case studies often rely on people's (faulty) memories. Reliance on memory is not unique to retrospective case studies, but the problems associated with memory appear most clearly in this research method.

In retrospective research, there is selectivity and distortion not only on the part of the researcher, but on the subject's part as well. What someone remembers is not only incomplete, it is systematically incomplete. Ordinary people, like scientists, have theories about the relationships between events, and what they judge as unim-

Table 3.2. Extraneous Variables Due to Incomplete Access, Selection, and Distortion

Extraneous Variables	Alternative Explanations	When a Problem	Methods of Control
Incomplete access	Unseen events may explain what is observed	Researcher is an outsider; those observed want to conceal information	Involve insiders in the research
Researcher selectivity	Events are due to causes researcher's theory considers unimportant; to causes someone in researcher's social position can't see	Researcher and subjects are from very different social groups; research lacks operational definitions	Specify selectivity by operationalizing variables; compare observations by people from different social positions or using different theories
Researcher distortion or bias	Researcher's evaluation of data may be colored by preconceptions	Researcher knows hypothesis; has stake in results; comes from different social group from those observed	Blind judges; misled judges; compare different observers

portant tends to be forgotten. These biases are usually unexpressed. Furthermore, memories can be distorted to fit the view that makes a person most comfortable at present. Suppose, for example, a researcher is interested in the predisposing factors in juvenile delinquency. A sample of delinquent boys is selected, and each is asked questions about his relationships with his parents. Most of the boys report that their fathers were frequently absent from the home and spent little time playing with them. Can their memories be trusted? It could well be that these delinquent boys are rebelling against their fathers' authority and are justifying their rebellion by remembering the times father was away and saying that father didn't care. It is hard to know what produced the boys' reports if their memories are the only evidence available. (This problem is not restricted to retrospective case studies—selective memory is a very serious problem in correlational research and even in experimental research when variables are measured by people's accounts of the past.) Memories are most likely to be distorted when distortion can be used to justify one's actions and maintain or enhance one's self-esteem.

METHODS OF CONTROL

The only ways to control the effects of selective and distorted memory involve using other sources of information. In a study of the causes of delinquency, for example, it is possible to ask the delinquent boy and his parents the same questions about the period of his childhood. This way the amount of distortion between different memories will be known, even if it is impossible to know whose memory was most accurate.

In some retrospective research, it is possible to rely on *archival records* that do not depend on memory. The Kerner Commission study of urban riots (Chapter 2) used records of incomes and unemployment rates to determine the economic conditions of cities where riots occurred.

Another approach is to use a research method that does not rely on memory. In the study of delinquency, for example, it is possible to do a *prospective study*, in which a large number of children is *directly observed* before some of them become delinquents, to identify the differences between the children who do and don't turn out delinquent. Another alternative is experimental research. In the study of delinquency, a group of young children can be given whatever delinquents are presumed to lack, to see if their rate of delinquency turns out to be lower than that of a control group.

Table 3.3 summarizes how selective or distorted memory can allow for alternative explanations of the results of studies that rely on memory.

SAMPLE STUDY: PROBLEMS OF OPERATIONAL DEFINITIONS AND GENERALIZING ABOUT POPULATIONS

Sample studies have three important characteristics not generally present in naturalistic observations and retrospective case studies.

1. Variables in sample studies are operationally defined.
2. Sample studies generalize about populations from information about samples.

Table 3.3. Extraneous Variables Due to Memory

Extraneous Variables	Alternative Explanations	When a Problem	Methods of Control
Selective or distorted memory (in subject)	Subject's memory may be distorted to fit his or her "theory" or current opinion	Retrospective research relying on memory; subject's self-esteem at stake	Compare two memories; use archival records; prospective research

3. Sample studies involve collecting the same information about a number of different people or events.

Since sample studies share these characteristics with correlational and experimental research, the validity problems that exist in sample studies are also present in the other forms of quantitative research.

Invalid Operational Definitions

Whenever operational definitions are used, the possibility exists that they are invalid. Unfortunately, there is no research design or procedure that will protect research from *invalid operational definitions*. In evaluating research, it is your job to think about the operational definitions used. Ask yourself if the definition of a variable being studied might be measuring something else. Here are some examples. Most intelligence tests require knowledge (often reading knowledge) of the language in which they are given—this means they are also measuring acquired language skills. Juvenile delinquency can be defined in terms of convictions in court, but convictions are more frequent when defendants don't have private counsel—this means that the definition of delinquency is also measuring economic status. If a researcher using this definition of delinquency discovers that delinquents are educationally deprived, the findings may only mean that poor people get poor educations. In general, when an operational definition measures more than one thing at a time, whatever is said of one of the variables could, with justification, be said of the other(s) as well. Operational definitions that measure more than one thing at a time are said to be *confounded,* and the variables measured together are said to be confounded with each other. When an operational definition is confounded, any conclusion drawn about the variable it is supposed to measure may just as well be drawn about the extraneous variable confounded with it. In evaluating research, keep constantly aware that operational definitions are not necessarily the same as the variables they are supposed to measure. If you should even suspect confounding, offer an alternative explanation based on the extraneous variable buried in the operational definition.

Biased Samples

There are some difficulties associated with drawing inferences about populations based on information about samples, and they can best be illustrated by an example. Suppose a researcher wants to determine the birth control practices of married couples in Vermont. There are, let us say, 120,000 such couples and, to make things easier, let us also assume a list of their names and addresses is available. Still, 120,000 is too many couples to survey, and so a sample of 500 couples is taken. Skipping the important details for now, let's say that of the couples surveyed, 27% use the pill, 19% use sterilization (either partner), 17% use intrauterine devices, 17% use diaphragms, condom, and/or foam, 5% use rhythm, and the remaining 15% use no birth control. Is it safe to say, for example, that the pill is the most commonly used method of birth control among Vermont couples? Not necessarily. Here are some problems.

Samples rarely contain exactly the same proportions of anything as the population from which they are drawn. (If you doubt this, toss a coin 100 times, and see if you get 50 tails. You will probably get *about* 50 tails, but you will probably not get exactly 50.) If the sample is a good one, it is fair to conclude that *about* 27% of the couples in the Vermont population use the pill, and that *about* 19% use sterilization. To decide whether the pill is more commonly used, you would need to test the hypothesis that "about 27%" in this sample is greater than "about 19%." To do this, you would have to determine the likelihood that, given a population in which the pill and sterilization are used with equal frequency, a sample of 500 couples would include 27% using the pill and 19% using sterilization. If this is highly *unlikely,* you can be reasonably sure that the pill and sterilization are *not* used with equal frequency in the whole population. There are statistical procedures to determine this likelihood. In general, the larger the sample, the more certain you can be that an observed difference corresponds to a difference in the whole population. (The more often you toss a loaded coin, the more certain you can be that it's loaded.) When samples of 500 are taken out of a population of 120,000, they are likely to be *somewhat* different from each other and from the population, and the generalizations you can make from a sample can be expected to be slightly inaccurate. The larger the sample, the less inaccurate it will be. This error of inference is called *sampling error.*

Sampling error is an unavoidable problem when a scientist attempts to make inferences about a population from less than complete data. However, it need not lead us to question the internal validity of research for two reasons. First, if the sample is chosen carefully, so as to be representative of the population, the amount of sampling error can be placed within known limits. You may see such statements as "We can say with 95% confidence that Dewey will win within 3% either way of 53% of the popular vote." This means that 5% of the time the error will be greater and that 2½% of the time Dewey will not win a majority. Although such an error may embarrass the prognosticator, it is predictable. We know how much error to expect how often.

Second, and more important, when a sample is representative of a population, the error is equally likely to go in either direction. Data from representative samples vary *randomly* around the data that would be collected from the population; the findings are not systematically distorted by the measurement of an extraneous variable. Thus, while sampling error does limit the certainty of any inference about a population, it is a weak argument for questioning the validity of a researcher's conclusions.

The above comments were all predicated on the assumption that the sample of 500 Vermont couples was *representative* of all couples in the state. The must serious problem with sampling involves being sure the sample is representative—that it is not systematically distorted by some extraneous variable. Suppose, for example, that the Vermont sample included only half the proportion of Catholics that exist in the state population. Such a sample is not representative; it is *biased*. A *biased sample* is one that contains a *systematic error:* it is consistently different from the population in a particular direction. In the present example, a sample with few Catholics probably underestimates the proportion of couples using rhythm and no birth control. A biased sample is one that consistently misrepresents the population from which it was drawn; data from such a sample differ from population data in a particular direction because of the presence of an extraneous variable. Name the extraneous variable, and an alternative explanation follows: "Rhythm was found to be the least popular birth control method in Vermont because the sample *underrepresented Catholics,* not because it is least popular."

METHODS OF CONTROL

The only way to be certain that a sample is representative is to use a truly *random sample*. This presumes a complete list of the population (which was available), and a systematic procedure that allows everyone in the population an equal chance of being chosen for the sample. This might be done by putting all the couples' names and addresses in a computer, assigning each couple a number, and using a program that generates random numbers. The first 500 numbers that correspond to numbers that had been assigned to couples would determine the people sampled. While this procedure is possible, it might exhaust the researcher's budget to travel to the remote locations where all these people may live. Therefore, random samples, while they are theoretically ideal, are rarely used in large-scale sample studies.

A usual procedure is to choose a sample on some convenient basis, assuring that the sample is equivalent to the population with respect to several variables considered important to the research. For the Vermont birth control study, we might agree that it is important to make sure the sample and the population are similar in age distribution, religion, rural or urban residence, and number of children already born, since these factors probably influence birth control methods. If the researcher took a sample of people from rural areas, towns, and cities (in the same proportion as the state population), chose individuals in these locations on a random basis, and showed us that the sample was very close to the overall population of couples in terms of the other variables mentioned, we might be willing to accept the sample as representative. Other than true random sampling, there is no absolute rule for drawing a representative sample. All we can ask of a researcher is that the sample is representative of the population in those things that are probably relevant to the research question. If we are assured of that, we can proceed on the assumption that the error in this sample is no different from the error in a true random sample.

When evaluating a piece of research that uses sampling techniques, consider the population being sampled, and then think about the method used to draw the sample. If you can think of a way in which the sample may be systematically different from the population, ask yourself whether this bias could have influenced the results. If it could have, an alternative explanation is possible.

The above discussion has concerned the difficulties in concluding that data from a sample accurately represented the population *from which the sample was drawn.*

To ask whether the findings are true of other populations is to raise another question, which is discussed in Chapter 5. In the Vermont example, we have discussed whether one can be justified in drawing conclusions about adult married Vermonters. If one can, these conclusions still may not apply to the birth control practices of unmarried Vermonters or of people living elsewhere. We emphasize this point because researchers often take samples from much more restricted and less interesting populations than the adult married couples of Vermont. Most educational and psychological research uses conveniently available populations, such as "third grade pupils in the Horseheads Central School District" or "introductory psychology students at Moreland University, spring term, 1993." The question of internal validity often becomes the question of whether results hold true even for such restricted populations as these.

Sampling bias is possible even with such restricted populations. One common source of sampling bias is the use of volunteer subjects for experiments. Unlike the average person, the person who volunteers for psychological research is likely to want to please (demand characteristics), and may also be unusually well motivated to perform. Consequently, what is true of volunteer subjects may not be true of the population from which they are drawn. Thus, when volunteers are used, their desire to please (extraneous variable) may provide an alternative explanation of their behavior.

Uncontrolled Variation in Information

It may seem easy to collect the same information from (or about) different people, but this is not always so. In a sample study using interviews, respondents may say different things to different interviewers depending on the interviewer's sex, age, race, or other characteristics that act as extraneous variables in the research. Sometimes it is possible to avoid this problem by using a single interviewer or interviewers who are similar in terms of characteristics that may influence a person's response. Still, *holding the interviewer constant* is not always an ideal solution. Consider a survey on interracial attitudes. People will respond differently to black and white interviewers, but it would not help to use only one race of interviewers. Any difference between the responses of whites and blacks may be due either to their different attitudes or to their different reactions to being interviewed by, for example, a black (extraneous variable). In this case, control may be achieved either by eliminating the interviewer entirely (a mailed questionnaire could be used if its contents did not reveal its author's race), or by using both black and white interviewers to collect data from both black and white respondents. The latter solution may be preferable because it allows one to both hold the interviewer's race constant and to measure its effects. If black and white interviewers get the same results from similar respondents, it can be concluded that the interviewer's race made no difference. This method of using both races of interviewer has created an experiment within the sample study: Race of interviewer is manipulated to see its effects on respondents. The strategy of measuring the effect of a potential extraneous variable is discussed further on pages 93 to 94.

Other problems exist in trying to get the same information from different people. It may go without saying that in a questionnaire everyone should be asked the same questions, but one cannot always assume that the questions are understood the same way by everyone. Some people may not understand because of limited vocabulary or reading ability, and it is not safe to assume their answers mean the same as those of other people. This problem can best be prevented by preliminary work by the researcher to make sure questions are understood.

The problem of "getting the same information" exists not only in interview and questionnaire situations, but in most forms of quantitative research, including laboratory experiments. In conducting an experiment on learning, for example, sounds from outside the lab may distract some subjects and constitute an extraneous variable that should be controlled because people are not all learning under the same conditions. You could do nothing, assuming that each subject is equally likely to be subjected to a distracting level of noise, or you could hold noise constant by placing the subject in a soundproof room, or putting plugs in his/her ears, or giving her/him a head set with a prerecorded tape of noise to listen to. When it is fairly easy to hold an extraneous variable constant by use of a standard procedure, this is the best method of control.

METHODS OF CONTROL

The information collected sometimes depends on who gathers it, or on how, when, or where it was collected. There are two main methods to control this problem.

Hold procedures constant. Ask questions in the same order, with the same wording; use one interviewer; always collect data in the same lab, at the same time of day, on the same apparatus, and so on.

Experimentally manipulate the variable causing responses to vary. The use of black and white interviewers in a survey of racial attitudes is the example used above. This method allows one to both control for and measure the effect of a potential extraneous variable.

When none of these controls is used, the researcher must assume (a better word is hope) that variations are random. The example of noise outside the learning lab is an illustration. With luck, this will influence the subjects in each group about equally. Even with luck, though, noise may so increase the variability between individuals as to hide any effect of the variables being studied.

The major validity problems of sample studies also exist in correlational and experimental research. All these quantitative methods operationalize variables, draw conclusions from samples to populations, and attempt to get the same information repeatedly. When evaluating quantitative research, watch out for:

Invalid operational definitions: ones that measure a variable other than or in addition to what they are supposed to measure.

Biased samples: samples that are systematically different in some way from the population they are drawn from.

Uncontrolled variation in information: information that depends on who collected it, or how, when or where it was collected.

If you suspect any of these problems, name the extraneous variable(s) that might be responsible, and try to explain how the extraneous variable(s) might account for the researcher's findings.

CORRELATIONAL RESEARCH: THE PROBLEM
OF SUBJECT VARIABLES

Correlational research assesses the relationship between variables without manipulating any variable. The essential problem with this procedure is that it is impossible to measure one variable at a time in existing populations. Any measure of occupational status, for example, is in part a measure of education, because in our society the status of an occupation is closely related to the amount of education required for it. To attempt to relate occupational status to any other variable (say, intelligence or leadership ability) is difficult because any relationship that appears to exist may, in fact, be due to either occupation or education. Such variables as occupational status, education, intelligence, political party affiliation, and others, when they are measured as things a subject possesses before the research begins, are called *subject variables,* or *organismic variables,* and they pose the validity problem most characteristic of correlational research.

A *subject variable* or *organismic variable* is any characteristic that a research subject brings along to the research setting. For individuals, these characteristics include such attributes as sex, religion, education, and so on; for groups, they include group structure, communication patterns, and coalitions within the group. Some variables may or may not be organismic, depending on how they are treated in research. Anxiety is a good example. Consider an investigation of the effect of anxiety on learning. One method for this investigation would categorize people as highly anxious, moderately anxious, or nonanxious, using a pretest instrument such as the Taylor Manifest Anxiety Scale. The subjects would be given standard material to learn, and their performances compared. This correlational study measures the anxiety subjects bring with them to the study; anxiety is a subject variable. An experimental study of the effect of anxiety on learning might attempt to create anxiety experimentally (e.g., by misleading some subjects to believe that they are about to take an intelligence test), and measure the performance of anxious and control subjects on the same learning task. In such a study, anxiety is manipulated and is not treated as an organismic variable. Both studies use between-subjects *designs,* because they draw conclusions by comparing one group of people to another. Only the second study is a between-subjects *experiment* because only this study manipulates anxiety and assigns people to the anxious or nonanxious groups.

The variables in correlational studies tend to be organismic variables. The problem this creates is that other organismic variables are invariably correlated with those measured. Anxiety may be related to low self-esteem, insecurity in the presence of authority figures, emotional instability, or any number of other things. Therefore, if a correlational study shows anxiety to be related to learning, several alternative explanations are plausible. Learning may be affected by anxiety, by any of the correlated variables mentioned, by some other correlated variable, or by any combination of the above. *Measures of organismic variables are always confounded by other organismic variables. Whenever one variable in a hypothesis is organismic, all correlates of this variable are extraneous variables in the study, and each one can potentially be used to suggest an alternative explanation.*

METHODS OF CONTROL

The example of anxiety and learning suggests one possible way to eliminate the problem.

Use an experimental design with random assignment. When a subject variable is the independent variable in a hypothesis and it is capable of manipulation, a *between-subjects experiment* that employs random assignment (equivalent-groups design) can minimize the threat to validity by manipulating the subject variable. Thus, in an experiment on the effect of anxiety on learning, the potential subjects are randomly assigned to two groups: the experimental (anxious group) and the control (not anxious group). The two groups are treated identically except for the procedure used to create anxiety. This means that subjects are greeted the same way and are given instructions that differ only in one respect. Let's say the "anxiety group" is told that what they are about to do is an intelligence test, while the controls are told that the experimenter wants to compare two word lists to see if they are of equal difficulty (or some other presumably non-anxiety-arousing instruction). Both groups are given the same word lists to memorize, and their learning is tested in the same way. Thus, the only systematic difference between the two groups is in the part of the instructions that was intended to produce (or not to produce) anxiety.

What about organismic variables? These subjects, like the subjects in a correlational study, differ in the anxiety they had when they arrived, and also in self-esteem, relationships to authority, and every other variable that may be related to anxiety or learning. However, the subjects who began with high anxiety, say, were equally likely to be assigned to either group; so also were the subjects with low self-esteem, emotional instability, and so on. Thus, it would be unreasonable to conclude that the reason the people in the anxious group performed better was that they were trying to bolster their low self-esteem by performing well. There is no reason to believe that this group had lower (or higher) self-esteem than the other group. When a researcher assigns subjects at random to groups in a between-subjects experiment, we say that organismic variables (self-esteem, anxiety before the experiment began, etc.) are *randomized. Random assignment to conditions eliminates any bias that might systematically put similar people in the same group.* Contrast the randomized experiment with a correlational study of the same variables. In the correlational study, the highly anxious people probably have other personality characteristics in common as well (some possibilities have already been mentioned), and any of these could explain any observed difference in learning. In the experiment, personality characteristics are randomized. They are not systematically related to anxiety, because each personality type is equally likely to be in the anxious and nonanxious groups of the experiment. Thus, personality differences between groups are unlikely explanations of any differences in learning.

It is important to note that randomization does not eliminate all the personality differences between the two groups, but only ensures that each personality type or characteristic is *equally likely* to be in either group. On occasion, the people with low self-esteem, for example, will be put in the same group by the luck of the draw, but this does not happen systematically. The errors due to randomization in experiments resemble those produced by representative or random sampling in sample studies. Random error exists in both, but it is tolerable because it is not biased in either direction, and because its magnitude can be estimated with statistical techniques. In short, while randomization does not eliminate extraneous variables, and it does not keep them from varying, it does minimize their power to offer alternative explanations for research findings.

Randomization controls organismic variables only when they are independent variables, and when they can be manipulated. In many cases, these criteria are not met. For example, most of the variables of interest to sociologists and political scientists are either impossible or very difficult to manipulate. Think of doing an experiment to measure the effects of religion, social class, stigmatization, alienation, cultural conflict, or social disorganization. All are variables that subjects (people or societies) carry with them, and which pretty much must be studied as they are. A general strategy for controlling the effects of correlates of organismic variables that cannot be manipulated is matching.

Matching. This is the strategy of comparing individuals or groups who are equal in terms of an extraneous variable in order to rule this variable out as an explanation of a hypothesized relationship. Wrightsman (1969) used matching in a study done to discover whether supporters of George Wallace for President in 1968 upheld "law and order" as much in their daily lives as their candidate did in his campaign. In Nashville, the local government had passed an ordinance requiring all cars to display a tax sticker (cost: $15) beginning November 1, 1968, a few days before the election. Wrightsman's study was simple: he and his students went around to parking lots after the law went into effect and noted the presence or absence of tax stickers on cars with political bumper stickers. Wallace supporters (operational definition: Wallace sticker on car) obeyed the law significantly less frequently than Humphrey or Nixon supporters, or cars without bumper stickers. This is a correlational study. Neither variable (candidate supported, obedience to law) was manipulated. It follows that organismic variables entered the study with the subjects (cars), and that some of these may be related to the variables being studied. One such variable is socioeconomic status. Wrightsman reasoned that Wallace supporters in Tennessee tended to come from the working class, and they might, therefore, be less likely to have the $15 for the sticker. If this were true, the findings could be explained without reference to the Wallace supporters' lawfulness.

Wrightsman used matching to rule out this explanation. Wrightsman's observers were instructed to proceed by looking for a car in a parking lot with a political bumper sticker, recording the necessary information about the car, and then recording the same information about the car parked closest on its left that had no bumper sticker. It was reasoned that cars parked next to each other in the same lot would likely belong to people of similar socioeconomic status who were on similar errands. Thus, each car was matched with a single other car of presumably equal socioeconomic status. Wallace cars were less law-abiding than the cars parked on their left, while Nixon and Humphrey cars were more law-abiding than the cars parked on their left.

It is important to realize that matching controls only those variables that are matched. It may still be, for example, that Wallace supporters who used bumper stickers were more generally rebellious people than the average Wallaceite. Since Wallace was not a major party candidate, affixing a Wallace sticker may have taken a streak of rebelliousness. The Humphrey and Nixon sticker-users may have been more typical of all supporters of their candidates. If this were true, Wrightsman's results would imply that it was rebelliousness that led some people both to use Wallace stickers and not to affix tax stickers. The conclusions would not apply to Wallace supporters in general. However far-fetched this hypothesis, the matching for socioeconomic status does nothing to rule out the alternative explanation based on rebelliousness.

Because matching controls only those variables that are matched, there is a practical limit to how many organismic variables can be controlled by matching. A researcher generally uses matching to control only those variables most likely to provide alternative explanations of the expected results. This is sometimes done even in experimental research, when a variable is so important that the researcher is unwilling to rely on randomization to equalize it. Such a situation might exist in research on learning, where intelligence is so important an organismic variable that subjects may be matched on it before being randomly assigned to experimental groups.

Occasionally, in an experimental study, a special sort of matching called the *yoked control* is used. Subjects are paired and then undergo treatments that are identical except for the independent variable. A good example is Brady's work with the "executive monkeys" (Brady, 1958). Two monkeys, strapped into identical apparatus, were either shocked or not shocked together. Although each monkey had a lever in front of it, only one lever had the power to turn off or prevent the shocks. (The monkeys with this lever—the "executives"—developed ulcers.) Another example comes from dream research. In studies in which subjects are deprived of dreaming, their sleep is also interrupted, so the two variables (dreaming and sleeping) are confounded. To control this, a second subject may be yoked with the dream-deprived subject so that whenever one subject starts to dream, both are awakened, regardless of whether the second subject is dreaming. Thus, both subjects are interrupted in sleep to the same extent, but only one is systematically dream-deprived.

The ultimate in matching, of course, is to *compare subjects with themselves*. This is possible in correlational research on such topics as emotional mood, intellectual development, and social change, all of which imply change over time within a single individual or society. Within-subjects experiments also control for subject variables by comparing subjects with themselves. More will be said below about this method for controlling organismic variables.

Statistical control of correlates of organismic variables. Similar in intent to matching are a number of procedures that attempt to accomplish matching after the fact. The researcher collects information about possible extraneous variables and then compares subjects who are equivalent in terms of these variables. Wrightsman used an elementary form of statistical control in his bumper-sticker study to deal with the extraneous variable of socioeconomic status. On the assumption that the age of a car was a good index of the socioeconomic status of its owner, Wrightsman recorded the model years of all cars observed. When Wallace supporters with new (less than four year old) cars were compared with Humphrey and Nixon supporters with new cars, the Wallaceites were less obedient of the law. The same relationship held when people with older cars were compared. By comparing groups of cars of the same age, Wrightsman was able to judge the relationship between political preference and obedience with socioeconomic status held constant. Since the relationship still held, one alternative explanation was ruled out.

In this procedure, Wrightsman did not match individual cars, but controlled status effects through data analysis. Status was measured (by age of car), and the data analysis was broken down according to status in the hope that, with status held constant, the hypothesized relationship would still hold.

More sophisticated methods of statistical control have been developed to deal with the problem of subject variables, and you will find them in reports of correlational research. The statistical procedures and rationales for such techniques as partial correlation (e.g., Friedman, 1972; Hays, 1963) and analysis of covariance (e.g., Kerlinger, 1973; Winer, 1962) are described in various books on research methodology, including those cited here.

Inclusion of extraneous variable(s) in the hypothesis. Randomization, matching, and the statistical controls discussed above all attempt to keep extraneous variables out of consideration. It is also possible to measure an extraneous variable specifically to assess its effect on the variables of the original hypothesis. Consider this example. An educator wished to study the effect of programmed instruction on performance in a college introductory psychology course. Since the researcher did not have the power to see that students were randomly assigned to programmed or nonprogrammed instruction, the study was correlational. The final exam performance in a section receiving programmed instruction was compared with that of another section receiving more traditional instruction. The programmed group scored higher on the final exam. It was later discovered that the students in the programmed section had higher verbal ability (as measured by Scholastic Aptitude Tests). Thus, their success on the final exam might have been due either to superior instruction or to superior verbal ability; the two variables were confounded.

Because the researcher had information on all three variables (type of instruction, verbal ability, and performance) for each subject, it was possible to examine the joint effect of the independent variable and the "third" variable on performance. This was done by dividing the students in each section into subgroups according to their SAT Verbal scores, and by summarizing the results (see Table 3.4).

This table summarizes what we already know and gives additional information. The last column shows that the programmed instruction group scored higher on the final exam (80.8 to 73.1), and the bottom row shows that students with high verbal ability (SAT Verbal over 500) did better than students of lower verbal ability (83.3

Table 3.4. Mean Final Examination Scores of Introductory Psychology Students of Low and High Verbal Ability Receiving Two Types of Instruction (Hypothetical Data)

Method of Instruction	SAT Verbal Scores				Grand Mean
	500 or Below	n^a	Over 500	n^a	
Programmed	77.0	9	83.0	16	80.8
Traditional	68.0	17	84.0	8	73.1
All students	71.1	26	83.3	24	76.6

[a] "n" denotes the number of people in each subgroup. In the programmed instruction section, nine students had SAT Verbal scores of 500 or below, and sixteen had scores over 500, and so on.

to 71.1). We can also see from the columns labeled *"n"* that more high-verbal students were in the programmed section (16 to 8, though each section had 25 students). This is information we already had. The special value of this table is that it also gives quantitative information on the effects of programmed instruction on each type of student (low and high verbal ability) separately. When we examine these data, we find that programmed instruction greatly improved the performance of low-verbal students, who scored 77, compared to 68 for similar students in the traditional class. However, programmed instruction was no help to the students with high verbal ability. In fact, these students performed slightly better in the traditional class (84 to 83). By measuring verbal ability, and including it as a variable for study, we have discovered that the effect of programmed instruction depends on the type of student being taught. The researcher started with a simple question about two variables—"Which instructional method is more effective?"—and was able to get an answer about three variables—"Programmed instruction is better with students of low verbal ability, but the method of instruction makes little difference with students of higher verbal ability." The joint effect of verbal ability and instructional method on performance is called an *interaction of variables*.

When the effect of one variable depends on the presence, absence, or amount of another variable, the two variables are said to interact. In the example, the effect of programmed instruction depends on the type of student. The reverse is also true: the performance of a given type of student depends on the type of instruction (at least for low-verbal students). An interaction exists whenever two or more independent variables, by virtue of acting at the same time, influence a dependent variable. In the programmed instruction example, both type of instruction and verbal ability are considered as independent variables which, when combined, have an influence on performance. That is, the effect of the two variables acting together is different from the sum of two separate effects. Programmed instruction increases performance, and so does verbal ability, but programmed instruction, when combined with high verbal ability, does nothing to increase performance.

Probably the most famous interaction is that of alcohol and barbiturates. Someone who is used to taking either drug knows what to expect when taking one alone, but the deaths of people who have taken both are proof that the interaction is different from the sum of the two drug effects. Each drug has an effect, and so does their interaction.

In the case of the drug interaction, each drug has an effect by itself, but the effect of the two taken together cannot be predicted from the effect of the single drugs alone. It is also possible for variables to interact even when it seems that neither of them has any effect by itself. Consider the example of a psychologist who tried out a new "energizing" drug on a sample of emotionally disturbed and mentally retarded children. The children's behavior changed after ingesting the drug, but the average change was zero. When the researcher divided the results between boys and girls, it became clear that the girls all became more active after taking the drug, while the boys became less active. When boys and girls were considered together, the increase and decrease canceled each other, and the net effect appeared to be zero. (This example and several others appear in a detailed article on the concept of interaction by Schaefer [1976].)

It is important to realize that the existence of an interaction changes the meaning of the information that was available before the interaction was examined. This is obvious in the example of the "energizing" drug, where the effect of the drug seems to be zero until the interaction with the child's sex is taken into account. The point applies equally well to the example of programmed instruction. Although it is true that, for the students studied, those receiving programmed instruction did better, this simple statement is misleading. The facile interpretation—that programmed instruction helps students learn better—is incorrect. If there is any causal relationship, it can only be for some (low-verbal) students. By explicitly studying the extraneous variable of verbal ability, something was learned about programmed instruction that would have been missed if verbal ability had been controlled by randomization or matching. The strategy of including additional variables in the hypothesis sometimes allows us to discover that the effect of an independent variable may depend on a variable that had previously been thought to be extraneous. Since extraneous variables commonly interact in this way with variables of more direct interest, the best way to handle "extraneous" variables is often to explicitly measure them to assess their importance. This strategy reaches its highest development when an extraneous variable can be experimentally manipulated to study its effects, as in the example of black and white interviewers on page 87.

A common method of including extraneous variables in the hypothesis is *multiple regression analysis*. It is beyond the scope of this book to explain the mathematics of this common technique of economics, sociology, and political science, but we can briefly explain how it works in general terms. An example will help. In a study we conducted with our colleague Tom Dietz (Stern, Dietz, and Kalof, 1993), we surveyed a sample of college students to examine the how different beliefs about the consequences of changes in the natural environment affected the students' willingness to take action on environmental problems. Our chief measure of action was a scale of political behavior made up of the respondents' expressed willingness to participate in proenvironmental demonstrations, contribute money, sign petitions, and take a job with a company that harms the environment. (We reversed the responses on the last survey item so we could combine them by addition.) We measured three kinds of beliefs as independent variables: beliefs that environmental problems cause harm to the respondent or his or her family (showing an egoistic concern), beliefs that other, more distant human beings might be harmed (altruistic concern), and beliefs that environmental conditions harm nonhuman organisms or the biosphere generally (biospheric concern). We reasoned that students would be more likely to take action when they believed an environmental problem threatened things they valued. Because some of the literature on environmentalism claims that women are more proenvironmental than men, we recorded the gender of each respondent. At first, we intended to treat gender as an extraneous variable, but we arranged our analysis so that we could interpret it as an independent variable as well. We thus had one dependent variable (willingness to act politically) and four variables treated as independent variables (three kinds of concerns or values, and gender).

We wanted to learn whether each kind of value had an effect on proenvironmental political behavior independently of the effects of the other values and independently of any effect of gender. (Actually, since this is a correlational study, we were measuring associations and not effects, but our hypothesis was causal and we intended to interpret any associations as effects.) We could have presented the data in a table like Table 3.4, but with four independent variables, it would be difficult to make sense of the numbers in the table. Instead, we used multiple linear regression analysis. This is a statistical technique that arrives at numbers (called *regression coefficients*) for each independent variable that allow a researcher to estimate each respondent's score on the dependent variable by multiplying the respondent's score on each independent variable by its coefficient and then adding. In our study, multiple regression results in something like this:

$$\begin{aligned} &(e \times \text{egoistic concern score}) \\ +\ &(s \times \text{social-altruistic concern score}) \\ +\ &(b \times \text{biospheric concern score}) \\ +\ &\underline{(g \times \text{gender [0 if male, 1 if female]})} \\ =\ &\text{estimated political action score.} \end{aligned}$$

In this equation, e, s, b, and g are the regression coefficients for each of the four independent variables. The equation allows the researcher to estimate an individual's political action score given knowledge of that individual's beliefs and gender. Larger coefficients mean that an independent variable has a large effect; coefficients close to zero mean that it has little effect on the political action score. In terms of controlling for extraneous variables, the importance of this equation is that each regression coefficient takes the other coefficients into account—it represents the effect of a particular independent variable with the other ones held constant by a statistical procedure.

In our study, we first compared women and men on the political action scale, and found that the women students expressed more willingness than the men to take proenvironmental action. The political action scale was a standardized scale, which means that the average score is zero, and 95% of the individuals have scores between -2 and $+2$. On average, women scored $+.23$ and men $-.28$, a difference of .51, which is strongly statistically significant. We then conducted the multiple regression with the three kinds of beliefs and gender as independent variables. It showed that each kind of belief had a statistically significant association with political behavior, but that gender had no significant effect. With beliefs controlled statistically, the average score for women was $+.07$ and for men, $-.10$, a difference of only .17.

We concluded several things from this. First, gender has some sort of effect on proenvironmental political behavior. Second, beliefs about all three kinds of effects of environmental conditions—on self, on others, and on the biosphere—also affect political behavior. Third, when gender and beliefs are considered together, the effect of gender disappears. We guessed that gender had an *indirect effect* on proenvironmental behavior by influencing environmentally relevant beliefs: that is, gender directly affected environmental beliefs, but only beliefs (and not gender) affected the behavioral measure directly. In support of this guess, we found that the college women in this population believed that environmental problems had more serious effects on self, on others, *and* on the biosphere than the men did.

This example shows how multiple regression techniques can be used to consider the effect of an extraneous variable (gender) by including it in the hypothesis. It also shows how regression can lead to a deeper understanding than can be obtained by holding the variable constant (for example, studying only female students), or by using techniques like matching that achieve control of the variable but not information about it. We concluded that gender was *not* extraneous to environmental concern. It seemed to somehow influence beliefs about the environment that, in turn, affected behavior. This conclusion has led us to conduct more research to try to understand the relationships that might explain the role of gender in environmental attitudes and behavior. In our new research, we are trying to learn more about differences between men's and women's beliefs about the environment.

The kind of findings we observed are sometimes reported in research articles as a *path diagram,* which represents statistically significant associations in a correlational study that are presumed to reflect causal relations with arrows, and the strengths of those associations with regression coefficients. Figure 3.1 is a path diagram that summarizes findings from our study. Each of the three arrows on the left side of the diagram represents a regression equation estimating scores on a belief scale from gender. The three arrows on the right side of the diagram represent the single regression equation estimating political action scores from the three kinds of beliefs *and* from gender. There is no arrow directly from gender to the political action scale because that regression coefficient was not statistically significant. So the diagram graphically represents our interpretation that gender has an effect on commitment to action indirectly, through environmental beliefs, but not directly, independent of beliefs.

The strategy of including extraneous variables in the hypothesis is limited in that it controls only those variables that are included. Other organismic variables are left uncontrolled. In the programmed instruction study, for example, an important organismic variable is the teacher's instructional style. Type of instruction is confounded with the style and personality of the teachers involved, and this cannot be changed by measuring students' verbal ability. In the study of environmentalism, political liberalism or conservatism is an extraneous variable that is left uncontrolled. It may affect both environmental beliefs and behavior, and it is not controlled by including gender in the hypothesis.

Often, researchers begin with a hypothesis stated in terms of the interaction of variables. The critical period hypothesis in developmental psychology is an example.

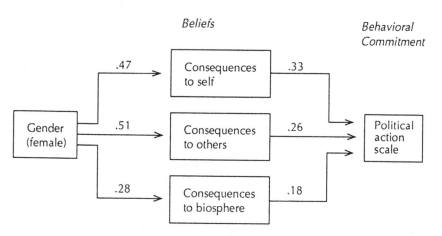

Figure 3.1 Effects of gender and beliefs on commitment to take proenvironmental action. (All the regression coefficients reported are statistically significant at the .05 level or beyond.

The effect of a life experience is held to be dependent on the stage of development during which it occurs. That is, the effect of experience depends on time. There are many other examples in the social sciences in which interactions are hypothesized. Such hypotheses can be tested either by correlational research, as in the programmed instruction example, or by experimental methods, if the independent variables can be manipulated. In any research of this type, the presence of an interaction changes the meaning of any effects of the variables that interact. The reasoning behind this is the same whether the interaction was predicted or not.

In summary, the chief problem in drawing conclusions from correlational research is that such research measures organismic variables. Any finding explained in terms of an organismic variable may alternatively be explained in terms of any other organismic variable that is correlated with the first, but was not studied. Four strategies are commonly used to solve this problem of inference:

Randomization. A between-subjects experiment allows organismic variables to vary randomly, and eliminates systematic error.

Matching. Individuals can be matched with others (or themselves) so that the only important differences are in terms of variables in the hypothesis.

Statistical control. Individuals can be matched after the fact to compare the effect of an independent variable on people who were initially comparable in terms of selected extraneous variable(s).

Inclusion of extraneous variable(s) in the hypothesis. An extraneous variable is measured and treated as an independent variable that may, either alone or in interaction with other variables in the study, influence a dependent variable of interest.

WITHIN-SUBJECTS EXPERIMENT: THE PROBLEM OF "TIME-TIED" EXTRANEOUS VARIABLES

The within-subjects experiment has already been mentioned as a technique for controlling organismic variables. By observing changes in a single individual, or group of individuals, the effects of a manipulated variable can be measured while achieving perfect control of organismic variables. A price is paid for this control, however. When a subject is observed over a period of time, to see when he/she changes, any variable that might have produced an observed change is confounded with the passage of time. The independent variable might have changed the subject, but any other events during the same time period may also be responsible. In short, *"time-tied" extraneous variables* (Agnew & Pyke, 1969) *pose the characteristic validity problem of within-subjects experiments.*

Consider this example of a within-subjects experiment. A researcher is studying the effect of a new drug, Memoraid, on learning. Because some people learn faster than others, the researcher decides to use subjects as their own controls. Each subject will get a chance to learn both with and without the drug. On the first day, each subject is tested with a placebo (no drug), on a task involving the learning of a series of nonsense syllables. On the next day the subjects are given the real drug, and are asked to learn a new list of nonsense syllables. The subjects learn better the second time. The experimenter might be tempted to conclude that Memoraid improves learning. However, many time-tied extraneous variables are confounded with the drug's effect. Subjects may have learned something about memorizing nonsense syllables on the first day and applied the knowledge by learning better on the second day. Or, they may have become bored with nonsense syllables. This would mean that the drug has a stronger effect than the results indicate. Subjects may have gotten to know the experimenter better, and, feeling comfortable, may have performed better the second time. On the other hand, familiarity may have lowered their anxiety level, leaving them less motivated to perform well. It's also possible that time-tied changes took place in the apparatus used to collect data. The wires in the memory drum used to display the nonsense syllables may have become worn, and resistance in the circuits might have increased, causing the drum to move slower and giving subjects more time to learn on the second day. The laboratory might have been visited by noisy plumbers on the first day, or the weather might have been rainy, making the subjects mentally sluggish. And so on and so on.

The above problems are not unique to experimental research; they also exist in case studies, naturalistic observations, and correlational research. Suppose the effects of Memoraid were first discovered by a scientist who accidentally ingested some of the drug. Her/his evidence would have been based on a retrospective case study, without *any* effort at systematic control. The effects attributed to the drug could have easily been due to any number of time-tied variables.

METHODS OF CONTROL

Three common procedures for controlling time-tied extraneous variables are described below.

Use of a comparison group. A group of subjects could be observed over the same time period as the experimental subjects, but without exposure to the independent variable. In the Memoraid experiment, this could be accomplished by randomly assigning subjects to get either the drug *or* the placebo (control). This would transform the study into a between-subjects experiment. The between-subjects design does not have serious problems with time-tied extraneous variables.

Comparison groups can be used to control time-tied extraneous variables in non-experimental research, and some special designs have been developed for this purpose. In the *multiple time-series design* (Campbell & Stanley, 1963; Gottman, McFall, & Barnett, 1969), a group that has been exposed to an independent variable is compared to a control group on several occasions both before and after exposure. Both groups are exposed to the passage of time, but if the independent variable makes a difference, they will change differently over time, and especially after the independent variable is introduced. More sophisticated procedures for making unambiguous inferences from correlational data over time include the cross-lagged panel design and methods of path analysis (e.g., Heise, 1969; Land, 1969).

Counterbalancing. In a counterbalanced design, two or more groups are used, one for each treatment condition. However, unlike the between-subjects experiment in which each group is exposed to different treatments, in a counterbalanced design, each group gets all treatments, but in different orders. To counterbalance the experiment on Memoraid and learning, one group would get the placebo on the first day, and Memoraid on the next day. The other subjects would get Memoraid first, and then the placebo. Thus, any effect of learning to memorize, or boredom, or noisy plumbers, or slow machines would be equally divided between subjects getting the drug and subjects getting the placebo. If any of these variables either aids or interferes with learning, it could not explain any difference between drug and placebo treatments. It is also possible to counterbalance the lists of nonsense syllables in this study. After all, one list may be easier to learn than the other. To control for this possibility, the two groups can be divided, with half of each group learning list A first, and then list B. The order would be reversed for the other half of each group. The counterbalanced design for the Memoraid experiment is given in Table 3.5.

ABA design (repeated experiments). In an ABA design, subjects are observed before and after an experimental treatment, as well as while they are getting the treatment. (A represents the condition in which the treatment is absent and B the condition in which it is present.) This experimental design is common to most studies in the field of behavior modification. For example, suppose a teacher wants to decrease the frequency of aggressive outbursts by one of the boys in the class. The teacher plans to reinforce nonaggressive behavior with praise, and remove the boy from his classmates when he acts aggressively toward them. First, a "baseline" is taken. That is, the child is observed for a while before the treatment begins, and the frequency of aggressive outbursts is tabulated. When treatment begins, the number of aggressive acts each day is recorded, and, it is hoped, it decreases. The experiment may go on, alternately starting and stopping the treatment a few times, to demonstrate a consistent relationship between onset of treatment and decreases in aggressive behavior. The subject has served as his own control.

Note that in this example, the within-subjects design is used with only one subject. Partly because of increased interest in behavior modification techniques, psychologists have paid considerable attention to experimental designs for single subjects. As a result, they have developed some subtle methods of within-subject experimentation (e.g., Kratochwill & Levin, 1992).

The ABA design controls for some of the important time-tied variables. If a time-tied variable operated continually, its effect should increase with time, independent of treatments. In the Memoraid experiment, the effect of learning to learn, or boredom, or acquaintance of the subject and the experimenter should get stronger and stronger, rather than coming and going with the drug. If subjects were given a placebo at both ends of the experiment, and if they learned best in the middle (under the drug), the above-mentioned variables could probably be discounted.

Both counterbalancing and the ABA design require that variables be manipulated. That is, these controls can be used only in experimental research. In correlational research, case studies, and naturalistic observations, the comparison group strategy

Table 3.5. A Counterbalanced Design

	First-Day Treatment		Second-Day Treatment	
Group	Drug	Syllable List	Drug	Syllable List
No. 1	Placebo	List A	Memoraid	List B
No. 2	Placebo	List B	Memoraid	List A
No. 3	Memoraid	List A	Placebo	List B
No. 4	Memoraid	List B	Placebo	List A

is the only feasible way to rule out alternative explanations dependent on the passage of time.

BETWEEN-SUBJECTS EXPERIMENTS: THE IMPORTANCE OF GROUP EQUIVALENCE

Recall from Chapter 2 that unless a between-subjects experiment randomly assigns subjects to treatment and comparison groups (the equivalent groups design), it cannot be assumed that the groups are comparable. In a nonequivalent groups design, subjects assigned to different treatments may be systematically different in terms of whatever organismic variables are associated with the particular group they are in. But between-subjects experiments often use naturally occurring comparison groups. In such experiments, it is generally possible to think of alternative explanations that depend on the noncomparability of the groups (Cook & Campbell, 1979). A few examples:

In educational research, treatments are often applied to whole classrooms, with other classrooms providing the comparison group. But pupils are rarely assigned to classrooms at random. They may be assigned by ability grouping, by pressure from parents who try to get their children into the classroom of the teacher they think is best, or by some other nonrandom procedure. Every deviation from randomness introduces extraneous variables into the experiment. In these examples, pupil ability and parental tendencies toward intervention may influence the dependent variable in an educational experiment as much as the independent variable does.

In marketing research, companies sometimes test-market a new version of a product in one city and use another city as the comparison group. When this happens, every difference between the cities is a confounding variable in the experiment. Among the variables that might matter in marketing are average income and educational levels, unemployment levels, and, for some products, cultural or religious variables that affect purchases of the product.

Sometimes a government agency or a company evaluates a new program by comparing the first people who participate with others in their vicinity. For example, to evaluate an energy-conservation program, a natural-gas company offered it to all its customers in a city. It surveyed the first 200 participants in the program and a random sample of 200 other households to see how many energy-conservation activities they had taken in their homes, and it attributed the difference between the groups to the program. But participation in the program was not by random assignment, and there are systematic differences between the participants and the nonparticipants. A very important difference is that the participants were obviously among the households most interested in energy conservation. Some of the energy conservation measures these households took might well be due to their own interest in conservation, and not to the program.

METHODS OF CONTROL

Matching. When random assignment is not possible or desirable in between-subjects experiments, the most common method of control for organismic variables is matching. As discussed in methods of control for correlational studies, matching subjects on important extraneous variables that might affect the dependent variable eliminates alternative explanations based on those extraneous variables. Using only first-year college students in the dormitory crowding experiment conducted by Baum and Valins (1977) eliminated the possibility that the student's year in college might have caused the observed differences between the crowded and uncrowded dorm residents. For example, third- or fourth-year dorm residents might feel less crowded than first-year residents because they have had more time to become adapted to dorm conditions.

Waiting-list control. Another method, useful in program-evaluation studies like the energy-conservation experiment above, is the waiting-list control group. The gas company might have randomly chosen half of its first 200 participants to be told that the program was oversubscribed and that they would have to wait a month to join. It could then have compared the energy activities these people undertook at the end of the month with those undertaken by the other half of the 200, who were allowed to join the program immediately. This kind of control achieves many of the benefits of random assignment to treatments. It automatically controls for interest in energy conservation, because all 200 customers can be assumed to be about equal on that variable and because the most highly interested were equally likely to be assigned to the treatment or the control group. But it is not as good a research design as one that randomly assigns treatments to a representative sample of all the company's customers, because the subjects in both groups are probably systematically different from the rest of the population that the company wants to learn about. What works well with the highly motivated first 200 might not work at all in the rest of the city.

Statistical control. Yet another way to eliminate alternative explanations in between-subjects, nonequivalent-groups experiments is through statistical control of organismic variables. Usually this is accomplished by including the variables in the data analysis. For example, in their quasi-experiment on crowding in dorms, Baum and Valins (1977) used a survey to collect background information on the dorm residents. The researchers included this information in the data analysis, and none of the background variables had an effect on the dependent measures (Epstein & Baum, 1978). As with correlational studies, the most common methods of statistical control for quasi-experiments are cross-tabulation, partial correlation, regression, and analysis of variance. More sophisticated statistical analyses have recently been developed. Many of these techniques have been reviewed by Achen (1986).

Even when subjects are randomly assigned to experimental treatments, the between-subjects experiment is not a foolproof design. "On stage" and other changes caused by research, as well as biases in judgment, are problems for this method. Just as for other quantitative methods (sample study and correlational study), sampling bias and invalid operational definitions can pose serious threats to the validity of a between-subjects experiment, with or without randomization.

The last sections of this chapter have outlined the major sources of alternative explanations for the results of quantitative research. Table 3.6 summarizes these sources, indicates when they are most likely to cause trouble, and describes some of the methods researchers use to rule out alternative explanations. This table, together with Tables 3.1, 3.2, and 3.3, constitute a summary of the common sources of alternative explanations for the findings of social scientific research.

The exercises for this chapter emphasize the ability to identify alternative expla-

Table 3.6. Sources of Alternative Explanation in Quantitative Research Methods

Source	Description	When a Problem	Methods of Control
Invalid operational definition	Operational definition measures another variable as well	Potential problem with all operational definitions	Prevent confounding
Sampling bias	Sample systematically different in some respects from population	Nonrandom sampling; volunteer subjects	Assure that sample is representative
Uncontrolled variation in information	Results depend on who collected them or how, when, or where collected	Whenever data are collected on several people or occasions	Hold procedures constant; manipulate the variable responsible
Organismic variables	Subject variables are measured and confounded with extraneous variables	When hypothesis contains an organismic variable; nonequivalent groups experiments	Randomization; matching; subject as own control; statistical control; waiting-list control; manipulate extraneous variable
Time-tied variables	Independent variable's effects confounded with the passage of time	Research with no comparison group	Add comparison group; counterbalancing; ABA design

nations for research results and to suggest controls that would improve the research. Specifically, the questions in the exercises directly test your ability to use the following terms:

Extraneous variable (defined on p. 63)
Alternative explanation (p. 63)
Holding procedures constant (p. 88)
Matching (p. 91)
Statistical control (p. 92)
Subjects as their own controls (p. 92)
Comparison group as a control (p. 99)
Sampling bias (p. 86)

The main point of this chapter is to build your skill in reading scientific reports with a critical eye to alternative explanations for reported findings. The exercises provide the opportunity to practice evaluating reports of research. A procedure for seeking alternative explanations may be helpful to you, until you develop enough experience to look in the right places.

Begin by identifying the research method used in the study you are evaluating. Table 3.7 identifies the most common sources of alternative explanation for each research method, and suggests the place to begin looking for validity problems in a

Table 3.7. Sources of Alternative Explanation in Six Methods of Scientific Research

Source	Research Method						
	Naturalistic Observation	Retrospective Case Study	Sample Study	Correlational Study	Within-Subjects Experiment	Between-Subjects, Nonequivalent Groups	Between-Subjects, Equivalent Groups
On stage effects (p. 65)	*	*	*	*	*	*	*
More persistent changes due to research (p. 69)	*	*	*	*	*	*	*
Incomplete access (p. 77)	**	**	*	*	*	*	*
Researcher selectivity (p. 78)	*	**	—	—	—	—	—
Researcher distortion (p. 80)	*	**	*	*	*	*	*
Selective or distorted memory (p. 82)	A source of alternative explanation when research relies on memory data						
Invalid operational definitions (p. 84)	—	—	**	**	**	**	**
Sampling bias (p. 86)	—	—	***	*	*	*	*
Uncontrolled variation in information (p. 87)	—	—	*	*	*	*	*
Organismic variables (p. 89)	*	*	—	***	— (Held constant)	**	—
Time-tied Variables (p. 98)	*	*	—	* (If subjects compared to selves)	***	**	—

*Asterisks indicate common sources of alternative explanation in a particular research method. The more asterisks, the more serious the problem. In looking for alternative explanations, start with sources given two or three asterisks, but do not ignore any column with an asterisk.

piece of research. By using the information in Table 3.7, you should be able to ask questions that will lead you to alternative explanations. With practice, you should become able to ask these questions and think of alternative explanations without consulting the table.

EXERCISES

The objective of this chapter and the following one is to help you learn to critically evaluate reports of empirical research. The exercises in this chapter provide practice on prepared summaries of (usually imaginary) research. In Chapter 4, you will apply your skills to actual published scientific reports.

The central skill in evaluating research is the skill of identifying plausible alternative explanations for researchers' findings. Because this ability is of greatest importance, the "briefer" exercises and problems that follow are provided for practice in offering alternative explanations. These are followed by other exercises that use all the skills of this chapter.

BRIEFER EXERCISES

For each research report summarized below, answer these questions in the spaces provided:

(a) What method was used to collect the data? (Use categories defined in Chapter 2.)

(b) What is the hypothesis (if any)? Identify the variables in the hypothesis, labeling the independent and dependent variables if the hypothesis is causal.

(c) Identify the findings (that is, what relationship of variables was observed?).

(d) Identify extraneous variables that suggest alternative explanations of these findings. State the alternative explanations, and suggest one method to control for each extraneous variable.

1. To assess the effects of psychotherapy as opposed to drug therapy, the progress of schizophrenic patients receiving these therapies was observed. All subjects were diagnosed schizophrenic, and were assigned to the treatments considered appropriate by their attending physicians. Subjects in the drug therapy condition were receiving a variety of drug treatments, but none was receiving psychotherapy. Those in the psychotherapy treatment included only subjects for whom no drugs were prescribed. After six months' observation, improvement, as judged by outside consultant psychiatrists, was greater in the psychotherapy group. It was concluded that psychotherapy is more effective than drug therapy in the treatment of schizophrenia.

(a)

(b)

(c)

(d)

2. To measure the effect of background music on retention of verbal material, volunteer subjects (drawn from an introductory psychology class on the basis of their interest) were randomly assigned to read a short story under one of three conditions: while listening to a recording of rock music (by the Grateful Dead), while listening to classical music (a recording of Beethoven's Second Symphony), or while listening to silence. All subjects wore headsets to screen out extraneous noises, and all were given the same multiple-choice test of their recall of details in the story. The group listening to silence remembered more details than either of the groups exposed to music, and it was concluded that music is a source of distraction leading to decreased retention.

(a)

(b)

(c)

(d)

3. An organization of newsmagazine publishers commissioned a researcher to get evidence concerning any relationship between reading newsmagazines and being well-informed on current events. The researcher carefully chose a representative sample of 1000 adults, collecting data from each on the number of newsmagazines read in the past month. Each person sampled also took a short test on current events. A significant relationship was found: the more newsmagazines a person reads, the higher she/he scored on the current events test. It was concluded that reading newsmagazines makes a person well-informed.

(a)

(b)

(c)

(d)

4. An experimental remedial math program was tested by using it on 30 fifth-graders all of whom were at least two years behind grade level in math. Subjects were all the fifth-graders who met this criterion in the school studied. After three months in the new program, the students had gained an average of eight months on their math achievement scores. Since this was a vast improvement over the three months' progress that might have been expected, the program was pronounced successful and instituted throughout the school system.

(a)

(b)

(c)

(d)

5. An investigator hypothesized that males perform better under competitive conditions than females. To test this hypothesis, a group of college students, participating as a course requirement, was given a series of arithmetic problems under instructions that these were part of an intelligence test, and that their scores would be compared with those of other adults across the country (these instructions were intended to make the situation competitive). The males in this group did significantly better than females. A second group of students, satisfying the same course

requirement, was given a series of nonsense syllables to learn, with instructions that the study concerned the relative ease of learning different kinds of meaningless material (these instructions were assumed to be noncompetitive). In this group, males and females performed equally well. The investigator concluded that males respond more favorably than females to competition (that is, the hypothesis was supported).

(a)

(b)

(c)

(d)

ANSWERS TO BRIEFER EXERCISES

1. (a) Method: *Between-subjects experiment, nonequivalent-groups design.* Since subjects were assigned to either of two treatments, this study meets our definition of a between-subjects experiment. But note that subjects were given the treatments their physicians considered appropriate, and were *not* assigned to treatments at random. This makes the study less than fully experimental (a quasi-experiment), and leaves the study open to a variety of alternative explanations.

(b) Hypothesis: Psychotherapy and drug *therapy* are not equally *effective in treating schizophrenics.* The independent variable is therapy, since the type of therapy is what is varied. The dependent variable is effectiveness.

(c) Findings: Improvement was greater in the psychotherapy group than the drug therapy group.

(d) Extraneous variables and alternative explanations:

   Changes caused by the research: Patients in psychotherapy spend more time with the doctor than patients receiving drugs. This fact may encourage the patient to "look good" to please the doctor (possibly in spite of a failure to improve). Patients might, for example, fail to report symptoms.

   Biases: No information is presented on the biases of the participating doctors (or the outside consultants) for either form of therapy. Doctors' biases may work in the therapy situation as self-fulfilling prophecies. It is certainly true that doctors who do psychotherapy have a personal stake in the process that may make them work harder than they do when treating patients with drugs. The *doctor's effort,* rather than the specific treatment, may cause improvement. Consultants, if they know who got which therapy, could distort what they see to fit their preconceptions.

Invalid operational definitions: "Psychotherapy" and "drug therapy" are inadequately defined. Any number of different drugs and schools of therapy may be involved. An evaluation of "drug therapy" presumes that the doctors know what drug to prescribe (not always true, especially in psychiatry). We could be rejecting drug therapy on the basis of the inappropriate choice of a particular drug in several cases. Improvement is "as judged by outside consultant psychiatrists," and the possible biases in this definition have already been discussed.

Organismic variables: By allowing the doctors to choose the treatments (perfectly good medical practice), we have made the *treatment* into an organismic variable—subjects are already in a treatment before the researcher does anything. This leads to confounding because other, related, organismic variables may affect the outcome of treatment. There are several possibilities. For example, doctors may habitually assign the more serious cases to drug therapy, thinking that they cannot benefit from psychotherapy. Thus, the improvement of the psychotherapy patients may be due to the fact that they weren't as sick in the first place. (Extraneous variable: *Severity of illness*). It is also possible that the doctors assigned patients to psychotherapy when they sensed the *personal compatibility* (extraneous variable) that may be necessary for successful therapy. Thus, their improvement may have been due to the doctors' screening, which allowed into psychotherapy only those patients who could be helped. Doctors could have screened their patients in many other ways (e.g., highly verbal patients tend to do better in psychotherapy, it is believed). Any organismic variable that differentiates the two groups may be responsible for the results.

Controls: Doctor-patient interaction can't be controlled entirely. In fact, it has been argued that the effect of psychotherapy may be due primarily to the relationship, rather than particular techniques. Biases might be lessened by assigning patients to doctors all of whom believe in the type of treatment they are asked to give, and by keeping the consultants blind to which patients receive what therapy. The problem of defining therapy can be handled by specifying which drug(s) and form(s) of psychotherapy are being studied. The results might not generalize to other treatments, but at least they would clearly apply to *some*. Organismic variables can best be controlled by random assignment to treatments. Doctors have sometimes agreed to this.

2. (a) Method: *Between-subjects experiment, equivalent-groups design.*
   (b) Hypothesis: *Music* affects the *retention of verbal material.* (Variables in italics.)
   (c) Findings: People listening to silence retained more verbal material than people listening to two kinds of background music.
   (d) Extraneous variables and alternative explanations:

   Biases: There is a sampling bias involved in using volunteers. Volunteers usually are more interested, motivated to please, and willing to work than a cross section of the same population. This causes confounding and suggests an alternative explanation only if some of the factors associated with volunteering might offer an explanation of the results. There is no obvious reason to expect that volunteers, in particular, would do better or worse with music or without (though they might do better than average under *all* conditions). If, however, the researcher had expectations about how subjects would perform, volunteers, being motivated to do what the experimenter wants, might confirm the hypothesis even if music had no effect.

Invalid operational definition of "music": "Music," in this study, is operationally defined as either the Grateful Dead or Beethoven, and "no music" is defined as silence. Isn't there something in between? You might say this study is comparing the effect of *sound* and *no sound* on retention. We can't tell if the effects are produced by sound or by *musical* sound; the two are confounded. This could be controlled by having the "no music" group hear a recording of conversation, or of white noise, at the same decibel level as the recorded music.

Organismic variables: These are controlled, since the subjects were assigned to the three conditions at random.

3. (a) Method: *correlational study*.

(b) Hypothesis: There is a relationship between *reading newsmagazines* and *being informed on current events*. The study started out to look for *a* relationship; only after the study was done was there any mention of a *causal* relationship. The hypothesis does not distinguish between independent and dependent variables.

(c) Findings: People who report having read a large number of newsmagazines are better informed about current events than people who report having read fewer newsmagazines. (Note that this statement is much different from the stated conclusion, which does not follow from this evidence.)

(d) Extraneous variables and alternative explanations:

"On stage" effects: Some subjects may lie to the researcher about how many magazines they read (it's hard to fake a current events test, unless you want to look stupid). This suggests an alternative explanation if (a) there is reason to expect that they may lie, and (b) their lying would change the results. These conditions may exist in this study. Suppose that some of the more educated subjects fear that they would look bad if they admitted how little they read. The same people may be informed about current events (maybe by watching the evening news), but without reading. The finding would then be a result of well-informed people trying to *appear* well-read, rather than any effect of actual reading of newsmagazines.

Organismic variables: In any correlational study, look for these. Here someone has used a correlation to "prove" a causal relationship; the reasoning is fallacious because any number of extraneous factors (organismic variables) might have produced the effect (of making some people better informed than others). Here are a few likely examples: People of higher *economic status* (extraneous variable) are well-informed (because they can have an impact on current events) and read more newsmagazines (because they can afford them). Or, people with more *education* are better informed (through their education) and read more magazines (because they like to); it may be, though, that it is their reading of *newspapers* that makes them well-informed. Or, maybe some people who must be well-informed about current events because their jobs require it read newsmagazines as a way to stay well-informed. And so on.

Controls: For organismic variables, you could use an experimental design or match or control statistically for extraneous variables. Since it would be hard to make people read newsmagazines (how could you be sure they read them?), it might make more sense to use matching or statistical after-the-fact control. We suggest controls for socioeconomic class, level of education, and the amount of exposure they have to sources of news other than magazines. If subjects matched on these variables knew more current events when they read more newsmagazines, we might start to believe that the magazines had something to do with it.

4. (a) Method: *within-subjects experiment*. Subjects are compared only to themselves (and to what they are expected to do).

(b) Hypothesis: *Remedial Math Program X* improves the *math achievement* of fifth graders who are behind grade level.

(c) Findings: Fifth-graders who were behind grade level in math gained an average of eight months on a math achievement test in the first three months of a new remedial program.

(d) Extraneous variables and alternative explanations:

Changes caused by research: There is a very real possibility that *the act of instituting the new program* (extraneous variable), rather than the program itself, could influence results. Students and teachers may try harder just because the method is new, and this effort may pay off (the Hawthorne effect). The new method may also give the slow students more *attention* than they would otherwise get. If the teachers believe in the new method, they may put unusual effort into it, and produce a self-fulfilling prophecy. Finally, the teachers, knowing that they are being observed, may try harder, regardless of the method they are using. Most of these criticisms take the form that teachers and/or students might work harder in the experimental situation regardless of the program they are using. (*Control:* It would help to give the comparison group some *other* program which is also different from what the teachers have used in the past. This would allow you to tell whether one program was better, even when both are "new" and "experimental.")

Time-tied variables: These are the big sources of trouble in within-subjects experiments. How do you *know* that fifth graders in this school should improve three months in three months? It seems to make sense, but it may not be so. The fifth grade teachers may be exceptionally good (or the fourth grade teachers exceptionally bad), so that everyone accelerates in fifth grade, regardless of special programs. Or these fifth-grade teachers may habitually give special attention to slow students, even when not using the new method. (*Control:* Use a comparison group. Really, these pupils should be divided in half, so that half the low-math fifth graders could be taught with a different system, for comparison.)

We can't resist commenting on this hypothetical school system's decision to adopt the new program systemwide on the basis of this faulty study. In terms of what's good for the slow learners in math, it may not matter whether the observed results are due to the program, the Hawthorne effect, or a self-fulfilling prophecy, on the principle that whatever works should be used. But if the truth of the matter is that the new program succeeded because it was implemented by enthusiastic teachers, it would be very unwise to force teachers to adopt the new methods. This is one of the reasons careful evaluation of evidence has practical importance.

5. (a) Method: *Between-subjects experiment, nonequivalent-group design.* According to our classification system, this is an experiment because one of the variables (competitiveness) is manipulated. It is important to remember, though, that one of the independent variables (gender) is *not* manipulated. Thus, with respect to gender, the study is correlational.

(b) Hypothesis: *Males perform* better under *competitive conditions* than *females.* There are *two* independent variables here: gender (male vs. female) and competitiveness of situation (competitive vs. noncompetitive). The dependent variable is performance.

(c) Findings: Under competitive instructions, males outperformed females on arithmetic problems. Under noncompetitive instructions, both sexes learned nonsense syllables equally well.

(d) Extraneous variables and alternative explanations:

Changes caused by research: Regardless of the instructions given, subjects may have tried to please the experimenter by doing what amounts to the gender-typed behavior on the task. Males may have tried harder on the math, while females may not have tried so hard. Thus, gender stereotypes, rather than response to competition, may have been responsible for the results. Furthermore, this sort of situation would have been most serious in the "competitive" situation. If neither group makes a special effort with noncompetitive instructions, and only males try hard in math under competitive conditions (because they are supposed to be good at math), we would expect the reported results. Maybe on a verbal task, women would do better with competitive instructions. (Control: Equalize the tasks. It's easy to see here why a task that isn't gender-typed would be advisable—subjects would have no idea what is expected in terms of gender roles, and might respond to competitiveness rather than to the nature of the task. One might also study the effect of gender-typing by manipulating this variable: you could assign male-stereotyped and female-stereotyped tasks under both competitive and noncompetitive conditions.)

Invalid operational definition of competitiveness: This operational definition is confounded because the competitive and noncompetitive groups differ not only in the instructions they were given but also in the type of material used to test their performance (an extraneous variable). Any gender difference attributed to competition may with equal reason be attributed to the type of task: men do better at math; but there is no ginder difference on verbal problems. You might also arrive at this explanation by considering:

Organismic variables: These may be a problem since one of the independent variables (gender) is organismic. If gender-related variables could explain the results, there is confounding. It turns out that such a problem exists. Males do better than females in mathematics, while females tend to excel on verbal tasks. In this study, the males did better on the mathematical task (the so-called competitive one) and the groups were equal on the verbal task (the "noncompetitive" one). This is consistent with what you might expect, even if the competitive instructions had no effect. (Control: The two tasks should have been equal in difficulty, and both should have been tasks on which men and women usually do equally well. Some pretesting of the tasks would have been necessary.) Note: we don't know how the two groups for this study were chosen. Were individuals assigned to groups at random? They came from one college course, but on what basis? One group may have been, for some reason, more verbal, more mathematical, or more competitive than the other.

Try the following problems; no answers are provided for them.

BRIEFER PROBLEMS

1. To test the effect of marijuana on time perception, the following experiment was performed. Subjects were given a standard dose of THC (the primary psychoactive ingredient of marijuana), and were asked to estimate the duration of a light that appeared on a screen in front of them. The light appeared three times, for durations of 10, 30, and 60 seconds. Each subject was presented with each duration once, in a random order (a different random order was chosen for each subject). The dependent variable was defined as the percent overestimation of time found for each duration. An average overestimation of 17% was found for the 10 second duration, 22% for the 30 second duration, and 20% for the 60 second duration. It was concluded that marijuana has a significant effect on time perception, resulting in an overestimation of time.

(a)

(b)

(c)

(d)

2. In another marijuana-time perception experiment, subjects were exposed to each of three dosages: zero (placebo), low THC, and high THC. Treatments were separated from each other by 24 hours, and all subjects first received the high-dose, then the placebo, and then the low-dose condition. All subjects in all conditions made a judgment of the duration of a light that was on for 30 seconds in all cases. The dependent variable was defined as percent overestimation of time, and was found to be 12%, 10% and 20% for zero, low, and high doses, respectively. Statistical results were not significant, and the investigator concluded that he had failed to support a conclusion that marijuana affected time perception.

(a)

(b)

(c)

(d)

3. To support an argument in favor of long prison terms for felonies, a prison administrator produced data to indicate that the older a prisoner is when released from prison, the less likely he or she is to commit another crime within the next four years. Specifically, Glaser (1964) found that federal prisoners released at ages 18–21, 22–25, 26–35, and 36 and over were returned to prison or sentenced for felony-like offenses 48%, 40%, 34%, and 27%, respectively, within four years. The prison administrator argued that these data showed that keeping prisoners locked up longer made them less likely to commit new crimes.

(a)

(b)

(c)

(d)

4. To compare the effectiveness of psychoanalytically oriented psychotherapy and behavior therapy, an experimenter randomly assigned neurotic patients to the psychiatric residents working under him on his hospital's staff. The residents were undergoing training in psychoanalytic techniques as part of their program, and were also given instruction in behavior therapy by an outside consultant, so that they could participate in the experiment. All patients were interviewed on admission to the hospital by the experimenter, who then assigned them to either behavior or psychoana-

lytic therapy. After six months of therapy, the patients were reinterviewed by the experimenter, and improvement was assessed by a checklist of symptoms filled out by the patient before and after therapy, and by the experimenter's rating of degree of improvement. Both groups improved significantly when patients' responses were used to measure improvement, but only the psychoanalytic group improved when the psychiatrist's ratings were used as the criterion. The investigator concluded that the results *favored psychoanalysis,* as patients' responses could have indicated denial of conflict, and that this possibility was more likely in behavior therapy patients.

(a)

(b)

(c)

(d)

5. A researcher hypothesized that anxiety would inhibit people from making new social contacts. To test this prediction, a group of 20 people was convened for an afternoon wine-and-cheese party. Five of the 20 were observers, each assigned to observe three other people and to keep track of the number of times each person initiated conversation with someone else at the party. Observers were instructed not to initiate conversation with anyone. The number of conversations initiated was the measure of making new social contacts, and the score on the Taylor Manifest Anxiety Scale (administered two weeks before the party) was the measure of anxiety. Subjects scoring high on anxiety made significantly fewer social contacts than low-anxiety subjects, and this was taken as support for the hypothesis.

(a)

(b)

(c)

(d)

A more complete exercise follows, in which a bit more information is given about the study described, and in which you are asked to evaluate the study in more detail. Answers follow the exercise.

COMPLETE EXERCISE

Answer the following questions about the research described below:

(a) What method was used to collect the data? (Use the categories from Chapter 2: naturalistic observation, retrospective case study, sample study, correlational study, within-subjects experiment, between-subjects experiment with equivalent-groups design, and between-subjects experiment with non-equivalent groups design).

(b) What is the hypothesis, if any? Is it causal or noncausal?

(c) Identify the variable(s) studied. If the hypothesis is causal, identify the independent and dependent variables. State the operational definition of each variable.

(d) Identify the findings (that is, what relationship of variables was observed?)

(e) Identify an extraneous variable that is controlled by holding it constant (e.g., by constant procedures, matching, statistical control, or comparing subjects to themselves).

Identify an extraneous variable that is randomized. (If there is none, say so.)

(f) Identify any extraneous variables that suggest an alternative explanation of the observed results. State the alternative explanation(s), and suggest one way to control for each extraneous variable involved.

(g) Identify the sample studied and the population from which it was drawn. If you detect any sampling bias, identify it.

(h) Identify any interactions of variables being studied.

The director of Hometown YMCA wanted to see if the "Y" program helps build leaders. He looked up the "Y" membership records, and found the names of all 52 boys aged 10–12 who were members in 1963. Using the school district's records of the same year, he randomly chose 52 boys of the same age, excluding from his sample any boy who was already on the "Y" list. He attempted to contact all of the 104 men (he could locate only 48 of the "Y" members and 41 of the nonmembers) and to determine their present occupations. Using a standard index of the socioeconomic status of occupations, a status rating was determined for each subject's present job. As the "Y" group had the higher average status rating, it was concluded that the "Y" builds leaders.

(a)

(b)

(c)

(d)

(e)

(f)

(g)

(h)

ANSWERS TO COMPLETE EXERCISE

(a) Method: Correlational study (no variable was manipulated.)
(b) Hypothesis: Membership in the "Y" increases the chances of a boy's becoming a leader. Causal.
(c) Variables: Membership in "Y"; leadership.
    Independent variable: Membership in "Y." Operational definition: being a boy, included on the membership list for 1963, and listed as between the ages of 10 and 12.
    Dependent variable: Leadership. Operational definition: the score of subject's present occupation on an index of socioeconomic status of occupations.
(d) Findings: Members of the Hometown YMCA had higher status occupations than non-"Y" members of the same age and gender.
(e) Held constant: age of subjects when their status is assessed, gender, city they lived in at age 10–12.
    Randomized: none. This was not a true experiment, and subjects were not randomly assigned to participate in the "Y" program or not to participate. Thus, there are a number of variables that may vary in an uncontrolled manner (see discussion of uncontrolled variables).

(f) Extraneous variables and alternative explanations:

Invalid operational definition of leadership: The researcher collected data about the socioeconomic status of the subject's present occupation, and drew a conclusion about leadership. While it is sometimes true that one can rise to a high-status occupation because of one's leadership qualities, one can also attain this position through personal connections, special training, or an agreeable personality. These factors are all extraneous variables that might explain subjects' scores on "leadership." The definition of leadership is an especially serious problem, because of other difficulties described below.

Organismic variables: This is a classic case of correlations being used to prove causes. We do not know that leadership was caused by the "Y" program, because there may be any number of organismic variables, correlated with membership, that may be more important. Here are some that suggest alternative explanations of the results:

Parents' socioeconomic status: If the "Y" was mainly an organization serving the middle and upper classes in Hometown in 1963, the boys who joined had an advantage over the average public school boy, even before they entered the "Y." Their later success may have been due to family influence in the town, or to socialization into the behavior patterns that allow one to become successful in the society. This explanation is strengthened by the fact that the measure of "leadership" is really a measure of socioeconomic status.

Neighborhood: The "Y" probably mainly served boys who lived nearby. If the "Y" was in a fancy part of town, it received a selected sample of boys, even if it did not exclude the lower class. These boys had the advantages of social class already mentioned.

School attendance: The comparison group all went to public school, while we don't know if that is also true of the "Y" boys. If this is a town in which richer families sent their boys to private or parochial schools, then the "Y" group is being compared to a relatively disadvantaged population.

Alternative explanation: Boys who come from high socioeconomic status homes (and therefore are likely to join the Hometown "Y") are likely to obtain high socioeconomic status jobs. This may be accomplished through family connections, increased access to education, or through any number of personal qualities, with leadership only one.

Controls: An experimental design, assigning some boys to "Y"-type programs and others to no treatment, would be one solution to the problem of organismic variables. Because the long-term follow-up would be impractical, another solution is desirable. Subjects could be matched on a few potentially important extraneous variables (e.g., socioeconomic status of father's job, attendance at public school in all groups), and then compared again. (It might be necessary to throw out the data of some subjects who could not be matched.) Or data on these extraneous variables could be collected and entered into a data analysis that would control for them statistically.

The problem of measuring leadership is more difficult. It might be necessary to design a standard group situation in which people would behave in ways that can be rated in terms of whether leadership is shown. All subjects could then be called in to participate in this "experiment," and the results could be the measure of leadership. At any rate, some measure should be used that is based more directly on what the "Y" is trying to produce in its boys.

(g) Sample: 104 men; 52 who were members of the Hometown YMCA at ages 10–12 in 1963, and 52 of the same age who attended Hometown public schools in 1963 but were not "Y" members.

Population: Boys in Hometown who were 10–12 years old in 1963.

Sampling bias: One source of bias has already been mentioned. A sample of boys in public school is an unrepresentative sample of all the boys of that age in Hometown. This bias creates a problem because, while the comparison group was drawn only from the public school population, we do not know if this was also true of the "Y" group. Thus the sampling procedure confounds "Y" membership with type of school attended.

Another source of bias exists. Not all the subjects sampled actually appeared in the results. Four "Y" boys and nine in the comparison group could not be located. We do not know how these boys would have scored on "leadership." This could suggest an alternative explanation if the uneven split favors one group. Suppose that Hometown is a depressed area, and that the boys with high ambition and strong leadership qualities all left town. This would mean that the non-"Y" group was underrated in terms of actual leadership ability. On the other hand, it may be that the boys who left town were mainly shiftless wanderers. If so, the "Y" group was underrated by the data. Thus, the loss of subjects from the sample (called "attrition") may be hiding an uncontrolled extraneous variable. At least we know that only 13 of 104 subjects are affected, so we may conclude that this is not a serious problem with the research.

This study seems to generalize its findings beyond the population it studied. The conclusion that the "Y" builds leaders clearly implies more than the 1963 program for 10–12-year-old boys, and it almost certainly is meant to generalize beyond Hometown. Such generalizations would not even be justified from an unbiased sample. Neither are these generalizations necessarily wrong. They require more information about the effects of "Y" programs on other populations.

(h) Interactions of variables: None is being investigated.

Now try answering the same questions about the research described in the following problems. No answers are provided for these.

COMPLETE PROBLEMS

For each of the reports below, answer the eight questions that were listed on page 116.

1. In a study of the effect of country music on suicide, Stack and Gundlack (1992) hypothesized that country music nurtures a suicidal mood through its key themes of marital discord, alcohol abuse, and alienation from work. Reasoning that country music appeals more to whites than to blacks, they expected that the relationship between suicide and music would be stronger for whites than for blacks. Their sample consisted of 49 large metropolitan areas for which data were available on

exposure to country music (measured as the proportion of radio airtime devoted to country music, compared to other forms of music, such as classical and rock). Suicide is measured as the number of suicides per 100,000 population, and rates were calculated for both whites and blacks (defined according to U.S. census criteria). To control for other factors commonly associated with suicide, the researchers included in their model four additional independent variables: the divorce rate; an index of structural poverty; location of the metropolitan area in one of the southern states, as defined by the census bureau; and gun availability (the number of retail outlets, per 100,000 population, listed under "guns" or firearms" in the telephone yellow pages). The results indicated that the greater the exposure to country music in the 49 metropolitan areas, the greater the suicide rate for whites. Airtime devoted to country music had no effect on the suicide rate for blacks.

(a)

(b)

(c)

(d)

(e)

(f)

(g)

(h)

2. To measure the effect of team teaching on school performance and attitudes, Gamsky (1970) conducted a study on ninth graders learning English and history. The two teachers involved in teaching these subjects used a team-teaching approach for one ninth-grade class, and their traditional approach for the other class. The classes were randomly assigned to treatment conditions, and were asserted to be composed of comparable students. The team-teaching approach used consisted of dividing the class periods (the English and history periods were back to back) into 20 minute segments, including large group work taught by each teacher, as well as individual and small group work. Teacher aides were available to help with the small groups. The traditional teaching approach was not described in detail. At the end of the year, achievement scores in both subjects were equal for the two classes, but the team-taught class scored higher on some measures of attitude toward school. It was concluded that team teaching had some benefits in the attitudinal area.

(a)

(b)

(c)

(d)

(e)

(f)

(g)

(h)

3. Malamuth and Check (1981) examined the effects on attitudes of exposure to films that portray sexual violence as having positive consequences. Female and male college students in introductory psychology classes were randomly assigned to view either a violent-sexual film that justifies violence against women or a film that excluded all forms of sexual violence. The movies were viewed in campus theaters as a course requirement on "movie ratings" and were being shown as part of a regular campus film program. Several days after exposure to the films, subjects completed a sexual attitudes survey during class. In addition to basic demographic information, the survey included a scale measuring attitudes of acceptance of interpersonal violence against women. Subjects were not aware that there was any relationship between the survey and the viewing of the movies. Some students were eliminated from the analysis because they did not show up for the film or were absent from class on the day that the sexual attitudes survey was administered. The results indicated that exposure to the sexually violent film increased male subjects' acceptance of interpersonal violence against women. Women exposed to the sexually violent film tended to be less accepting of interpersonal violence than control subjects.

(a)

(b)

(c)

(d)

(e)

(f)

(g)

(h)

4. Shoham et al. (1987) attempted to explain the violent criminal offenses of a sample of 60 violent and 60 nonviolent prisoners by investigating their relationships with their families. Specifically, they hypothesized that violent prisoners grow up in tension-ridden families. Prison officials were asked to designate prisoners as either violent or nonviolent, and the researchers selected 60 prisoners from each group to study. From the prisoners' criminal records, the total number of violent offenses was recorded for each participant in the study (murder, manslaughter, attempted murder, assault, armed robbery, rape, quarrels, and causing physical injury). Each prisoner completed a family-background questionnaire, and the researchers constructed a family agreement/disagreement index from the number of incidents of disagreement reported between the parents, between the parents and the school, and between the parents and the prisoner. The researchers employed statistical controls for father's dominance, mother's dominance, impunitive parents, attachment to family, age, and education. The results indicated that parental disagreements in childhood had no effect on the number of violent offenses. However, as education level increased, there was a significant decrease in the number of violent offenses.

(a)

(b)

(c)

(d)

(e)

(f)

(g)

(h)

4

EVALUATING SCIENTIFIC EVIDENCE IN THE PUBLISHED LITERATURE

Chapter 3 was designed to provide a guide for judging the internal validity of social scientific studies. In the exercises and problems, you practiced finding extraneous variables and the alternative explanations they suggest for observed data, and you learned how to identify and suggest controls for extraneous variables. You also distinguished between the samples of people studied and the populations from which the samples were drawn, and identified the interactions being studied. In short, Chapter 3 gave you the tools to evaluate the internal validity of a summarized scientific study.

To be able to use these tools to evaluate *real* scientific reports, as they appear in the academic and professional journals, you must learn how to find what you are looking for in a scientific report. This chapter offers some pointers about evaluating evidence as it appears in the journals.

There is no new language to learn, though you will surely be exposed to new language in the journal articles you read. It may be best to be guided through a scientific article before you try to understand one on your own. The discussion that follows uses as an example the article by Baron and Straus, "Cultural and Economic Sources of Homicide in the United States" (1988), which follows.

Cultural and Economic Sources of Homicide in the United States

Larry Baron
University of California, Los Angeles

Murray A. Straus
University of New Hampshire

Are high rates of homicide better explained by cultural or economic factors? Some research suggests that a regional culture of violence underlies high rates of homicide, whereas other research suggests that poverty or economic inequality increases the likelihood of homicide. A major limitation of this body of research has been the failure of researchers to include an indicator of cultural support for violence that is analytically separate from measures of southern region. In this article, a 12-item Legitimate Violence Index (LVX) is introduced that measures cultural support for violence. Using the 50 states as the units of analysis, hypotheses derived from cultural and economic theories of homicide are investigated using multiple regression. Several additional variables are included in the analysis to control for spurious relationships. The results show that legitimate violence, poverty, and economic inequality are significantly associated with state-to-state differences in the incidence of homicide.

Southern states have a higher average homicide rate than states in other regions of the country. Although a substantial amount of research has been devoted to explaining the predominance of lethal violence in the South, there appears to be little consensus. The major point of contention concerns whether southern homicide is best explained by cultural or economic factors. Some research seems to suggest that the high rate of southern homicide is due to a regional culture of violence (Gastil 1971; Hackney 1969; Messner 1983; Reed 1971; Simpson 1985), whereas other research suggests that it reflects conditions of poverty (Bailey 1984; Loftin and Hill 1974; Loftin and Parker 1985; McDowall 1986; Smith and Parker 1980; Williams 1984) or economic inequality (Blau and Blau 1982).

A major obstacle to resolving this controversy has been the absence of a measure of the cultural approval of violence. Because such a measure has not been available, researchers have resorted to using southern region as a substitute for violent cultural norms (e.g., Bailey 1984; Blau and Blau 1982; Loftin and Parker 1985; Messner 1982; Smith and Parker 1980). This strategy is questionable, however, because it presupposes that cultural support for violence and southern region are identical. Equating southern *region* with *culture* only skirts the empirical issue of the extent to which the South represents a regional culture of violence. Consequently, region and culture must be measured independent of one another and their degree of association empirically assessed if the southern culture of violence thesis is to be adequately tested.

To accomplish this task, a Legitimate Violence Index (LVX) was constructed. This index is composed of 12 indicators of noncriminal violence and is conceptualized as a measure of one aspect of the cultural approval of violence (i.e., socially acceptable or legitimate violence). The Legitimate Violence Index makes it possible to study the geographic distribution of cultural support for violence in the United States.

The purpose of this article is to investigate whether cultural support for violence is more heavily concentrated in the South than any other region of the country, and to estimate the relative effects of cultural and economic variables on rates of homicide. The unit of analysis and population for this study is the 50 American states.[1] Multiple regression is used to test hypotheses derived from cultural and economic theories of homicide.

SOUTHERN CULTURE OF VIOLENCE AND HOMICIDE

The relatively high rate of southern homicide predates the Civil War and has been attributed to such factors as frontier living, a history of slavery and lynching, the widespread use of guns and knives, and the conviction that violence is an integral and unavoidable feature of everyday life in the South (Doerner 1978; Reed 1977). Some researchers suggest that this legacy of violence has become embedded in the culture of southern states and is now a major source of lethal violence (Gastil 1971; Hackney 1969; Reed 1977).

The argument that the South repre-sents a culture of violence has prompted researchers to employ a measure of southern region as an indicator of cultural support for violence. In one study, Hackney (1969) regressed the 1940 state homicide rate on a variable composed of the 11 Confederate States and variables measuring urbanization, education, unemployment, per capita personal income, the state's per capita income, and median age. In order to control for race, the analysis was run separately for blacks and whites. Hackney found that among whites, Confederate South was the best predictor of homicide; among blacks, Confederate South followed age as the second best predictor. Hackney interpreted these findings as showing that southerners share a collective perception of violation and persecution, and a cultural tradition that approves of violence as an appropriate response to such perceptions.

In a related article, Gastil (1971) advanced the argument that the high rates of lethal violence in the South are due to a "regional culture of violence." In order to test this idea, Gastil constructed a Southernness Index that is based on the extent to which states are populated by individuals born and reared in the South. Gastil predicted that states with a higher proportion of indigenous southerners would also have higher rates of homicide. He tested this hypothesis by regressing the 1960 state homicide rate on the Southernness Index and nine control variables. The results showed that Southernness explained a greater proportion of the variance in homicide than the percent black, percent age 20–34, median income, urbanization, median years of education, city size, physicians per 1,000 population, hospital beds per 1,000 population, and population size. These results held up when the analysis was run separately for blacks and whites. Gastil concluded that a regional culture of violence is central to understanding the genesis and persistence of the high rates of southern homicide.

Critical of these findings, Loftin and Hill (1974) charged that Gastil and Hackney overestimated the effect of southern region on rates of homicide because they failed to include adequate controls for structural variables. To test this contention, Loftin and Hill replicated the two studies, but added a Gini Index and a Structural Poverty Index to the analysis. The Structural Poverty Index is composed of infant mortality rates, percent of persons age 25 and older with less than 5 years of education, percent of the population illiterate, percent of families with annual incomes under $1,000, armed forces mental test failures, and percent of children living with one parent. In the two replicated regressions, the Structural Poverty Index emerged as the best predictor of the average homicide rate for the years 1959–1961. The indicators of southern region were rendered statistically insignificant. These findings confirmed Loftin and Hill's contention that Gastil and Hackney misspecified their models by omitting important variables from their regression equations.

In a recent contribution to the southern culture of violence controversy, Huff-Corzine, Corzine, and Moore (1986) performed a replication of Loftin and Hill's research using 1970 state data and a 3-year average homicide rate (1969–1971).[2] According to Huff-Corzine et al., Loftin and Hill (1974) were unable to find a relationship between their measures of southern region and homicide because of two flaws in their analysis: (1) the failure to use a measure of southernness that was powerful enough to find an effect; and (2) the presence of multicollinearity that diminished the interpretability of their ordinary least squares estimates. In an effort to surmount the problem of

using an ineffective measure of southern region, Huff-Corzine et al. introduced a new measure based on the proportion of the state's population born in the South. In order to gauge the relative influence of poverty and violent cultural norms on rates of homicide, Huff-Corzine et al. employed a modified version of Loftin and Hill's Structural Poverty Index and computed separate regression analyses using either Gastil's Southernness Index or proportion of the state's population born in the South. Multicollinearity was dealt with by employing ridge regression. Separate analyses were performed using the white homicide rate, nonwhite homicide rate, and the homicide rate for the total population. We will restrict our discussion to their analysis of the total population.

The results showed that the homicide rate for the total population was significantly influenced by Gastil's Southernness Index, proportion of the population born in the South, Loftin and Hill's Structural Poverty Index, and percent of the population nonwhite. The percent of the population between the ages 20 to 34, the proportion of the population residing in rural areas, the Gini Index of Income Inequality, and the availability of hospital beds per 100,000 population were not significantly related to the homicide rate.[3] Huff-Corzine et al. (1986, p. 919) concluded that, contrary to the implications of Loftin and Hill's (1974) study, violent cultural norms emanating from the South cannot be "explained away" by poverty, economic inequality, or other demographic characteristics of Southern states, but represent an independent source of high rates of homicide.

Despite Huff-Corzine et al.'s conclusion that a southern culture of violence affects state-to-state differences in rates of homicide, questions can be raised regarding the validity of their cultural indicators—Gastil's Southernness Index and proportion of the population born in the South. The assumption underlying both of these measures is that all individuals who are born and reared in the South are inculcated with beliefs and conduct norms supportive of violence. Consequently, states with a higher proportion of indigenous southerners are presumed to be more heavily saturated with a culture of violence. Whereas we cannot dismiss the possibility that the migration of native southerners to other parts of the country might provide a clue to the social distribution of violent cultural norms, a more plausible interpretation of these two indicators of southern influence is that they are measuring social disorganization rather than cultural support for violence. Because the two measures used by Huff-Corzine et al., Gastil's Southernness Index and proportion of the population born in the South, are based on migration flows of the southern population, these variables may be measuring the adverse consequences of in-migration.[4] If this interpretation is correct, the Huff-Corzine et al. findings could be reinterpreted as indicating that high southern rates of homicide reflect the influence of poverty and social disorganization, not a southern culture of violence.

As it presently stands, the controversy regarding the relative influence of cultural and economic factors on rates of homicide is a long way from being settled.[5] A resolution to this debate requires the availability of a measure of cultural support for violence that is conceptually and empirically distinct from measures of southern influence. As Loftin and Hill (1974, p. 723) cogently argue: "Unless culture can be measured distinctly and independently of region, the validity of our studies will always be threatened by the large number of non-cultural variables that are systematically related to region."

The Legitimate Violence Index was constructed to avoid the problem of confounding region and culture and permits us to estimate their separate effects on state-level rates of homicide. The following hypotheses were tested.

> HYPOTHESIS 1. States in the southern region are more likely to have a higher level of support for legitimate violence than states in any other region of the country.
>
> HYPOTHESIS 2. The higher the level of legitimate violence, the higher the homicide rate.
>
> HYPOTHESIS 3. As poverty increases, the homicide rate increases.
>
> HYPOTHESIS 4. As economic inequality increases, the homicide rate increases.

LEGITIMATE VIOLENCE INDEX[6]

Conceptual Basis of the Index

The indicators included in the LVX were selected on the assumption that, if there are group differences in values concerning violence, they should be observable in many different activities such as education, recreation, and law enforcement. Consequently, we searched for indicators that might reflect an underlying belief in the efficacy and desirability of physical force. However, to avoid the circularity of inferring a culture of violence from high rates of violent crime, it was necessary to restrict the indicators to violent activities that are noncriminal and socially approved. The index constructed to measure this aspect of cultural support for violence is the LVX.

It should be noted that the indicators comprising the LVX are aggregate behaviors (e.g., the audience for television programs with violent content) or cultural products (e.g., legislation authorizing corporal punishment in the schools), rather than verbal expression of beliefs, attitudes, and values. This roughly corresponds to Durkheim's "collective representations" (Durkheim 1938; Lukes 1972). It is also consistent with much anthropological research (Geertz 1973), and with several ethnomethodological studies (e.g., Garfinkel 1967; Leiter 1980). The choice of behavioral and cultural product indicators was partly based on the lack of comparative opinion survey data for states, but also on the limitations of such data. Specifically, there are cultural contradictions in the evaluation of violence that makes it extraordinarily difficult for people to verbalize their true beliefs and attitudes (Dibble and Straus 1980; Greenblat 1983). Therefore, public opinion survey data, even if it were available for states, might not accurately reflect the extent to which there are proviolence elements in American culture.

Indicators

The 12 indicators included in the LVX are summarized and may be grouped in the following categories.

Mass Media Preferences The variables in this category are intended to represent the degree of public interest in magazine and television media with violent content. Two variables are included in this group. The first is the 1979 circulation rates per 100,000 population of five magazines that depict violence or serve a segment of the population involved in violence. The second is an index of the most violent television programs during the Fall of 1980.[7]

Govermental Use of Violence This group of indicators is based on the assumption that legal support of violent acts may be seen as reflecting public sentiment about the acceptability of violence. The 5 variables in this category include laws permitting corporal punishment by school teachers in 1979, execution per 100 homicide arrests for the years 1940–1959, executions per 100 homicide arrests fot the years 1960–1978, blacks sentenced to death per 100 blacks arrested for homicide in 1980, and whites sentenced to death per 100 whites arrested for homicide in 1980.[8]

Participation in Socially Approved Violent Activities The variables included in this category were chosen because they were judged to reflect violent, yet socially approved, activities. The five variables comprising this category are hunting licenses sold per 1,000 population in 1980, the state of origin of college football players per capita in 1972, National Guard enrollment per 100,000 population in 1976, National Guard expenditures per capita in 1976, and lynchings per million population during the years 1882–1927.[9]

Indexing Method and Reliability

Prior to computing the LVX, the 12 indicators were transformed to Z scores. The indicators were then summed and the composite index was standardized through a procedure called "ZP" scoring (Straus 1980). ZP scores have a theoretical range of zero to 100, a mean of 50, and a standard deviation of 20. Through the ZP scaling method, index scores acquire the characteristics of both Z scores and percentages. Thus a change of one ZP score point can be interpreted as a change of 1% of the zero to 100 score range, whereas a change of 20 ZP score points can be viewed as a change of 20% of the score range or as one standard deviation. The internal consistency reliability of the LVX was tested with the

SPSS reliability program. Cronbach's standardized alpha for the 12 composite indicators is .71.[10]

DATA AND VARIABLES

Homicide Rate

The variables analyzed in this study were derived from existing data sources. The dependent variable is the 1980 rate per 100,000 population of homicides known to the police, as reported in the Uniform Crime Reports (UCR). Although the UCR is known to underestimate the volume of violent crime, comparison of vital statistics with the UCR suggests that the homicide data are extremely accurate (Gove, Hughes, and Geerken 1985; Hindelang 1974).

Gini Index and Percent Poor

In addition to the Legitimate Violence Index, the variables of central theoretical interest are the Gini Index of income inequality and percent of the population with family incomes below the poverty level. The reason for including two economic indicators is that, in principle, each represents a different dimension of impoverishment. The Gini Index is a measure of relative deprivation, whereas the percent poor is a measure of absolute deprivation.

The Gini Index was computed using 1979 data on family income. The theoretical range of scores on the Gini Index is from 0 to 100; however, the actual range is from 31 to 40. States with higher index scores have greater income inequality. The measure of absolute deprivation is the proportion of families in 1980 with incomes below the poverty level, as set by the Office of Management and Budget. State ranks and regional breakdowns of the Gini Index and percent poor are presented in Appendices 1A and 1B.

Control Variables

Several variables were included in the analysis to control for spurious associations. As was previously noted, empirical support for a culture of violence explanation of homicide has been based primarily on the relation between southern region and rates of homicide. Consequently, a Confederate South dummy variable (1 = Confederate States, 0 = non-confederate states) was used as a measure of southern location.[11]

A substantial amount of research indicates that, relative to their representation in the population, a disproportionate amount of criminal homicide is perpetrated by blacks (Curtis 1975; Harries 1974; Willie and Edwards 1983; Wilson 1984; Wolfgang 1958; Wolfgang, Figlio, and Sellin 1972) and young people (Greenberg 1983; Hindelang 1981; Hirschi and Gottfredson 1983). Thus, two variables were included to control for the racial and age compositions of the population: percent of the population black, 1980; and the percent of the population age 18–24, 1980. Studies also show that violent crime is more prevalent in urban than in rural areas (Friday 1983; Harries 1974, 1980; Nettler 1984). As a result, percent of the 1980 population residing in Standard Metropolitan Statistical Areas (SMSAs) was included as a control variable.

Some researchers have found an association between the proportion of the population divorced and criminal violence, suggesting that violent crime is a reflection of social disorganization (Baron and Straus In Press; Blau and Blau 1982; Smith and Bennett 1985). Therefore, a Family Integration Index was constructed to measure the degree of connectedness or social stability in states. The inverse of the Family Integration Index may be interpreted as the degree of social disorganization.[12] A complete list of the variables and source documents can be found in Appendix 2.

STATE AND REGIONAL VARIATIONS IN RATES OF HOMICIDE AND LEGITIMATE VIOLENCE

Homicide

The ranking of each state according to its 1980 homicide rate and its score on the

Legitimate Violence Index (LVX) is presented in Table 1. The first column of Table 1 shows the array of homicide rates. As can be seen, Nevada led the rest of the country with 20 homicides per 100,000 population and South Dakota trailed with less than one homicide per 100,000 population. Consistent with previous research (Harries 1971; Kowalski, Dittman, and Bung 1980; Lottier 1938; Shannon 1954), southern states are heavily represented in the upper level of the distribution. Specifically, 6 of the 10 states with the highest homicide rates are located in the South (Texas, Louisiana, Mississippi, Florida, Georgia, and Alabama), two are located in the Southwest

Table 1. Rank Order of the States with Respect to the Homicide Rate, 1980 and Legitimate Violence, 1882–1980

| Rank | Homicides Known to the Police per 100,000 Population | | Legitimate Violence | |
	State	Homicide Rate	State	Index Score
1	Nevada	20.0	Wyoming	98
2	Texas	16.9	Montana	87
3	Louisiana	15.7	Mississippi	85
4	California	14.5	Idaho	83
5	Mississippi	14.5	Utah	83
6	Florida	14.5	Georgia	78
7	Georgia	13.8	Nevada	77
8	Alabama	13.2	Arkansas	74
9	New Mexico	13.1	Vermont	71
10	New York	12.7	Louisiana	66
11	South Carolina	11.4	Alaska	64
12	Missouri	11.1	Florida	63
13	Tennessee	10.8	Alabama	62
14	North Carolina	10.6	Oklahoma	62
15	Illinois	10.6	Texas	61
16	Arizona	10.3	Arizona	60
17	Michigan	10.2	South Carolina	60
18	Oklahoma	10.0	South Dakota	59
19	Alaska	9.7	North Dakota	57
20	Maryland	9.5	Oregon	56
21	Arkansas	9.2	Delaware	54
22	Indiana	8.9	New Mexico	54

(continued)

Table 1. (continued)

	Homicides Known to the Police per 100,000 Population		Legitimate Violence	
Rank	State	Homicide Rate	State	Index Score
23	Kentucky	8.8	Colorado	54
24	Hawaii	8.7	Kansas	52
25	Virginia	8.6	North Carolina	47
26	Ohio	8.1	Virginia	47
27	West Virginia	7.1	Washington	45
28	Colorado	6.9	Hawaii	45
29	New Jersey	6.9	Tennessee	44
30	Kansas	6.9	Nebraska	42
31	Delaware	6.9	Iowa	41
32	Pennsylvania	6.8	Ohio	41
33	Wyoming	6.2	West Virginia	38
34	Washington	5.5	Kentucky	36
35	Oregon	5.1	Pennsylvania	35
36	Connecticut	4.7	Maine	34
37	Nebraska	4.4	Illinois	34
38	Rhode Island	4.4	California	33
39	Massachusetts	4.1	Minnesota	32
40	Montana	4.0	Indiana	31
41	Utah	3.8	Missouri	30
42	Idaho	3.1	New Hampshire	30
43	Wisconsin	2.9	Connecticut	29
44	Maine	2.8	Michigan	29
45	Minnesota	2.6	Wisconsin	27
46	New Hampshire	2.5	New York	27
47	Vermont	2.2	Maryland	26
48	Iowa	2.2	New Jersey	22
49	North Dakota	1.2	Massachusetts	19
50	South Dakota	0.7	Rhode Island	18

(Nevada and New Mexico), one in the far West (California), and only one in the Northeast (New York).

Regional variations in homicide and legitimate violence were examined by computing the mean for each of the 4 census regions. As expected, the South has the highest homicide rate (11.3 per 100,000 population), followed by the West (8.5 per 100,000), the North Central (5.8 per 100,000), and the Northeast (5.2 per 100,000). The results indicate that a resident of the South is approxi-

mately twice as likely to be a victim of homicide than a resident of the Northeast or North Central regions.

Legitimate Violence

The second column of Table 1 shows the state-to-state differences in legitimate violence. If the proponents of the southern culture of violence thesis are correct, we would expect to see a heavy concentration of southern states in the first quintile of the distribution. Perusal of the state ranks shows that this is only partially the case; Western states tend to be more strongly represented in the upper level of the distribution than southern states. In fact, four out of the top 5 states are located in the West (Wyoming, Montana, Idaho, and Utah). Nonetheless, southern states also tend to have high index scores as 4 of the 10 highest legitimate violence states are located in the South (Mississippi, Georgia, Arkansas, and Louisiana). The states with the lowest scores on the LVX appear to be concentrated in the Northeast.

Contrary to the hypothesis that the South has the highest level of legitimate violence, Table 2 indicates that the West has the highest average score. It should be noted, though, that the South has the second highest regional score and is slightly above the national average in legitimate violence.[13] The two areas of the country with the lowest levels of legitimate violence are the North Central and Northeastern regions. One interesting finding from the Census Bureau's divisional breakdown (not reported here) is that the Pacific States (California, Hawaii, Oregon, Washington, and Alaska) are below the national average in legitimate violence, indicating that the Mountain states (Arizona, Colorado, Idaho, Montana, Nevada, New Mexico, Utah, and Wyoming) are responsible for the high score of the Western region on the LVX.

CORRELATION ANALYSIS

The zero-order correlations are displayed in Table 3.[14] Contrary to the argument that high rates of homicide reflect cultural support for violence, the correlation of homicide with the LVX is low and not statistically significant ($r = .19$). The strongest associations with homicide are for the percent black ($r = .63$), Confederate South ($r = .53$), the Gini Index ($r = .53$), and percent of families with poverty level incomes ($r = .43$). The Family Integration Index has a significant inverse relationship with homicide ($r = -.38$), whereas the proportion of the population residing in SMSAs is positively associated ($r = .35$). This pattern of correlations suggests that a combination of residence in the South, a large black population, a high degree of relative and absolute deprivation, a low level of family integration, and a high level of urbanization constitute a mix of societal characteristics that increases the risk of homicide.

There are good reasons to exercise caution in the interpretation of the zero-order correlations. First, although the bivariate associations run counter to a

Table 2. Regional Differences in the Homicide Rate, 1980, and Legitimate Violence, 1882–1980

Region	Homicide Rate	Legitimate Violence Index Score
South	11.3	56.4
West	8.5	64.5
North Central	5.8	39.6
Northeast	5.2	31.7
National Average	8.2	50.0

Note: Regional differences for the Homicide Rate and Legitimate Violence are significant at $p < .005$.

Table 3. Zero-Order Correlations ($N = 50$)

Variable	1	2	3	4	5	6	7	8	9
1 Homicide Rate, 1980	1.00								
2 Legitimate Violence Index, 1882–1980	.19	1.00							
3 Confederate South	.53***	.33**	1.00						
4 Percent Residing in SMSAs, 1980	.35**	−.54***	−.02	1.00					
5 Gini Index, 1979	.53***	.28*	.67***	−.18	1.00				
6 Percent below Poverty Level Income, 1980	.43***	.35**	.65***	−.34*	.93***	1.00			
7 Percent Black, 1980	.63***	.10	.77***	.19*	.61***	.60***	1.00		
8 Percent Age 18–24, 1980	−.09	.29*	−.04	−.17	−.10	−.08	−.10	1.00	
9 Family Integration Index, 1976	−.38**	.34**	−.17	−.42**	−.19	−.10	−.26*	.64***	1.00
Mean	8.19	50.04	.22	61.37	34.48	12.48	9.14	13.46	16.49
Standard Deviation	4.51	19.96	.42	22.85	1.81	3.42	9.22	.75	13.37

Notes: *Significant at $p < .05$.
   **Significant at $p < .01$.
   ***Significant at $p < .001$.

cultural explanation of homicide, it is possible that one or more of the control variables is suppressing the relationship between the LVX and homicide. Second, examination of Table 3 shows that several of the independent variables are moderately intercorrelated. This increases the likelihood that some of the correlations with homicide may be spurious. These possibilities are explored in the next section where the results of two multiple regression analyses are reported.

MULTIPLE REGRESSION ANALYSES

The upper half of Table 4 reports the regression of homicide on all the indepen-

dent variables except the Gini Index. In the lower section, the same regression model was used with the exception that percent below poverty level incomes was replaced with the Gini Index. As was previously noted, separate regressions were performed due to the prohibitively high correlation between the Gini Index and percent poor.

A comparison of the upper and lower panels of Table 4 shows very similar results. The adjusted R^2 indicates that 60% and 61% of the state-to-state variation in the homicide rate is accounted for by each equation, respectively.[15] In both models, the percent of the population residing in SMSAs provides the best param-

Table 4. Multiple Regression Analyses of the Homicide Rate, 1980

Independent Variable	Standardized Coefficient	Unstandardized Coefficient	Standard Error	t value
Percent Residing in SMSAs, 1980	.533	.105	.027	3.879***
Legitimate Violence Index, 1882–1980	.418	.094	.027	3.413**
Percent Below Poverty Level Income, 1980	.317	.418	.195	2.139*
Family Integration Index, 1976	−.276	−.093	.045	−2.033*
Percent Black, 1980	.297	.145	.081	1.791
Percent Age 18–24	.113	.680	.737	.922
Confederate South	−.074	−.806	1.770	−.456
				Adjusted $R^2 = .60$
Percent Residing in SMSAs, 1980	.488	.096	.024	3.972***
Legitimate Violence Index, 1882–1980	.414	.092	.027	3.450**
Gini Index, 1979	.343	.857	.330	2.591*
Percent Black, 1980	.320	.156	.076	2.055*
Family Integration Index, 1976	−.252	−.084	.045	−1.884
Percent Age 18–24	.101	.606	.720	.842
Confederate South	−.111	−1.201	1.754	.685
				Adjusted $R^2 = .61$

Notes: *Significant at $p < .05$.
**Significant at $p < .01$.
***Significant at $p < .001$.

eter estimate of the homicide rate. The relative explanatory power of the predictor variables is also equivalent in the two regressions. The major differences between the two analyses are that percent black has a significant association with homicide in the regression using the Gini Index, but it does not attain significance when percent poor is used; and a low level of family integration is significantly related to homicide in the equation using percent poor, but it is not significantly associated in the equation using the Gini Index. This difference notwithstanding, the results show considerable consistency regardless of which measure of economic deprivation is employed.

The most noteworthy finding from the multivariate analysis is that the LVX emerged as a significant predictor of homicide, once the effects of the other predictor variables were held constant.[16] Inspection of the first-order partial correlations showed that the substantial negative association between percent of the population residing in SMSAs and the LVX was suppressing the bivariate relationship of the LVX with homicide. When percent of the population residing in SMSAs is partialed out of the equation, legitimate violence is significantly related to the homicide rate. Thus, the regression analyses confirm the hypotheses that homicide rates have a significant tendency to increase in proportion to increases in the levels of legitimate violence, poverty, and economic inequality.

SUMMARY AND CONCLUSIONS

Southern states average a higher rate of homicide than states in any other section of the country. One line of argument attributes this to a regional culture of violence that began prior to the Civil War and is now presumably woven into the cultural fabric of Southern states. Another line of argument suggests that the high rate of Southern homicide is a function of economic deprivation, which is more prevalent in the South. Despite the many studies examining this issue, it has not been possible to settle this controversy. This is because no previous study employed a measure of cultural support for violence that is conceptually and empirically independent of southern region.

As a step toward investigating the extent to which the cultural approval of violence affects the homicide rate independent of southern region, a Legitimate Violence Index was constructed and employed in the present analysis. State ranks and regional differences were examined to test the hypothesis that southern states have the highest level of legitimate violence. This hypothesis was not confirmed as the western region showed the greatest magnitude of support for legitimate violence, although the difference between the West and South was not statistically significant. This finding casts doubt on the argument that the South represents a distinctive culture of violence. It also raises questions about the validity of using southern region as an indicator of cultural support for violence.

Two multiple regression analyses were performed to assess the partial effects of Confederate South, legitimate violence, poverty, economic inequality, and a set of control variables on the homicide rate. The results provide support for the predictions that legitimate violence, poverty, and economic inequality each have a significant relationship to homicide. Although the Confederate South indicator was significantly related to homicide in the bivariate case, it did not attain a greater than chance association in the regression analyses. Therefore, southern location and cultural support for violence do not have parallel effects on the homicide rate. Again, this suggests that southern region represents something other than cultural support for violence and should not be conceptualized as a proxy for culture.

The results also indicate that cultural support for violence is widely distributed throughout the United States. Thus, it is not the South per se or a cultural legacy of violence in the South that precipitates high rates of homicide; rather, the association of homicide with the LVX suggests that there may be a diffusion or spillover from socially approved forms of violence to criminal violence. The positive evaluation of violence by government, mass media, and sports seems to be carried over to social contexts in which the use of violence is illegitimate, such as homicidal assaults. Thus, socially approved forms of violence may provide cultural support for homicide and perhaps other types of criminal violence. However, one must be cautious about generalizing from homicide to other violent crimes such as as-sault, robbery, or rape because homicide represents the most extreme type of criminal violence and may therefore be unique. Consequently, the extent to which the "spillover" explanation applies to other types of criminal violence is an important area for future research.[17]

Finally, this study helps to move us beyond the unproductive debate between adherents of cultural and economic explanations of homicide. Previous authors have tended to argue in favor of one position or the other. The present results show that cultural support for violence is one factor, but not the only factor, contributing to the incidence of lethal violence. More urbanized states and states with greater poverty and economic inequality also tend to have higher rates of homicide. Thus, cultural and economic factors are not at odds in the explanation of homicide; rather, each accounts for a significant proportion of the state-to-state variation.

Appendix 1A. Ranking of the States on the Gini Index, 1979, and Percent Below Poverty Level Income, 1980

	Gini Index, 1979		Percent Below Poverty Level Income, 1980	
Rank	State	Index Score	State	Percent Poor
1	Mississippi	39.6	Mississippi	24.5
2	Louisiana	37.9	Louisiana	18.9
3	Georgia	37.5	Arkansas	18.7
4	Kentucky	37.4	Kentucky	18.4
5	Tennessee	37.3	Alabama	17.9
6	Alabama	37.1	New Mexico	17.4
7	Arkansas	36.9	Tennessee	17.0
8	New Mexico	36.8	Georgia	16.4
9	Florida	36.3	South Dakota	16.1
10	Texas	36.2	South Carolina	15.9
11	Oklahoma	36.0	Texas	14.8
12	New York	35.8	North Carolina	14.6
13	South Carolina	35.7	West Virginia	14.5
14	South Dakota	35.6	New York	13.7
15	West Virginia	35.2	Oklahoma	13.3
16	North Dakota	35.0	Florida	13.0
17	California	35.0	Maine	12.9

(*continued*)

Appendix 1A. (continued)

	Gini Index, 1979		Percent Below Poverty Level Income, 1980	
Rank	State	Index Score	State	Percent Poor
18	North Carolina	35.0	North Dakota	12.8
19	Missouri	34.9	Idaho	12.7
20	Delaware	34.8	Arizona	12.4
21	Virginia	34.8	Missouri	12.4
22	Arizona	34.7	Montana	12.4
23	Idaho	34.6	Delaware	11.9
24	Hawaii	34.2	Virginia	11.5
25	Nebraska	34.0	Illinois	11.5
26	Michigan	33.9	Vermont	11.4
27	Maine	33.9	California	11.3
28	Oregon	33.9	Oregon	11.3
29	Montana	33.8	Michigan	11.1
30	Colorado	33.7	Utah	10.7
31	New Jersey	33.7	Pennsylvania	10.5
32	Vermont	33.6	Ohio	10.5
33	Kansas	33.6	Nebraska	10.4
34	Alaska	33.5	Rhode Island	10.3
35	Illinois	33.3	Kansas	10.2
36	Massachusetts	33.3	Colorado	10.2
37	Rhode Island	33.2	Washington	10.2
38	Maryland	33.2	Alaska	10.1
39	Ohio	33.0	Hawaii	10.0
40	Washington	33.0	Maryland	9.9
41	Minnesota	32.9	Indiana	9.8
42	Pennsylvania	32.9	Massachusetts	9.8
43	Iowa	32.8	New Jersey	9.7
44	Utah	32.7	Iowa	9.4
45	Indiana	32.5	Minnesota	9.3
46	Nevada	32.4	Connecticut	8.7
47	Connecticut	32.3	New Hampshire	8.7
48	Wisconsin	32.1	Nevada	8.5
49	New Hampshire	31.8	Wisconsin	8.5
50	Wyoming	31.1	Wyoming	8.0

Appendix 1B. Regional Differences on the Gini Index, 1979, and Percent Below Poverty Level Income, 1980

Region	Gini Index	Percent Poor
South	36.6	15.9
West	33.8	11.2
North Central	33.6	11.0
Northeast	33.4	10.6
National Average	34.3	12.5

Note: Regional differences for the Gini Index and Percent Below Poverty Level Income are significant at $p < .001$.

Appendix 2. References to Data Sources

Variable Name*	Variable Label and Source Document
ckf24	Homicides Known to the Police per 100,000 Population, 1980 Federal Bureau of Investigation, 1981. *Crime in the United States, 1980.* Washington, DC: U.S. Government Printing Office.
blk80	Percent Black of the Population, 1980 Bureau of the Census, 1982. *State and Metropolitan Area Data Book.* Washington, DC: U.S. Government Printing Office.
met80	Percent of the Population Residing in SMSAs, 1980 Bureau of the Census, 1982. *State and Metropolitan Area Data Book.* Washington, DC: U.S. Government Printing Office.
yng80	Percent of the Population Age 18–24, 1980 Bureau of the Census, 1982. *State and Metropolitan Area Data Book.* Washington, DC: U.S. Government Printing Office.
gini79fx	Gini Index, 1979 Bureau of the Census, 1979. *Provisional Estimates of Social, Economic, and Housing Characteristics of States and Selected Standard Metropolitan Areas* (Publication No. PHCBO-S1-1). Washington, DC: U.S. Government Printing Office.
pov80	Percent of the Population Below Poverty Level Income, 1980 Bureau of the Census, 1983. *Statistical Abstract of the United States—1984.* Washington, DC: U.S. Government Printing Office.
vlc	Confederate South Dummy Variable, 1861–1865 Faulkner, H. U. 1957. *American Political and Social History.* 7th ed. New York: Appleton-Century-Crofts.
xcv12zp	Legitimate Violence Index, 1882–1980 Straus, M. A. 1985. "The Legitimate Violence Index." Mimeographed paper available on request from the Family Research Laboratory, 128 Horton Social Science Center, University of New Hampshire, Durham, NH 03824. (This paper provides the sources and a state-by-state listing of the 12 indicators. It also describes the procedures used to construct the index and the scores for each state.)
xinf3	Family Integration Index, 1976 Linsky, A. S., and M. A. Straus, 1986. *Social Stress in the United States: Links to Regional Patterns of Crime and Illness.* Dover, MA: Auburn House. (The sources for the three indicators are provided in the appendix to the book.)

Note: *The variable names are the identifiers used in the codebooks of the State and Regional Indicators Archive (SRIA) at the University of New Hampshire. These codebooks give the source documents, and in the case of indexes or rates, the SPSS commands used to compute them.

ACKNOWLEDGMENTS

The research reported in this article is part of the Family Violence Research Program (FVRP), and the State and Regional Indicators Archive (SRIA). A bibliography listing papers and books of the FVRP and SRIA is available from the Family Research Laboratory, University of New Hampshire, 128 Horton Social Science Center, Durham, NH 03824. We are grateful to the Graduate School of the University of New Hampshire and the National Institute of Mental Health (grant

T32 MH15161 to the University of New Hampshire, and grant 5T32MH15123 to Yale University) for financial support for this research.

NOTES

1. There is a heated controversy concerning the appropriateness of using states as the units of analysis for macrosociological research. The predominant view seems to be that smaller units such as cities, counties, and SMSAs are preferable to states. Critics of state-level analysis argue that due to the heterogeneity of states, a single statistic masks the immense variation within states (Loftin and Hill 1974; Messner 1982). However, despite the prevailing wisdom that "smaller is better," we have not been able to find any empirical support for the contention that data at a lower level of aggregation yields more valid results than data at a higher level of aggregation. Surely, there are studies that show that researchers sometimes obtain different results when using different units of analysis (Bailey 1984); but these studies do not indicate which set of findings is correct. In fact, Straus (1985a) presents empirical data showing that dissimilar results are an exception.

2. Consistent with Loftin and Hill's (1974) study, Huff-Corzine et al. excluded Hawaii and Alaska from their analysis.

3. Huff-Corzine et al. also found that Gastil's Southernness Index, the proportion of the population born in the South, and the Structural Poverty Index were significantly related to the white homicide rate. This study further showed that neither the Structural Poverty Index nor the proportion of the population born in the South were significantly related to the nonwhite homicide rate, although Gastil's Southernness Index was significantly related to the homicide rate among nonwhites.

4. Theoretically, the criminogenic consequences of in-migration could be explained in two ways. First, in-migrants tend to lack social ties through which informal social control operates. Second, in-migrants tend to bring with them beliefs and behaviors that, to the

extent that they differ from those of the established community, can undermine the legitimacy of community norms among the resident population (cf. Blau and Blau 1982; Crutchfield, Geerken, and Gove 1982).

5. In addition to the state-level studies reviewed, a number of researchers have investigated the southern culture of violence thesis using city- or SMSA-level data (Bailey 1984; Blau and Blau 1982; Blau and Golden 1986; Loftin and Parker 1985; McDowall 1986; Messner 1982, 1983; Simpson 1985). Although these researchers use a different unit of analysis, their studies share the same limitation as the state-level research of the failure to include an independent measure of cultural support for violence.

6. In our description of the Legitimate Violence Index (LVX), it was necessary to omit a great deal of information in order to fit within the space limitations of a journal article. A comprehensive discussion of the index can be found in an article devoted entirely to the LVX (Straus 1985b). That article discusses the theoretical rationale of the index, the reason for using indicators as diverse as possible rather than homogeneous indicators, state ranks of the 12 indicators, and a complete list of the source documents.

7. The magazines included in the Violent Magazine Circulation Index are the combined circulation of the *Army, Air Force, and Navy Times, Easy Riders, Guns and Ammo, Heavy Metal,* and *Shooting Times.* These magazines were chosen from a larger group of magazines on the basis of a principal components analysis. The 6 most violent television programs were selected on the basis of ratings published by the National Coalition on Television Violence. The programs are "Charlie's Angels," "Enos," "Incredible Hulk," "Hart to Hart," "Dukes of Hazzard," and "Fantasy Island."

8. Because capital punishment is typically a response to murder, we took this into account when computing these variables by using arrests for homicide as the denominator. This enabled us to control for contamination with homicide. See Straus (1985b) for elaboration on this and other aspects of the Legitimate Violence Index.

9. At first glance it might seem inappro-

priate to use lynching as an indicator of legitimate violence. However, Brown's (1979) analysis of vigilante violence suggests that, although illegal, lynching in Post-Reconstruction America had cultural support among dominant groups in society. Also, because lynching is an historical indicator, it provides a measure of the historical legacy of violence in states.

10. An alpha coefficient of .71 would ordinarily be considered acceptable, but on the low side. However, given the deliberate heterogeneity of the 12 indicators, the alpha level represents a greater degree of internal consistency than was expected. The theory that guided the construction of the LVX does not assume that the indicators are strongly related to each other, only that each of them is a manifestation of legitimate violence. For this reason, we chose not to use item analysis or factor analysis as a basis for deleting items from the overall index. Rather, we made the theoretical assumption that each manifestation of legitimate violence makes an independent contribution to legitimizing criminal violence. If that assumption is correct, the sum of the 12 indicators represents a measure of the cumulative effect, and this cumulative effect does not depend on the items being highly intercorrelated. In fact, it is maximized if the items have a zero correlation with each other (Nunnally 1978).

11. We considered using Gastil's (1971) Southernness Index but decided not to do so for three reasons. First, the index does not reflect the large migration flows since the 1960s. Second, Gastil did not provide sufficient information to guide the construction of a revised index. For instance, one of Gastil's (1971, p. 425) coding rules is: "Give 15 to definitely non-Southern states with a strong representation of Southern population in either the formative period or more recently." Assuming that one could deduce which states are "definitely non-Southern" and which years are included in the "formative period," there is no unambiguous way of determining the percentage that fall into the category of "strong representation." Third, although it would have been possible to use the original Southernness Index, there is no evidence that

it is a better measure of southern influence than measures of Confederate South or Southern Region. Finally, because the Southernness Index is based on migratory patterns, it could be measuring the effects of social disorganization (i.e., population turnover), rather than the effects of cultural support for violence.

12. The Family Integration Index is the average of three Z scored variables. These variables are intended to be indicators of the extent to which the population of each state lives in households that maximize family ties or interactions. The three variables comprising the Family Integration Index are percent of households with both the husband and wife present, the inverse of the percent of persons living alone, and the number of families per 100,000 population.

13. Scheffe's test was employed to examine each possible pair of means and to determine if any two means were significantly different from one another. We were unable to find a significant difference between the West and South in legitimate violence, although the West and South were found to have significantly higher levels of legitimate violence than the Northeast and North Central regions. While the higher average index score of the West compared to the South in legitimate violence was not statistically significant, the fact that the South does not lead the country in legitimate violence raised doubts about the argument that violent cultural norms are disproportionately concentrated in the South.

14. As a preliminary step to calculating correlations and regression coefficients, a number of diagnostic tests were performed to inspect the data for departures from normality, linearity, and the presence of outliers. Normality was checked by examining descriptive statistics and scatter plots of residuals. Nonlinear trends were examined by plotting the decile version of each independent variable against the homicide rate and checking the Eta test of linearity. Frequency distributions, studentized residuals, and Cook's D statistics were computed to test for outliers. The results did not show any significant deviations from normality or linearity, nor did they show any bivariate or multivariate outliers.

A correlation matrix containing all the independent variables was inspected for high coefficients that might denote the presence of multicollinearity. A correlation of .93 was observed between the Gini Index and the percent of families below poverty level incomes. Because an association of such magnitude can increase the standard error and produce unstable regression coefficients, it was decided to use each of these variables in separate regression equations.

15. Readers familiar with Loftin and Hill's (1974) study may note that they obtained a higher coefficient of determination ($R^2 = .92$) than we obtained in the present study ($R^2 = .60$ and $.61$). There could be several reasons for this difference. One possible explanation is that changes in American society during the last two decades have diminished the predictability of homicide (Loftin and Hill used 1959–1960 data, whereas we used 1980 data). Although this is a possible explanation, we are reluctant to make a strong case in support of this argument because the difference could be due to methodological characteristics. For example, inspection of the correlation matrix from Loftin and Hill's study reveals a pattern of excessively high correlations. This raises the possibility that Loftin and Hill's high R^2 is partially due to multicollinearity. Another possible explanation is that Loftin and Hill used a different set of independent variables in their analysis. Any or all of these factors could have contributed to the difference in R^2.

16. When such terms as "held constant" and "partial effect" are used, they are intended to be interpreted in the statistical sense. We do not presuppose that economic and cultural indicators are uncorrelated with one another. On the contrary, we assume, and in fact find, a relationship between measures of the economic structure of society and legitimate violence. This relationship is shown by the correlations of .43 between the percent poor and the LVX, and .53 between the Gini Index and the LVX. These correlations indicate that impoverishment and economic inequality are related to legitimate violence. They also show that the relationship is far from perfect, thus making it possible statistically for each to

exert an independent influence on the incidence of homicide.

17. We have carried out one such study using the UCR rape rate as the measure of criminal violence and found a significant indirect relationship between legitimate violence and rape. More precisely, we found that the association between legitimate violence and rape is mediated by the level of sexual inequality in society. For details see Baron and Straus (1987).

REFERENCES

Bailey, W. C. 1984. "Poverty, Inequality, and City Homicide Rates." *Criminology* 22: 531–550.

Baron, L., and M. A. Straus. 1987. "Four Theories of Rape: A Macrosociological Analysis." *Social Problems* 34: 501–521.

———. In press. "Legitimate Violence, Violent Attitudes, and Rape: Test of the Cultural Spillover Theory." *Annals of the New York Academy of Sciences*.

Blau, J. R., and P. M. Blau. 1982. "The Cost of Inequality: Metropolitan Structure and Violent Crime." *American Sociological Review* 47: 114–128.

Blau, P. M., and R. M. Golden. 1986. "Metropolitan Structure and Criminal Violence." *The Sociological Quarterly* 27: 15–26.

Brown, R. M. 1979. "The American Vigilante Tradition." Pp. 153–185 in *Violence in American Historical and Comparative Perspectives,* edited by H. D. Graham and T. R. Gurr. Beverly Hills: Sage.

Crutchfield, R. D., M. R. Geerken, and W. R. Gove. 1982. "Crime Rate and Social Integration." *Criminology* 20: 467–478.

Curtis, L. A. 1975. *Violence, Race, and Culture.* Lexington, MA: Lexington.

Dibble, U., and M. A. Straus. 1980. "Some Social Structural Determinants of Inconsistency Between Attitudes and Behavior: The Case of Family Violence." *Journal of Marriage and the Family* 42: 71–80.

Doerner, W. G. 1978. "The Deadly World of Johnny Reb: Fact, Foible, or Fantasy?" Pp. 91–98 in *Violent Crime: Historical and Contemporary Issues,* edited by J. A. Inciardi and A. E. Pottieger. Beverly Hills: Sage.

Durkheim, E. (1897) (1938). *The Rules of Sociological Method.* New York: Free Press.

Friday, P. C. 1983. "Urban Crime." Pp. 1582–1587 in *Encyclopedia of Criminal Justice,* vol. 4, edited by S. H. Kadish. New York: Free Press.

Garfinkel, H. 1967. *Studies in Ethnomethodology.* New York: Prentice-Hall.

Gastil, R. D. 1971. "Homicide and a Regional Culture of Violence." *American Sociological Review* 36: 412–427.

Geertz, C. 1973. *The Interpretation of Cultures.* New York: Basic Books.

Gove, W. R., M. Hughes, and M. Geerken. 1985. "Are Uniform Crime Reports a Valid Indicator of the Index Crimes? An Affirmative Answer with Minor Qualifications." *Criminology* 23: 451–491.

Greenberg, D. F. 1983. "Age and Crime." Pp. 30–35 in *Encyclopedia of Criminal Justice,* vol. 1, edited by S. H. Kadish. New York: Free Press.

Greenblat, C. S. 1983. "A Hit is a Hit is a Hit . . . or is it? Approval and Tolerance of the Use of Physical Force by Spouses." Pp. 235–260 in *The Dark Side of Families,* edited by D. Finkelhor, R. J. Gelles, G. Hotaling, and M. A. Straus. Beverly Hills: Sage.

Hackney, S. 1969. "Southern Violence." *American Historical Review* 74: 906–925.

Harries, K. D. 1971. "The Geography of Crime, 1968." *Journal of Geography* 70: 204–213.

———. 1974. *The Geography of Crime and Justice.* New York: McGraw-Hill.

———. 1980. *Crime and the Environment.* Springfield, IL: Charles C. Thomas.

Hindelang, M. J. 1974. "The Uniform Crime Reports Revisited." *Journal of Criminal Justice* 2: 1–17.

———. 1981. "Variations in Sex-Race-Age-Specific Incidence Rates of Offending." *American Sociological Review* 46: 461–474.

Hirschi, T., and M. Gottfredson. 1983. "Age and the Explanation of Crime." *American Journal of Sociology* 89: 552–584.

Huff-Corzine, L., J. Corzine, and D. C. Moore. 1986. "Southern Exposure: Deciphering the South's Influence on Homicide Rates." *Social Forces* 64: 907–924.

Kowalski, G. S., R. L. Dittman, Jr., and W. L. Bung. 1980. "Spatial Distribution of Criminal Offenses by States 1970–1976." *Journal of Research in Crime and Delinquency* 17: 4–25.

Leiter, K. 1980. *A Primer on Ethnomethodology.* New York: Oxford.

Loftin, C., and R. H. Hill. 1974. "Regional Subculture and Homicide: An Examination of the Gastil-Hackney Thesis." *American Sociological Review* 39: 714–724.

Loftin, C., and R. N. Parker. 1985. "An Errors-In-Variable Model of the Effect of Poverty on Urban Homicide Rates." *Criminology* 23: 269–285.

Lottier, S. 1938. "Distribution of Criminal Offenses in Sectional Regions." *Journal of Criminal Law, Criminology and Police Science* 29: 329–344.

Lukes, S. 1972. *Emile Durkheim: His Life and Work.* New York: Harper.

McDowall, D. 1986. "Poverty and Homicide in Detroit, 1926–1978." *Violence and Victims* 1: 23–24.

Messner, S. F. 1982. "Poverty, Inequality, and the Urban Homicide Rate: Some Unexpected Findings." *Criminology* 20: 103–114.

———. 1983. "Regional and Race Effects on the Urban Homicide Rate: The Subculture of Violence Revisited." *American Journal of Sociology* 88: 997–1007.

Nettler, G. 1984. *Explaining Crime.* 3rd ed. New York: McGraw-Hill.

Nunnally, J. C. 1978. *Psychometric Theory.* 2nd ed. New York: McGraw-Hill.

Reed, J. S. 1971. "To Live-and-Die-in Dixie: A Contribution to the Study of Southern Violence." *Political Science Quarterly* 86: 429–443.

———. 1977. "Below the Smith and Wesson Line: Reflections on Southern Violence." Paper presented at the second annual Hugo L. Black Symposium, University of Alabama, Birmingham, April 21.

Shannon, L. W. 1954. "The Spatial Distribution of Criminal Offenses by States." *Journal of Criminal Law, Criminology and Police Science* 45: 264–273.

Simpson, M. E. 1985. "Violent Crime, Income Inequality, and Regional Culture: Another Look." *Sociological Focus* 18: 199–208.

Smith, M. D., and R. N. Parker. 1980. "Type of Homicide and Variation in Regional Rates." *Social Forces* 59: 136–147.

Smith, M. D., and N. Bennett. 1985. "Poverty, Inequality, and Theories of Forcible Rape." *Crime and Delinquency* 31: 295–305.

Straus, M. A. 1980. "Indexing and Scaling for Social Science Research with SPSS." Unpublished manuscript.

———. 1985a. "The Validity of U.S. States as Units for Sociological Research." Paper presented at the annual meeting of the American Sociological Association, Washington, DC.

———. 1985b. *Index of Legitimate Violence.* Durham, NH: Family Research Laboratory, University of New Hampshire.

Willie, C. V., and O. L. Edwards. 1983. "Race and Crime." Pp. 1347–1351 in *Encyclopedia of Criminal Justice,* vol. 4, edited by S. H. Kadish. New York: Free Press.

Williams, K. R. 1984. "Economic Sources of Homicide: Reestimating the Effects of Poverty and Inequality." *American Sociological Review* 49: 283–289.

Wilson, W. J. 1984. "The Urban Underclass." Pp. 75–117 in *Minority Report,* edited by L. W. Dunbar. New York: Pantheon Books.

Wolfgang, M. E. 1958. *Pattern of Criminal Homicide.* Philadelphia: University of Pennsylvania Press.

Wolfgang, M. E., R. M. Figlio, and T. Sellin. 1972. *Delinquency in a Birth Cohort.* Chicago: University of Chicago Press.

In the social sciences, articles that report empirical research have a fairly standard organization. If you look at Baron and Straus' article, you will notice that it is divided into sections and subsections. In this article, sections are set off by headings centered and in CAPITALS, subsections are centered with the first letter of each word capitalized, and sub-subsections are flush left with initial words capitalized. In a typical scientific report in the social sciences, there are four or five standard sections, and the author has some latitude for using subsections. Baron and Straus' article has seven sections and eight subsections—somewhat more than in the usual organization.

Most articles in scientific journals include an ABSTRACT (which appears at the beginning, often in fine print, set off from the text of the article) and a SUMMARY or CONCLUSIONS (which appears at the end of the article). *These sections are the first things to read in a scientific report.* The ABSTRACT and SUMMARY give you an overview of the purpose of the research, its methods, its findings, and the author's conclusions, where often you can find the answers to several of the questions you have without looking further. In Baron and Straus' article, the abstract is set off at the beginning and the last section summarizes the research.

The first section of the text of any article is generally called the INTRODUCTION. It is usually not labeled as such, since the first section is obviously the introduction; so it is with Baron and Straus. The introduction will tell you something about the general question being investigated. It first reports what previous researchers have found out about this question, then tells you what this particular study will try to find out, and usually ends with a formal statement of the hypotheses. Thus, the introduction puts the present study in a context of previous, related research. In Baron and Straus' article, the introduction includes the section labeled SOUTHERN CULTURE OF VIOLENCE AND HOMICIDE that continues the discussion of the issues in the literature that their work addresses. Such a section is often called BACKGROUND and reviews the literature regarding the general question under study. As is common in research articles, Baron and Straus end their discussion of the literature with formal statements of the hypotheses that were tested in their research.

The second section of a scientific study is usually called the METHOD section. Baron and Straus have opted to describe their method in two separate sections: one describes the way they operationalized the key independent variable of interest (LEGITIMATE VIOLENCE INDEX) and the other describes the remaining variables analyzed in the study and their data sources (DATA AND VARIABLES). The method section gives specific, detailed information about how a particular study was conducted. The rule of thumb for *writing* this section (which you will not be doing) is to give the reader all the information he or she would need to replicate the study. Thus, in this section we will find information about who or what, exactly, the *subjects* (a common subheading) were, how the variables were operationalized, what *procedures* (a common subheading) were used to conduct the research, what *measures* (a common subheading) were used to get the numbers that represent the variables, and what specialized equipment, if any, was employed.

The third section of a typical scientific article is called RESULTS, and offers a summarized report of the findings of the research. Sometimes only the findings relevant to the main hypothesis are reported in this section, but sometimes auxiliary data are reported here as well. In this section you will encounter the technical language and notation of statistics, which are used to summarize and draw conclusions from data in the majority of empirical articles in the social sciences. Baron and Straus' results are divided into three sections: one that presents the descriptive statistical analyses of homicide and legitimate violence and one each for a description of two inferential analyses (correlation and multiple regression).

Scientific articles often present next a section labeled DISCUSSION (sometimes this section is combined with RESULTS). Here the implications of the results are stated and the author's conclusions appear. If the results supported the hypothesis, the author might note other hypotheses also supported by the data. If the results were a surprise, the author might offer possible explanations. In the discussion section the author evaluates those alternative explanations of the data that he or she considers plausible or at least worthy of mention. In Baron and Straus' article, the discussion appears in the SUMMARY AND CONCLUSIONS section, the last section in the report. As we noted above in the discussion of the abstract, the summary provides a brief overview of the research and includes all of the important information about the research method, findings, and conclusions.

The above is a brief view of the structure of scientific research reports; more detailed accounts are available elsewhere (e.g., American Psychological Association, 1983).

The *first question* to answer about scientific reports is: *What method was used* (from among the categories defined in Chapter 2) to collect the data? If you look at the ABSTRACT, you will note that the authors are studying the cultural and economic factors that explain variations in homicide rates among the 50 states. States are being compared, the authors are studying the independent variables (cultural and economic factors) as organismic variables, and nothing is being manipulated. The test of method in this case is in the way the independent variables are operationally defined. If they are defined by an experimental manipulation, you have an experiment; if they are defined by the measurement of something already there, the study is nonexperimental. This study is correlational.

You can also identify the method used by looking in the METHOD section. The approach is the same, but it may take longer to find the answer. Once you see that the independent variables are operationalized in terms of differences between states, you know the study is nonexperimental.

The *second question* to answer is: *What is the hypothesis,* if any? Is it causal or noncausal? The first place to look for the hypothesis is in the title of an article. The titles of scientific articles are noted for being dull but full of information. More often than not, the hypothesis and the major variables studied are all packed into the title. The Baron and Straus article is a good example. The title, "Cultural and Economic Sources of Homicide in the United States," suggests that the hypothesis concerns a relationship between homicide and "culture" and "economy." Further, the title tells us that the hypothesized relationship is causal because it uses a key word in causality: the *sources* of homicide. Sometimes, as in this case, a title will use words or phrases that imply causal relationships between variables, e.g., "the effect of" something, or "the influence of" something. However, often you cannot tell anything about whether the hypothesis is causal from the title alone and further reading is necessary to decide. For example, in the Baron and Straus article, if you missed the clues about the general hypothesis in the title and their report of "hypotheses derived" in the abstract, it would be hard not to find the four hypotheses listed at the end of the introduction or background section. Before they present their formal hypotheses, Baron and Straus review the more general questions that their study addresses: Is cultural support for violence more heavily concentrated in the South than any other region of the country, and what are the effects of cultural and economic variables on rates of homicide? Baron and Straus discuss the background of these general questions in their introduction: The homicide rate in southern states is higher than in states in other regions of the country. Some researchers argue that southern homicide reflects a culture of violence that is unique to the southern region, while others argue that it reflects economic inequality or poverty. Prior research has used southern region as a proxy for a cultural support for violence; that is, it has used southern location as the operational definition of cultural support for violence. Baron and Straus correctly criticize the validity of inferences about culture that are made from such an operational definition. Their study uses a different strategy: it creates an operational definition of cultural support for violence (the legitimate violence index) that is independent of region (Confederate South) and examines the independent effects of each variable on homicide rates.

There are four hypotheses in this study: (1) States in the southern region are more likely to have a higher level of support for legitimate violence than states in any other region of the country. (2) The higher the level of legitimate violence, the higher the homicide rate. (3) As poverty increases, the homicide rate increases. (4) As economic inequality increases, the homicide rate increases. It is important to note that these hypotheses could be interpreted as noncausal. Consider Hypothesis (2): the higher the level of legitimate violence, the higher the homicide rate. This does not say which variable causes which, only that they are correlated. Hypotheses (3) and (4) are worded in a more ambiguous way. The word "increases" may have the same meaning as getting "higher" in Hypothesis (2), or it may imply a prediction, as in: "if poverty increases, the homicide rate will increase [as a result]." The wording is not clearly causal because the researchers know that their correlational data can never confirm a causal hypothesis. Nevertheless, a reading of the article makes quite clear that all the debate in this literature is about the *causes* of the higher homicide rates in the South. So we conclude that all the hypotheses in this study are causal, except Hypothesis (1), which remains ambiguous. It does not hypothesize about *why* some states have higher rates of legitimate violence, only about where those states are to be found. (The literature contains some causal hypotheses about why southern states might have higher rates of legitimate violence.)

Third question: Identify the variables being studied. Then, if applicable, what is the independent variable? What is its operational definition? What is the dependent variable? What is its operational definition?

With the hypotheses stated clearly, as in Baron and Straus' research, the variables are fairly easy to identify. With multiple hypotheses, however, it is best to consider each separately: In Hypothesis 1, support for legitimate violence is a dependent variable, but "southern region" is not exactly an independent variable. The text clearly indicates that support for legitimate violence is presumed to depend on a number of cultural and historical factors and not on the southern region in itself. These cultural and historical factors are the true independent variables, and the study does not measure them. Hypothesis 2: level of legitimate violence is independent, homicide rate is dependent. Hypothesis 3: poverty is independent, homicide rate is dependent. Hypothesis 4: economic inequality is independent, homicide rate is dependent.

Operational definitions often take some digging, and they are usually found in the METHOD section. Recall that Baron and Straus' methods are discussed in two sections, one that describes the operationalization of one variable, support for legitimate violence, and one headed DATA AND VARIABLES. The rest of the variables in the hypotheses are operationalized in the Data and Variables section. An entire section is devoted to the LEGITIMATE VIOLENCE INDEX (LVX), primarily because this operational definition of support for legitimate violence is quite complex. The LVX is an *index* that is constructed from 12 indicators (or variables) that "reflect an underlying belief in the efficacy and desirability of physical force." The indicators are based on noncriminal, socially approved violent activities, and the LVX is conceptualized as a measure of this noncriminal aspect of cultural support for violence. Baron and Straus explain in footnote 6 that much of the information on the LVX had to be omitted because of space limitations. They refer us to an article by Straus that provides a detailed description of the index. Unfortunately, the article that they refer us to is an unpublished manuscript (at least as of the publication date of the article you read here), and we would have to write the author for a copy. When you are doing a careful review, do not hesitate to ask for copies of unpublished manuscripts that are cited in the published literature. What we know about the LVX from Baron and Straus' article follows.

The LVX is composed of 12 indicators or variables that are grouped into three categories. Each of these categories has at least two indicators. The first category is *mass media preferences,* which "represent the degree of public interest in magazine and television media with violent content." Public interest in violent media is measured by two variables: (1) A Violent Magazine Circulation Index, which consists of the 1979 circulation rates per 100,000 population of five magazines that depict violence or serve a segment of the population involved in violence. Footnote 7 provides the names of the five magazines *(Army, Air Force, and Navy Times, Easy Riders, Guns and Ammo, Heavy Metal,* and *Shooting Times).* (2) An index of the six "most violent television programs" in the fall of 1980 ("Charlie's Angels," "Enos," "Incredible Hulk," "Hart to Hart," "Dukes of Hazzard," and "Fantasy Island"), based on ratings by the National Coalition on Television Violence. The article does not actually state what the index was. Perhaps it was based on TV viewership of the six programs in the largest city in each state. We would have to consult the unpublished manuscript to be certain.

The second category of indicators in the LVX is *governmental use of violence,* or legal support of violent acts, which "may be seen as reflecting public sentiment about the acceptability of violence." Governmental use of violence is composed of five variables: (1) laws permitting *corporal punishment* by schoolteachers in 1979, (2) *executions* per 100 homicide arrests for the years *1940–1959,* (3) *executions* per 100 homicide arrests for the years *1960–1978,* (4) *blacks sentenced to death* per 100 blacks arrested for homicide in 1980, and (5) *whites sentenced to death* per 100 whites arrested for homicide in 1980.

The third LVX category is *participation in socially approved violent activities.* The five variables in this category and their operationalizations are: (1) *hunting licenses* sold per 1,000 population in 1980, (2) the *state of origin of college football players* per capita in 1972 (we cannot tell from the article how this is operationalized), (3) *National Guard enrollment* per 100,000 population in 1976, (4) *National Guard expenditures* per capita in 1976, and (5) *lynchings* per million population during the years 1882–1927. (In footnote 9, the authors justify the use of lynchings as a measure of socially approved activities because "it provides a measure of the historical legacy of violence in states."). The LVX itself is a composite of these 12 indicators created by a statistical technique (the use of Z scores) that gives each indicator the same mean score and the same variability. This ensures that each indicator has equal weight in the LVX even though the indicators were originally measured in very different units. It is the final LVX score that is the operational definition of "support for legitimate violence" in a state.

In addition to the LVX, there are two additional independent variables, the *Gini Index* of income inequality and the *percent poor.* The Gini Index measures relative deprivation and was computed using 1979 family income. This index is a measure that is used often in research on social stratification, and has a possible range of 0 to 100, with 0 indicating perfect equality (each person or household has equal wealth) and 100 indicating perfect inequality (one person or one household has all of the wealth). In this case, the Gini Index has a range of scores from 31 to 40, with higher scores indicating greater income inequality in the state. The percent poor measures absolute deprivation and is the proportion of families in 1980 with incomes below the poverty level.

The dependent variable is the homicide rate, which is operationalized as "the 1980 rate per 100,000 population of homicides known to the police, as reported in the Uniform Crime Reports (UCR)."

Variable operationalizations are often long and involved, as in the Baron and Straus study. You know you have found a complete operational definition when there is a number to represent a variable (Gini Index score = 40), or a category system for a variable (e.g., the presence or absence of a variable, such as whether or not the state was a member of the Confederacy).

Fourth question: Identify the findings. Findings always appear in the RESULTS section, although they are also summarized in the ABSTRACT and SUMMARY. Newcomers to research in the social sciences often have more trouble with this section than with any other part of scientific reports. We digress here to give a brief guide to deciphering the statistics that typically appear in RESULTS sections.

In social science research, the phenomena are usually not so obvious that you can tell at a glance what is happening. For this reason, statistics are used to get mathematical statements about the magnitude of the observed effects, and about the probability that these effects might have occurred "by chance."

The most important thing to know about the use of statistics is the logic of statistical inference. Statistics are most commonly used to make inferences about populations from data on samples. Statistics allow a researcher to take into account sampling error—the possibility that the sample happens, by the luck of the draw, to contain many individuals that differ from what is typical in the population. If it does, the data from the sample will differ from the value that would have been obtained if every individual in the population had been measured. With experiments, statistics are used to estimate the size of error introduced by randomization—the possibility that the individuals assigned to one experimental condition happen to differ systematically from those assigned to other conditions in ways that affect the dependent variable. In Baron and Straus' research, statistics were used to allow the researchers to take into account measurement error—the possibility that states happen to differ, for example, in the frequency of unreported homicides or in errors in measuring parts of the legitimate violence scale, such as the frequency of watching violent television programs.

Regardless of what kinds of random error enter into the data reported in a study, the logic of statistical inference is the same. As an illustration, consider Baron and Straus' comparison of homicide rates and legitimate violence in the four major regions of the United States. The researchers want to determine the likelihood that the regional differences in homicide rates they observe could have resulted from some random process that happens, by chance, to produce higher reports of homicide in some states than in others. For example, it could be that, even after the effects of urbanization, poverty or proportion of young adults are taken into account, there are random differences from state to state in the extent to which homicide is underreported or misreported. By chance, these random measurement errors might work out so that states in the South and West have higher reported homicide rates than those in the North Central and Northeastern regions. The statistical tests of significance indicate the probability that the results observed in the data were the result of purely random processes. If that probability is low, instead of thinking that regional differences in homicide rates are due to chance, we can conclude that it's likely they result from a real, causal factor that is related to region.

Statisticians have calculated a number of different mathematical functions that tell exactly how likely it is that, by this kind of accident, a difference of a certain size across the groups would appear. For any difference that is observed, a researcher can perform the appropriate calculations and find out how likely it is that this difference would have occurred by chance between individuals (or states) that are actually equal. Baron and Straus report in Table 2 that regional differences for the homicide rate and legitimate violence are significant at $p < .005$. They do not indicate in the table the observed value of the statistic that they used to test regional differences on the two variables, but footnote 13 provides the information: Scheffé's test was used to determine if any two means were significantly different from one another. Their test found that there was not a significant difference between the South and West regions in support for legitimate violence (Hypothesis 1 is not supported) but that the South and West regions were significantly higher in LVX than the Northeast and North Central regions. The test statistic is used to determine the chances of observing differences as great as those reported in Table 2 if legitimate violence and homicide rates were in fact unrelated to region and the observed differences reflected only errors in measurement or other random factors unrelated to region. The "$p < .005$" indicates that the *probability* of observing such a large difference in regions by chance is less than .005, or less than five in 1000. If it is very unlikely that the difference is due to chance, it is correspondingly more likely that it is due to regional characteristics of states (or at least to some variable related to regional characteristics). If you understand what the p values refer to, you have understood the most important single part of the RESULTS section.

This, in very simple terms, is the logic of statistical inference. It is assumed that the variables under study are *not* related (this is called the "null hypothesis," and is generally what a researcher wants to be able to *reject* as a likelihood). If it can be shown statistically that what is observed is inconsistent with the null hypothesis, this is rejected in favor of the alternative, namely that the variables under study *are* related.

Researchers have many ways of telling you about whether their data confirm their hypotheses or not. The simplest way, and the one to look for first, is the value of "p" associated with the statistical test of a hypothesis. Usually, in the social sciences, if p is less than .05, the null hypothesis is considered unlikely enough to be rejected. Look for p values, and interpret them as follows:

If	Then the Probability of the Result Occurring by Chance Is
$p = .02$	.02, or 2%
$p < .05$	less than .05; less than 5%
$p < .001$	less than .001; less than $1/10$ of 1%
$.01 < p < .025$	between 1% and $2\frac{1}{2}$%
$p > .10$	greater than 10% (in this case, the null hypothesis cannot be rejected)

Sometimes you may see the notation "n.s." where you expect a value of p. This stands for "not significant," and means that p is too large to reject the null hypothesis.

In the text of a RESULTS section, there are many ways an investigator may tell you whether a hypothesis is confirmed. Read the text, and translate words into p values as follows:

If the Text Says	It Means
The results are statistically significant (or reliable) at the .01 level	$p < .01$
Alpha (α) was set at .05, and the result was significant	$p < .05$
The null hypothesis was rejected with 95% confidence	$p < .05$
The difference was statistically reliable at the .05 level	$p < .05$

All of the above mean that the null hypothesis was rejected, and that the variables (whose relationship is being tested) *are* related to each other. This should give you the idea.

Many of the different statistics used in research are ultimately converted into p values. Thus, if you have no background in statistics, you may do best to ignore the values of such statistics as t, F, r, chi-square (X^2), W, rho, tau, U, T, and z, and look for p. By doing this, you are taking the author's word that the statistic is appropriate for the data. It is true that scientists do sometimes err in their choice of statistics, but this is not the place to give you the background you would need to draw your own conclusions about whether such an error has been made.

It is worth mentioning one of the limits to the usefulness of a p value. A low p implies that the null hypothesis can be rejected with strong (but not perfect) confidence. It implies that there is some nonzero relationship between the variables being compared. It does *not*, however, say anything about the *strength* of that relationship. We know only that the effect is not zero.

In short, not every *statistically significant* relationship is a *strong* relationship. Sometimes there are ways to judge the strength of the relationship from the results reported in a study. The simplest way is to look at the size of the sample that produced the reported p value. Common sense and statistics both tell us that the greater the effect of a variable, the easier it will be to prove that the influence exists. In general, $p < .05$ can indicate a strong relationship if the number of individuals in the sample is less than, say, 50. With sample sizes in the hundreds, any respectable effect will yield a $p < .001$.

In Baron and Straus' article, the strength of the relationship between variables is estimated with CORRELATION ANALYSIS. Two variables are correlated if the values of one variable consistently rise or fall with the values of another variable. The statistic that describes the relationship is the correlation coefficient, or *Pearson's r*. Pearson's r can have values between $+1.0$ and -1.0, with the absolute value of the coefficient indicating the magnitude (or strength) of the relationship. A perfect relationship would yield a coefficient of 1.0 (positive or negative), and a coefficient of 0 would indicate no relationship between the variables. The sign of the coefficient gives the direction of the relationship. A positive sign means that as one variable increases, the other variable also increases (or, as one variable decreases, the other variable decreases). A negative sign means that there is an inverse relationship between the variables: increases in one are associated with decreases in the other (or decreases in one are associated with increases in the other).

Baron and Straus report the "zero-order," or bivariate, correlations in Table 3. They report that there is no statistically significant relationship between legitimate violence and homicide. However, homicide has significant positive relationships with the Gini Index and the percent poor families, as well as with other variables. Quantitative research reports usually do not end their analyses with correlation; the goal is very often to specify the nature of more complex multivariate relationships. For example, Baron and Straus were interested to find out whether the correlation between homicide rates and southern region (which had been noted by previous researchers) was really due to cultural support for violence, or to poverty. Bivariate correlations do not go far toward answering this question, because it concerns more than two variables.

This is why the authors conduct a multivariate analysis of the determinants of homicide, reported in the section MULTIPLE REGRESSION ANALYSES. If you followed the discussion in Chapter 3 of multiple regression, the interpretation of the coefficients reported in Table 4 should not be too difficult. Note that the table presents two regression analyses, one with percent poor and one with the Gini Index. The analyses are very similar, and the logic behind performing two multiple regressions is explained in the first paragraph of the section. Whenever variables are highly correlated (e.g., $r = .93$ for Gini Index and percent poor), they are considered collinear, or almost linear combinations of each other. Because they are nearly equivalent, researchers use one or the other in the analysis, but not both (unless they are combined or scaled to represent one variable).

Table 4 presents additional information. The regression coefficients (called partial coefficients) are given in both standardized form (sometimes called beta coefficients) and unstandardized form (sometimes called B coefficients). The interpretation of the unstandardized regression coefficient is straightforward: for each change of one unit in the independent variable, the dependent variable changes by the number of units represented by the coefficient. So, the unstandardized regression coefficient of .094 ($B = .094$) for the legitimate violence index indicates that for each additional increase of one point on the LVX score, the homicide rate increased by .094 per 100,000 population, holding the effects of the other independent variables constant statistically. Or, a 1% increase in percent poor was associated with an increase in the homicide rate of 0.418 per 100,000 population. Standardized regression coefficients use standard units instead of the original units in which the variables were measured. Thus, while they cannot be interpreted in terms of the original units of measurement, they do allow us to compare the relative importance of the independent variables in a multivariate model. Table 4 illustrates how standardized regression coefficients help us understand the relative importance of variables. Examination of the standardized coefficient column in the table shows clearly that the percent residing in SMSAs is the most important predictor variable (the coefficient is .533), the legitimate violence index is the next most important variable (.418), and the Confederate South variable contributes almost nothing to the explanation of homicide rates ($-.074$), when the other independent variables are taken into account. This conclusion is supported by the information provided in the last column of the table, the t value. This t is a significance test for partial regression coefficients (standardized or unstandardized), and we have already discussed the interpretation of p values. R^2 (in this case "adjusted" to correct for the number of cases and variables) indicates the proportion of the variation (technically, the variance) in the dependent variable that is explained by a set (or combination) of independent variables. R^2 can have any value from 0 to 1. Thus, R^2 tells us how well the regression equation fits the data. In Baron and Straus' study, the seven independent variables together explain about 60% of the variance in U.S. states' 1980 homicide rates.

We emphasize that although the bivariate correlation between the LVX and homicide rates was not significant ($r = .19$), the multiple regression uncovered an important pattern: the LVX is a significant predictor of state variations in homicide rates when controlling for the other independent variables. As the authors explain the finding, the large negative relationship between percent of the population residing in SMSAs and the LVX ($-.54$) was suppressing what would have otherwise been a strong bivariate relationship between LVX and homicide. To explain this in another way, if separate analyses were carried out for highly urbanized states (most people living in SMSAs) and for rural states, the data would have shown strong positive relationships between LVX and homicide rates in both kinds of states. Based on these findings, Baron and Straus conclude that "homicide rates have a significant tendency to increase in proportion to increases in the levels of legitimate violence, poverty, and economic inequality." So, Hypotheses 2, 3, and 4 are confirmed. (Recall that Hypothesis 1 was not supported by the data, e.g., southern states are not more likely to have a higher level of support for legitimate violence than states in any other region.)

Fifth question: Identify an *extraneous variable that is controlled* by holding it constant. Identify an extraneous variable that is randomized (if there is one).

Controls for extraneous variables generally get first mention in the METHOD section. In experimental studies, look for carefully followed *procedures* during the manipulation of the independent variable. In all studies, look for care in the measurement of nonmanipulated variables. Baron and Straus were careful to include extraneous variables in the hypotheses by analyzing them as independent variables in the multiple regression (percent residing in SMSAs, family integration index, percent black, percent age 18–24). This is the same method of control that we discussed in Chapter 3 regarding our study of proenvironmental political behavior. Including variables in the analysis serves as a *statistical control* for spuriousness. A spurious relationship is one that disappears when a third variable is introduced. For example, in their background review of the southern culture of violence argument, Baron and Straus discuss a study that reported a spurious relationship between a southernness index (extent to which states are populated by individuals who migrated from the South) and homicide rates: the relationship between the southernness index and homicide rates disappeared when structural poverty was taken into account (included in the regression equation). Statistical control could have been achieved in other ways, for example, by comparing states in only one region, e.g., the South. This would prevent variation introduced by the region variable, so that variations in the dependent variable could not be attributed to region. But as we show in Chapter 3, it is generally more informative to introduce a potentially extraneous variable into the analysis as an explanatory variable.

Although the concept of randomization is relevant to statistical inference in the

Baron and Straus study, the study did not control any variables by randomization. Randomization by definition can be used only in experimental research. In between-subjects experiments that compare equivalent groups, organismic variables are randomized when subjects are randomly assigned to treatment groups. In correlational research, organismic variables are allowed to vary.

Sixth question: Identify any *extraneous variables* that suggest an alternative explanation of the observed results. State the alternative explanation(s) and suggest one way to control for each extraneous variable involved.

In a carefully written scientific report, the author will mention any important extraneous variables that were not controlled. It may have been impossible to obtain control, or the variable may have been overlooked until after the data were collected. In either case, interpretation of the results depends on the extent to which extraneous variables were controlled, and possible alternative explanations are generally discussed along with the results in the DISCUSSION section. Uncontrolled extraneous variables may also be mentioned in the METHOD section while explaining the controls for other extraneous variables.

Even though Baron and Straus took great care to conduct a rigorous scientific study, they could not have controlled for all extraneous variables that might affect homicide rates. They do not directly address alternative explanations for their findings—a practice that is not uncommon in published research reports. Nevertheless, it is always worth your while to try to identify extraneous variables the author has not thought of. To do this, refer to the discussion of extraneous variables in Chapter 3 (Tables 3.1, 3.2, 3.3, 3.6, and 3.7) and try to think of types of variables that are likely to be left uncontrolled in the type of study you are reading. If you can think of a type of variable, try to come up with an example of that type that leads to an alternative explanation of the results. For example, in correlational studies, organismic variables are the primary source of alternative explanations. In the Baron and Straus study, this means that characteristics of states must be considered organismic, and while they did include some state characteristics (urbanization, poverty, LVX score, percent black, percent poor, and so on), surely you can think of some characteristics that are missing. What about environmental conditions, such as climate? Perhaps the high homicide rates in the South and West regions are due to uncomfortably hot climates. Some research supports this assumption of a connection between weather and aggressive behavior. For example, Anderson and Anderson (1984) found that aggressive crimes (murder and rape) in Chicago and in Houston increased as temperature increased (see also Harries and Stadler, 1983, for a similar finding for aggravated assault in Dallas). Another source of alternative explanation may be the LVX scale. Any source of invalidity in this scale would suggest an alternative explanation because the scale may actually be measuring something other than "cultural support for violence." We do not see any invalidity in the scale, but a more careful examination might reveal some.

You can use the same tables in Chapter 3 to suggest controls for the uncontrolled variables you find. Be specific about how you would use the method of control you suggest in the particular study you are reviewing. In the Baron and Straus study, including a measure of temperature (e.g., the state-to-state average annual, or average summer temperature) in the regression model might be suitable as a control for the effects of this extraneous variable on homicide rates.

Seventh question: Identify the sample studied and the population from which it was drawn. If you detect any sampling bias, identify it.

Information on the sample and the population sampled is almost always found in the METHOD section. Some research reports will then have a subsection within the METHOD section called "Subjects" or "Unit of Analysis" or, sometimes, "Data." If the METHOD section is not subdivided, the information usually comes very early in the section. Baron and Straus did not use a sample—they analyzed data on the entire population of the 50 U.S. states. Their "unit of analysis" (the 50 states) is first mentioned in the ABSTRACT and again at the end of the INTRODUCTION where they present the purpose of their research and the general question being investigated. Although the issues of generalizing from samples to populations and sampling bias are not of concern in this study, Baron and Straus acknowledge that some researchers question whether state-level analysis yields valid results (see footnote 1). It has been argued that as data are aggregated into large units (such as states), a single statistic (for example, a score on the legitimate violence index) cannot capture the large variation within states, and it is better to study smaller units such as cities, counties, or SMSAs. Baron and Straus maintain that there is no empirical support for the claim that data at lower levels of aggregation are more valid than state-level data. They cite research indicating that, with few exceptions, research using different units of analysis yields similar results.

There are a number of reasons why we should be cautious when evaluating research based on data that combine, or aggregate, the behavior of many individuals into large units of analysis like U.S. states. Some of the reasons are statistical. For example, the data on a small group of units like the states often fail to show the normal distribution that statistical techniques like regression analysis assume they have. The result may be to alter the results of ordinary regression analysis. For this reason, statistical analysts recommend that research on aggregates (e.g., cities, counties, states, countries) use analytic methods that perform well with non-normal data (Dietz, Kalof, & Frey, 1991). Baron and Straus were aware of this issue. The information provided in footnote 14 suggests that the data used in this study meet the requirements necessary for ordinary regression analysis.

A second reason for caution in interpreting aggregate-level research concerns using data on aggregates to make inferences about individual behaviors. Consider that states have poverty rates and income distributions, but only individuals commit homicide. It is fair to ask how state characteristics might affect an individual who lives there. Baron and Straus make such an inference when they claim, based on their analysis of state-to-state variation in homicide rates, that the positive evaluation of violence in the culture is "carried over to social contexts in which the use of violence is illegitimate, such as homicidal assaults." They do not present any evidence for this inference, however. Researchers can also run into trouble when generalizations are made about large-scale social groups or processes on the basis of data collected from individuals.

Eighth question: Identify any interactions being studied. This question tells us to look for interactions in the hypothesis or hypotheses of the research. If the hypothesis suggests that the effects of one variable depends on a second variable, and if this interrelationship of effects is being investigated, there are interactions being studied. If not, there are none being studied. Some research may encounter unexpected interactions during the analysis of the data. You will have to read the RESULTS and SUMMARY sections to find these unanticipated interactions. Baron and Straus neither hypothesized nor encountered any variable interactions in their study.

With the information you have just read, and with the practice on Baron and Straus' article, you should be ready to try an article on your own. The scientific report entitled "On Being Sane in Insane Places," by D. L. Rosenhan, is the example for this chapter.

Rosenhan's article is similar to Baron and Straus' in that it is not divided into sections titled INTRODUCTION, METHODS, RESULTS, and DISCUSSION, the way many scientific articles are. You must find the answers to the eight questions by reading through the report. Don't be too discouraged; even though the formal headings are not there, the material is presented in the same logical order.

Another difference between Rosenhan's article and Baron and Straus' is that Rosenhan's article is clearly more than one piece of research (that is, different kinds of data were collected, in different ways, to test different hypotheses). For the purposes of this exercise, consider only the main study, the one in which pseudopatients were admitted to mental hospitals, and the hospital's response (diagnosis, treatment, length of stay, etc.) was observed. Omit the section called "The Experience of Psychiatric Hospitalization," which contains some interesting, but separate, data.

At the end of Rosenhan's article is a place for you to answer the questions about it. Our answers follow.

On Being Sane in Insane Places

D. L. Rosenhan

If sanity and insanity exist, how shall we know them?

The question is neither capricious nor itself insane. However much we may be personally convinced that we can tell the normal from the abnormal, the evidence is simply not compelling. It is common-place, for example, to read about murder trials wherein eminent psychiatrists for the defense are contradicted by equally eminent psychiatrists for the prosecution on the matter of the defendant's sanity. More generally, there are a great deal of conflicting data on the reliability, utility,

Reprinted with permission from *Science*, 1973, *179*, 250–258. Copyright © 1973 American Association for the Advancement of Science.

The author is professor of psychology and law at Stanford University, Stanford, California 94305. Portions of these data were presented to colloquiums of the psychology departments at the University of California at Berkeley and at Santa Barbara; University of Arizona, Tucson; and Harvard University, Cambridge, Massachusetts.

and meaning of such terms as "sanity," "insanity," "mental illness," and "schizophrenia" (1). Finally, as early as 1934, Benedict suggested that normality and abnormality are not universal (2). What is viewed as normal in one culture may be seen as quite aberrant in another. Thus, notions of normality and abnormality may not be quite as accurate as people believe they are.

To raise questions regarding normality and abnormality is in no way to question the fact that some behaviors are deviant or odd. Murder is deviant. So, too, are hallucinations. Nor does raising such questions deny the existence of the personal anguish that is often associated with "mental illness." Anxiety and depression exist. Psychological suffering exists. But normality and abnormality, sanity and insanity, and the diagnoses that flow from them may be less substantive than many believe them to be.

At its heart, the question of whether the sane can be distinguished from the insane (and whether degrees of insanity can be distinguished from each other) is a simple matter: do the salient characteristics that lead to diagnoses reside in the patients themselves or in the environments and contexts in which observers find them? From Bleuler, through Kretchmer, through the formulators of the recently revised *Diagnostic and Statistical Manual* of the American Psychiatric Association, the belief has been strong that patients present symptoms, that those symptoms can be categorized, and, implicitly, that the sane are distinguishable from the insane. More recently, however, this belief has been questioned. Based in part on theoretical and anthropological considerations, but also on philosophical, legal, and therapeutic ones, the view has grown that psychological categorization of mental illness is useless at best and downright harmful, misleading, and pejorative at worst. Psychiatric diagnoses, in this view, are in the minds of the observers and are not valid summaries of characteristics displayed by the observed (3–5).

Gains can be made in deciding which of these is more nearly accurate by getting normal people (that is, people who do not have, and have never suffered, symptoms of serious psychiatric disorders) admitted to psychiatric hospitals and then determining whether they were discovered to be sane and, if so, how. If the sanity of such pseudopatients were always detected, there would be prima facie evidence that a sane individual can be distinguished from the insane context in which he is found. Normality (and presumably abnormality) is distinct enough that it can be recognized wherever it occurs, for it is carried within the person. If, on the other hand, the sanity of the pseudopatients were never discovered, serious difficulties would arise for those who support traditional modes of psychiatric diagnosis. Given that the hospital staff was not incompetent, that the pseudopatient had been behaving as sanely as he had been outside of the hospital, and that it had never been previously suggested that he belonged in a psychiatric hospital, such an unlikely outcome would support the view that psychiatric diagnosis betrays little about the patient but much about the environment in which an observer finds him.

This article describes such an experiment. Eight sane people gained secret admission to 12 different hospitals (6). Their diagnostic experiences constitute the data of the first part of this article; the remainder is devoted to a description of their experiences in psychiatric institutions. Too few psychiatrists and psychologists, even those who have worked in such hospitals, know what the experience is like. They rarely talk about it with former patients, perhaps because they dis-

trust information coming from the previously insane. Those who have worked
in psychiatric hospitals are likely to have
adapted so thoroughly to the settings that
they are insensitive to the impact of that
experience. And while there have been
occasional reports of researchers who
submitted themselves to psychiatric hospitalization (7), these researchers have
commonly remained in the hospitals for
short periods of time, often with the
knowledge of the hospital staff. It is difficult to know the extent to which they
were treated like patients or like research
colleagues. Nevertheless, their reports
about the inside of the psychiatric hospital
have been valuable. This article extends
those efforts.

PSEUDOPATIENTS AND THEIR
SETTINGS

The eight pseudopatients were a varied
group. One was a psychology graduate
student in his 20's. The remaining seven
were older and "established." Among
them were three psychologists, a pediatri-
cian, a psychiatrist, a painter, and a
housewife. Three pseudopatients were
women, five were men. All of them employed pseudonyms, lest their alleged diagnoses embarrass them later. Those who
were in mental health professions alleged
another occupation in order to avoid the
special attentions that might be accorded
by staff, as a matter of courtesy or caution, to ailing colleagues (8). With the
exception of myself (I was the first pseudopatient and my presence was known
to the hospital administrator and chief
psychologist and, so far as I can tell, to
them alone), the presence of pseudopatients and the nature of the research program was not known to the hospital
staffs (9).

The settings were similarly varied. In

order to generalize the findings, admission into a variety of hospitals was
sought. The 12 hospitals in the sample
were located in five different states on
the East and West coasts. Some were old
and shabby, some were quite new. Some
were research-oriented, others not. Some
had good staff-patient ratios, others were
quite understaffed. Only one was a
strictly private hospital. All of the others
were supported by state or federal funds
or, in one instance, by university funds.

After calling the hospital for an ap-
pointment, the pseudopatient arrived at
the admissions office complaining that he
had been hearing voices. Asked what the
voices said, he replied that they were
often unclear, but as far as he could tell
they said "empty," "hollow," and "thud."
The voices were unfamiliar and were of
the same sex as the pseudopatient. The
choice of these symptoms was occasioned
by their apparent similiarity to existential
symptoms. Such symptoms are alleged
to arise from painful concerns about the
perceived meaninglessness of one's life.
It is as if the hallucinating person were
saying, "My life is empty and hollow."
The choice of these symptoms was also
determined by the *absence* of a single
report of existential psychoses in the literature.

Beyond alleging the symptoms and
falsifying name, vocation, and employment, no further alterations of person,
history, or circumstances were made. The
significant events of the pseudopatient's
life history were presented as they had
actually occurred. Relationships with parents and siblings, with spouse and children, with people at work and in school,
consistent with the aforementioned exceptions, were described as they were or
had been. Frustrations and upsets were
described along with joys and satisfac-
tions. These facts are important to remember. If anything, they strongly biased

the subsequent results in favor of detecting sanity, since none of their histories or current behaviors were seriously pathological in any way.

Immediately upon admission to the psychiatric ward, the pseudopatient ceased simulating *any* symptoms of abnormality. In some cases, there was a brief period of mild nervousness and anxiety, since none of the pseudopatients really believed that they would be admitted so easily. Indeed, their shared fear was that they would be immediately exposed as frauds and greatly embarrassed. Moreover, many of them had never visited a psychiatric ward; even those who had, nevertheless had some genuine fears about what might happen to them. Their nervousness, then, was quite appropriate to the novelty of the hospital setting, and it abated rapidly.

Apart from that short-lived nervousness, the pseudopatient behaved on the ward as he "normally" behaved. The pseudopatient spoke to patients and staff as he might ordinarily. Because there is uncommonly little to do on a psychiatric ward, he attempted to engage others in conversation. When asked by staff how he was feeling, he indicated that he was fine, that he no longer experienced symptoms. He responded to instructions from attendants, to calls for medication (which was not swallowed), and to dining-hall instructions. Beyond such activities as were available to him on the admissions ward, he spent his time writing down his observations about the ward, its patients, and the staff. Initially these notes were written "secretly," but as it soon became clear that no one much cared, they were subsequently written on standard tablets of paper in such public places as the dayroom. No secret was made of these activities.

The pseudopatient, very much as a true psychiatric patient, entered a hospital with no foreknowledge of when he would be discharged. Each was told that he would have to get out by his own devices, essentially by convincing the staff that he was sane. The psychological stresses associated with hospitalization were considerable, and all but one of the pseudopatients desired to be discharged almost immediately after being admitted. They were, therefore, motivated not only to behave sanely, but to be paragons of cooperation. That their behavior was in no way disruptive is confirmed by nursing reports, which have been obtained on most of the patients. These reports uniformly indicate that the patients were "friendly," "cooperative," and "exhibited no abnormal indictions."

THE NORMAL ARE NOT DETECTABLY SANE

Despite their public "show" of sanity, the pseudopatients were never detected. Admitted, except in one case, with a diagnosis of schizophrenia *(10)*, each was discharged with a diagnosis of schizophrenia "in remission." The label "in remission" should in no way be dismissed as a formality, for at no time during any hospitalization had any question been raised about any pseudopatient's simulation. Nor are there any indications in the hospital records that the pseudopatient's status was suspect. Rather, the evidence is strong that, once labeled schizophrenic, the pseudopatient was stuck with that label. If the pseudopatient was to be discharged, he must naturally be "in remission"; but he was not sane, nor, in the institution's view, had he ever been sane.

The uniform failure to recognize sanity cannot be attributed to the quality of the hospitals, for, although there were considerable variations among them, several are considered cxcellent. Nor can it be alleged that there was simply not enough time to observe the pseudopatients. Length of hospitalization ranged from 7 to 52 days, with an average of 19 days. The pseudopatients were not, in fact, carefully observed, but this failure clearly speaks more to traditions within psychiatric hospitals than to lack of opportunity.

Finally, it cannot be said that the failure to recognize the pseudopatients' sanity was due to the fact that they were not behaving sanely. While there was clearly some tension present in all of them, their daily visitors could detect no serious behavioral consequences—nor, indeed, could other patients. It was quite common for the patients to "detect" the pseudopatients' sanity. During the first three hospitalizations, when accurate counts were kept, 35 of a total of 118 patients on the admissions ward voiced their suspicions, some vigorously. "You're not crazy. You're a journalist, or a professor [referring to the continual notetaking]. You're checking up on the hospital." While most of the patients were reassured by the pseudopatient's insistence that he had been sick before he came in but was fine now, some continued to believe that the pseudopatient was sane throughout his hospitalization (11). The fact that the patients often recognized normality when staff did not raises important questions.

Failure to detect sanity during the course of hospitalization may be due to the fact that physicians operate with a strong bias toward what statisticians call the type 2 error (5). This is to say that physicians are more inclined to call a healthy person sick (a false positive, type 2) than a sick person healthy (a false negative, type 1). The reasons for this are not hard to find: it is clearly more dangerous to misdiagnose illness than health. Better to err on the side of cau-

tion, to suspect illness even among the healthy.

But what holds for medicine does not hold equally well for psychiatry. Medical illnesses, while unfortunate, are not commonly pejorative. Psychiatric diagnoses, on the contrary, carry with them personal, legal, and social stigmas (12). It was therefore important to see whether the tendency toward diagnosing the sane insane could be reversed. The following experiment was arranged at a research and teaching hospital whose staff had heard these findings but doubted that such an error could occur in their hospital. The staff was informed that at some time during the following 3 months, one or more pseudopatients would attempt to be admitted into the psychiatric hospital. Each staff member was asked to rate each patient who presented himself at admissions or on the ward according to the likelihood that the patient was a pseudopatient. A 10-point scale was used, with a 1 and 2 reflecting high confidence that the patient was a pseudopatient.

Judgments were obtained on 193 patients who were admitted for psychiatric treatment. All staff who had had sustained contact with or primary responsibility for the patient—attendants, nurses, psychiatrists, physicians, and psychologists—were asked to make judgments. Forty-one patients were alleged, with high confidence, to be pseudopatients by at least one member of the staff. Twenty-three were considered suspect by at least one psychiatrist. Nineteen were suspected by one psychiatrist *and* one other staff member. Actually, no genuine pseudopatient (at least from my group) presented himself during this period.

The experiment is instructive. It indicates that the tendency to designate sane people as insane can be reversed when the stakes (in this case, prestige and diagnostic acumen) are high. But what can be said of the 19 people who were suspected of being "sane" by one psychiatrist and another staff member? Were these people truly "sane," or was it rather the case that in the course of avoiding the type 2 error the staff tended to make more errors of the first sort—calling the crazy "sane"? There is no way of knowing. But one thing is certain: any diagnostic process that lends itself so readily to massive errors of this sort cannot be a very reliable one.

THE STICKINESS OF PSYCHODIAGNOSTIC LABELS

Beyond the tendency to call the healthy sick—a tendency that accounts better for diagnostic behavior on admission than it does for such behavior after a lengthy period of exposure—the data speak to the massive role of labeling in psychiatric assessment. Having once been labeled schizophrenic, there is nothing the pseudopatient can do to overcome the tag. The tag profoundly colors others' perceptions of him and his behavior.

From one viewpoint, these data are hardly surprising, for it has long been known that elements are given meaning by the context in which they occur. Gestalt psychology made this point vigorously, and Asch *(13)* demonstrated that there are "central" personality traits (such as "warm" versus "cold") which are so powerful that they markedly color the meaning of other information in forming an impression of a given personality *(14)*. "Insane," "schizophrenic," "manic-depressive," and "crazy" are probably among the most powerful of such central traits. Once a person is designated abnormal, all of his other behaviors and characteristics are colored by that label. Indeed, that label is so powerful that many of the pseudopatients' normal behaviors were

overlooked entirely or profoundly misinterpreted. Some examples may clarify this issue.

Earlier I indicated that there were no changes in the pseudopatient's personal history and current status beyond those of name, employment, and, where necessary, vocation. Otherwise, a veridical description of personal history and circumstances was offered. Those circumstances were not psychotic. How were they made consonant with the diagnosis of psychosis? Or were those diagnoses modified in such a way as to bring them into accord with the circumstances of the pseudopatient's life, as described by him?

As far as I can determine, diagnoses were in no way affected by the relative health of the circumstances of a pseudopatient's life. Rather, the reverse occurred: the perception of his circumstances was shaped entirely by the diagnosis. A clear example of such translation is found in the case of a pseudopatient who had had a close relationship with his mother but was rather remote from his father during his early childhood. During adolescence and beyond, however, his father became a close friend, while his relationship with his mother cooled. His present relationship with his wife was characteristically close and warm. Apart from occasional angry exchanges, friction was minimal. The children had rarely been spanked. Surely there is nothing especially pathological about such a history. Indeed, many readers may see a similar pattern in their own experiences, with no markedly deleterious consequences. Observe, however, how such a history was translated in the psychopathological context, this from the case summary prepared after the patient was discharged.

> This white 39-year-old male . . . manifests a long history of considerable

ambivalence in close relationships, which begins in early childhood. A warm relationship with his mother cools during his adolescence. A distant relationship to his father is described as becoming very intense. Affective stability is absent. His attempts to control emotionality with his wife and children are punctuated by angry outbursts and, in the case of the children, spankings. And while he says that he has several good friends, one senses considerable ambivalence embedded in those relationships also. . . .

The facts of the case were unintentionally distorted by the staff to achieve consistency with a popular theory of the dynamics of a schizophrenic reaction (15). Nothing of an ambivalent nature had been described in relations with parents, spouse, or friends. To the extent that ambivalence could be inferred, it was probably not greater than is found in all human relationships. It is true the pseudopatient's relationships with his parents changed over time, but in the ordinary context that would hardly be remarkable—indeed, it might very well be expected. Clearly, the meaning ascribed to his verbalizations (that is, ambivalence, affective instability) was determined by the diagnosis: schizophrenia. An entirely different meaning would have been ascribed if it were known that the man was "normal."

All pseudopatients took extensive notes publicly. Under ordinary circumstances, such behavior would have raised questions in the minds of observers, as, in fact, it did among patients. Indeed, it seemed so certain that the notes would elicit suspicion that elaborate precautions were taken to remove them from the ward each day. But the precautions proved needless. The closest any staff member came to questioning these notes occurred when one pseudopatient asked his physician what kind of medication he was

receiving and began to write down the response. "You needn't write it," he was told gently. "If you have trouble remembering, just ask me again."

If no questions were asked of the pseudopatients, how was their writing interpreted? Nursing records for three patients indicate that the writing was seen as an aspect of their pathological behavior. "Patient engages in writing behavior" was the daily nursing comment on one of the pseudopatients who was never questioned about his writing. Given that the patient is in the hospital, he must be psychologically disturbed. And given that he is disturbed, continuous writing must be a behavioral manifestation of that disturbance, perhaps a subset of the compulsive behaviors that are sometimes correlated with schizophrenia.

One tacit characteristic of psychiatric diagnosis is that it locates the sources of aberration within the individual and only rarely within the complex of stimuli that surrounds him. Consequently, behaviors that are stimulated by the environment are commonly misattributed to the patient's disorder. For example, one kindly nurse found a pseudopatient pacing the long hospital corridors. "Nervous, Mr. X?" she asked. "No, bored," he said.

The notes kept by pseudopatients are full of patient behaviors that were misinterpreted by well-intentioned staff. Often enough, a patient would go "berserk" because he had, wittingly or unwittingly, been mistreated by, say, an attendant. A nurse coming upon the scene would rarely inquire even cursorily into the environmental stimuli of the patient's behavior. Rather, she assumed that his upset derived from his pathology, not from his present interactions with other staff members. Occasionally, the staff might assume that the patient's family (especially when they had recently visited) or other patients had stimulated the outburst. But never were the staff found to assume that one of themselves or the structure of the hospital had anything to do with a patient's behavior. One psychiatrist pointed to a group of patients who were sitting outside the cafeteria entrance half an hour before lunchtime. To a group of young residents he indicated that such behavior was characteristic of the oral-acquisitive nature of the syndrome. It seemed not to occur to him that there were very few things to anticipate in a psychiatric hospital besides eating.

A psychiatric label has a life and an influence of its own. Once the impression has been formed that the patient is schizophrenic, the expectation is that he will continue to be schizophrenic. When a sufficient amount of time has passed, during which the patient has done nothing bizarre, he is considered to be in remission and available for discharge. But the label endures beyond discharge, with the unconfirmed expectation that he will behave as a schizophrenic again. Such labels, conferred by mental health professionals, are as influential on the patient as they are on his relatives and friends, and it should not surprise anyone that the diagnosis acts on all of them as a self-fulfilling prophecy. Eventually, the patient himself accepts the diagnosis, with all of its surplus meanings and expectations, and behaves accordingly *(5)*.

The inferences to be made from these matters are quite simple. Much as Zigler and Phillips have demonstrated that there is enormous overlap in the symptoms presented by patients who have been variously diagnosed *(16)*, so there is enormous overlap in the behaviors of the sane and the insane. The sane are not "sane" all of the time. We lose our tempers "for no good reason." We are occasionally depressed or anxious, again for no good reason. And we may find it difficult to get along with one or another person—

again for no reason that we can specify. Similarly, the insane are not always insane. Indeed, it was the impression of the pseudopatients while living with them that they are sane for long periods of time—that the bizarre behaviors upon which their diagnoses were allegedly predicated constituted only a small fraction of their total behavior. If it makes no sense to label ourselves permanently depressed on the basis of an occasional depression, then it takes better evidence than is presently available to label all patients insane or schizophrenic on the basis of bizarre behaviors or cognitions. It seems more useful, as Mischel *(17)* has pointed out, to limit our discussions to *behaviors,* the stimuli that provoke them, and their correlates.

It is not known why powerful impressions of personality traits, such as "crazy" or "insane," arise. Conceivably, when the origins of and stimuli that give rise to a behavior are remote or unknown, or when the behavior strikes us as immutable, trait labels regarding the *behaver* arise. When, on the other hand, the origins and stimuli are known and available, discourse is limited to the behavior itself. Thus, I may hallucinate because I am sleeping, or I may hallucinate because I have ingested a peculiar drug. These are termed sleep-induced hallucinations, or dreams, and drug-induced hallucinations, respectively. But when the stimuli to my hallucinations are unknown, that is called craziness, or schizophrenia—as if that inference were somehow as illuminating as the others.

THE EXPERIENCE OF PSYCHIATRIC HOSPITALIZATION

The term "mental illness" is of recent origin. It was coined by people who were humane in their inclinations and who wanted very much to raise the station of (and the public's sympathies toward) the psychologically disturbed from that of witches and "crazies" to one that was akin to the physically ill. And they were at least partially successful, for the treatment of the mentally ill *has* improved considerably over the years. But while treatment has improved, it is doubtful that people really regard the mentally ill in the same way that they view the physically ill. A broken leg is something one recovers from, but mental illness allegedly endures forever *(18)*. A broken leg does not threaten the observer, but a crazy schizophrenic? There is by now a host of evidence that attitudes toward the mentally ill are characterized by fear, hostility, aloofness, suspicion, and dread *(19)*. The mentally ill are society's lepers.

That such attitudes infect the general population is perhaps not surprising, only upsetting. But that they affect the professionals—attendants, nurses, physicians, psychologists, and social workers—who treat and deal with the mentally ill is more disconcerting, both because such attitudes are self-evidently pernicious and because they are unwitting. Most mental health professionals would insist that they are sympathetic toward the mentally ill, that they are neither avoidant nor hostile. But it is more likely that an exquisite ambivalence characterizes their relations with psychiatric patients, such that their avowed impulses are only part of their entire attitude. Negative attitudes are there too and can easily be detected. Such attitudes should not surprise us. They are the natural offspring of the labels patients wear and the places in which they are found.

Consider the structure of the typical psychiatric hospital. Staff and patients are strictly segregated. Staff have their own living space, including their dining facilities, bathrooms, and assembly places. The glassed quarters that contain the professional staff, which the pseudopatients came to call "the cage," sit out on every dayroom. The staff emerge primarily for caretaking purposes—to give medication, to conduct a therapy or group meeting, to instruct or reprimand a patient. Otherwise, staff keep to themselves, almost as if the disorder that afflicts their charges is somehow catching.

So much is patient-staff segregation the rule that, for four public hospitals in which an attempt was made to measure the degree to which staff and patients mingle, it was necessary to use "time out of the staff cage" as the operational measure. While it was not the case that all time spent out of the cage was spent mingling with patients (attendants, for example, would occasionally emerge to watch television in the dayroom), it was the only way in which one could gather reliable data on time for measuring.

The average amount of time spent by attendants outside of the cage was 11.3 percent (range, 3 to 52 percent). This figure does not represent only time spent mingling with patients, but also includes time spent on such chores as folding laundry, supervising patients while they shave, directing ward cleanup, and sending patients to off-ward activities. It was the relatively rare attendant who spent time talking with patients or playing games with them. It proved impossible to obtain a "percent mingling time" for nurses, since the amount of time they spent out of the cage was too brief. Rather, we counted instances of emergence from the cage. On the average, daytime nurses emerged from the cage 11.5 times per shift, including instances when they left the ward entirely (range, 4 to 39 times). Late afternoon and night nurses were even less available, emerging on the average 9.4 times per shift (range, 4 to 41 times). Data on early morning nurses, who arrived usually after midnight and departed at 8 a.m., are not available because patients were asleep during most of this period.

Physicians, especially psychiatrists, were even less available. They were rarely seen on the wards. Quite commonly, they would be seen only when they arrived and departed, with the remaining time being spent in their offices or in the cage. On the average, physicians emerged on the ward 6.7 times per day (range, 1 to 17 times). It proved difficult to make an accurate estimate in this regard, since physicians often maintained hours that allowed them to come and go at different times.

The hierarchical organization of the psychiatric hospital has been commented on before (20), but the latent meaning of that kind of organization is worth noting again. Those with the most power have least to do with patients, and those with the least power are most involved with them. Recall, however, that the acquisition of role-appropriate behaviors occurs mainly through the observation of others, with the most powerful having the most influence. Consequently, it is understandable that attendants not only spend more time with patients than do any other members of the staff—that is required by their station in the hierarchy—but also, insofar as they learn from their superiors' behavior, spend as little time with patients as they can. Attendants are seen mainly in the cage, which is where the models, the action, and the power are.

I turn now to a different set of studies, these dealing with staff response to patient-initiated contact. It has long been known that the amount of time a person spends with you can be an index of your significance to him. If he initiates and maintains eye contact, there is reason to believe that he is considering your requests and needs. If he pauses to chat or actually stops and talks, there is added

reason to infer that he is individuating you. In four hospitals, the pseudopatient approached the staff member with a request which took the following form: "Pardon me, Mr. [or Dr. or Mrs.] X, could you tell me when I will be eligible for grounds privileges?" (or ". . . when I will be presented at the staff meeting?" or ". . . when I am likely to be discharged?"). While the content of the question varied according to the appropriateness of the target and the pseudopatient's (apparent) current needs the form was always a courteous and relevant request for information. Care was taken never to approach a particular member of the staff more than once a day, lest the staff member became suspicious or irritated. In examining these data, remember that the behavior of the pseudopatients was neither bizarre nor disruptive. One could indeed engage in good conversation with them.

The data for these experiments are shown in Table 1, separately for physicians (column 1) and for nurses and attendants (column 2). Minor differences between these four institutions were overwhelmed by the degree to which staff avoided continuing contacts that patients had initiated. By far, their most common response consisted of either a brief response to the question, offered while they were "on the move" and with head averted, or no response at all.

The encounter frequently took the following bizarre form: (pseudopatient) "Pardon me, Dr. X. Could you tell me when I am eligible for grounds privileges?" (physician) "Good morning, Dave. How are you today?" (Moves off without waiting for a response.)

It is instructive to compare these data with data recently obtained at Stanford University. It has been alleged that large and eminent universities are characterized by faculty who are so busy that they have no time for students. For this comparison, a young lady approached individual faculty members who seemed to be walking purposefully to some meeting or teaching engagement and asked them the following six questions.

1) "Pardon me, could you direct me to Encina Hall?" (at the medical school: ". . . to the Clinical Research Center?").
2) "Do you know where Fish Annex is?" (there is no Fish Annex at Stanford).
3) "Do you teach here?"
4) "How does one apply for admission to the college?" (at the medical school: ". . . to the medical school?").
5) "Is it difficult to get in?"
6) "Is there financial aid?"

Without exception as can be seen in Table 1 (column 3), all of the questions were answered. No matter how rushed they were, all respondents not only maintained eye contact, but stopped to talk. Indeed, many of the respondents went out of their way to direct or take the questioner to the office she was seeking, to try to locate "Fish Annex," or to discuss with her the possibilities of being admitted to the university.

Similar data, also shown in Table 1 (columns 4, 5, and 6), were obtained in the hospital. Here too, the young lady came prepared with six questions. After the first question, however, she remarked to 18 of her respondents (column 4), "I'm looking for a psychiatrist," and to 15 others (column 5), "I'm looking for an internist." Ten other respondents received no inserted comment (column 6). The general degree of cooperative responses is considerably higher for these university groups than it was for pseudopatients in psychiatric hospitals. Even so, differences are apparent within the medical

school setting. Once having indicated that she was looking for a psychiatrist, the degree of cooperation elicited was less than when she sought an internist.

POWERLESSNESS AND DEPERSONALIZATION

Eye contact and verbal contact reflect concern and individuation; their absence, avoidance and depersonalization. The data I have presented do not do justice to the rich daily encounters that grew up around matters of depersonalization and avoidance. I have records of patients who were beaten by staff for the sin of having initiated verbal contact. During my own experience, for example, one patient was beaten in the presence of other patients for having approached an attendant and told him, "I like you." Occasionally, punishment meted out to patients for misdemeanors seemed so excessive that it could not be justified by the most radical interpretations of psychiatric canon. Nevertheless, they appeared to go unquestioned. Tempers were often short. A patient who had not heard a call for medication would be roundly excoriated, and the morning attendants would often wake patients with: "Come on, you m——f——s, out of bed!"

Neither anecdotal nor "hard" data can convey the overwhelming sense of powerlessness which invades the individual as he is continually exposed to the depersonalization of the psychiatric hospital. It hardly matters *which* psychiatric hospital—the excellent public ones and the very plush private hospital were better than the rural and shabby ones in this regard, but, again, the features that psychiatric hospitals had in common overwhelmed by far their apparent differences.

Powerlessness was evident every-

Table 1. Self-Initiated Contact by Pseudopatients with Psychiatrists and Nurses and Attendants, Compared to Contact with Other Groups

Contact	Psychiatric Hospitals		University Campus (Nonmedical)	University Medical Center Physicians		
	(1) Psychiatrists	(2) Nurses and Attendants	(3) Faculty	(4) "Looking for a Psychiatrist"	(5) "Looking for an Internist"	(6) No Additional Comment
Responses						
Moves on, head averted (%)	71	88	0	0	0	0
Makes eye contact (%)	23	10	0	11	0	0
Pauses and chats (%)	2	2	0	11	0	10
Stops and talks (%)	4	0.5	100	78	100	90
Mean number of questions answered (out of 6)	*	*	6	3.8	4.8	4.5
Respondents (No.)	13	47	14	18	15	10
Attempts (No.)	185	1283	14	18	15	10

*Not applicable.

where. The patient is deprived of many of his legal rights by dint of his psychiatric commitment (21). He is shorn of credibility by virtue of his psychiatric label. His freedom of movement is restricted. He cannot initiate contact with the staff, but may only respond to such overtures as they make. Personal privacy is minimal. Patient quarters and possessions can be entered and examined by any staff member, for whatever reason. His personal history and anguish is available to any staff member (often including the "grey lady" and "candy striper" volunteer) who chooses to read his folder, regardless of their therapeutic relationship to him. His personal hygiene and waste evacuation are often monitored. The water closets may have no doors.

At times, depersonalization reached such proportions that pseudopatients had the sense that they were invisible, or at least unworthy of account. Upon being admitted, I and other pseudopatients took the initial physical examinations in a semipublic room, where staff members went about their own business as if we were not there.

On the ward, attendants delivered verbal and occasionally serious physical abuse to patients in the presence of other observing patients, some of whom (the pseudopatients) were writing it all down. Abusive behavior, on the other hand, terminated quite abruptly when other staff members were known to be coming. Staff are credible witnesses. Patients are not.

A nurse unbuttoned her uniform to adjust her brassiere in the presence of an entire ward of viewing men. One did not have the sense that she was being seductive. Rather, she didn't notice us.

A group of staff persons might point to a patient in the dayroom and discuss him animatedly, as if he were not there.

One illuminating instance of depersonalization and invisibility occurred with regard to medications. All told, the pseudopatients were administered nearly 2100 pills, including Elavil, Stelazine, Compazine, and Thorazine, to name but a few. (That such a variety of medications should have been administered to patients presenting identical symptoms is itself worthy of note.) Only two were swallowed. The rest were either pocketed or deposited in the toilet. The pseudopatients were not alone in this. Although I have no precise records on how many patients rejected their medications, the pseudopatients frequently found the medications of other patients in the toilet before they deposited their own. As long as they were cooperative, their behavior and the pseudopatients' own in this matter, as in other important matters, went unnoticed throughout.

Reactions to such depersonalization among pseudopatients were intense. Although they had come to the hospital as participant observers and were fully aware that they did not "belong," they nevertheless found themselves caught up in and fighting the process of depersonalization. Some examples: a graduate student in psychology asked his wife to bring his textbooks to the hospital so he could "catch up on his homework"—this despite the elaborate precautions taken to conceal his professional association. The same student, who had trained for quite some time to get into the hospital, and who had looked forward to the experience, "remembered" some drag races that he had wanted to see on the weekend and insisted that he be discharged by that time. Another pseudopatient attempted a romance with a nurse. Subsequently, he informed the staff that he was applying for admission to graduate school in psychology and was very likely to be admitted, since a graduate professor was one of his regular hospital visitors. The same person began to engage in psychotherapy with other patients—all of this as a way of becoming a person in an impersonal environment.

THE SOURCES OF DEPERSONALIZATION

What are the origins of depersonalization? I have already mentioned two. First are attitudes held by all of us toward the mentally ill—including those who treat them—attitudes characterized by fear, distrust, and horrible expectations on the one hand, and benevolent intentions on the other. Our ambivalence leads, in this instance as in others, to avoidance.

Second, and not entirely separate, the hierarchical structure of the psychiatric hospital facilitates depersonalization. Those who are at the top have least to do with patients, and their behavior inspires the rest of the staff. Average daily contact with psychiatrists, psychologists, residents, and physicians combined ranged from 3.9 to 25.1 minutes, with an overall mean of 6.8 (six pseudopatients over a total of 129 days of hospitalization). Included in this average are time spent in the admissions interview, ward meetings in the presence of a senior staff member, group and individual psychotherapy contacts, case presentation conferences, and discharge meetings. Clearly, patients do not spend much time in interpersonal contact with doctoral staff. And doctoral staff serve as models for nurses and attendants.

There are probably other sources. Psychiatric installations are presently in serious financial straits. Staff shortages are pervasive, staff time at a premium. Something has to give, and that something is patient contact. Yet, while financial stresses are realities, too much can be made of them. I have the impression that the psychological forces that result in depersonalization are much stronger than the fiscal ones and that the addition of more staff would not correspondingly improve patient care in this regard. The incidence of staff meetings and the enormous amount of record-keeping on patients, for example, have not been as substantially reduced as has patient contact. Priorities exist, even during hard times. Patient contact is not a significant priority in the traditional psychiatric hospital, and fiscal pressures do not account for this. Avoidance and depersonalization may.

Heavy reliance upon psychotropic medication tacitly contributes to depersonalization by convincing staff that treatment is indeed being conducted and that further patient contact may not be necessary. Even here, however, caution needs to be exercised in understanding the role of psychotropic drugs. If patients were powerful rather than powerless, if they were viewed as interesting individuals rather than diagnostic entities, if they were socially significant rather than social lepers, if their anguish truly and wholly compelled our sympathies and concerns, would we not *seek* contact with them, despite the availability of medications? Perhaps for the pleasure of it all?

THE CONSEQUENCES OF LABELING AND DEPERSONALIZATION

Whenever the ratio of what is known to what needs to be known approaches zero, we tend to invent "knowledge" and assume that we understand more than we actually do. We seem unable to acknowledge that we simply don't know. The needs for diagnosis and remediation of behavioral and emotional problems are enormous. But rather than acknowledge that we are just embarking on understanding, we continue to label patients "schizophrenic," "manic-depressive," and "insane," as if in those words we had captured the essence of understanding. The facts of the matter are that we have known for a long time that diagnoses are often not useful or reliable, but we have nevertheless continued to use them. We now know that we cannot distinguish insanity from sanity. It is depressing to consider how that information will be used.

Not merely depressing, but frightening. How many people, one wonders, are sane but not recognized as such in our psychiatric institutions? How many have been needlessly stripped of their privileges of citizenship, from the right to vote and drive to that of handling their own accounts? How many have feigned insanity in order to avoid the criminal consequences of their behavior, and, conversely, how many would rather stand trial than live interminably in a psychiatric hospital—but are wrongly thought to be mentally ill? How many have been stigmatized by well-intentioned, but nevertheless erroneous, diagnoses? On the last point, recall again that a "type 2 error" in psychiatric diagnosis does not have the same consequences it does in medical diagnosis. A diagnosis of cancer that has been found to be in error is cause for celebration. But psychiatric diagnoses are rarely found to be in error. The label sticks, a mark of inadequacy forever.

Finally, how many patients might be "sane" outside the psychiatric hospital but seem insane in it—not because craziness resides in them, as it were, but because they are responding to a bizarre setting, one that may be unique to institutions which harbor nether people? Goffman (4) calls the process of socialization to such institutions "mortification"—an apt metaphor that includes the processes of depersonalization that have been described here. And while it is impossible to know whether the pseudopatients' responses to these processes are characteristic of all inmates—they were, after all, not real patients—it is difficult to believe that these processes of socialization to a psychiatric hospital provide useful attitudes or habits of response for living in the "real world."

SUMMARY AND CONCLUSIONS

It is clear that we cannot distinguish the sane from the insane in psychiatric hospitals. The hospital itself imposes a special environment in which the meanings of behavior can easily be misunderstood. The consequences to patients hospitalized in such an environment—the powerlessness, depersonalization, segregation, mortification, and self-labeling—seem undoubtedly countertherapeutic.

I do not, even now, understand this problem well enough to perceive solutions. But two matters seem to have some promise. The first concerns the proliferation of community mental health facilities, of crisis intervention centers, of the human potential movement, and of behavior therapies that, for all of their own problems, tend to avoid psychiatric labels, to focus on specific problems and behaviors, and to retain the individual in a relatively nonpejorative environment. Clearly, to the extent that we refrain from sending the distressed to insane places, our impressions of them are less likely to be distorted. (The risk of distorted perceptions, it seems to me, is always present, since we are much more sensitive to an individual's behaviors and verbalizations than we are to the subtle contex-

tual stimuli that often promote them. At issue here is a matter of magnitude. And, as I have shown, the magnitude of distortion is exceedingly high in the extreme context that is a psychiatric hospital.)

The second matter that might prove promising speaks to the need to increase the sensitivity of mental health workers and researchers to the *Catch 22* position of psychiatric patients. Simply reading materials in this area will be of help to some such workers and researchers. For others, directly experiencing the impact of psychiatric hospitalization will be of enormous use. Clearly, further research into the social psychology of such total institutions will both facilitate treatment and deepen understanding.

I and the other pseudopatients in the psychiatric setting had distinctly negative reactions. We do not pretend to describe the subjective experiences of true patients. Theirs may be different from ours, particularly with the passage of time and the necessary process of adaptation to one's environment. But we can and do speak to the relatively more objective indices of treatment within the hospital. It could be a mistake, and a very unfortunate one, to consider that what happened to us derived from malice or stupidity on the part of the staff. Quite the contrary, our overwhelming impression of them was of people who really cared, who were committed and who were uncommonly intelligent. Where they failed, as they sometimes did painfully, it would be more accurate to attribute those failures to the environment in which they, too, found themselves than to personal callousness. Their perceptions and behavior were controlled by the situation, rather than being motivated by a malicious disposition. In a more benign environment, one that was less attached to global diagnosis, their behaviors and judgments might have been more benign and effective.

REFERENCES AND NOTES

1. P. Ash, *J. Abnorm. Soc. Psychol.* 44, 272 (1949); A. T. Beck, *Amer. J. Psychiat.* 119, 210 (1962); A. T. Boisen, *Psychiatry* 2, 233 (1938); N. Kreitman, *J. Ment. Sci.* 107, 876 (1961); N. Kreitman, P. Sainsbury, J. Morrisey, J. Towers, J. Scrivener, *ibid.,* p. 887; H. O. Schmitt and C. P. Fonda, *J. Abnorm. Soc. Psychol.* 52, 262 (1956); W. Seeman, *J. Nerv. Ment. Dis.* 118, 541 (1953). For an analysis of these artifacts and summaries of the disputes, see J. Zubin, *Annu. Rev. Psychol.* 18, 373 (1967); L. Phillips and J. G. Draguns, *ibid.* 22, 447 (1971).

2. R. Benedict, *J. Gen. Psychol.* 10, 59 (1934).

3. See in this regard H. Becker, *Outsiders: Studies in the Sociology of Deviance* (Free Press, New York, 1963); B. M. Braginsky, D. D. Braginsky, K. Ring, *Methods of Madness: The Mental Hospital as a Last Resort* (Holt, Rinehart & Winston, New York, 1969); G. M. Crocetti and P. V. Lemkau, *Amer. Social. Rev.* 30, 577 (1965); E. Goffman, *Behavior in Public Places* (Free Press, New York, 1964); R. D. Laing, *The Divided Self: A Study of Sanity and Madness* (Quadrangle, Chicago, 1960); D. L. Phillips, *Amer. Sociol. Rev.* 28, 963 (1963); T. R. Sarbin, *Psychol. Today* 6, 18 (1972); E. Schur, *Amer. J. Sociol.* 75, 309 (1969); T. Szasz, *Law, Liberty and Psychiatry* (Macmillan, New York, 1963); *The Myth of Mental Illness: Foundations of a Theory of Mental Illness* (Hoeber-Harper, New York, 1963). For a critique of some of these views, see W. R. Gove, *Amer. Sociol. Rev.* 35, 873 (1970).

4. E. Goffman, *Asylums* (Doubleday, Garden City, N.Y., 1961).

5. T. J. Scheff, *Being Mentally Ill: A Sociological Theory* (Aldine, Chicago, 1966).

6. Data from a ninth pseudopatient are not incorporated in this report because, although his sanity went undetected, he falsified aspects of his personal history, including his marital status and parental relationships. His experimental behaviors therefore were not identical to those of the other pseudopatients.

7. A. Barry, *Bellevue Is a State of Mind* (Harcourt Brace Jovanovich, New York, 1971); I. Belknap, *Human Problems of a State Mental Hospital* (McGraw-Hill, New York, 1956); W. Caudill, F. C. Redlich, H. R. Gilmore, E. B. Brody, *Amer. J. Orthopsychiat.* 22, 314 (1952); A. R. Goldman, R. H. Bohr, T. A. Steinberg, *Prof. Psychol.* 1, 427 (1970); unauthored, *Roche Report* 1 (No. 13), 8 (1971).

8. Beyond the personal difficulties that the pseudopatient is likely to experience in the hospital, there are legal and social ones that, combined, require considerable attention before entry. For example, once admitted to a psychiatric institution, it is difficult, if not impossible, to be discharged on short notice, state law to the contrary notwithstanding. I was not sensitive to these difficulties at the outset of the project, nor to the personal and situational emergencies that can arise, but later a writ of habeas corpus was prepared for each of the entering pseudopatients and an attorney was kept "on call" during every hospitalization. I am grateful to John Kaplan and Robert Bartels for legal advice and assistance in these matters.

9. However distasteful concealment is, it was a necessary first step to examining these questions. Without concealment, there would have been no way to know how valid these experiences were; nor was there any way of knowing whether whatever detections occurred were a tribute to the diagnostic acumen of the staff or to the hospital's rumor network. Obviously, since my concerns are general ones that cut across individual hospitals and staffs, I have respected their anonymity and have eliminated clues that might lead to their identification.

10. Interestingly, of the 12 admissions, 11 were diagnosed as schizophrenic and one, with the identical symptomatology, as manic-depressive psychosis. This diagnosis has a more favorable prognosis, and it was given by the only private hospital in our sample. On

the relations between social class and psychiatric diagnosis, see A. deB. Hollingshead and F. C. Redlich, *Social Class and Mental Illness: A Community Study* (Wiley, New York, 1958).

11. It is possible, of course, that patients have quite broad latitudes in diagnosis and therefore are inclined to call many people sane, even those whose behavior is patently aberrant. However, although we have no hard data on this matter, it was our distinct impression that this was not the case. In many instances, patients not only singled us out for attention, but came to imitate our behaviors and styles.

12. J. Cumming and E. Cumming, *Community Ment. Health* 1, 135 (1965); A. Farina and K. Ring, *J. Abnorm. Psychol.* 70, 47 (1965); H. E. Freeman and O. G. Simmons, *The Mental Patient Comes Home* (Wiley, New York, 1963); W. J. Johannsen, *Ment. Hygiene* 53, 218 (1969); A. S. Linsky, *Soc. Psychiat.* 5, 166 (1970).

13. S. E. Asch, *J. Abnorm. Soc. Psychol.* 41, 258 (1946); *Social Psychology* (Prentice-Hall, New York, 1952).

14. See also I. N. Mensh and J. Wishner, *J. Personality* 16, 188 (1947); J. Wishner, *Psychol. Rev.* 67, 96 (1960); J. S. Bruner and R. Tagiuri, in *Handbook of Social Psychology*, G. Lindzey, Ed. (Addison-Wesley, Cambridge, Mass., 1954), vol. 2, pp. 634–654; J. S. Bruner, D. Shapiro, R. Tagiuri, in *Person Perception and Interpersonal Behavior*. R. Tagiuri and L. Petrullo, Eds. (Stanford Univ. Press, Stanford, Calif., 1958), pp. 277–288.

15. For an example of a similar self fulfilling prophecy, in this instance dealing with the "central" trait of intelligence, see R. Rosenthal and L. Jacobson, *Pygmalion in the Classroom* (Holt, Rinehart & Winston, New York, 1968).

16. E. Zigler and L. Phillips, *J. Abnorm. Soc. Psychol.* 63, 69 (1961). See also R. K. Freudenberg and J. P. Robertson, *A.M.A. Arch. Neurol. Psychiatr.* 76, 14 (1956).

17. W. Mischel, *Personality and Assessment* (Wiley, New York, 1968).

18. The most recent and unfortunate instance of this tenet is that of Senator Thomas Eagleton.

19. T. R. Sarbin and J. C. Mancuso, *J. Clin. Consult. Psychol.* 35, 159 (1970); T. R. Sarbin, ibid., 31, 447 (1967); J. C. Nunnally, Jr., *Popular Conceptions of Mental Health* (Holt, Rinehart & Winston, New York, 1961).

20. A. H. Stanton and M. S. Schwartz, *The Mental Hospital: A Study of Institutional Participation in Psychiatric Illness and Treatment* (Basic, New York, 1954).

21. D. B. Wexler and S. E. Scoville, *Ariz. Law Rev.* 13, 1 (1971).

22. I thank W. Mischel, E. Orne, and M. S. Rosenhan for comments on an earlier draft of this manuscript.

QUESTIONS ABOUT "ON BEING SANE IN INSANE PLACES"

(a) What method was used to collect the data? (Use Chapter 2 categories.)

(b) What is the hypothesis, if any? Is it causal or noncausal?

(c) Identify the variables being studied. If the hypothesis is causal, what is the independent variable? What is its operational definition? What is the dependent variable? What is its operational definition?

(d) Identify the findings (what relationship of variables was observed?)

(e) Identify an extraneous variable controlled by holding it constant. Identify an extraneous variable controlled by randomization.

(f) Identify any uncontrolled extraneous variables. For each, give an alternative explanation of the observed results, based on the uncontrolled variable. Suggest a way to control for each uncontrolled variable.

(g) Identify the sample studied and the population from which it was drawn. If you detect any sampling bias, identify it.

(h) Identify any interactions being studied.

ANSWERS

(a) *Method:* Within-subjects experiment.

    The essence of the study was this: people complained of psychiatric symptoms (to gain admission) and then acted sane. The responses of the hospital staffs were observed. The experimenter deliberately created a situation (i.e., manipulated a variable) by having people identified as psychiatric patients act sane, and observed responses (dependent variables). There is no other group to compare with the one observed here.

(b) *Hypothesis:* Nowhere in Rosenhan's article is there a clear statement of a hypothesis, though it's obvious that there is one and that it involves the relationship of variables. One way to state Rosenhan's hypothesis is this: When a diagnosed psychiatric patient behaves normally, it has no effect on his/her diagnosis. In slightly different words, it is: Normality will not be recognized as such when it occurs in a hospitalized psychiatric patient. The hypothesis is causal. Rosenhan is saying that once someone is in the role of patient, sane behavior will *not cause* hospital staffs to treat the person as a sane person.

(c) *Variables:* normality (or normal behavior) and hospital's response (or recognition of normality). "Reports of hearing voices" is not a variable here. It's true that all pseudopatients simulated psychotic symptoms to get into the hospital, but the experiment wasn't done to see if symptoms could get them in. The question was whether sanity could get them out. The way to test this was to get sane people admitted as patients.

Independent variable: Normality (normal behavior). The operational definition is a long one. The last four paragraphs of the section "Pseudopatients and Their Settings" provide the operational definition of normality, since they describe what the pseudopatients did after they were admitted. These paragraphs can be summarized as follows: Pseudopatients gave their accurate life histories, except for name, vocation, employment, and the alleged symptoms. They ceased simulating symptoms when they arrived on the ward, and acted and interacted as they normally would, with the exception of taking extensive notes. They were cooperative, and sought release from the hospital.

Dependent variable: Hospital's response (recognition of normality). Whatever you call it, the dependent variable was whether or not the pseudopatients were ever recognized, or diagnosed, as sane. Rosenhan seems to use several operational definitions, some more concrete than others (see the section "The Normal Are Not Detectably Sane"). The more concrete operational definitions are diagnosis at discharge and length of stay in the hospital. Less concrete ones are questions raised about pseudopatients' simulations and "indications in the hospital records that the pseudopatient's status was suspect." The section "The Stickiness of Psychodiagnostic Labels" contains several examples of the hospital's response, but these are based on nonsystematic observation and cannot really be called operational definitions or measures of any variable.

(d) *Findings:* Again, there are a number of findings, some quantitative, and others qualitative. They are reported in two sections of the article: "The Normal are Not Detectably Sane" and "The Stickiness of Psychodiagnostic Labels." Some of the major findings are: all were discharged with a diagnosis of schizophrenia "in remission"; length of hospitalization averaged 19 days; there is no evidence in the pseudopatients' records that their status was suspect. Other findings concerned staff response to pseudopatients' note-taking, other patients' responses to the pseudopatients, and so on.

(e) *Extraneous variables held constant:* Some aspects of the pseudopatients' behavior were held constant. They reported the same symptoms, they all said the symptoms were gone, and all began reporting this at the same point in their hospitalization. All the pseudopatients (almost) did not take any medication, despite prescriptions. The general behavior of the pseudopatients was reportedly fairly well controlled, with respect to the ways in which they responded to ward staff, at least. Also, staff knowledge of the existence of pseudopatients was controlled by telling them nothing.

Extraneous variables controlled by randomization: None, in this design. There is no comparison group, so subjects cannot be assigned randomly to groups.

(f) *Uncontrolled extraneous variables:* Rosenhan discusses some of these. One is the *amount of time the staff had* to detect sanity. There are no data on whether detection might increase with time or with doctor-patient contact. While it's true that in 7 to 52 days the staff *should* have had enough time, Rosenhan's data show that doctors didn't spend much time with the patient. Thus, failure to detect sanity may have been due to a hospital social structure that discourages professional contact, instead of any inability of the professional staff to diagnose if they *do* make contact. This is an alternative explanation. Rosenhan would probably counter-argue that as all pseudopatients' discharge diagnoses were "schizophrenia in remission," the physicians must have felt capable of making a professional diagnosis at discharge. Still, the doctors were wrong.

Rosenhan also mentions the *tendency of doctors to err in the direction of caution*—to diagnose an illness if there is doubt. Rosenhan tries to rule out this variable by conducting an experiment-within-an-experiment; psychiatric staffs were told to expect a pseudopatient, and their diagnoses and suspicions were recorded. Many patients were "diagnosed" incorrectly as pseudopatients. Rosenhan did not make the proper test of this extraneous variable. Suppose he had told the hospital staff to expect pseudopatients and then actually had some admitted. It would be instructive to see if the pseudopatients could be correctly identified. If they could be discovered, then we would know that sanity can be recognized in a mental hospital, if only the doctors would look for it there.

Let us see if we can identify any extraneous variables Rosenhan has not discussed. We might look for comparison groups that should have been included (since the design is within-subjects). What should Rosenhan have controlled for? You might not think of these, but Lieberman (1973) came up with two interesting suggestions. First, Lieberman noted that ward conditions are designed to make insane people more manageable. The *effect of the ward environment* is extraneous to the question of whether sanity can be diagnosed. The results are explained on the grounds that staff may think nothing of sane behavior because patients often appear more sane than they actually are. Lieberman suggested that Rosenhan attempt to take insane people out of the hospital, to see if the people on the outside can detect insanity.

Lieberman also suggested that the pseudopatients were "not just sane persons; they were sane persons *feigning insanity*." The results may only mean that the doctors can not tell the insane from the sane feigning insanity (alternative explanation). A comparison group could have pseudopatients feign a regular medical problem (presumably one such as lower-back pain or chronic fatigue, for which diagnosis relies heavily on self-report, as it does for schizophrenia). If the doctors were unable to diagnose normality in these patients, the cause of misdiagnosis must lie in the pseudopatients' dissimulation, and not in the diagnostic category "schizophrenia."

(g) *Sample and Population:* The sample consisted of twelve hospitals in five East and West Coast states, and their psychiatric staffs. The population sampled seems to be U.S. hospital psychiatric facilities, both public and private, and their staffs.

Rosenhan's conclusions are meant to apply to hospitals and their psychiatric staffs everywhere, and by implication to all mental health professionals. He says,

"We now know that we cannot distinguish insanity from sanity," and this "we" would seem to mean anyone presumably qualified to make that distinction.

Sampling bias: Twelve hospitals in five states on the East and West Coasts were used, and Rosenhan tells us that they differed from each other on several dimensions. Still, we do not know the basis for choosing these twelve hospitals. As we are not told they were chosen at random from some psychiatric directory, we must presume that they were chosen for convenience (e.g., to the pseudopatients' homes). It is impossible to know whether this bias has seriously affected the results. My guess (and it is just that) is that sampling bias is not a serious problem with this study. Even so, the sampling procedure was not ideal.

(h) *Interactions:* None. Only two variables were investigated in the main study.

If you are interested, you might want to answer these same questions about the other studies Rosenhan reports. The one on the responses of psychiatric staffs, professors, and hospital doctors to people's questions (summarized in Rosenhan's Table 1) is an interesting piece of research.

5

REVIEWING A BODY OF LITERATURE: THE PROBLEM OF GENERALIZATION

In introducing Chapter 3, we mentioned two questions that should be asked about a piece of research before accepting its conclusions. The first was whether the conclusions were supported by the data for the people or events studied. This was the question of internal validity, and Chapters 3 and 4 were devoted to it. By now, you should be fairly skilled at looking for alternative explanations and evaluating the internal validity of single scientific studies.

The second validity question has been left unasked until now. It was the question of whether the conclusions of a study apply to any people or events beyond the particular ones that were studied. This question is one of overriding importance, since our interest in research is rarely restricted to the specific situation studied. We are not so much interested in the stories of Rosenhan's pseudopatients as we are in the broader question of whether psychiatric diagnoses have anything to do with the patient, or whether they are only responses to the abnormal setting of the psychiatric facility. Our interest is in the variables, not the specific details of a piece of research. But by reading a single study, we cannot be sure to what extent the findings depend on the particular way the variables were measured. In Rosenhan's study, we can only guess whether the patients would have been treated differently if they had entered the hospitals with some other set of symptoms, and we cannot be sure whether they would have been discovered if the hospital staffs had been warned to expect pseudopatients. The answers to these questions are critical, but we cannot get the answers from Rosenhan's study alone.

Thus, a major reason for evaluating a group of studies is to determine the strength of evidence supporting or refuting a general statement about the relationships between variables. Two studies of the same variables may differ in many ways: their operational definitions of either variable, the subject population studied, and any number of procedural details in the ways the studies are conducted.

The act of drawing conclusions from a study involves a process of generalizing beyond these particulars to the broader question about the variables. The process is risky because there is no way to tell by examining a single study whether some apparently unimportant detail of its procedure is responsible for its findings, or whether its results would generalize to other subject populations. These determinations are best made by observing whether similar findings emerge from studies that use different procedures, different populations, or different observers. External validity is best evaluated by comparing studies that deal with the same general question in different ways.

An example of this was presented in Chapter 2, with some studies dealing with the relationship between crowding and aggression. The idea that these two variables are related derives from a theory of territoriality in animal behavior. This theory holds that animals maintain and defend territories against invaders of the same species (sometimes also of the same sex). The territoriality hypothesis implies, among other things, that when members of the same species are crowded together in a small space, the incidence of aggression will increase. Thus, research relating crowding and aggression provides one way to test the territoriality hypothesis. Still, there are many ways to study the relation of crowding to aggression. One may study it in any species, in animals of various ages and either sex. One may look at crowding in living spaces over the length of a lifetime or crowding in a narrow passageway over a matter of seconds. Finally, aggression may be measured in any form from physical violence to negative comments about a person's ideas. If a relationship between crowding and aggression is found that holds across species, types of crowding, and types of aggression, we would have general support for the existence of the relationship, and also support for the territoriality hypothesis (though not conclusive support until the other implications of territoriality are investigated).

More often than not, hypotheses in the social sciences are not supported over such a wide range of situations and subjects. Studies of the "same" relationship find different, even contradictory, results. One of the ways in which theories evolve is through testing their implications and finding that the predictions do not always come true. If it is possible to define the difference between the situations where the theory works and the situations where it doesn't, a step has been taken toward refining and improving the theory.

When you set out to evaluate the scientific support for a generalization, you can expect that the original statement may have to be reformulated to account for negative evidence. Often this is done by identifying variables not previously considered important, but which seem to make the difference between when the old theory works and when it doesn't.

The purpose of this chapter is to give you some skills you will need to draw appropriate conclusions after you have read several scientific reports that provide data about the same general question. You will be using the skills you have already developed, but you will also need to have some way to compare the results of different studies, because they will not always point to the same conclusion.

A good general procedure for comparing studies is to summarize each article you read on a separate page, using an outline such as the one provided in Table 8. It will be helpful if your outlines are set up so that they can be placed side by side when you want to compare the articles.

If you look at Table 5.1, you will see that most of the information called for involves answers to the questions you have been answering in the last two chapters. Here are some brief notes about summarizing articles.

Leave space for several *independent and dependent variables* in your outline, as it is common for studies to test several hypotheses at once. Make careful note of the operational definitions used, since the same variable may be operationalized differ-

Table 5.1. Format for Summaries of Empirical Research Reports

---

Author(s), *date*—other bibliographic information should be noted here.
Method (classify according to categories in Chapter 2)

Hypothesis (list more than one, if there are several)

Independent variable(s)/Operational definition(s)
    (1)
    (2)
    (3)

Dependent variables(s)/Operational definition(s)
    (1)
    (2)
    (3)

Findings (What relationship of variables was observed?)

Controlled extraneous variables (note the ones you consider important)

Uncontrolled extraneous variables/alternative explanations
    (1)
    (2)

Sample/population sampled

Sampling biases

Interactions studied

Conclusion(s) of author(s)

---

ently in two different studies. A frequent reason studies get different results is that they do not define the same variables in the same way.

There is a space for *findings* in the summary table because research on the same question does not always lead to the same result. Try to write the findings down in operational terms, because this will make it easier to identify differences among studies.

Make careful note of *alternative explanations* of the results of each study. If you are lucky, data from other studies may help rule out some alternative explanations. On the other hand, if all the research is open to the same alternative explanation, you have identified an important conclusion about the research.

The *population sampled* is important to note. A finding that holds for one population may or may not be true of another population. The *only* way to know is by looking at research using other populations. If research using different populations uncovers the same results, you can have some confidence in the generality of the findings. If results do not generalize across populations, you can look to differences between the populations for possible explanations of the results.

It is important to note *interactions* reported in research. One study may find a general relationship between two variables, while another may suggest that this general relationship depends on a third variable. An example of an interaction is found in research on how the use of personal space in faculty offices reflects power and status. Early research found that professors with higher academic rank were more likely to create social distance by positioning their desks between themselves and their students. In a replication of that research, Seyfrit and Martin (1985) found that higher status was related to social distance between professors and students in the faculty office for males but not for females—status of female faculty members was unrelated to desk placement. Regardless of status, female professors, like the nontenured male professors, placed their desks so that they did not create a barrier between them and students. High-ranking female professors typically used a desk arrangement that allowed them to sit behind their desks, while allowing students to sit at a chair to the side of the desk.

The last part of the summary table calls for a brief statement of the *author(s)' conclusion(s)*. Conclusions are general statements about variables that are made on the basis of the operationally stated findings. Rosenhan concluded, on the basis of his study with the pseudopatients, that "the normal are not detectably sane" and "we cannot distinguish sanity from insanity." It is important to distinguish conclusions from findings because it is possible to accept an author's findings while disputing the conclusions that are presumed to follow. In the controversy over Rosenhan's article, there was little or no criticism of the findings—many critics do not even doubt that they could be reproduced in other hospitals—but there is loud disagreement about Rosenhan's conclusions. Try to state the author(s)' conclusion(s) clearly; yours may ultimately be different.

On the following pages, there are reprints of three studies that deal with the general question of whether arrest for domestic assault deters future violence.

Read the studies and summarize all three, using the format in Table 5.1. Our summaries begin after the reprints. With summaries, we can then discuss how to draw conclusions from the three studies and how to write a report evaluating the group of articles and giving your own conclusions.

The Specific Deterrent Effects of Arrest for Domestic Assault

Lawrence W. Sherman

University of Maryland, College Park and Police Foundation

Richard A. Berk

University of California, Santa Barbara

with 42 Patrol Officers of the Minneapolis Police Department, Nancy Wester, Donileen Loseke, David Rauma, Debra Morrow, Amy Curtis, Kay Gamble, Roy Roberts, Phyllis Newton, and Gayle Gubman

The specific deterrence doctrine and labeling theory predict opposite effects of punishment on individual rates of deviance. The limited cross-sectional evidence available on the question is inconsistent, and experimental evidence has been lacking. The Police Foundation and the Minneapolis Police Department tested these hypotheses in a field experiment on domestic violence. Three police responses to simple assault were randomly assigned to legally eligible suspects: an arrest; "advice" (including, in some cases, informal mediation); and an order to the suspect to leave for eight hours. The behavior of the suspect was tracked for six months after the police intervention, with both official data and victim reports. The official recidivism measures show that the arrested suspects manifested significantly less subsequent violence than those who were ordered to leave. The victim report data show that the arrested subjects manifested significantly less subsequent violence than those who were advised. The findings falsify a deviance amplification model of labeling theory beyond initial labeling, and fail to falsify the specific deterrence prediction for a group of offenders with a high percentage of prior histories of both domestic violence and other kinds of crime.

Sociologists since Durkheim ([1893] 1972: 126) have speculated about how the punishment of individuals affects their behavior. Two bodies of literature, specific deterrence and labeling, have developed competing predictions (Thorsell and Klemke, 1972). Durkheim, for example, implicitly assumed with Bentham that the pains of punishment deter people from repeating the crimes for which they are punished, especially when punishment is certain, swift and severe. More recent work has fostered the ironic view that punishment often makes individuals more likely to commit crimes because of altered interactional structures, foreclosed

Reprinted with permission from Lawrence W. Sherman, Richard A. Berk, "The Specific Deterrant Effects of Arrest for Domestic Assault," *American Sociological Review*, vol. 49, 1984, pp. 261–72.

legal opportunities and secondary deviance (Lemert, 1951, 1967; Schwartz and Skolnick, 1962; Becker, 1963).

Neither prediction can muster consistent empirical support. The few studies that allege effects generally employ weak designs in which it is difficult, if not impossible, to control plausibly for all important factors confounded with criminal justice sanctions and the rulebreaking behavior that may follow. Thus, some claim to show that punishment deters individuals punished (Clarke, 1966; F.B.I., 1967: 34–44; Cohen and Stark, 1974: 30; Kraut, 1976; Murray and Cox, 1979; McCord, 1983), while others claim to show that punishment increases their deviance (Gold and Williams, 1969; Shoham, 1974; Farrington, 1977; Klemke, 1978). Yet all of these studies suffer either methodological or conceptual flaws as tests of the effects of punishment (Zimring and Hawkins, 1973; Gibbs, 1975; Hirschi, 1975; Tittle, 1975), especially the confounding of incarceration with attempts to rehabilitate and the frequent failure to differentiate effects for different types of offenders and offenses (Lempert, 1981–1982).

Perhaps the strongest evidence to date comes from a randomized experiment conducted by Lincoln et al. (unpubl.). The experiment randomly assigned juveniles, who had already been apprehended, to four different treatments ranked in their formality: release; two types of diversion; and formal charging. The more formal and official the processing, the more frequent the repeat criminality over a two-year follow-up period. This study supports labeling theory for arrested juveniles, although it cannot isolate the labeling or deterrent effects of arrest per se.

In all likelihood, of course, punishment has not one effect, but many, varying across types of people and situations (Chambliss, 1967; Andenaes, 1971). As Lempert (1981–1982: 523) argues, "it is only by attending to a range of such offenses that we will be able to develop a general theory of deterrence." The variables affecting the deterrability of juvenile delinquency, white-collar crime, armed robbery and domestic violence may be quite different. Careful accumulation of findings from different settings will help us differentiate the variables which are crime- or situation-specific and those which apply across settings.

In this spirit, we report here a study of the impact of punishment in a particular setting, for a particular offense, and for particular kinds of individuals. Over an eighteen-month period, police in Minneapolis applied one of three intervention strategies in incidents of misdemeanor domestic assault: arrest; ordering the offender from the premises; or some form of advice which could include mediation. The three interventions were assigned randomly to households, and a critical outcome was the rate of repeat incidents. The relative effect of arrest should hold special interest for the specific deterrence-labeling controversy.

POLICING DOMESTIC ASSAULTS

Police have been typically reluctant to make arrests for domestic violence (Berk and Loseke, 1981), as well as for a wide range of other kinds of offenses, unless victims demand an arrest, the suspect insults the officer, or other factors are present (Sherman, 1980). Parnas's (1972) qualitative observations of the Chicago police found four categories of police action in these situations: negotiating or otherwise "talking out" the dispute; threatening the disputants and then leaving; asking one of the parties to leave the premises; or (very rarely) making an arrest.

Similar patterns are found in many other cities. Surveys of battered women who tried to have their domestic assailants arrested report that arrest occurred in 10 percent (Roy, 1977: 35) or 3 percent (see Langley and Levy, 1977: 219) of the cases. Surveys of police agencies in Illinois (Illinois Law Enforcement Commission, 1978) and New York (Office of the Minority Leader, 1978) found explicit policies against arrest in the majority of the agencies surveyed. Despite the fact that violence is reported to be present in one-third (Bard and Zacker, 1974) to two-thirds (Black, 1980) of all domestic disturbances police respond to, police department data show arrests in only 5 percent of those disturbances in Oakland (Hart, n.d., cited in Meyer and Lorimer, 1977:21), 6 percent of those disturbances in a Colorado city (Patrick et al., n.d., cited in Meyer and Lorimer, 1977: 21) and 6 percent in Los Angeles County (Emerson, 1979).

The best available evidence on the frequency of arrest is the observations from the Black and Reiss study of Boston, Washington and Chicago police in 1966 (Black, 1980: 182). Police responding to disputes in those cities made arrests in 27 percent of violent felonies and 17 percent of the violent misdemeanors. Among married couples (Black, 1980: 158), they made arrests in 26 percent of the cases, but tried to remove one of the parties in 38 percent of the cases.

An apparent preference of many police for separating the parties rather than arresting the offender has been attacked from two directions over the last fifteen years. The original critique came from clinical psychologists, who agreed that police should rarely make arrests (Potter, 1978: 46; Fagin, 1978: 123–24) in domestic assault cases, and argued that police should mediate the disputes responsible for the violence. A highly publicized demonstration project teaching police special counseling skills for family crisis intervention (Bard, 1970) failed to show a reduction in violence, but was interpreted as a success nonetheless. By 1977, a national survey of police agencies with 100 or more officers found that over 70 percent reported a family crisis intervention training program in operation. While it is not clear whether these programs reduced separation and increased mediation, a decline in arrests was noted for some (Wylie et al., 1976). Indeed, many sought explicitly to reduce the number of arrests (University of Rochester, 1974; Ketterman and Kravitz, 1978).

By the mid-1970s, police practices were criticized from the opposite direction by feminist groups. Just as psychologists succeeded in having many police agencies respond to domestic violence as "half social work and half police work," feminists began to argue that police put "too much emphasis on the social work aspect and not enough on the criminal" (Langley and Levy, 1977: 218). Widely publicized lawsuits in New York and Oakland sought to compel police to make arrests in every case of domestic assault, and state legislatures were lobbied successfully to reduce the evidentiary requirements needed for police to make arrests for misdemeanor domestic assaults. Some legislatures are now considering statutes requiring police to make arrests in these cases.

The feminist critique was bolstered by a study (Police Foundation, 1976) showing that for 85 percent of a sample of spousal homicides, police had intervened at least once in the preceding two years. For 54 percent of the homicides, police had intervened five or more times. But it was impossible to determine from the cross-sectional data whether making more or fewer arrests would have reduced the homicide rate.

In sum, police officers confronting a domestic assault suspect face at least three conflicting options, urged on them by different groups with different theories. The officers' colleagues might recommend forced separation as a means of achieving short-term peace. Alternatively, the officers' trainers might recommend mediation as a means of getting to the underlying cause of the "dispute" (in which both parties are implicitly assumed to be at fault). Finally, the local women's organizations may recommend that the officer protect the victim (whose "fault," if any, is legally irrelevant) and enforce the law to deter such acts in the future.

RESEARCH DESIGN

In response to these conflicting recommendations, the Police Foundation and the Minneapolis Police Department agreed to conduct a randomized experiment. The design called for random assignment of arrest, separation, and some form of advice which could include mediation at the officer's discretion. In addition, there was to be a six-month follow-up period to measure the frequency and seriousness of domestic violence after each police intervention. The advantages of randomized experiments are well known and need not be reviewed here (see, e.g., Cook and Campbell, 1979).

The design only applied to simple (misdemeanor) domestic assaults, where both the suspect and the victim were present when the police arrived. Thus, the experiment included only those cases in which police were empowered (but not required) to make arrests under a recently liberalized Minnesota state law; the police officer must have probable cause to believe that a cohabitant or spouse had assaulted the victim within the last four hours (but police need not have witnessed the assault). Cases of life-threatening or severe injury, usually labeled as a felony (aggravated assault), were excluded from the design for ethical reasons.

The design called for each officer to carry a pad of report forms, color coded for the three different police actions. Each time the officers encountered a situation that fit the experiment's criteria, they were to take whatever action was indicated by the report form on the top of the pad. We numbered the forms and arranged them in random order for each officer. The integrity of the random assignment was to be monitored by research staff observers riding on patrol for a sample of evenings.

After police action was taken, the officer was to fill out a brief report and give it to the research staff for follow-up. As a further check on the randomization process, the staff logged in the reports in the order in which they were received and made sure that the sequence corresponded to the original assignment of treatments.

Anticipating something of the victims' background, a predominantly minority, female research staff was employed to contact the victims for a detailed face-to-face interview, to be followed by telephone follow-up interviews every two weeks for 24 weeks. The interviews were designed primarily to measure the frequency and seriousness of victimizations caused by the suspect after the police intervention.[1] The research staff also collected criminal justice reports that mentioned the suspect's name during the six-month follow-up period.

[1] The protocols were based heavily on instruments designed for an NIMH-funded study of spousal violence conducted by Richard A. Berk, Sarah Fenstermaker Berk, and Ann D. Witte (Center for Studies of Crime and Delinquency, Grant #MH-34616–01). A similar protocol was developed for the suspects, but only twenty-five of them agreed to be interviewed.

CONDUCT OF THE EXPERIMENT

As is common in field experiments, implementation of the research design entailed some slippage from the original plan. In order to gather data as quickly as possible, the experiment was originally located in the two Minneapolis precincts with the highest density of domestic violence crime reports and arrests. The 34 officers assigned to those areas were invited to a three-day planning meeting and asked to participate in the study for one year. All but one agreed. The conference also produced a draft order for the chief's signature specifying the rules of the experiment. These rules created several new situations to be excluded from the experiment, such as if a suspect attempted to assault police officers, a victim persistently demanded an arrest, or if both parties were injured. These additional exceptions, unfortunately, allowed for the possibility of differential attrition from the separation and mediation treatments. The implications for internal validity are discussed later.

The experiment began on March 17, 1981, with the expectation that it would take about one year to produce about 300 cases (it ran until August 1, 1982, and produced 330 case reports.) The officers agreed to meet monthly with the project director (Sherman) and the project manager (Wester). By the third or fourth month, two facts became clear: (1) only about 15 to 20 officers were either coming to meetings or turning in cases; and (2) the rate at which the cases were turned in would make it difficult to complete the project in one year. By November, we decided to recruit more officers in order to obtain cases more rapidly. Eighteen additional officers joined the project, but like the original group, most of these officers only turned in one or two cases. Indeed, three of the original officers pro-

duced almost 28 percent of the cases, in part because they worked a particularly violent beat, and in part because they had a greater commitment to the study. Since the treatments were randomized by officer, this created no internal validity problem. However, it does raise construct validity problems to which we will later return.

There is little doubt that many of the officers occasionally failed to follow fully the experimental design. Some of the failures were due to forgetfulness, such as leaving the report pads at home or at the police station. Other failures derived from misunderstanding about whether the experiment applied in certain situations; application of the experimental rules under complex circumstances was sometimes confusing. Finally, from time to time there were situations that were simply not covered by the experiment's rules.

Whether any officers intentionally subverted the design is unclear. The plan to monitor randomization with ride-along observers broke down because of the unexpectedly low incidence of cases meeting the experimental criteria. The observers had to ride for many weeks before they observed an officer apply one of the treatments. We tried to solve this problem with "chase-alongs," in which the observers rode in their own car with a portable police radio and drove to the scene of any domestic call dispatched to any officer in the precinct. Even this method failed.

Thus, we are left with at least two disturbing possibilities. First, police officers anticipating (e.g., from the dispatch call) a particular kind of incident, and finding the upcoming experimental treatment inappropriate, may have occasionally decided to void the experiment. That is, they may have chosen to exclude certain cases in violation of the experimental design. This amounts to differential attrition, which is clearly a threat to internal validity. Note that if police officers blindly decided to exclude certain cases (e.g., because they did not feel like filling out the extra forms on a given day), all would be well for internal validity.

Second, since the recording officer's pad was supposed to govern the actions of each pair of officers, some officers may also have switched the assignment of driver and recording officer after deciding a case fit the study in order to obtain a treatment they wanted to apply. If the treatments were switched between driver and recorder, then the internal validity was again threatened. However, this was almost certainly uncommon because it was generally easier not to fill out a report at all than to switch.

Table 1 shows the degree to which the treatments were delivered as designed.[2] Ninety-nine percent of the suspects targeted for arrest actually were arrested, while only 78 percent of those to receive advice did, and only 73 percent of those to be sent out of the residence for eight hours were actually sent. One explanation for this pattern, consistent with the experimental guidelines, is that mediating and sending were more difficult ways for police to control the situation, with a greater likelihood that officers might resort to arrest as a fallback position. When the assigned treatment is arrest, there is no need for a fallback position. For example, some offenders may have refused to comply with an order to leave the premises.

Such differential attrition would potentially bias estimates of the relative effectiveness of arrest by removing uncooperative and difficult offenders from the mediation and separation treatments. Any deterrent effect could be underestimated and, in the extreme, artifactual support for deviance amplification could be

found. That is, the arrest group would have too many "bad guys" *relative* to the other treatments.

We can be more systematic about other factors affecting the movement of cases away from the designed treatments. The three delivered treatments represent a polychotomous outcome amenable to multivariate statistical analysis. We applied a multinominal logit formulation (Amemiya, 1981: 1516–19; Maddala, 1983: 34–37), which showed that the designed treatment was the dominant cause of the treatment actually received (a finding suggested by Table 1). However, we also found that five other variables had a statistically significant effect on "upgrading" the separation and advice treatments to arrests: whether police reported the suspect was rude; whether police reported the suspect tried to assault one (or both) of the police officers; whether police reported weapons were involved; whether the victim persistently demanded a citizen's arrest; and whether a restraining order was being violated. We found no evidence that the background or characteristics of the suspect or victim (e.g., race) affected the treatment received.

Overall, the logit model fit the data very well. For well over 80 percent of the cases, the model's predicted treatment was the same as the actual treatment (i.e., correct classifications), and minor alterations in the assignment threshold would have substantially improved matters. Moreover, a chi-square test on the residuals was not statistically significant (i.e., the observed and predicted treatments differed by no more than chance). In summary, we were able to model the assignment process with remarkable success simply by employing the rules of the experimental protocol (for more details, see Berk and Sherman, 1983).

We were less fortunate with the inter-

[2] Sixteen cases were dropped because no treatment was applied or because the case did not belong in the study (i.e., a fight between a father and son).

Table 1. Designed and Delivered Police Treatments in Spousal Assault Cases

Designed Treatment	Delivered Treatment			
	Arrest	Advise	Separate	Total
Arrest	98.9%	0.0%	1.1%	29.3%
	(91)	(0)	(1)	(92)
Advise	17.6%	77.8%	4.6%	34.4%
	(19)	(84)	(5)	(108)
Separate	22.8%	4.4%	72.8%	36.3%
	(26)	(5)	(83)	(114)
Total	43.4%	28.3%	28.3%	100%
	(136)	(89)	(89)	(314)

views of the victims; only 205 (of 330, counting the few repeat victims twice) could be located and initial interviews obtained, a 62 percent completion rate. Many of the victims simply could not be found, either for the initial interview or for follow-ups: they either left town, moved somewhere else or refused to answer the phone or doorbell. The research staff made up to 20 attempts to contact these victims, and often employed investigative techniques (asking friends and neighbors) to find them. Sometimes these methods worked, only to have the victim give an outright refusal or break one or more appointments to meet the interviewer at a "safe" location for the interview.

The response rate to the bi-weekly follow-up interviews was even lower than for the initial interview, as in much research on women crime victims. After the first interview, for which the victims were paid $20, there was a gradual falloff in completed interviews with each successive wave; only 161 victims provided all 12 follow-up interviews over the six months, a completion rate of 49 percent. Whether paying for the follow-up interviews would have improved the response rate is unclear; it would have added over $40,000 to the cost of the research. When the telephone interviews yielded few reports of violence, we moved to conduct every fourth interview in person, which appeared to produce more reports of violence.

There is absolutely no evidence that the experimental treatment assigned to the offender affected the victim's decision to grant initial interviews. We estimated a binary logit equation for the dichotomous outcome: whether or not an initial interview was obtained. Regressors included the experimental treatments (with one necessarily excluded), race of the victim, race of the offender, and a number of attributes of the incident (from the police sheets). A joint test on the full set of regressors failed to reject the null hypothesis that all of the logit coefficients were zero. More important for our purposes, none of the t-values for the treatments was in excess of 1.64; indeed, none was greater than 1.0 in absolute value. In short, while the potential for sample selection bias (Heckman, 1979; Berk, 1983) certainly exists (and is considered later), that bias does not stem from obvious sources, particularly the treatments. This implies that we may well be able to meaningfully examine experimental effects for the subset of individuals from whom initial interviews were obtained.

The same conclusions followed when the follow-up interviews were considered.

In sum, despite the practical difficulties of controlling an experiment and interviewing crime victims in an emotionally charged and violent social context, the experiment succeeded in producing a promising sample of 314 cases with complete official outcome measures and an apparently unbiased sample of responses from the victims in those cases.

RESULTS

The 205 completed initial interviews provide some sense of who the subjects are, although the data may not properly represent the characteristics of the full sample of 314. They show the now familiar pattern of domestic violence cases coming to police attention being disproportionately unmarried couples with lower than average educational levels, disproportionately minority and mixed race (black male, white female), and who were very likely to have had prior violent incidents with police intervention. The 60 percent suspect unemployment rate is strikingly high in a community with only about 5 percent of the workforce unemployed. The 59 percent prior arrest rate is also strikingly high, suggesting (with the 80 percent prior domestic assault rate) that the suspects generally are experienced lawbreakers who are accustomed to police interventions. But with the exception of the heavy representation of Native Americans (due to Minneapolis' unique proximity to many Indian reservations), the characteristics in Table 2 are probably close to those of domestic violence cases coming to police attention in other large U.S. cities.

Two kinds of outcome measures will be considered. One is a *police-recorded* "failure" of the offender to survive the six-month follow-up period without having police generate a written report on the suspect for domestic violence, either through an offense or an arrest report written by any officer in the department, or through a subsequent report to the project research staff of a randomized (or other) intervention by officers participating in the experiment. A second kind of measure comes from the *interviews with victims,* in which victims were asked if there had been a repeat incident with the same suspect, broadly defined to include an actual assault, threatened assault, or property damage.

The two kinds of outcomes were each formulated in two complementary ways: as a dummy variable (i.e., repeat incident or not) and as the amount of time elapsed from the treatment to either a failure or the end of the follow-up period. For each of the two outcomes, three analyses were performed: the first using a linear probability model; the second using a logit formulation; and the third using a proportional hazard approach. The dummy outcome was employed for the linear probability and logit analyses, while the time-to-failure was employed for the proportional hazard method.[3]

Given the randomization, we began in traditional analysis of variance fashion. The official measure of a repeat incident was regressed on the treatment received for the subset of 314 cases (out of 330) that fell within the definition of the experiment. Compared to the baseline treatment of separation, which had the highest recidivism rate in the police data, the arrest treatment reduced repeat occur-

[3] In addition to the linear probability model, the logit and proportional hazard formulations can be expressed in forms such that the outcome is a probability (e.g., the probability of a new violent incident). However, three slightly different response functions are implied. We had no theoretical basis for selecting the proper response function, and consequently used all three. We expected that the substantive results could be essentially invariant across the three formulations.

Table 2. Victim and Suspect Characteristics: Initial Interview Data and Police Sheets

A. Unemployment			
Victims	61%		
Suspects	60%		
B. Relationship of Suspect to Victim			
Divorced or separated husband		3%	
Unmarried male lover		45%	
Current husband		35%	
Wife or girlfriend		2%	
Son, brother, roommate, other		15%	
C. Prior Assaults and Police Involvement			
Victims assaulted by suspect, last six months		80%	
Police intervention in domestic dispute,			
last six months		60%	
Couple in Counseling Program		27%	
D. Prior Arrests of Male Suspects			
Ever Arrested For Any Offense		59%	
Ever Arrested For Crime Against Person		31%	
Ever Arrested on Domestic Violence Statute		5%	
Ever Arrested On An Alcohol Offense		29%	
E. Mean Age			
Victims	30 years		
Suspects	32 years		
F. Education		Victims	Suspects
< high school		43%	42%
high school only		33%	36%
> high school		24%	22%
G. Race		Victims	Suspects
White		57%	45%
Black		23%	36%
Native American		18%	16%
Other		2%	3%

N = 205 (Those cases for which initial interviews were obtained)

rences by a statistically significant amount ($t = -2.38$). Twenty-six percent of those separated committed a repeat assault, compared to 13 percent of those arrested. The mediation treatment was statistically indistinguishable from the other two. To help put this in perspective, 18.2 percent of the households failed overall.

The apparent treatment effect for arrest in this conventional analysis was suggestive, but there was a danger of biased estimates from the "upgrading" of some separation and advise treatments. In response, we applied variations on the corrections recommended by Barnow et al. (1980: esp. 55). In brief, we inserted instrumental variables in place of the delivered treatments when the treatment effects were analyzed. These instruments, in turn, were constructed from the multinomial logit model described earlier.[4]

Table 3 shows the results of the adjusted models. The first two columns report the results for the linear probability approach. Again, we find a statistically

[4] We did *not* simply use the conditional expectations of a multinomial logit model. We used an alternative procedure to capitalize on the initial ran-

Table 3. Experimental Results for Police Data

Variable	Linear		Logistic		Proportional Hazard Rate	
	Coef	t-value	Coef	t-value	Coef	t-value
Intercept (separate)	0.24	5.03*	−1.10	−4.09*	—	—
Arrest	−0.14	−2.21*	−1.02	−2.21*	−0.97	−2.28*
Advise	−0.05	−0.79	−0.31	−0.76	−0.32	−0.88
	F = 2.01		Chi-square = 5.19		Chi-square = 5.48	
	P = .07		P = .07		P = .06	
N = 314						

*$p < .05$, two-tailed test.

significant effect for arrest ($t = -2.21$). However, it is well known that the linear probability model will produce inefficient estimates of the regression coefficients and biased (and inconsistent) estimates of the standard errors. Significance tests, therefore, are suspect. Consequently, we also estimated a logit model, with pretty much the same result. At the mean of the endogenous variable (i.e., 18.2 percent), the logit coefficient for arrest translates into nearly the same effect (i.e., $-.15$) found with the linear probability model ($t = -2.21$).

One might still object that the use of a dummy variable outcome neglects right-hand censoring. In brief, one cannot observe failures that occur after the end of the experimental period, so that biased (and inconsistent) results follow. Thus, we applied a proportional hazard analysis (Lawless, 1982: Ch. 7) that adjusts for right-hand censoring. In this model the time-to-failure dependent variable is transformed into (roughly) the probability at any given moment during the six-month follow-up period of a new offense occurring, given that no new offenses have yet been committed. The last two columns of Table 3 indicate that, again, an effect for arrest surfaces ($t = -2.28$).

dom assignment. The details can be found in Berk and Sherman (1983).

The coefficient of -0.97 implies that compared to the baseline of separation, those experiencing an arrest were less likely to commit a new battery by a multiplicative factor of .38 (i.e., e raised to the -0.97 power). If the earlier results are translated into comparable terms, the effects described by the proportional hazard formulation are the largest we have seen (see footnote 4). But the major message is that the arrest effect holds up under three different statistical methods based on slightly different response functions. Overall, the police data indicate that the separation treatment produces the highest recidivism, arrest produces the lowest, with the impact of "advise" (from doing nothing to mediation) indistinguishable from the other two effects.

Table 4 shows the results when self-report data are used. A "failure" is defined as a new assault, property destruction or a threatened assault. (Almost identical results follow from a definition including only a new assault.) These results suggest a different ordering of the effects, with arrest still producing the lowest recidivism rate (at 19%), but with advice producing the highest (37%).

Overall, 28.9 percent of the suspects in Table 4 "failed." Still, the results are much the same as found for the official failure measure. However, given the effective sample of 161, we are vulnerable

Table 4. Experimental Results for Victim Report Data

Variable	Linear		Logistic		Proportional Hazard Rate	
	Coef	t-value	Coef	t-value	Coef	t-value
Intercept (advise)	0.37	5.54*	−0.53	−1.70	—	—
Arrest	−0.18	−2.00*	−0.94	−2.01*	−0.82	−2.05*
Separate	−0.04	−0.35	−0.15	−0.10	−0.27	−0.09
	F = 2.31		Chi-square = 4.78		Chi-square = 4.36	
	P = .10		P = .09		P = .11	

N = 161 (Those cases for which *all* follow-up interviews were obtained)

*$p < .05$, two-tailed test.

to sample selection bias. In response, we applied Heckman's (1979) sample selection corrections. The results were virtually unchanged (and are therefore not reported).

An obvious rival hypothesis to the deterrent effect of arrest is that arrest incapacitates. If the arrested suspects spend a large portion of the next six months in jail, they would be expected to have lower recidivism rates. But the initial interview data show this is not the case: of those arrested, 43 percent were released within one day, 86 percent were released within one week, and only 14 percent were released after one week or had not yet been released at the time of the *initial* victim interview. Clearly, there was very little incapacitation, especially in the context of a six-month follow-up. Indeed, virtually all those arrested were released before the first follow-up interview. Nevertheless, we introduced the length of the initial stay in jail as a control variable. Consistent with expectations, the story was virtually unchanged.

Another perspective on the incapacitation issue can be obtained by looking at repeat violence which occurred shortly after the police intervened. If incapacitation were at work, a dramatic effect should be found in households experiencing arrest, especially compared to households experiencing advice. Table 5

shows how quickly the couples were reunited, and of those reunited in one day, how many of them, according to the victim, began to argue or had physical violence again. It is apparent that *all* of the police interventions effectively stopped the violence for a 24-hour period after the couples were reunited. Even the renewed quarrels were few, at least with our relatively small sample size. Hence, there is again no evidence for an incapacitation effect. There is also no evidence for the reverse: that arrested offenders would take it out on the victim when the offender returned home.

DISCUSSION AND CONCLUSIONS

The experiment's results are subject to several qualifications. One caution is that both kinds of outcome measures have uncertain construct validity. The official measure no doubt neglects a large number of repeat incidents, in part because many of them were not reported, and in part because police are sometimes reluctant to turn a family "dispute" into formal police business. However, the key is whether there is *differential* measurement error by the experimental treatments; an undercount randomly distributed across the three treatments will not bias the estimated experimental effects (i.e., only the

Table 5. Speed of Reunion and Recidivism by Police Action

| | Time of Reunion | | | | | |
Police Action	Within One Day	More than One Day but Less Than One Week	Longer or No Return	(N)	New Quarrel Within A Day	New Violence Within A Day
Arrested (and released)	38%	30%	32%	(N = 76)	(2)	(1)
Separated	57%	31%	10%	(N = 54)	(6)	(3)
Advised	—	—	—	(N = 72)	(4)	(1)
N = 202 (Down from 205 in Table 2 due to missing data)						

estimate of the intercept will be biased). It is hard to imagine that differential undercounting would come solely from the actions of police, since most officers were not involved in the experiment and could not have known what treatment had been delivered.

However, there might be differential undercounting if offenders who were arrested were less likely to remain on the scene after a new assault. Having been burned once, they might not wait around for a second opportunity. And police told us they were less likely during the follow-up period (and more generally) to record an incident if the offender was not present. For example, there would be no arrest forms since the offender was not available to arrest. If all we had were the official outcome measures, there would be no easy way to refute this possibility. Fortunately, the self-report data are *not* vulnerable on these grounds, and the experimental effects are found nevertheless.

It is also possible that the impact for arrest found in the official outcome measure represents a reluctance of *victims* to call the police. That is, for some victims, the arrest may have been an undesirable intervention, and rather than face the prospect of another arrest from a new incident, these victims might decide not to invoke police sanctions. For example, the arrest may have cost the offender

several days' work and put financial stress on the household. Or the offender may have threatened serious violence if the victim ever called the police again. However, we can again observe that the self-report data would not have been vulnerable to such concerns, and the experimental effects were found nevertheless. The only way we can see how the self-report data would fail to support the official data is if respondents in households experiencing arrest became more hesitant to admit to *interviewers* that they had been beaten a second time. Since there was no differential response rate by treatment, this possibility seems unlikely. If the arrested suspects had intimidated their victims more than the other two treatment groups, it seems more likely that such intimidation would have shown up in noncooperation with the interviews than in differential underreporting of violence in the course of the interviews.

This is not to say that the self-report data are flawless; indeed there is some reason to believe that there was undercounting of new incidents. However, just as for the official data, unless there is differential undercounting by the experimental treatments, all is well. We can think of no good reasons why differential undercounting should materialize. In summary, internal validity looks rather sound.

The construct validity of the treatments is more problematic. The advice and separation interventions have unclear content. Perhaps "good" mediation, given consistently, would fare better compared to arrest. The more general point is that the treatment effects for arrest are only relative to the impact of the other interventions. Should their content change, the relative impact of arrest could change as well.

Likewise, we noted earlier that a few officers accounted for a disproportionate number of the cases. What we have been interpreting, therefore, as results from different intervention strategies could reflect the special abilities of certain officers to make arrest particularly effective relative to the other treatments. For example, these officers may have been less skilled in mediation techniques. However, we re-estimated the models reported in Tables 3 and 4, including an interaction effect to capture the special contributions of our high-productivity officers. The new variable was not statistically significant, and the treatment effect for arrest remained.

Finally, Minneapolis is hardly representative of all urban areas. The Minneapolis Police Department has many unusual characteristics, and different jurisdictions might well keep suspects in custody for longer or shorter periods of time. The message should be clear: external validity will have to wait for replications.

Despite these qualifications, it is apparent that we have found no support for the deviance amplification point of view. The arrest intervention certainly did not make things worse and may well have made things better. There are, of course, many rejoinders. In particular, over 80 percent of offenders had assaulted the victims in the previous six months, and in over 60 percent of the households the police had intervened during that interval.

Almost 60 percent of the suspects had previously been arrested for something. Thus, the counterproductive consequences of police sanction, if any, may for many offenders have already been felt. In labeling theory terms, secondary deviation may already have been established, producing a ceiling for the amplification effects of formal sanctioning. However, were this the case, the arrest treatment probably should be less effective in households experiencing recent police interventions. No such interaction effects were found. In future analyses of these data, however, we will inductively explore interactions with more sensitive measures of police sanctioning and prior criminal histories of the suspects.

There are, of course, many versions of labeling theory. For those who theorize that a metamorphosis of self occurs in response to official sanctions over a long period of time, our six-month follow-up is not a relevant test. For those who argue that the development of a criminal self-concept is particularly likely to occur during a lengthy prison stay or extensive contact with criminal justice officials, the dosage of labeling employed in this experiment is not sufficient to falsify that hypothesis. What this experiment does seem to falsify for this particular offense is the broader conception of labeling implicit in the prior research by Lincoln et al. (unpubl.), Farrington (1977) and others: that for every possible increment of criminal justice response to deviance, the more increments (or the greater the formality) applied to the labeled deviant, the greater the likelihood of subsequent deviation. The absolute strength of the dosage is irrelevant to this hypothesis, as long as some variation in dosage is present. While the experiment does not falsify all possible "labeling theory" hypotheses, it does at least seem to falsify this one.

The apparent support for deterrence

is perhaps more clear. While we certainly have no evidence that deterrence will work in general, we do have findings that swift imposition of a sanction of temporary incarceration may deter male offenders in domestic assault cases. And we have produced this evidence from an unusually strong research design based on random assignment to treatments. In short, criminal justice sanctions seem to matter for this offense in this setting with this group of experienced offenders.

A number of police implications follow. Perhaps most important, police have historically been reluctant to make arrests in domestic assault cases, in part fearing that an arrest could make the violence worse. Criminal justice sanctions weakly applied might be insufficient to deter and set the offender on a course of retribution. Our data indicate that such concerns are by and large groundless.

Police have also felt that making an arrest was a waste of their time: without the application of swift and severe sanctions by the courts, arrest and booking had no bite. Our results indicate that only three of the 136 arrested offenders were formally punished by fines or subsequent incarceration. This suggests that arrest and initial incarceration alone may produce a deterrent effect, regardless of how the courts treat such cases, and that arrest makes an independent contribution to the deterrence potential of the criminal justice system. Therefore, in jurisdictions that process domestic assault offenders in a manner similar to that employed in Minneapolis, we favor a *presumption* of arrest; an arrest should be made unless there are good, clear reasons why an arrest would be counterproductive. We do not, however, favor *requiring* arrests in all misdemeanor domestic assault cases. Even if our findings were replicated in a number of jurisdictions, there is a good

chance that arrest works far better for some kinds of offenders than others and in some kinds of situations better than others.[5] We feel it best to leave police a loophole to capitalize on that variation. Equally important, it is widely recognized that discretion is inherent in police work. Simply to impose a requirement of arrest, irrespective of the features of the immediate situation, is to invite circumvention.

REFERENCES

Amemiya, Takeshi. 1981. "Qualitative response models: a survey." Journal of Economic Literature 19: 1483–1536.

Andenaes, Johannes. 1971. "Deterrence and specific offenses." University of Chicago Law Review 39: 537.

Bard, Morton. 1970. "Training police as specialists in family crisis intervention." Washington, D.C.: U.S. Department of Justice.

Bard, Morton and Joseph Zacker. 1974. "Assaultiveness and alcohol use in family disputes—police perceptions." Criminology 12: 281–92.

Barnow, Burt S., Glen G. Cain and Arthur S. Goldberger. 1980. "Issues in the analysis of selectivity bias." Pp. 53–59 in Ernst W. Stromsdorfer and George Farkas (eds.), Evaluation Studies Review Annual, Volume 5. Beverly Hills: Sage.

Becker, Howard. 1963. The Outsiders. New York: Free Press.

Berk, Richard A. 1983. "An introduction to sample selection bias in sociological data." American Sociological Review, 48: 386–98.

Berk, Richard A. and Lawrence W. Sherman. 1983. "Police responses to family violence incidents: an analysis of an experi-

---

[5] Indeed, one of the major policy issues that could arise from further analysis of the interaction effects would be whether police discretion should be guided by either achieved or ascribed relevant suspect characteristics.

mental design with incomplete randomization." Unpublished manuscript. Department of Sociology, University of California at Barbara.

Berk, Sarah Fenstermaker and Donileen R. Loseke. 1981. "Handling family violence: situational determinants of police arrest in domestic disturbances." Law and Society Review 15: 315–46.

Black, Donald. 1980. The Manners and Customs of the Police. New York: Academic Press.

Chambliss, William. 1967. "Types of deviance and the effectiveness of legal sanctions." Wisconsin Law Review 1967: 703–19.

Clarke, Ronald V. G. 1966. "Approved school boy absconders and corporal punishment." British Journal of Criminology: 6: 364–75.

Cohen, Lawrence E. and Rodney Stark. 1974. "Discriminatory labeling and the five-finger discount." Journal of Research in Crime and Delinquency 11: 25–39.

Cook, Thomas D. and Donald T. Campbell. 1979. Quasi-Experimentation: Design and Analysis Issues for Field Settings. Chicago: Rand McNally.

Durkheim, Emile. [1893] 1972. Selected Writings. Edited with an Introduction by Anthony Giddens. [Selection from Division of Labor in Society, 6th edition, 1960 (1893)] Cambridge: Cambridge University Press.

Emerson, Charles D. 1979. "Family violence: a study by the Los Angeles County Sheriff's Department." Police Chief 46(6): 48–50.

Fagin, James A. 1978. "The effects of police interpersonal communications skills on conflict resolution." Ph.D. Dissertation, Southern Illinois University Ann Arbor: University Microfilms.

Farrington, David P. 1977. "The effects of public labeling." British Journal of Criminology 17: 112–25.

Federal Bureau of Investigation. 1967. Uniform Crime Reports. Washington, D.C.: U.S. Department of Justice.

Gold, Martin and Jay Williams. 1969. "National study of the aftermath of apprehension." Prospectus 3: 3–11.

Gibbs, Jack P. 1975. Crime, Punishment and Deterrence. New York: Elsevier.

Heckman, James. 1979. "Sample selection bias as a specification error." Econometrica 45: 153–61.

Hirschi, Travis. 1975. "Labeling theory and juvenile delinquency: an assessment of the evidence." Pp. 181–203 in Walter R. Gove (ed.), The Labeling of Deviance. New York: Wiley.

Illinois Law Enforcement Commission. 1978. "Report on technical assistance project—domestic violence survey." (Abstract). Washington, D.C.: National Criminal Justice Reference Service.

Ketterman, Thomas and Marjorie Kravitz. 1978. Police Crisis Intervention: A Selected Bibliography. Washington, D.C.: National Criminal Justice Reference Service.

Klemke, Lloyd W. 1978. "Does apprehension for shoplifting amplify or terminate shoplifting activity?" Law and Society Review 12: 391–403.

Kraut, Robert E. 1976. "Deterrent and definitional influences on shoplifting." Social Problems 23: 358–68.

Langley, Richard and Roger C. Levy 1977. Wife Beating: The Silent Crisis. New York: E. P. Dutton.

Lawless, Jerald F. 1982. Statistical Models and Methods for Lifetime Data. New York: Wiley.

Lemert, Edwin M. 1951. Social Pathology. New York: McGraw-Hill.

———.1967. Human Deviance, Social Problems and Social Control. Englewood Cliffs, NJ: Prentice-Hall.

Lempert, Richard. 1981–1982. "Organizing for deterrence: lessons from a study of child support." Law and Society Review 16: 513–68.

Lincoln, Suzanne B., Malcolm W. Klein, Katherine S. Teilmann and Susan Labin. unpubl. "Control organizations and labeling theory: official versus self-reported delinquency." Unpublished manuscript, University of Southern California.

Maddala, G. S. 1983. Limited, Dependent and Qualitative Variables in Econometrics. Cambridge: Cambridge University Press.

McCord, Joan. 1983. "A longitudinal appraisal of criminal sanctions." Paper presented to the IXth International Congress on Criminology, Vienna, Austria, September.

Meyer, Jeanie Keeny and T. D. Lorimer. 1977. Police Intervention Data and Domestic Violence: Exploratory Development and Validation of Prediction Models. Report prepared under grant #RO1MH27918 from National Institute of Mental Health. Kansas City, Mo., Police Department.

Murray, Charles A. and Louis A. Cox, Jr. 1979. Beyond Probation. Beverly Hills: Sage.

Office of the Minority Leader, State of New York. 1978. Battered Women: Part I (Abstract). Washington, D.C.: National Criminal Justice Reference Service.

Parnas, Raymond I. 1972. "The police response to the domestic disturbance." Pp. 206–36 in Leon Radzinowicz and Marvin E. Wolfgang (eds.), The Criminal in the Arms of the Law. New York: Basic Books.

Police Foundation. 1976. Domestic Violence and the Police: Studies in Detroit and Kansas City. Washington, D.C.: The Police Foundation.

Potter, Jane. 1978. "The police and the battered wife: the search for understanding." Police Magazine 1: 40–50.

Roy, Maria (ed.). 1977. Battered Women. New York: Van Nostrand Reinhold.

Schwartz, Richard and Jerome Skolnick. 1962. "Two studies of legal stigma." Social Problems 10: 133–42.

Sherman, Lawrence W. 1980. "Causes of police behavior: the current state of quantitative research." Journal of Research in Crime and Delinquency 17: 69–100.

Shoham, S. Giora. 1974. "Punishment and traffic offenses." Traffic Quarterly 28: 61–73.

Thorsell, Bernard A. and Lloyd M. Klemke. 1972. "The labeling process: reinforcement and deterrent." Law and Society Review 6: 393–403.

Tittle, Charles. 1975. "Labeling and crime: an empirical evaluation." Pp. 157–79 in Walter R. Gove (ed.), The Labeling of Deviance. New York: Wiley.

University of Rochester. 1974. "FACIT—Family Conflict Intervention Team Experiment—Experimental Action Program." (Abstract). Washington, D.C.: National Criminal Justice Reference Service.

Wylie, P. B., L. F. Basinger, C. L. Heinecke and J. A. Reuckert. 1976. "Approach to evaluating a police program of family crisis interventions in six demonstration cities—Final report." (Abstract). Washington, D.C.: National Criminal Justice Reference Service.

Zimring, Franklin E. and Gordon T. Hawkins. 1973. Deterrence: The Legal Threat in Crime Control. Chicago: University of Chicago Press.

The Role of Arrest in Domestic Assault: The Omaha Police Experiment*

Franklyn W. Dunford
David Huizinga
Delbert S. Elliott
University of Colorado, Boulder

This paper reports on a replication of the Minneapolis Domestic Violence Experiment in Omaha, Nebraska. Suspects who were eligible for the experiment were randomly assigned to one of three police dispositions: mediation, separation, or arrest. No differences by disposition were found in prevalence or frequency of repeat offending, using five measures of recidivism to assess outcome six months after police intervention. A survival analysis, using three of the measures for which dates of failure were available, also produced no differences by disposition.

In what has come to be known as a landmark study, the Minneapolis Domestic Violence Experiment (Sherman and Berk, 1984a, 1984b) assessed the effects of different police responses on the future violence of individuals apprehended for domestic assault. The authors (1984a:1) reported that

> arrest was the most effective of three standard methods police use to reduce domestic violence. The other police methods—attempting to counsel both parties or sending assailants away—were found to be considerably less effective in deterring future violence in the cases examined.

Sherman and Berk specified arrest and initial incarceration, "alone," as deterring continued domestic assault and recommended that the police adopt arrest as the favored response to domestic assault *on the basis* of its deterrent power. These findings and recommendations came at a time when advocacy for increased sensitivity to women's rights was strong and pressure was mounting to change the social service approach to domestic violence that had dominated law enforcement and court policy over the preceding two decades (Morash, 1986). Sherman and Berk's recommendations were uniquely appealing for the times and were received by many women's advocates and enforcement administrators as justification for change (Cohn and Sherman, 1987; Sherman and Cohn, 1989).

The overwhelming reaction of the research community to the Minneapolis experiment, with its recommendation for presumptory arrests in cases of misdemeanor domestic assault, was a call for additional studies to corroborate its conclusions (Binder and Meeker, 1988; Elliott, 1989; Lempert, 1989; Williams and Hawkins, 1989). The Omaha Domestic

Reprinted with permission from Franklyn W. Dunford, et al., "The Role of Arrest in Domestic Assault: The Omaha Police Experiment," *Criminology*, vol. 28 (2), 1990, pp. 183–206.

Violence Police Experiment, funded by the National Institute of Justice, was conceived and designed to determine if the findings reported for the Minneapolis experiment could be duplicated elsewhere.[1]

THE OMAHA RESEARCH DESIGN

Omaha is a city of approximately 400,000 inhabitants, 10% of whom are black and 2% of Hispanic origin (U.S. Department of Commerce, 1983). The city is split into three sectors (south, west, north) for police purposes. In concert with Chief Robert Wadman of the Omaha Police Division and after surveying 911 dispatch records, it was determined that approximately 60% of disturbance calls were reported during the hours of "C" shift (4 p.m. to midnight). On this basis, the decision was made to limit the replication experiment in Omaha to eligible domestic assaults coming to the attention of the police throughout the city (all three sectors) during the hours of "C" shift.[2] In this way, no segment of the city (e.g., socioeconomic status [SES] or ethnic group) would be excluded from participation in the experiment by the research design, and the majority of domestic violence calls would be included in the study.

Following the design of the Minneapolis experiment, police calls for domestic violence found to be eligible for the study were randomly assigned to "arrest," "separation," or "mediation" for all instances

in which both victims and suspects were present when the police arrived. A case was eligible for the experiment if (1) probable cause for an arrest for misdemeanor assault existed, (2) the case involved a clearly identifiable victim and suspect, (3) both parties to the assault were of age (18 or older), (4) both parties had lived together sometime during the year preceding the assault, and (5) neither party to the offense had an arrest warrant on file. Cases for which the police had no legal authority to make an arrest (i.e., no probable cause to believe that an assault had occurred) were excluded from the experiment, as were more serious cases (i.e., felony cases).

After responding officers determined eligibility, they contacted (by radio or telephone) the Information Unit of the Omaha Police Division and gave a civilian operator the date and time of the call, names and birth dates of the victims and suspects, and their own police identification number(s). A treatment was then assigned by a computer-generated randomization program initiated by the Information Unit operators. In this manner, eligibility decisions always preceded requests for randomized dispositions and permanent and protected records of the particulars of each transaction were recorded and stored within the computer used to make the assignment.

DESCRIPTION OF THE EXPERIMENT

In February 1986 all of the command and patrol officers assigned to "C" (and "D") shift were trained during a succession of three-day training sessions. Training focused on the rationale, content, and mechanics of the experiment. At each shift change thereafter, officers new to "C" shift were similarly trained. A total of 194 officers were ultimately assigned

[1] Shortly after funding the Omaha project, the National Institute of Justice (1986) announced a general initiative for replications for the Minneapolis experiment and funded additional studies, which are now in progress: Dade County, Florida; Atlanta, Georgia; Charlotte, North Carolina; Milwaukee, Wisconsin; Colorado Springs, Colorado. The Omaha project is thus one of six replications.

[2] "D" shift (8 p.m. to 4 a.m.) was also trained and used until it was disbanded approximately six months into the experiment.

to the participating shifts and received training on the methods and procedures of the experiment. Of that number, 31 (16%) did not refer any cases to the study, and 61 (31%) accounted for approximately 75% of the referrals.

One of the greatest challenges faced when implementing random assignment in field settings is monitoring and identifying all violations of randomized outcomes. Although researchers may not be able to prevent violations of randomly designated treatments (e.g., arresting when treatment is randomized to mediating), they should be able to ensure that such violations do not go undetected when they occur. Because there were some violations of the randomly assigned treatment dispositions, four treatment classifications were possible: Treatment as Assigned, Treatment as Officially Recorded, Treatment Immediately Delivered, and Treatment Ultimately Delivered. The first measure, Treatment as Assigned, was the treatment that was randomly assigned by computer and communicated to officers in the field by the Information Unit: arrest, separate, or mediate. The treatment variable used for the analyses presented in this paper is Treatment as Assigned. The second measure, Treatment as Officially Recorded, was treatment as recorded by responding officers on the Domestic Violence Report form. After receiving a randomized treatment from the Information Unit, officers recorded the disposition on the Domestic Violence Report form, along with other relevant information, and forwarded the report to headquarters. When the 330 Treatments as Assigned were compared with the Treatments as Officially Recorded on the Domestic Violence Report forms, one discrepancy was found. The third measure, Treatment as Immediately Delivered, reflects estimates of the initial treatment that was actually delivered at the scene of an eligible case. This measure was determined by asking victims about treatments delivered to suspects and by reviewing what police officers wrote on the Domestic Violence Report form about the treatment delivered and comparing the two. Some of the discrepancies between Treatment as Assigned and Treatment as Immediately Delivered appear to have involved differences in perceptions of what happened rather than any real differences, while others were clear misdeliveries of treatment.[3]

The final treatment category consisted of Treatment as Ultimately Delivered. This classification was determined by comparing treatments as assigned with what victims reported as ultimately happening and what police officers recorded on the Domestic Violence Report forms as ultimately happening and by comparing Arrests with official records of police, prosecuting attorney, and court actions. If, for example, in the course of delivering Mediation a suspect assaulted an officer and was arrested, the case was defined as follows: Treatment as Assigned = Mediation; Treatment as Immediately Delivered = Mediation; Treatment as Ultimately Delivered = Arrest. Also, if the assigned treatment was Arrest and no official record could be found that an arrest was made, the case was

---

[3] Victims were not always sure of what happened as a result of police interventions. Some of their confusion was to be expected. The police, for example, would mediate a dispute, after which the suspect would leave, but at the time of the interview the victim would report a separation as the intervention. Or, after the police left, one of the parties to a separation treatment would return and the event would be recalled as a mediation. This kind of confusion is even more understandable given that (by responding officer estimates) over 30% of the victims had been drinking at the time of the police intervention, which may have affected what victims remembered as happening during those time periods. Further, many victims were clearly traumatized by the presenting assault, which also may have affected their recall.

Table 1. Assigned and Delivered Treatments

Assigned Disposition	As Delivered		
	Mediate	Separate	Arrest
Mediate*			
N	102	8	2
%	89	7	2
Separate			
N	5	98	3
%	5	92	3
Arrest			
N	3	2	104
%	3	2	95

*Three cases assigned to mediate were delivered as no warrants
$\chi^2 = 3.502$ d.f. = 2   p = .174

classified on the Treatment as Ultimately Delivered measure as Mediation.[4] Treatment as Ultimately Delivered is problematic in that the absence of an officially recorded arrest is not foolproof evidence that an arrest was not made. In several cases, for example, no record of arrest was found in the police record bureau even though the case had been officially recorded as "booked" into the jail. Conversely, cases were found in the police record bureau that were not found in the "jail" booking records.

As a check on the misapplication of treatment, the disparities between Treatments as Assigned and Treatments as Delivered were examined.[5] As presented in Table 1, 95% of the cases assigned to an arrest received an arrest, 92% of those assigned to be separated were separated, and 89% of the mediation cases were

mediated; overall, 92% of the treatments were delivered as assigned. When Mediate and Separate were collapsed and made into an "informal" or nonpunitive treatment category, as suggested by Binder and Meeker (1988), to be eventually used in comparisons with a "formal" or punitive treatment (arrest) group, the overall delivered-as-assigned rate was 97%. When the prevalence of misapplied cases was compared by treatment groups (following Glass and Stanley, 1970), the null hypothesis that misapplications were independent of treatment assignments, could not be rejected ($\chi^2 = 3.50$, $p \leq .174$). Given the relatively small number of misapplications, the suspicion that many of the cases conservatively defined as misapplications may not in actuality have been misapplied, and the provision to collapse mediation and separation into one nonpunitive treatment class for some analyses, the misapplication rates shown in Table 1 were judged to be acceptable (i.e., did not affect the adequacy of the test or otherwise provide a serious threat to internal validity), and subsequent attention was focused on the distribution of the misapplied cases.

The purpose of random assignment

[4]The decision to call an unconfirmable arrest a mediation rather than separation or something else was arbitrary. This was done, however, with the understanding that comparisons of treatments as Ultimately Delivered would always be between the arrest treatment and a nonarrest treatment (mediation and separation combined).

[5]Treatment as Delivered will refer to Treatment as Immediately Delivered from this point on, unless noted otherwise.

within experiments is to ensure the equivalence of experimental groups within probability limits at the point of assignment. One check on how well random assignment worked involved a comparison of the randomly assigned treatment groups on variables thought to have some relevance for an assignment bias (e.g., ethnicity, SES, employment status, level of violence, prior arrest history). Six (6.2%) of the 96 comparisons proved to be statistically different at probability levels of .10 or less (about the number that would be expected to be different by chance), and the differences did not consistently favor any one of the treatment groups (see Dunford et al., 1989, for this comparison).[6]

[6] A question about the internal validity of the Omaha experiment is of interest. Although the cases randomly assigned to different treatments may have been equivalent at the point of random assignment, their equivalency by the time the police left the scene of the presenting assault is at issue. The concern focuses on the consequences that the systematic granting or denial of victim requests for the arrest of suspects at the presenting offense has on future calls to the police. Those victims who requested the arrest of suspects randomly assigned to the arrest treatment were always successful. Victims who requested the arrest of suspects randomly assigned to mediation or separation were never successful. Subsequent official recidivism may thus have been a function of the motivation victims received to call the police for new assaults because of their prior positive or negative experiences at the presenting offense. When this issue was examined, no evidence could be found for its support. First, *victim reports* of subsequent violence were not subject to this source of bias, which, as will be shown below, is entirely consistent with findings based on the official measures of recidivism. Second, victim willingness to call the police for subsequent conflicts did not appear to be related to treatment. At the six-month interview, victims were asked whether they had become more or less willing to call the police in the event of a new fight with the offender. There were no statistically significant differences between treatments in willingness to call the police again. Victims were also asked, approximately one week after the presenting offense, whether they were satisfied with the action the police had taken. Again, no statistically significant differences among treatments were found (mediation scored lowest and separation

An additional assessment for bias in the self-reported victim data involved comparing arrest recidivism among respondents who were interviewed and those not interviewed. The prevalence of rearrest was 10.6% for those interviewed and 10.4% for those not interviewed, and the average number of rearrests was .126 and .104, respectively. These differences were not statistically significant.

Two types of outcome measures were included in the research design. The first was official recidivism as measured by new arrests and complaints for any crimes committed by suspects against victims, as found in official police records. The second was a victim report of three forms of repeated violence: (1) fear of injury, (2) pushing-hitting, and (3) physical injury. Both types of outcome measures permit assessment of the effects of differential treatment on preventing subsequent conflict. The design called for interviewing victims twice over a six-month follow-up period; the initial interview was held at the end of the first week after the presenting offense and the second six months later.[7] All of the interviewers were women and were matched on ethnicity to victim respondents. Almost all of the interviews were conducted in the homes of respondents and *always* in absolute privacy. Twenty percent of the sampled victims did not complete their initial interview (see Table 2). When participa-

highest in satisfaction). Finally, when victims were asked whether they were better or worse off because the police came, there were no statistically significant differences between the treatment groups in their responses. Although not conclusive, these data suggest that motivation to call the police for new conflicts was not affected by the treatment received at the presenting offense.

[7] Twelve-month follow-up interviews were also conducted. However, due to funding limitations, 12-month interviews and record searches were conducted during the data analysis and write-up periods of the original grant and were thus not available to be included in this presentation.

Table 2. Interview Completion Information, Initial and Six-Month Follow-Up Interviews

	Initial Interviews					Eligible Follow-up Interviews				Total Interviews	
	Completed		Not Completed		Total	Completed		Not Completed		Completed	
Disposition	N	%	N	%	Cases	N	$\%^a$	N	%	N	$\%^b$
Mediate	91	79.1	24	20.9	115	85	93.4	6	6.6	85	73.9
Separate	89	84.0	17	16.0	106	80	89.9	9	10.1	80	75.5
Arrest	83	76.2	26	23.8	109	77	92.8	6	7.2	77	70.6
Total	263	79.7	67	20.3	330	242	92.0	21	8.0	242	73.3

[a] The proportion of cases with initial interviews completing six-month follow-up interviews.
[b] The proportion of cases with initial and six-month follow-up interviews.

tion was dichotomized and compared (chi-square) by treatment groups to determine if rates were disproportionate to any particular treatment, no statistically significant differences were found. The overall completion rate for the six-month interview (including initial losses) was 73%. Again, losses were not disproportionate for any particular treatment group. Of the 21 cases lost from the first to the second interview, all but 2 (90%) were lost because victims had moved and could not be located.

TREATMENT CONTENT

Apart from instructing officers to advise suspects assigned to separation to stay away from victims for a minimum of eight hours, no attempt was made to standardize treatments. Precise treatment content, as a result, is not easily determined. The sources of descriptive information about treatment content include police records of police actions (Domestic Violence Report) and victim reports of what the police did. Such reports were not always definitive, however. The reports the police provided were brief, involving demographic information, a short checklist of action taken, and a narrative of the presenting offense and injuries. Victim reports were problematic in other ways. First, not all victims were interviewed (80% completed an initial interview). Second, victims were not always sure of what happened during, and as a result of, police interventions. Standard police practice often involves separating victims and suspects for interrogation while at the scene of a crime, and victims sometimes made poorly informed assumptions about the content of the treatment given to suspects. When the interviewers asked victim respondents about the action taken by the police (treatment), the interviewers were instructed to follow up on the treatment that the victims reported as being given rather than the treatment that was assigned. It was not practical, it was reasoned, to ask respondents questions about treatments that were not perceived as being delivered.

The substance of treatment is probably best described by respondents who reported themselves or their assailants as receiving a given treatment, irrespective of the treatments randomly assigned. However, when the proportion of victims randomly assigned to a treatment and reporting on that treatment is specified, the extent to which characteristics of that treatment are delivered as assigned can be assessed. The following descriptions of treatment content were obtained from police reports and from interviews with victims who reported on treatments.

Eighty-one victims reported that a *mediation* treatment had been given. The most common counsel given in mediation was to advise victims to leave (21%) or to give victims legal advice (17%; how to get a restraining order, what constitutes probable cause for an arrest, etc.). Very little was done in the way of referral or actual counseling. Thirty percent of the victims identifying the treatment as mediation reported that the police did advise them to seek outside help, and 24% reported that the police told them where to go to get help. According to victims, the presence of the police tended to stop the fights they were having with suspects (77%), and the explanation most frequently given for this effect was that they or the suspects left as a result of police intervention. Finally, victims reported that the police seldom took sides (17% of the time) when responding to calls for assistance and that when they did it was evenly divided between them and suspects. The mean time spent in the mediation process was estimated by victims to be 23 minutes, and the length of time the police were on site was estimated to be 29 minutes. Mediation, as delivered in Omaha, was generally little more than the restoration of order. With few exceptions the police simply calmed the protagonists and then left, doing so as quickly as circumstances permitted. No informed or systematic approach to counseling could be said to describe the mediation delivered. Finally, 76% (69 cases) of the 91 victims interviewed who were randomly assigned to mediation reported on mediation.

Ninety-one victims reported on their experiences in the *separation* treatment. The police achieved separation by asking suspects to leave in 68% of the cases (n = 62) and victims to leave in the other 32% of the cases (n = 29). The majority went to stay with a relative (40%) or friend (16%). The average length of separation was almost three full days (70 hours). Two-thirds (67%) of the victims reported the separation as lasting eight hours or longer and 23% were apart for two hours or less. Eighty-seven percent of the victims reported that the presence of the police stopped the trouble they were having with suspects. The reason most often given was that one or the other left as a result of the police intervention. The police were also reported by victims as taking sides 23% of the time and that they (victims) were favored two-thirds of the time when the police did so. The mean length of time police were present as estimated by victims was 37 minutes. Given the lack of authority to force people legally living together to separate, the success that officers had in getting people to separate was notable, and the average length of time that couples remained apart (three days) was striking. Eighty-four percent (75 cases) of the 89 interviewed victims whose cases were randomly assigned to separation answered questions about this disposition.

Ninety-seven victims responded to questions about the *arrest* treatment. Sixty percent of the total reporting an arrest indicated that they did not want the police to arrest suspects, 65% reported that suspects blamed them for the arrests, and 21% indicated that suspects threatened them because of the arrests. Ninety-three percent of the victims reported that the police presence stopped the violence, two-thirds (66%) of whom cited the arrest as the reason for the restoration of order. This was not surprising given that 95% of the victims reported that suspects went to jail. Twenty-nine percent of the victims reported the police as taking sides, 78% of whom reported the police as taking their (victims') side. The mean estimated length of time that the police were on site was 37 minutes. The total time in custody (the time from the point of cuffing the suspect at arrest through release) was not available. Time in custody was measured as the period from booking to release. However, the *minimum* time an arrested person could be in custody, from the point of arrest to the point of booking, was estimated by police officers to be a little over one hour. Less than 20% of those booked as part of the experiment were released from custody within two hours. The average length of time in jail (from the point of booking through release to post bond,[8] as measured by the jail) was 15 hours and 46 minutes for those randomly assigned to arrest. Jail records also indicated that bond amounts assessed against suspects ranged from $50 to $850, most frequently for either $350 (65%) or $100 (26%). About half (47%) of the suspects were released on bond and the other half (50%) were released after going to court. Three percent received pretrial release or were transferred to other facilities. An arrest for domestic assault in Omaha was not a trivial issue. Ninety percent (75 cases) of the 83 victims whose assailants were randomly assigned to arrest reported on the arrest experience.

DATA SOURCES

Data for the Omaha replication experiment came from three general sources: victim reports, Domestic Violence Report forms, and police and court records.

[8] Jail records list the time at which a suspect is sent from the jail up to the third floor of the department to post bond as the point of release from jail. This should not be confused with a release from custody, which does not occur until the bonding process is completed.

Victim Reports

Victims were interviewed three times over a one-year period about prior experiences with domestic violence, the presenting offense, and subsequent feelings about and experiences with suspects. Although the information obtained from victims was quite comprehensive, the only victim-reported information used in the analyses for this paper involved demographic characteristics, a few background measures used as control variables, and four outcome measures. Inasmuch as this paper focuses on the replication of the Minneapolis experiment, variables used in the Omaha study were limited to the kinds of variables used in the analyses of that experiment. Additional analyses are currently in progress, however, in which most of the victim-reported measures obtained in Omaha are used extensively to test a large number of hypotheses about domestic violence (Dunford and Elliott, 1989).

Domestic Violence Reports

When police officers encountered domestic disturbances of any sort they were to fill out a Domestic Violence Report and send it to headquarters at the end of each shift, along with all their other reports. Although it was impossible to determine how faithful officers were in this regard, Domestic Violence Reports were turned in for all but two of the eligible cases referred to the experiment. The reports contained the officers' accounts of the presenting offense, along with demographic information for victims and suspects.

Official Records

The records of the Police Record Bureau, the jail, and the court were searched at six- and twelve-month intervals after the presenting offense to determine the incidence of arrests, complaints, and warrants for old and new offenses. The date and type of each offense were recorded for each offense record found, the records were read to determine if the presenting victims and suspects were involved, and the results of court actions were noted, when they were known.

FINDINGS

Omaha-Minneapolis Comparisons

The major characteristics of the Minneapolis and Omaha experiments are presented in Table 3 for comparative purposes. Although the two experiments are quite similar across most of the comparisons specified in Table 3, they differ on a few key points. Differences in the penalties resulting from court appearances associated with random assignment to arrest, differences in the areas of the cities covered by the experiments, differences in interview completion rates, and differences in outcome measures and the way they were aggregated may affect the relevance of the two experiments for one another.

Treatment Effects

The effects of treatments/dispositions as randomly assigned were examined using each of the five outcome measures (official arrest and complaints and three victim reports of repeated violence) obtained during the six-month period following the date of entry into the experiment. Data are presented for each comparison and statistical assessments of differences in the prevalence and frequency of repeat offending are made. In comparisons using victim reports, missing cases were included in the analyses to allow for the examination of the effect of missing data on the experimental design.[9]

Findings for the two official measures of failure (arrests and complaints) are presented in Table 4. The two are presented separately to facilitate interpretation. Arrest was defined as a subsequent arrest for any incident in which the original suspect victimized the original victim or an incident in which an original victim and suspect pair came back into the experiment as an eligible case (i.e., a misdemeanor assault). Repeat cases (e.g., cases referred by officers to the study for a second time) were considered to be repeat arrests, because eligibility for inclusion in the experiment required the existence of probable cause for an arrest for a misdemeanor assault. Complaints were defined as official reports taken by police officers from the original victims implicating original suspects, as found in the records of the Police Record Bureau.

A review of the prevalence rates and mean frequencies in Table 4 tells the outcome of the experiment, by and large, independent of statistical tests: arresting suspects had no more effect on deterring future arrests or complaints (involving the same suspects and victims) than did separating or counseling them. The overall statistical comparisons revealed no significant differences in the prevalence or frequency of offending between treatment groups.

When the crimes associated with the repeat arrests noted in Table 4 were tabulated by offense charge, 27 of the charges (68%) were for assault, 8 (20%) were for disorderly conduct, 2 (5%) were for criminal mischief, and one each (2.5%)

---

[9] The extent of missing data in the arrest and complaint data is unkown since the absence of an official record may be due to recording failures or to official actions taken in other police-court jurisdictions.

Table 3. Comparison of Selected Characteristics in the Minneapolis and Omaha Experiments

	Minneapolis Experiment	Omaha Replication
Relationship of Suspect to Victim		
Divorce or Separated Husband	3%	1%
Unmarried Lover/Boyfriend	45%	39%
Ex-lover/Boyfriend	—	9%
Current Husband	35%	42%
Wife/Girlfriend/Ex-girlfriend	2%	4%
Relative, Roommate, Other	15%	5%
Inclusiveness of the Experiments		
Total City Coverage	No[a]	Yes
Twenty-four Hour Coverage	Yes	No[b]
All Officers on Shift Involved	No[c]	Yes
Every Day	Yes	Yes
Police Information		
Number of Officers Eligible to Make Referrals	52	194
Concentration of Refusals		
3 Officers	28%	12%
Sampling Period (mo.)	16½	18
Sample sizes		
Mediate	92	115
Separate	108	106
Arrest	114	109
Total	314	330
Mean Number of Referrals per Month	18.5	18.3
Follow-up Period (mo.)	6	6[d]
Proportion of Cases Misapplied	17.8[e]	7.9
Interview Data		
Proportion of Initial Interviews Completed	62%	80%
Proportion of Interviews Completed after 6-month Follow-up	49%	73%
Face-to-face Interviews Only	No	Yes
Incentive Payments—All Interviews	No	Yes
Outcome Measures		
Official Arrest for Repeated Domestic Conflict of Any Sort	Yes	Yes
Official Complaint Reports Taken from Victims by Police Officers	Yes	Yes
Reports by Project Staff of Police Interventions for Repeated Domestic Conflict	Yes	No
Victim Reports of Episodes in Which She/He		
a. Was Actually Assaulted	Yes	Yes[f]
b. Was Threatened with Assault	Yes	No
c. Had Property Damage	Yes	No
d. Felt in Danger of Being Physically Hurt	No	Yes
e. Was Pushed, Hit, or Hands Laid on Them	No	Yes
f. Was Physically Injured	No	Yes
g. Date of 1st, 2nd, 3rd Victim-reported Repeat Episodes with Injury	No	Yes

(continued)

Table 3. (continued)

	Minneapolis Experiment	Omaha Replication
Proportion of Repeat Offenders Sentenced to Jail/Probation/Fines	2%	64%
Unemployment		
Victims	61%	50%
Suspects	60%	31%
Prior Assaults and Police Involvement		
Victims Assaulted by Suspect in Prior 6 Months	80%	52%[g]
Police Intervention in Domestic Dispute, Last 6 Months	60%	—
Victims Reporting the Police Ever Coming to Victim's Assistance Because the Suspect Was Hitting or Threatening Her/Him	—	64%
Couple in Counseling Program	27%	11%
Prior Arrests of Male Suspects		
Ever Arrested for Any Offense	59%	65%
Ever Arrested on Domestic Violence Statute	5%	—
Ever Arrested for Any Offense Against Victim	—	11%
Arrested for Any Offense Against Victims in Prior 6 Months	—	3%
Mean Age (yr.)		
Victims	30	31
Suspects	32	31

	Minneapolis		Omaha	
	Victims	Suspects	Victims	Suspects
Education				
> High School	43%	42%	34%	31%
High School Only	33%	36%	43%	50%
< High School	24%	22%	23%	19%
Ethnicity				
White	57%	45%	56%	50%
Black	23%	36%	37%	43%
Hispanic	—	—	3%	4%
Native American	18%	16%	4%	3%
Other	2%	3%	.3%	—

[a]Two precincts.

[b]4 p.m. to midnight.

[c]Specifically trained domestic violence officers only.

[d]12-month follow-up measures were also obtained in Omaha, but were not available for this report.

[e]Because of the variability between definitions of misapplication, care must be exercised in the interpretation of these proportions.

[f]Victim reports of assault were determined in Omaha on the basis of four measures (see d through g), each measure providing a different dimension of assault.

Victim reported data are based upon 205 initial interviews in Minneapolis and 263 initial interviews in Omaha.

[g]Assault was determined in Omaha by victim reports of being physically hurt by suspects in the 6 months prior to the presenting offense.

Table 4. Prevalence and Mean Frequency ($\bar{X}$) of Arrest and Complaint Recidivism Six Months after the Presenting Offense

Number of Official Actions	Arrest Recidivism				Complaint Recidivism			
	Mediate	Separate	Arrest	Total	Mediate	Separate	Arrest	Total
0	105 91.3	94 88.7	96 88.1	295	98 85.2	87 81.1	90 82.6	275
1	9 7.8	12 11.3	10 9.2	31	15 13.0	15 14.2	12 11.0	42
2	—	—	3 2.8	3	2 1.7	3 2.8	5 4.6	10
3	1 .9	—	—	1	—	1 .9	1 .9	2
4	—	—	—		—	—	1 .9	1
Total N (Cases)	115	106	109	330	115	106	109	330
Total Number Events	12	12	16	40	19	24	29	72
Prevalence*	8.7	11.3	11.9		14.8	17.9	17.4	
$\bar{X}$x Frequency**	.104	.113	.147		.165	.226	.266	

*χ^2 = .700 d.f. = 2 p = .705
**F = .385 p = .681
t value = .19 d.f. = 217 p = .851
t value = .78 d.f. = 216 p = .435
t value = .66 d.f. = 200 p = .513

*χ^2 = .460 d.f. = 2 p = .794
**F = .950 p = .388
t value = .94 d.f. = 197 p = .350
t value = 1.34 d.f. = 178 p = .183
t value = .48 d.f. = 205 p = .635

**Mediate vs. Separate
**Mediate vs. Arrest
*Separate vs. Arrest

were for trespassing, failing to leave on request, and destruction of property. When statistical tests for differences in arrest outcome were limited to the 27 repeat assault cases, no differences by treatment were found.

Comparisons of victim reports of repeated violence, as shown in Table 5, also resulted in no statistically significant differences between treatment groups, although the interpretation of the findings was complicated somewhat by the presentation of missing data. When the analyses presented in Table 5 were repeated without including missing data as an outcome (to check the possible effect missing data had on the statistical tests), again there were no statistically significant differences (table not shown). In comparing the two analyses (with and without missing data), the prevalence and frequency of victim reported injury for the arrest treatment group were slightly lower, but not statistically significant, and this difference was not found in comparisons involving official measures of failure. Given the absence of any statistically significant differences, the hypothesis of no differences among groups cannot be rejected. Thus, it was concluded that victims whose partners were arrested were no less likely to experience repeated violence from that partner than were victims whose partners received a randomized "separate" or "mediate" disposition from the police.

It is important to note that the data do not favor any specific type of treatment. Repeated domestic violence did not appear to be related to police decisions to arrest suspects, to separate them from victims, or to mediate disputes in which they were involved. Further, the same outcome was observed[10] when similar

analyses were conducted to control for (1) prior arrests, (2) ethnicity, or (3) time spent in jail;[11] or to cases limited to (4) couples in conjugal relationships at the time of the presenting offense, (5) cohabitants who had lived together for the entire six-month follow-up period,[12] or (6) persons who had lived together for at least some time during the follow-up period.

The 7% misapplication rate reported earlier prompted the collapsing of the two unofficial police responses (mediate and separate) into one category in order to reduce the effects of misapplication. This procedure also facilitated tests for the effects of arrest (or punishment) versus no arrest (or no punishment), as sug-

---

[10] In addition, the analyses conducted experimentally for Treatment as Assigned were repeated for Treatment as Immediately and as Ultimately Deliv-ered with quite similar results. The conclusions based on the former were not changed by the latter. These data are available on request from the first author.

[11] A common question concerning the finding of no difference for the replication experiment focuses on the amount of time that suspects randomly assigned to arrest spent in jail. The assumption is that the no-difference finding might be attributable to the fact that those randomly assigned to arrest did not spend a fixed amount of time in jail, as they did in Minneapolis. That is, not all arrested suspects spent at least eight hours in jail. To test the effects that time in jail might have had in deterring continued domestic violence, the outcome analyses were repeated controlling for the amount of time spent in jail by those assigned to the arrest treatment. When the original outcome analyses were repeated limiting the samples to suspects who had spent in excess of 2, 4, 8, 12, or 24 hours in jail, no differences in the effect of the three treatments in the replication experiment were found. Further, an inverse relation characterized the correlations between the time spent in jail and each of the three victim-reported outcome measures, but positive correlations were found for the two official outcome measures. The size of the negative correlations (r), however, was quite small (.02 to .04) and none was statistically significant.

[12] When treatments were compared on whether cohabiting couples had lived together at any time during the six-month follow-up period, no significant statistical differences were found (mediate = 72%, separate = 72%, arrest = 75%). Further, when those living together for the full six months were compared with all others, again no statistical differences were found (mediate = 65%, separate = 58%, arrest = 59%).

Table 5. Victim-reported Outcomes During the Six-Month Follow-up Period by Treatment

Outcome	Victim Felt Endangered[a]				Victim Pushed or Hit[b]				Victim Physically Injured[c]			
	Mediate	Separate	Arrest	Total	Mediate	Separate	Arrest	Total	Mediate	Separate	Arrest	Total
Yes	41	39	44	124	35	34	29	98	23	22	16	61
	35.7	36.8	40.4		30.4	32.1	26.6		20.0	20.8	14.7	
No	44	41	33	118	50	46	48	144	62	58	61	181
	38.7	38.7	30.3		43.5	43.4	44.0		53.9	54.7	56.0	
Missing	30	26	32	88	30	26	32	88	30	26	32	88
	26.1	24.5	29.4		26.1	24.5	29.4		26.1	24.5	29.4	
Total N (Cases)	115	106	109	330	115	106	109	330	115	106	109	330
Frequency**	2.576	1.875	2.416		1.482	1.750	2.104		.635	.800	.558	

[a] Question: How many times since the event we talked about six months ago have you and (Offender) been involved in a fight or disagreement *in which you felt* that you were in danger of being physically hurt?

[b] Question: How many times since the event we talked about six months ago has (Offender) actually pushed, hit or laid hands on you in some way as part of a fight or disagreement you were having?

[c] Question: In how many fights or disagreements were you physically injured (e.g., knocked down, bruised, scratched, cut, choked, bones broken, eyes or teeth injured)?

	Victim Felt Endangered	Victim Pushed or Hit	Victim Physically Injured
	$\chi^2 = 2.220$ d.f. = 4 p = .695	$\chi^2 = 1.072$ d.f. = 4 p = .899	$\chi^2 = 1.828$ d.f. = 4 p = .767
	**F = .176 p = .838	**F = .319 p = .727	**F = .244 p = .784
**Mediate vs. Separate	t value = .54 d.f. = 115 p = .590	t value = .40 d.f. = 156 p = .689	t value = -.45 d.f. = 129 p = .654
**Mediate vs. Arrest	t value = .12 d.f. = 137 p = .908	t value = .76 d.f. = 127 p = .452	t value = .26 d.f. = 151 p = .794
**Separate vs. Arrest	t value = .61 d.f. = 139 p = .545	t value = .41 d.f. = 140 p = .685	t value = .62 d.f. = 142 p = .536

gested by Binder and Meeker (1988). The two nonarrest treatments are conceptualized as informal police responses to domestic violence. This "informal" treatment group could then be compared with an arrest group, where arrest is considered a "formal" police response to assault. This conceptualization limits the assumptions made about the content of treatment to the presence or absence of an arrest. Collapsing the data in this way reduced the level of misapplication to 3%, which eliminated over 50% of the disjunction between treatment assigned and treatment delivered while maintaining the integrity of the experimental design. The results of the comparisons involving formal and informal treatments, which are shown in Tables 6 and 7, do not alter any of the conclusions drawn thus far. No statistical tests or consistent trends in the data favored arresting suspects as opposed to not arresting them,

for any of the five outcome measures used to assess failure.[13]

Time-To-Failure Analysis

Notwithstanding an inability to find differences in the prevalence and frequency of repeat offending between treatment groups six months after the presenting offense, it is still possible that one treatment may delay repeated instances of conflict longer than other treatments. If, for example, the Minneapolis experiment's (Sherman and Berk, 1984b) finding that arrest delayed recidivism for sig-

---

[13] To replicate the methodology of the Minneapolis experiment, in which repeat cases were treated as new cases, the analyses conducted here were repeated on a reconstructed data set in which repeat cases in Omaha were counted not only as failures for originally submitted cases, but as new cases as well. Analyses of this reconstructed data set did not alter the findings previously reported (Dunford et al., 1989).

Table 6. Prevalence (P) and Mean Frequency ($\bar{X}$) of Arrest and Complaint Recidivism Six-Months after the Presenting Offense, Informal vs. Formal Treatment

Number of Official Actions	Arrest Recidivism			Complaint Recidivism		
	Informal	Formal	Total	Informal	Formal	Total
0	199	96	295	185	90	275
	90.0	88.1		83.7	82.6	
1	21	10	31	30	12	42
	9.5	9.2		13.6	11.0	
2	—	3	3	5	5	10
		2.8		2.3	4.6	
3	1	—	1	1	1	2
	.5			.5	.9	
4	—	—	—		1	1
					.9	
Total N (Cases)	221	109	330	221	109	330
Total Number Events	24	16	40	43	29	72
Prevalence*	10.0	11.9		16.3	17.4	
Frequency**	.109	.147		.195	.266	

$*\chi^2 = .299$ d.f. = 1 p = .584 $*\chi^2 = .068$ d.f. = 1 p = .794
$**$F = .742 p = .390 $**$F = 1.224 p = .269
t value = .81 d.f. = 183 p = .420   t value = .99 d.f. = 163 p = .324

Table 7. Victim-reported Outcome of Fear of Being Physically Hurt; Pushed, Hit, or Manhandled; or of Being Physically Injured by the Suspect During the Six-Month Follow-up Period, Informal vs. Formal Treatment

	Victim Felt Endangered			Victim Pushed or Hit			Victim Physically Injured		
Prevalence	Informal	Formal	Total	Informal	Formal	Total	Informal	Formal	Total
Yes	80	44	124	69	29	98	45	16	61
	36.2	40.4		31.2	26.6		20.4	14.7	
No	85	33	118	96	48	144	120	61	181
	38.5	30.3		43.4	44.0		54.3	56.0	
Missing	56	32	88	56	32	88	56	32	88
	25.3	29.4		25.3	29.4		25.3	29.4	
Total N (Cases)	221	109	330	221	109	330	221	109	330
Frequency**	2.236	2.416		1.612	2.104		.715	.558	
Informal vs. Formal	$*\chi^2=2.148$ d.f.=2 p=.342 **F=.027 p=.869 t value=.18 d.f.=193 p=.855			$*\chi^2=.972$ d.f.=2 p=.615 **F=.520 p=.472 t value=.63 d.f.=111 p=.529			$*\chi^2=1.754$ d.f.=2 p=.416 **F=.262 p=.609 t value=.54 d.f.=171 p=.589		

nificantly longer periods of time than other treatments could be replicated, it would have policy implications quite independent of the failure to replicate the Minneapolis prevalence outcomes in Omaha.

The analytical approach used in the time-to-failure analysis involved a simple, nonparametric life-table and survival-analysis procedure employing the Kaplan and Meier (1958) product-limit estimate of the survival distribution. As implemented, the procedure (Dixon et al., 1985) calculated the number of days to failure for arrest, complaints, and victim-reported injuries using the date of the presenting offense as the starting point and the date of the first failure (arrest, complaint, or injury) per case as the point of failure. The survival curves were then compared for equality over time, using the Mantel–Cox (1966) test for differences. The results of these procedures are illustrated in Figure 1.

The survival curves plotted for each of the three outcome measures reveal no consistent differences between groups, and the results of the statistical tests indicate that the hypothesis of no differences in time to failure should not be rejected. There were no real differences between the treatment survival curves, and when the small differences that did appear were reviewed, the results were inconsistent— arrest treatment tended to fail earliest when rearrest was the outcome, latest when victim-reported injury was the outcome, and in between the other two when complaint was the outcome.[14]

Right-hand censoring is an obvious problem for the survival analysis in the sense that a repeat conflict had not occurred for all cases by the end point of the analysis (Tuma and Hannan, 1984). Only 11% of the suspects in the replication experiment were rearrested for a crime against the original victim during the six-month follow-up period. Note, however, that the failures were evenly spread across the three treatment groups (mediate = 10, separate = 12, arrest = 13). The magnitude of the right-hand censoring problem was similar for the other outcome measures: 17% of the suspects had at least one official complaint filed against them, and 18% of the victims reported that suspects had physically injured them in the interim six-month period. Given the paucity and distribution of repeat cases found for the treatment groups and the obvious lack of substantive or statistical differences, the continued use of more elaborate and complex life-table analyses was deemed unwarranted. After six months at risk, no one treatment group could be described as requiring more time to fail than any other treatment group.

DISCUSSION

Conclusions based on the results of the research conducted in Omaha must be considered together with the outcomes of the five other research efforts currently funded by the National Institute of Justice to replicate the Minneapolis experiment. Since the results from all of these studies are not yet available, what follows must

---

[14] As additional checks on the effects of experimental treatments, composite measures of the prevalence of recidivism were developed based on the three victim-reported measures of recidivism and the two official measures of recidivism. These measures were aggregated a number of different ways and compared by experimental treatments. No statistically significant differences were found. When survival analyses were completed for Total

Failure (repeat arrests + repeat complaints + victim-reported reinjury) and for Total Assault (repeat arrests for assault + repeat complaints for assault + victim-reported reinjury), no statistically significant differences in the survival curves were found.

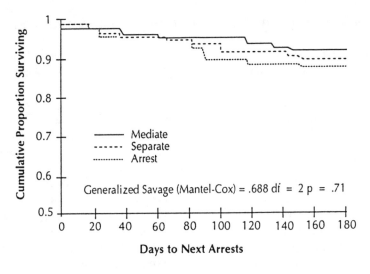

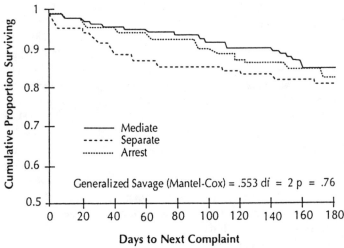

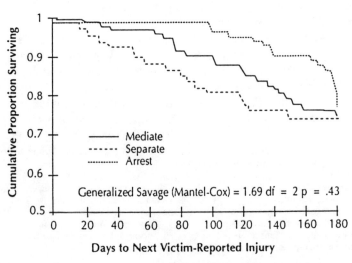

Figure 1. Survival Functions for Arrest, Complaint, and Victim-reported Injury, by Treatment Groups

be considered tentative. It must also be remembered that the results of the Omaha experiment cannot be generalized beyond Omaha nor beyond the types of cases defined as eligible during the hours of the experiment. Finally, although a serious attempt was made to replicate the Minneapolis experiment in Omaha, comparisons of the details of the two experiments reveal a number of significant differences. Whether these differences account for the differences in the findings of the two experiments is uncertain.

Given the strength of the experimental design used in Omaha and the absence of any evidence that the design was manipulated in any significant way, the inability to replicate findings associated with the Minneapolis experiment calls into question any generalization of the Minneapolis findings to other sites. First, arrest in Omaha, by itself, did not appear to deter subsequent domestic conflict any more than did separating or mediating those in conflict. Arrest, and the immediate period of custody associated with arrest, was not the deterrent to continued domestic conflict that was expected. If the Omaha findings should be replicated in the other five sites conducting experiments on this issue, policy based on the presumptory arrest recommendation coming out of the Minneapolis experiment may have to be reconsidered. Second, although arrest, by itself, did not act as a deterrent to continued domestic conflict for the misdemeanor domestic assault cases coming to the attention of the Omaha police, neither did it increase continued domestic conflict between parties to an arrest for assault. That is, victim-reported measures of repeated conflict, which are measures of behavior (as opposed to arrest and complaint data, which are measures of official police reaction to known violations of the law), clearly did not indicate that victims whose partners were arrested were at greater risk of subsequent conflict than were those whose partners were handled informally (mediated or separated) by the police. Arrest did not appear to place victims in greater danger of increased conflict than did separation or mediation. It would appear that what the police did in Omaha after responding to cases of misdemeanor domestic assault (arrest, separate, mediate), neither helped nor hurt victims in terms of subsequent conflict.

The failure to replicate the Minneapolis findings will undoubtedly cast some doubt on the deterrent power of a mandatory or even a presumptory arrest policy for cases of misdemeanor domestic assault. At this point, researchers and policymakers are in the awkward position of having conflicting results from two experiments and no clear, unambiguous direction from the research on this issue. Nevertheless, the data from the Omaha police experiment clearly suggest that the adoption of an arrest policy for cases of misdemeanor domestic assault may not, by itself, have any impact on the likelihood of repeated violent acts. For those who are directly involved in responding to domestic assaults, it might be profitable to begin thinking about new or additional strategies for dealing with this problem.

REFERENCES

Binder, Arnold and James W. Meeker. 1988. Experiments as reforms. Journal of Criminal Justice 16(4): 347–358.

Cohn, Ellen G. and Lawrence W. Sherman. 1987. Police policy on domestic violence. Paper presented at the annual meeting of the Academy of Criminal Justice Sciences, St. Louis.

Dixon, Wilfrid J., Morton B. Brown, L. Engelman, J. W. Frane, M. A. Hill, R. I. Jennrich, and J. D. Toporek. 1985.

BMDP Statistical Software. Berkeley: University of California Press.

Dunford, Franklyn W. and Delbert S. Elliott. 1989. Extension of the Omaha Spousal Assault Experiment. Grant No. CVR1R01 MH45082-01, National Institute of Mental Health, Bethesda, Md.

Dunford, Franklyn W., David Huizinga, and Delbert S. Elliott. 1989. The Omaha Domestic Violence Police Experiments. Final report to the National Institute of Justice, Washington, D.C.

Elliott, Delbert S. 1989. The evaluation of criminal justice procedures in family violence crimes. In Lloyd Ohlin and Michael Tonry (eds.), Crime and Justice: An Annual Review of Research. Vol. 11, Family Violence. Chicago: University of Chicago Press.

Glass, Gene V. and Julian C. Stanley. 1970. Statistical Methods in Education and Psychology. Englewood Cliffs, N.J.: Prentice-Hall.

Kaplan, E. L. and Paul Meier. 1958. Nonparametric estimation from incomplete observations. Journal of the American Statistical Association 53: 457–481.

Lempert, Richard. 1989. Humility is a virtue: On the publicization of policy-relevant research. Law and Society Review 23(1): 145–161.

Mantel, Nathan. 1966. Evaluation of survival data and new rank order statistics arising in its consideration. Cancer Chemotherapy Reports 50: 163–170.

Morash, Merry. 1986. Wife battering. Criminal Justice Abstracts 18: 252–271.

National Institute of Justice. 1986. Replicating an experiment in specific deterrence: Alternative police response to spouse assault. Research Solicitation. U.S. Department of Justice, Washington, D.C.

Sherman, Lawrence W. and Richard A. Berk. 1984a. The Minneapolis Domestic Violence Experiment. Police Foundation Reports. Washington, D.C.: Police Foundation.

———. 1984b. The specified deterrent effects of arrest for domestic assault. American Sociological Review 49(2): 261–272.

Sherman, Lawrence W. and Ellen G. Cohn. 1989. The impact of research on legal policy: The Minneapolis domestic violence experiment. Law and Society Review 23(1): 117–144.

Tuma, Nancy B. and Michael T. Hannan. 1984. Social Dynamics: Models and Methods. Orlando, Fla.: Academic Press.

U.S. Department of Commerce. 1983. Census of Population and Housing. Omaha: Bureau of Census.

Williams, Kirk R. and Richard Hawkins. 1989. The meaning of arrest for wife assault. Criminology 27: 163–181.

Coordinated Criminal Justice Interventions and Recidivism Among Batterers

Michael Steinman
University of Nebraska—Lincoln

INTRODUCTION

A major theme of this book is that treating woman battering effectively requires agencies with different roles and kinds of expertise to coordinate their efforts. Using a before and after research design, this chapter examines whether arrest policies coordinated with other criminal justice interventions are related to recidivism among batterers.*

POLICY RESPONSES TO BATTERING

The Minneapolis domestic violence experiment raised expectations that a single intervention, arrest, and temporary incarceration, could lower battering rates (Sherman & Berk, 1984). However, findings from the Omaha replication of this experiment (Dunford, Huizinga & Elliott, 1989) and conversations with researchers involved in other replications indicate that police action alone is not a panacea.

This news will disappoint those who were influenced by publicity about the Minneapolis experiment to think that the police could lower battering rates signifi-

cantly by themselves. It will not disappoint conservatives committed to patriarchal authority and to traditional roles for women. They are likely to use the replications' findings to criticize arrest policies and to demand that police chiefs do away with them.

The results of the replications will not surprise students of the policy process familiar with the difficulties of treating complex problems. Nor will it surprise personnel in shelters and men's anger control programs who are sensitive to the many causes, symptoms, and effects associated with battering. They know how little any one intervention can accomplish by itself.

Complex strategies are needed to treat complex problems. Earlier chapters have reported the benefits of coordinated, multiagency efforts. This chapter's purpose is to see if coordination between the police and other criminal justice agencies is associated with recidivism rates.

Three kinds of police intervention are examined: arrest, citation, and responding to a call for service but taking no formal action. Information on these interventions comes from two periods. One is an experimental period marked by

Reproduced by permission of Anderson Publishing Co. From *Woman Battering: Policy Responses.* Copyright © 1991 by Anderson Publishing Co. and Academy of Criminal Justice Sciences.

*This study was funded by state and local government agencies, businesses, and foundations in Lincoln, Nebraska and by the National Institute of Justice.

the enforcement of arrest policies coordinated with aggressive prosecution; the other is a baseline period before arrest policies and aggressive prosecution went into effect. The three police interventions represent a continuum of potentially deterrent costs. Arrest imposes the most costs and no formal action imposes the fewest. The costs imposed by arrest include a brief time in jail or the chance of it and the possibility of being prosecuted and suffering court-mandated penalties like a fine or a jail term. Arrest may also trigger indirect costs for offenders such as humiliation, divorce or separation from their partners, and loss of job (Williams & Hawkins, 1989).

Aggressive prosecution means more than prosecutors deciding to charge offenders. It also includes commitments to work with victims to gain their trust and cooperation, to prosecute offenders when they cannot get victims' cooperation, and to seek appropriate treatment for each offender (e.g., pretrial diversion services or court-ordered penalties). Thus, aggressive prosecution imposes its own costs which may include interventions by other criminal justice agencies.

Effective coordination between police and prosecutors requires certain actions. For example, police chiefs must define battering as a crime, be willing to promote this view in their departments and communities, adopt arrest policies, and monitor rank and file compliance with the policies. Chiefs must also require officers to undergo training about the dynamics of abusive relationships and why arrest policies are needed and how to implement them. Moreover, chiefs must work with prosecutors to make sure the enforcement of arrest policies is supported by prosecutions and that a track record of support is documented and publicized to officers and the community. In addition, prosecutors must take similar steps. They must define battering as a crime, charge batterers with criminal offenses, educate their staffs and the community about battering, and make sure staff are aware of police efforts.

Studies reported in earlier chapters indicate that police officers who do not see prosecutions flowing from arrest are less apt to consider battering a crime and more likely to think that arrest wastes time and contributes to more violence. Likewise, prosecutors are unlikely to give battering much time if they think they are acting alone. Taking the actions noted in the preceding paragraph forces line personnel to decide for themselves whether battering is a crime and how to respond to it. Confronted with these choices, line personnel tend to arrest and prosecute more offenders when they know others are treating battering like a crime too.

This chapter examines whether police action coordinated with other criminal justice interventions is related to recidivism rates. It is expected that coordinated interventions will be related to less recidivism when policies, training, and experience indicate to line police and prosecutors that their superiors want them to treat battering as a crime and that their efforts will be supported. This chapter also examines the relationship between coordinated criminal justice interventions and recidivism controlling for evidence that offenders have violent histories and for the nature of victim/offender relationships.

RESEARCH SETTING

The research setting is Lincoln/Lancaster County, Nebraska which has a mostly white (96%), middle-class population of over 200,000 people. Its white-collar economy is based on state government, the main campus of the state university, insurance companies, banks, and a variety of service industries. It also has a highly regarded public school system.

Coordinated efforts to stop battering began in 1985 when representatives of the local commission on the status of women, a victim support program, and a shelter approached Lincoln's police chief to persuade him that battering is a problem and that officers could reduce its incidence and protect victims by arresting offenders. These advocates for change had information from victims indicating that officers responded slowly to calls for help and that their typical response was to separate offenders and victims so the former could "cool off." These advocates argued that the police were not protecting victims from more harm.

The chief responded by identifying problems that prevented him from adopting arrest policies. Foremost among them were a disinclination among officers to get involved in what they considered domestic "disputes" and a concern that arresting or citing offenders would be wasted effort because most would avoid prosecution. At this time, most battering cases in which police did arrest or cite offenders were sent to the city attorney's office which typically gave them a very low priority. The chief's concerns led advocates for change to talk to the county attorney who said he would not give battering a priority because most victims did not cooperate with his office by filing charges when told they had to pay a $50 filing fee.

While these reactions were disappointing, the police chief and county attorney did agree that battering is a public problem and called for a multiagency approach to treat it. They pointed to the work of their own agencies to argue that policy changes in one or a few agencies would be ineffective without the coopera-

tion of all agencies with relevant missions. With their encouragement, the Justice Council, a local criminal justice coordinative body, created a special task force to develop and promote the adoption and implementation of appropriate policy options. Many agency heads were asked to serve on it in addition to those involved in earlier discussions: the county sheriff, the chair of the Judges Council, the city attorney, the public defender, the head of corrections, the head of the probation office, and the top counselor of a private men's anger control program. Since its creation, what has come to be known as the Domestic Violence Coalition (DVC) has grown to include pretrial diversion programs, the Lincoln Council on Alcoholism and Drugs, other men's anger control programs, and the police department's Victim Witness Unit. The DVC is an example of what Edleson calls a Community Intervention Project.

A major DVC-supported innovation was the adoption of arrest policies. The police department's policy states: "When violence has occurred or been threatened, irrespective of the victim's wishes, the primary responsibility of the responding officers is to investigate a crime, and if probable cause exists, to arrest the person responsible." It notes that many victims have "strong and complex reasons" not to report and testify against offenders and that the proximity of those involved makes more abuse possible. It also notes that not taking action can produce liability problems. The county sheriff's policy is similar.

The policies require officers to file reports on all incidents, including those in which they take no formal action, and to note explicitly when cases involve battering. This is meant to encourage effective enforcement and to stop officers from using radio reports when they take no formal action, a much-used practice before the policies were adopted that leaves no paper trail. Officers are also directed to give victims cards noting the telephone numbers and addresses of agencies that provide victim services. Both the police chief and sheriff require in-service training for their officers that stresses the criminal nature of battering. They did not do this before DVC efforts began. Neither department reports serious compliance problems.

The police chief and sheriff were moved to adopt arrest policies by a combination of influences including local demands for change, the well-publicized findings of the Minneapolis experiment (Sherman & Berk, 1984), and the possibility of judicial penalties for not protecting victims. In addition, they were influenced by the county attorney's decisions to handle misdemeanor cases and to prosecute offenders without requiring victims to file charges and pay a fee. The latter decision was an important step to take the onus of prosecuting off victims, to protect them from reprisal, and to inform offenders that the community does not tolerate battering. The latter decision was a major change since most cases are misdemeanors and had been handled by the city attorney's office.

The county attorney assigned all battering cases to one deputy and directed her to prosecute whenever possible, even when victim cooperation is doubtful or absent. Part of her standard operating procedure is to subpoena victims to encourage their cooperation and inform offenders that the decision to prosecute is not the victims'. She does not penalize victims who ignore the subpoenas.

The county attorney's new policies were key because they removed a significant police objection to arresting batterers by promising to support officers whenever possible. These policies and arrest policies went into effect on June 1,

1986. The DVC is committed to implementing as many coordinated interventions as possible. Its goals include putting larger numbers of carefully selected offenders in pretrial diversion programs and ensuring that other offenders appear in court to be judged guilty and punished. As will be shown later, this expectation has been realized to a large degree. In addition, DVC goals originally included commitments by one public and one private agency to contact victims within two days of every incident to make sure they get whatever help they need. Available evidence indicates that few victims, especially those in misdemeanor cases, have been contacted. As a result, this chapter focuses exclusively on criminal justice interventions. The DVC is currently considering ways to contact and service victims more effectively.

METHODOLOGY

This study compares associations between criminal justice interventions and recidivism before and after policies governing arrest and prosecution went into effect. Police incident reports and county attorney files were used to collect archival data on the first case in which every male offender was involved after June 1, 1986. Archival information was also collected from police reports when officers took no formal action. From July, 1987 to May 31, 1989, archival data on initial incidents were collected one year after each occurred. The data describe factual details about cases, the parties involved, how cases were handled by law enforcement officers, the county attorney, and other agencies, and whether the county attorney charged men with battering in subsequent cases.

After collecting archival data, efforts were made to locate and interview victims on the telephone. In addition to collecting information about initial incidents, interviews identified which victims were attacked again by offenders using a modified version of Straus's Conflict Tactics Scales (1979). Interviews were conducted by the Bureau of Sociological Research at the University of Nebraska-Lincoln. Interviewers were middle-aged women with considerable experience with telephone interviews. Their scripts introduced them to victims by stressing their university employment and invited respondents to verify their identity and purpose by calling a university extension.

Archival and interview data were also collected on cases from a 12-month baseline period running from June 1, 1985 to May 31, 1986. These cases were identified by a Lincoln police officer working in her spare time. She reviewed all police reports from this period and collected archival data on cases she believed involved battering. Given the time it took to do this, efforts to interview baseline victims did not begin until the spring, 1988.

Bureau staff located 322 victims from the experimental period, 47 of whom refused to be interviewed. The 275 victims who were interviewed represent 28.2 percent of the 974 victims in cases from this period. Interviews were conducted from 12 to 33 months after the incidents took place. The average number of months between initial incident and interview is 14.7. In addition, Bureau staff located 91 baseline victims, 28 of whom refused to be interviewed. The 63 who were interviewed represent 24 percent of the victims in 262 baseline incidents. Interviews of baseline victims were conducted from 24 to 48 months after initial incidents. The average number of months between initial baseline incident and interview is 33.1.

As with other samples of reported

cases of battering in other studies, disproportionately high percentages of cases involved minority group members and low-income people. While 4 percent of the local population is minority, minorities were involved in 27 percent of the experimental and 32 percent of the baseline cases on which archival data were collected. That most experimental (76%) and baseline (78%) incidents occurred in low-income census tracts suggests that they involved low-income people too. The often transient residential and employment histories of low-income/minority group people, their relative inability to pay for telephone service, and waiting a year to do the interviews made it difficult to find many victims. To interview as many of them as possible, Bureau staff contacted their neighbors, searched marriage license applications, used telephone and city directory records, called individuals with victims' last names hoping they were relatives and knew victims' whereabouts, and contacted victims' employers if they were noted in archival records and hospitals if victims used them after the incidents.

Very few important differences distinguish victims who were interviewed from those who were not. Not surprisingly, these few differences concern minority group status and income. Compared to figures in the above paragraph, smaller percentages of minority group members are in the experimental (18%) and baseline (16%) samples of interviewed victims; there are smaller percentages of cases from low-income census tracts (64% and 67% respectively) too. Nevertheless, minority and low-income people are still represented disproportionately compared to the community's minority and low-income populations.

The DVC's mission statement calls for the reduction of "domestic violence and its recidivism rate in Lincoln and

Lancaster County." The statement defines domestic violence as abuse "of any kind [i.e., verbal abuse and intimidating behavior as well as physical assault] . . . between two adults living under the same roof." This definition is expanded for this study to include adults who are or were in any intimate relationship, that is adults who are dating as well as those who had dated, lived together, or been married.

Recidivism is defined in this study using victim reports of physical battering. The reason for this is related to a core policy goal: protecting victims from physical violence and injury. Examining associations between interventions and post-incident physical assaults may help achieve this goal by contributing to the design and implementation of more effective policy responses.

Table 1 identifies the kinds of physical battering victims were asked about and the percentages of victims from both samples that reported experiencing them.

That the percentages are larger in the baseline data for most types of battering is a welcome finding. According to victims, 71 percent (n = 45) of the offenders from baseline cases repeated by engaging in at least 1 kind of post-incident physical abuse compared to 53 percent (n = 146) of the offenders from experimental cases.

Archival data were used to measure recidivism too. Six baseline and 11 experimental offenders whose victims did not report post-incident violence to interviewers were charged with more battering by prosecutors. Among the 11 from experimental cases, the county attorney charged 3 with attacking different victims. Information is unavailable on how many of the 6 baseline offenders attacked different victims because the city attorney's records are incomplete.

A dummy dependent variable was created and coded "1" for offenders who recidivated according to victim reports or

Table 1. Victim Reports of Post-Incident Battering Using a Modified Version of Straus' Conflict Tactics Scales*

	Baseline Period (n = 63) %	Experimental Period (n = 275) %
Has (the offender):		
Pushed, grabbed, or shoved you?	65	50
Hit or tried to hit you with something?	54	29
Slapped or spanked you?	40	27
Punched or kicked you?	41	24
Thrown you bodily?	43	27
Thrown something at you?	35	26
Bitten or scratched you?	22	11
Choked or strangled you?	25	17
Forced sex on you or forced you to do something sexual you didn't want to do?	18	14
Used a knife, gun, or other weapon on you?	6	6
Beat you until you were unconscious?	5	4
Burned you?	5	2
Hurt you with some other physical battering?	11	6

*The author is grateful to Jeffrey Edleson for advice in modifying and administering these items.

prosecutors' files and "0" for offenders who did not. Among offenders from experimental cases, 57 percent (n = 157) were coded "1" compared to 83 percent (n = 51) of the baseline offenders. All offenders are men and all victims are women.

The major independent variables are dummy variables indicating 3 police responses: taking no formal action, issuing citations to offenders, and arresting and transporting offenders to police headquarters where they were booked and often jailed for a time. In addition, the police took no action in a few cases but sent reports on them to the county attorney's office for prosecutors to decide whether to file charges. The men in these cases were grouped in the analysis with men who were cited. While they were not charged by police, their experience resembled those who were cited because they did not experience immediate costs but faced potential costs later. Finally, it was not possible to distinguish arrestees who were released after being booked from those who were jailed. However, police executives who monitor daily operations report that most arrestees spend at least a brief time in jail.

Table 2 reports police responses in the baseline and experimental periods to calls for service related to battering. While DVC innovations seem to have had little impact on whether officers took formal action in the experimental period,

their effects were major but impossible to document. Officers in the baseline period did not have to tag cases as battering-related or write reports when they took no formal action. Because they typically used their radios to report taking no formal action, the paper trail describing baseline police responses is incomplete. The actual number of battering cases is unknown as is the number of cases in which police took no formal action. This means that the percentage of baseline cases in which police took no formal action is understated in Table 2 and the percentages of baseline cases in which citations were issued and arrests were made are much smaller than reported.

Analysis compared associations between police responses and recidivism controlling for whether coordinated interventions were in place, whether offenders had criminal records or had been accused of battering before incidents, and type of victim/offender relationship. A one-tailed test of significance was applied in multiple regression analyses because it was expected that arrest policies coordinated with other interventions would be related to less recidivism.

FINDINGS

The DVC's goal is to expose offenders to certain and consistent sanctions to motivate them to avoid more sanctions by not repeating their violence. Table 3 de-

Table 2. Police Actions

	Baseline Period (n = 63) %	Experimental Period (n = 275) %
No formal police action	19	22
Citation issued	52	46
Suspect arrested	29	32
Total:	100	100

Table 3. Degrees of Offender Exposure to the Criminal Justice System*

	Baseline Period (n = 63) %	Experimental Period (n = 275) %
Only contacted by police	19	22
Cited only	27	14
Arrested only	6	4
Put in pretrial diversion	0	20
Charged by prosecutors		
but charges were dropped later for various reasons	33	19
Found not guilty in court	0	<.5
Put in probation or men's anger program	0	2
Fined under $100	5	5
Fined over $100	6	13
Jailed: For up to 90 days	2	3
For over 90 days	2	0

*Rounding off and the fact that some offenders received more than one punishment (e.g., some were fined and jailed) explains why the percentages in the experimental period total more than 100 percent.

scribes the handling of offenders during the baseline and experimental periods. It shows that more offenders were exposed to more criminal justice sanctions in the experimental period. For example, fewer men had the charges against them dismissed by prosecutors in the experimental period and more men in this period were put in pretrial diversion programs or court-ordered counseling services and were fined than in the baseline period. Additionally, 19 percent of baseline offenders were only contacted by police and not arrested or cited according to police reports. As was noted earlier, this percentage would be much larger than its experimental counterpart if the number of baseline cases in which police took no formal action was known. Likewise, the percentages of men who were only cited or arrested in the baseline period would be smaller.

The data in Table 4 suggest that coordinated efforts are useful. They show significantly less recidivism (Pearson's $r = -.19$, $p \leq .000$) among offenders from the experimental period. Eighty-three percent of the men in baseline cases re-offended compared to 57 percent of the men in experimental cases.

Table 4. DVC Interventions and Recidivism

	Baseline Period (6/1/85 to 5/31/86)	Experimental Period (After 6/1/86)
No Recidivism	12	118
	(19%)	(42.9%)
Recidivism	51	157
	(83.3%)	(57.1%)
Totals:	63	275
	(100%)	(100%)

Pearson's $r = -.19$, $p \leq .000$

Table 5. Regression of Recidivism on Police Actions Controlling for Experimental Effects (n = 338)

Police Actions:	b	t
No formal action	—omitted—	
Citation	−.01	−.10
Arrest	−.11	−1.44
Cases occurred in the experimental period	−.24	−3.52*
Constant	.84	10.62*

*≥1.64 significant at .05, one-tailed test

Determining if police responses are related to this finding required analysis regressing recidivism on them controlling for general experimental effects. A dummy variable was created measuring whether cases occurred before (=0) or after (=1) DVC efforts began. Table 5 reports the results of regressing recidivism on police responses and that dummy variable. Compared to no formal action, arrest and citation lack significant associations with recidivism although arrest's is deterrent and strong. While this analysis explained very little variance, it produced a significant coefficient indicating that offenders in experimental cases were 24 percent less likely to re-offend controlling for police responses. To understand this finding, recidivism was regressed on po-

lice responses separately for baseline and experimental cases. Table 6 reports the results.

Findings in Table 6 show that arrest is associated with about 18 percent less re-offending in the experimental period compared to no-formal action; the direction of citation's relationship with recidivism is the same but insignificant. In baseline cases, both arrest and citation are significantly related to more recidivism compared to no formal action. These results indicate that arrest coordinated with other interventions is related to significantly less recidivism and that uncoordinated police action, both arrest and citation, is related to significantly more recidivism. These are interesting findings but low rates of explained variance indicate that other influences are at work.

Table 6. Regression of Recidivism on Police Actions in Baseline and Experimental Periods

	Baseline Period (n=63)		Experimental Period (n=275)	
	b	t	b	t
Police Actions:				
No formal action (constant term)	.58	5.24*	.66	10.30*
Citation	.30	2.27*	−.07	−.91
Arrest	.25	1.74*	−.18	−2.15*
	R² = .08		R² = .02	

*≥1.64 significant at .05, one-tailed test

One such set of influences may be other criminal justice interventions. A dummy variable was created to identify men who were prosecuted ($=1$) and men who were not ($=0$). Bivariate analysis indicated that the decision to prosecute was not related to recidivism in experimental cases. However, a relationship emerged between the prosecution of cases and more violence in the baseline period (Pearson's $r = .26$). Since the city attorney handled most of these cases and gave battering a low priority, his office may have tended to prosecute men who committed more serious or violent offenses and who were less treatable. That no relationship emerged between prosecution and recidivism in experimental cases suggests that prosecution has an indirect utility because it reinforces the effects of police action.

Another bivariate analysis examined whether judicial findings of guilt and court-ordered penalties (fines, jail, or probation) were related to recidivism. A dummy variable was created to measure whether men were found guilty and sentenced ($=1$) or not ($=0$). Too few men received each kind of penalty to examine its independent association with recidivism. For example, only 7 men from experimental cases were jailed, 5 for 30 days, 1 for 60 days, and 1 for 90 days. Although all 22 percent ($n = 61$) of the offenders coded "1" from experimental cases had time to repeat, no relationship emerged between the dummy variable and recidivism. As with decisions to prosecute, the association between judicial actions and recidivism may be indirect. The courts may influence recidivism by taking battering cases seriously, thereby encouraging prosecutors to file charges and police to take formal action. Too few offenders were coded "1" ($n = 9$) to report findings from the baseline period.

Thus far, analysis has focused on DVC interventions in the expectation that

their costs will deter men from reoffending. However, some offenders may be more or less treatable. Others have reported that men with more violent histories tend to be more difficult to treat (e.g., Dutton & McGregor in this book; Sonkin et al., 1985). Two measures of whether offenders have violent histories are whether they had a criminal record at the time incidents occurred or had been accused of battering in the past. This information was available from archival sources. It is possible that men without criminal records or men who had not been accused of battering before incidents are more likely to be deterred by criminal justice interventions.

A dummy variable was created measuring whether men had a criminal record or had been accused of battering before incidents. Men with such records were coded "1" and men without them were coded "0". Fifty-four percent ($n = 34$) of the men from baseline cases were coded "1" as were 48 percent ($n = 133$) of the men from experimental cases. Bivariate analysis indicated that men coded "1" did not re-offend significantly more than men coded "0" in the baseline sample. Eighty-two percent ($n = 28$) of the baseline offenders coded "1" repeated as did 79 percent ($n = 23$) of the men coded "0". However, a small relationship (Pearson's $r = .12$) emerged in the experimental data: 63 percent ($n = 84$) of the men coded "1" repeated compared to 51 percent ($n = 73$) of the men coded "0".

Finally, analysis examined whether the nature of victim/offender relationships affects associations between interventions and recidivism. Marriage and cohabitation generally involve longer, more intimate relationships than dating and give offenders more opportunity to develop violent habits of interacting with their partners. As a result, men who were or had been in these relationships may be less treatable than daters. This possibility

Table 7. DVC Interventions and Recidivism Among Offenders Who Were or Had Been Married to or Cohabiting with Victims When Incidents Occurred

	Baseline Period (6/1/85 to 5/31/86)	Experimental Period (After 6/1/86)
No Recidivism	11 (20%)	101 (43.7%)
Recidivism	44 (80%)	130 (56.3%)
Totals:	55 (100%)	231 (100%)

Pearson's $r = -.19$, $p \leq .000$

was tested in a bivariate analysis including only offenders who were or had been married to or living with victims when incidents occurred. Another analysis examined only offenders who were dating or had dated victims when incidents occurred. Table 7 reports that DVC interventions are still related to significantly less recidivism when only offenders with marital or cohabiting histories with victims are included. The same association emerges in Table 8 regarding daters. That just eight pairs of daters are in the baseline period limits the drawing of hard and fast conclusions, however.

CONCLUSION

This chapter examined the association between police responses and recidivism among batterers when the enforcement of arrest policies is coordinated with other criminal justice interventions. It com-

pared this association with one from a baseline period before arrest policies and other new criminal justice responses were adopted and coordinated. As reported in Table 4, bivariate analysis indicated that the enforcement of arrest policies in coordination with other interventions is related to significantly less re-offending.

Regressing recidivism on particular police responses revealed that coordination was indeed related significantly to recidivism. As reported in Table 6, this analysis showed that, compared to taking no formal action, arresting and citing offenders were related to significantly more re-offending in baseline cases. It also showed that arrest was related to significantly less re-offending when the enforcement of arrest policies was coordinated with other criminal justice responses. That no police training on battering occurred in the baseline period may be important too. Bard argues that intervention

Table 8. DVC Interventions and Recidivism Among Offenders Who Were or Had Been Dating Victims When Incidents Occurred

	Baseline Period (6/1/85 to 5/31/86)	Experimental Period (After 6/1/86)
No Recidivism	1 (12.5%)	17 (38.6%)
Recidivism	7 (87.5%)	27 (61.4%)
Totals	8 (100%)	44 (100%)

by poorly trained officers can produce more violence (1971:3).

That uncoordinated police intervention is tied to significantly more recidivism shows that a traditional police argument for not taking action has some merit. Police intervention can be linked with more violence. As Chief Bouza noted in an earlier chapter, arrest policies are not an "automatic winner." However, this chapter's findings indicate that police action need not have this effect. Coordinating hierarchically supported arrest policies with prosecution and other interventions can turn police action into a deterrent. In fact, bivariate analyses suggested that the major value of other interventions is that they encourage the enforcement of arrest policies and strengthen their deterrent effects. These analyses found that prosecutors' decisions to charge offenders and judicial sanctions were not related to recidivism directly.

Other bivariate analyses indicated that coordinated effort is related to less recidivism among men who do not have a criminal record or a history of battering. This is consistent with findings reported elsewhere that interventions tend to be more effective among men who do not have violent histories. Other bivariate analyses also found that coordinated interventions were related to significantly less recidivism controlling for the kind of relationships offenders had with victims when incidents occurred. There was significantly less recidivism in the experimental period than in the baseline period among offenders who were or had been married to or living with victims when incidents occurred. The same association emerged among men who were or had been dating victims.

Finding that coordinated criminal justice interventions are related to less battering is good news. However, two caveats must be noted. The first is that the

findings reported here may not be generalizable to more socioeconomically and racially heterogeneous communities than Lincoln. The other is that low reported levels of explained variance indicate that stronger correlates remain to be found. Nevertheless, these findings are welcome because replications of the Minneapolis experiment revealing the inutility of isolated police action may produce a conservative reaction demanding a repudiation of arrest policies and the need for government intervention.

Finally, researchers looking for stronger policy correlates of recidivism should remember that identifying useful policies does not ensure their adoption or use. Service providers with responsibilities related to battering will continue to do their jobs according to their own styles and priorities. Given public expectations that the many parts of our fragmented policy system represent diverse views, most Americans would not have it any other way.

REFERENCES

Bard, M. (1971). "Iatrogenic Violence." *The Police Chief,* January: 16–17.

Dunford, F. W., D. Huizinga & D. S. Elliott (1989). *The Omaha Domestic Violence Police Experiment: Final Report.* Washington, DC: National Institute of Justice.

Sherman, L. W. & R. A. Berk (1984). "Deterrent Effects of Arrest for Domestic Assault." *American Sociological Review,* 49: 261–272.

Sonkin, D. J., D. Martin & L. Walker (1985). *The Male Batterer: A Treatment Approach.* New York: Springer Publishing.

Straus, M. A. (1979). "Measuring Intrafamily Conflict and Violence: The Conflict Tactics (CT) Scales." *Journal of Marriage and the Family,* 41: 75–88.

Williams, K. R. & R. Hawkins (1989). "The Meaning of Arrest for Wife Assault." *Criminology,* 27: 163–181.

Summary of Sherman, L. W., & Berk, R. A. (1984). The specific deterrent effects of arrest for domestic assault. *American Sociological Review, 49,* 261–272.

Method.   Between-subjects experiment, equivalent-groups design.

Hypothesis.   Police intervention in domestic violence has an influence on repeat incidence of assault. The hypothesis is causal.

Independent variables/operational definitions.   Police intervention strategy:

1. Arrest and temporary incarceration (for at least 8 hours)
2. Separation (ordering the offender from the premises for 8 hours)
3. Advice/mediation (a range of possible actions from doing nothing to mediation at the officer's discretion)

All offenders in cases of misdemeanor domestic assault were randomly assigned to receive one of the three interventions, or treatments.

Dependent variables/operational definitions.   Repeat incidence of domestic assault over a 6-month follow-up period as reported by police and victims. *Police reports* were based on official records of repeat offenses. This official outcome variable measured the amount of time elapsed between the experimental intervention and either a report of a repeat offense or the end of the 6-month follow-up period (authors refer to a "failure to survive" the follow-up period without a police-recorded report of domestic violence). The police reports came from either an offense or an arrest report written by a police officer, or a subsequent report to the project staff of "a randomized (or other) intervention by officers participating in the experiment." Thus, repeat cases of violence during the follow-up returned to the experiment as new cases. The second outcome measure was based on *victim reports* of whether or not there had been a repeat incident of "actual assault, threatened assault, or property damage" by the same suspect during the 6-month follow-up period. These data were collected in follow-up interviews with victims. Initial victim interviews were conducted in person, followed by telephone interviews every 2 weeks for 6 months (every fourth interview was conducted in person).

Findings.   Hypothesis was supported; police intervention strategy had an influence on repeat incidence of domestic assault. The police follow-up data showed that "the separation treatment produces the highest recidivism, arrest produces the lowest, with the impact of 'advise' (from doing nothing to mediation) indistinguishable from the other two effects." Victim interview data also indicated that arrested offenders had the lowest recidivism rate for assault, threatened assault, or property damage. The advice condition, however, had the highest rate of recidivism.

Controlled extraneous variables

1. Scene of assault (both suspect and victim present when police arrived)
2. Type of assault (only simple misdemeanor domestic assault)
3. Length of initial stay in jail
4. Some subject variables (see below for exceptions)

Uncontrolled extraneous variables/alternative explanations

1. There was a pattern of "upgrading" the treatments to arrest if police reported the suspect was rude or tried to assault at least one of the officers, if weapons were involved, if the victim persistently demanded a citizen's arrest, and if a restraining order was being violated. The authors inferred that "upgrading" would have led to an *underestimate* of the deterrent effects of arrest because the most difficult, and presumably, hardest-to-deter offenders were disproportionately placed in the arrest condition. (Sherman and Berk speculated that the experimental design was sometimes violated by officers who excluded or switched certain cases after deciding that the upcoming experimental treatment was inappropriate.)

2. The authors pointed out that the construct validity of the interventions was a major problem of the study, particularly because of the unclear content of the separation and advice treatments. For example, intervention through advice could have meant anything from doing nothing to some form of mediation at the officers' discretion—a very wide range of possible actions. The authors noted that the effects of arrest are "only relative to the impact of the other interventions . . . Should their content change, the relative impact of arrest could change as well" (p. 193).

3. Since victims were contacted every two weeks for 6 months, biases in their self reports may have affected the results. For example, they might have been embarrassed to report repeat assaults. Also, we could speculate that researcher expectations may have influenced victims to over- or underestimate repeat violence.

Sample/Population Sampled.   The sample consisted of 314 cases of misdemeanor domestic assault that occurred in the two precincts with the largest number of domestic violence reports in Minneapolis, Minnesota, between March 1981 and August 1982. Outcomes based on police data included all 314 cases, whereas the victim-reported data included only 161 cases for which all follow-up interviews were completed. The experiment included all cases where both suspect and victim were present when police arrived and where there was reason to believe that a cohabitant or spouse had assaulted the victim in the previous 4 hours. Felony cases were excluded.

Sampling biases.   The sample did not include domestic violence cases that occurred in low-domestic-violence areas in Minneapolis (presumably the more affluent neighborhoods) and was overrepresentative of couples that had violent histories, high unemployment, alcohol abuse, and prior arrests. Therefore, conclusions about the deterrent effect of arrest may not generalize to more affluent couples. The authors were appropriately cautious in generalizing their findings, noting that "there is a good chance that arrest works far better for some kinds of offenders than others and in some kinds of situations better than others" (p. 194).

Interactions.   Since more than a fourth of the cases were turned in by three officers, the authors investigated the interaction between "high-productivity officers" and treatments. They reported that the interaction was not significant. The authors also examined whether the arrest treatment was less effective for those who had experienced recent police intervention. No interaction was found.

Conclusions.   Arrest and temporary incarceration for misdemeanor domestic assault deters subsequent domestic violence. The authors concluded that "arrest makes an

independent contribution to the deterrence potential of the criminal justice system
. . . we favor a presumption of arrest; an arrest should be made unless there are
good, clear reasons why an arrest would be counterproductive" (p. 194.

Summary of Dunford, F. W., Huizinga, D., & Elliott, D. S. (1990). The role of arrest in domestic assault: The Omaha police experiment. *Criminology, 28,* 183–206.

Method.   Between-subjects experiment, equivalent-groups design.

Hypothesis.   Police intervention in domestic violence has an influence on repeat
incidence of assault (research hypothesis). Note that this study presents a traditional
test of a null hypothesis: that police intervention in domestic violence cases has no
influence on repeat incidence of assault. The hypothesis is causal.

Independent variables/operational definitions.   Police intervention strategy:

1. Arrest (taking offenders into custody and booking them; there was no fixed
   amount of jail time)
2. Separation (asking the suspects to leave the premises for at least 8 hours, or
   asking the victims to leave)
3. Mediation (giving counsel to the victims, such as providing legal advice and,
   occasionally, some referral or actual counseling)

The authors also examined police intervention collapsed into two categories: formal (arrest) and informal (separation and mediation).

All offenders were randomly assigned to one of the three interventions by a computerized program.

Dependent variables/operational definitions.   Five measures of repeat domestic
assault were obtained from official police records and victim reports over a 6-month
follow-up period. *Repeat arrest* was any subsequent arrest for an incident in which
the original offender victimized the original victim or an incident in which the original pair were involved in another misdemeanor assault. *Complaints* were official
police reports taken from the original victims incriminating the original suspects.
Victim reported outcomes consisted of three measures of repeated violence during the
6-month period after the police intervention. Victims reported on the number of times
they *felt endangered*, were *actually pushed or hit*, or were *physically injured*. The
victim data were collected through two personal interviews conducted just after the
presenting incident and 6 months later.

Findings.   The research hypothesis of a difference between intervention groups was
rejected (or as authors noted, they "fail to reject" the null hypothesis): police intervention strategy had no influence on repeat incidence of domestic assault. Official
records of recidivism showed no difference between the three types of police intervention in the prevalence or frequency of repeat offending. Victim reports also
showed no significant influence of treatment type on the three indicators of repeat
offending. Increased jail time also had no statistically significant effect on recidivism.
There were no differences in treatment groups in analyses of "failure to survive"
using three outcome measures of reoffending during the follow-up period (arrest,
complaint, and victim-reported injury).

Controlled extraneous variables

1. Scene of assault (both suspect and victim present when police arrived)
2. Type of assault (only simple misdemeanor domestic assault)
3. Suspect and victim at least 18 years old and cohabited sometime during the year prior to the assault
4. Subject variables (through random assignment of subjects to treatment groups)
5. Interviewers at follow-up were all female, and were matched on ethnicity with victim respondents
6. Statistical comparisons were made for prior arrests, ethnicity, time spent in jail, and couple status as married or cohabiting at the time of offense and during the 6-month follow-up period

Uncontrolled extraneous variables/alternative explanations

1. Because of some violations of the randomly assigned treatment dispositions, the authors coded each treatment into one of four categories: (1) treatment as assigned (randomly by computer), (2) treatment as officially recorded (by responding officers), (3) treatment immediately delivered (treatment actually delivered at the scene as estimated by comparing victim reports with police reports), and (4) treatment as ultimately delivered. The fourth category, treatment as ultimately delivered, was "determined by comparing treatments as assigned with what victims reported as ultimately happening and what police officers recorded . . . as ultimately happening and by comparing Arrests with official records of police, prosecuting attorney, and court actions" (p. 199). The treatment variable that was used in the analysis was *treatment as assigned*. The authors regarded the treatment as ultimately delivered category as "problematic in that the absence of an officially recorded arrest is not foolproof evidence that an arrest was not made" (p. 200). Thus, while officers arrested some offenders who were to receive mediation or separation (as they did in Minneapolis), these cases were not considered arrests. The authors explain: "If, for example, in the course of delivering Mediation a suspect assaulted an officer and was arrested, the case was defined as follows: Treatment as Assigned = Mediation; Treatment as Immediately Delivered = Mediation; Treatment as Ultimately Delivered = Arrest" (p. 199). The authors did not say how many offenders randomly assigned to mediation or separation were actually arrested; their overall 92% "delivered as assigned" rate was based on the comparison of treatments as assigned and treatments as *immediately delivered,* not ultimately delivered (see footnote 5 and Table 1). It is not difficult to speculate that the Omaha officers decided to arrest instead of mediate or separate based on similar conditions found in Minneapolis (rude offenders, use of weapons, etc.). But in Omaha these cases were counted as mediation or separation (the treatment as assigned). While the authors claim in footnote 10 that they reanalyzed the data for treatment as immediately and as ultimately delivered and found "quite similar results," they do not present these data. Footnote 10 assures us that the different measures of treatment made little difference statistically in the Omaha experiment. But in comparing results from Omaha and Minneapolis, it might matter that a treatment that was coded as arrest in Minneapolis was coded as nonarrest in Omaha.

2. There were other problems with variable operationalizations in the Omaha study. Treatments were not standardized, and the interventions had unclear content.

The authors noted that victim reports were often unreliable: "victims were not always sure of what happened during, and as a result of, police interventions" (p. 202). For example, while 95% of the victims interviewed from the arrest treatment group reported that the offenders were jailed after the incident, we do not know how many of the arrested offenders were actually jailed (recall that there was no minimum jail time attached to the arrest condition).

3. In footnote 6, the authors note that because of random assignment to treatments, some of the victims who requested that an arrest be made had to have their requests denied. This may have made these victims less likely to call the police in the follow-up period, resulting in measured recidivism lower than actual recidivism for the non-arrest groups. In the footnote, the authors present a number of lines of evidence to suggest that this mechanism probably did not operate.

Sample/population sampled.   The sample included all 330 eligible cases of simple misdemeanor domestic violence that occurred between 4 P.M. and midnight throughout the city of Omaha, Nebraska. The experiment ran for 18 months, beginning around February 1986. Cases were eligible if 1) both victim and suspect were present when the police arrived, 2) there was probable cause for a misdemeanor assault arrest, 3) a clearly identifiable victim and suspect were involved, 4) both parties were at least 18 years old and had lived together sometime during the year prior to the assault, and 5) neither party had an arrest warrant on file. Felony cases were excluded. Official police outcomes of repeat arrests and complaints were available on all 330 cases, and victim-reported outcomes were collected in 242 of the 330 cases (73% of the victims completed both the initial interview and the 6-month interview). The sample included a large number of minority, unmarried, underemployed couples with violent histories. The authors did not generalize the experimental results beyond Omaha or the eligible cases that were called in during the hours of the experiment.

Sampling biases.   The Omaha sample included only those domestic violence cases that were called in between 4 P.M. and midnight. While the authors noted that 60% of all disturbance calls occur during that period, 40% of the calls remain unaccounted for, and these cases may be different in significant ways from those that occur between 4 P.M. and midnight. Suppose, for example, that the most serious misdemeanor domestic violence incidents occur after midnight. Then this study would have relevance only to the deterrent effect of arrest in less serious misdemeanor domestic violence cases. This would be a source of bias if the results are used to generalize about domestic violence in Omaha at all hours.

Interactions.   The authors examined the interaction between victim willingness to call police for subsequent violence and type of intervention received at presenting offense. No interaction was found.

Conclusions.   Arrest is no more effective than mediation or separation in deterring subsequent domestic violence. Victims of arrested offenders were at no greater risk of subsequent assault than were victims whose partners received the separation or mediation treatments. Thus, the adoption of arrest policies for misdemeanor domestic assault does not, by itself, have any influence on the likelihood of repeated violence.

Summary of Steinman, M. (1991). Coordinated criminal justice interventions and recidivism among batterers. In M. Steinman (Ed.), *Woman battering: Policy responses* **(pp. 221–236). Cincinnati, Ohio: Anderson Publishing.**

Method. This quasi-experimental study actually combines two methods. In some respects, it is a between-subjects experiment, nonequivalent-groups design. This is so because it reports data on two groups of offenders: those who had police contact in the year before June 1, 1986, and those who had contact over a 2-year period beginning on that date. These two groups, clearly not made equivalent by randomization, were treated under different criminal justice policies.

The study also contains important elements of a within-subjects experiment, if it is considered as an experiment on the criminal justice system in Lincoln, which in an important sense it was. One June 1, 1986, the Domestic Violence Coalition (DVC) initiated a new set of policies throughout the system, and the study gathered data on the effects of that experiment. As we show, the study is subject to influence by extraneous variables associated with both of these research designs.

Hypothesis. Police response coordinated with other criminal justice interventions in domestic violence cases has an influence on repeat incidence of assault. The hypothesis really concerns an interaction effect, as can be seen from the introduction of the study and the presentation in Table 6. Steinman proposes that the effect of formal police interventions (e.g., arrest) on recidivism depends on the degree of coordination between the police and other elements of the local criminal justice system. The hypothesis is causal.

Independent variables/operational definitions

1. One independent variable is coordination between police and prosecutors. Its operational definition is the DVC program, which included an aggressive policy of prosecution for domestic violence, training for police officers about issues in abusive relationships and arrest policies, gaining trust and cooperation of victims, treatment for offenders, and various changes of policy in the police department and the county attorney's office. The adoption of the DVC program was a "natural experiment" in criminal justice policy—all those changes came about at once as a matter of policy. Steinman's role was basically to analyze the data—he did not, it appears, personally manipulate the variable.

2. The other independent variable was the police response. At both the baseline and experimental periods, there were two formal police actions: arrest and citation. The *arrest* action consisted of arresting and transporting suspects to police headquarters, where they were booked (the author claimed that most offenders who were arrested were jailed for "at least a brief time"). The *citation* category was not clearly defined, but it is assumed that cited offenders had to answer to the charge at a later time. In *no formal action* cases, police responded to a call but took no further official action.

Thus, there were six treatment conditions in all: three police actions in the baseline period and three in the experimental period.

Dependent variables/operational definitions. Repeat incidence of domestic assault was measured primarily by using *victim reports* of subsequent battering over a

12–33-month postincident period for victims in the experimental period, and 24–48 months postincident for victims in the baseline period. These data were based on information gathered during telephone interviews with victims that were conducted from 12 to 48 months after the incidents took place. It appears that only one follow-up interview was conducted with each victim. Victim reports were operationalized by using a modified version of a conflict tactics scale that assesses whether the original offender victimized the original victim with 13 kinds of physical assault or battering. Archival records were also used to measure recidivism for 17 offenders (6 baseline and 11 experimental) whose victims did not report any repeat violence during the interview. Among the 11 experimental offenders, 3 were officially charged with attacking different victims; information on repeated violence by baseline offenders was not available.

Findings.   Hypothesis was supported; formal police response coordinated with other intervention reduced repeat violence. Offenders who were arrested during the experimental period (with DVC intervention) had significantly fewer repeat violent incidents. Cited offenders also had fewer repeat incidents, but the relationship was not significant. In the baseline period (without DVC intervention), arrest and citation significantly increased repeat violence.

Controlled extraneous variables

1. Female interviewers collected victim follow-up data
2. Author reports that he controlled "for evidence that offenders have violent histories and for the nature of victim/offender relationships"

Uncontrolled extraneous variables/alternative explanations

1. Since the offenders were not randomly assigned to the baseline or experimental periods, we must examine the possible impact of uncontrolled subject variables on recidivism. It is possible that the offenders who received formal and informal police intervention were systematically different in terms of whatever variables may have caused the police to assign them to the particular intervention they got. For example, rude, uncooperative, or dangerous subjects may have been more likely to receive formal action (this would be similar to the pattern of upgrading found in the Minneapolis study). While the author noted that DVC innovations did not influence officers' decisions to take formal action in the experimental period, we could still speculate that formal action was more likely to be taken in the experimental period with certain kinds of offenders (or presenting offenses). Thus, even though approximately the same proportion of offenders received formal action in the baseline and experimental periods, arrest may have been more likely with certain kinds of offenders in the experimental period because of the increased emphasis on intervention. If so, recidivism may have been due to the particular characteristics of the cases that received formal police action during DVC intervention rather than by the DVC alone. However, the effect of arrest was different in the baseline and experimental periods. If arrest policy was no different in the two periods, it is difficult to see how nonrandom assignment to the arrest condition could account for the observed results.

The chief systematic differences between the groups concerned time. All the subjects in the experimental condition had police contact later than those in the baseline condition, so time-tied differences between the groups are potentially serious threats to validity. One such time-tied variable is change in attitudes toward battering in Lincoln. There was undoubtedly an increase in public debate about domestic violence in the period around June 1986—otherwise, the policy change could not have been accomplished. So perhaps the widespread attention of the community to battering somehow changed the responses of the batterers to police interventions, independent of the DVC policy itself.

While the introduction of the DVC may have changed attitudes about domestic violence (it may even have been an effect of changed attitudes), there may have been other extraneous variables associated with the different time periods used to compare recidivism rates. For example, the community may have experienced an episode of layoffs with the closing of a factory or a plant, or a losing football season, or an environmental disaster—all of which might have had some influence on domestic violence recidivism. Thus, any extraneous variables that are time-tied to the control and experimental periods pose problems for internal validity for this study.

2. Another time-tied difference concerns the data collection. The data on recidivism were collected an average of 14.7 months after the initial incident for victims in the experimental period and 33.1 months after the incident for victims in the baseline period. We should therefore expect higher rates of recidivism in the baseline group, simply because more time had passed in which a repeat incident might occur. Fortunately, Steinman's conclusions were not based only on reduced recidivism rates (83% in the baseline, 57% in the experimental), but also on an interaction effect: arrest lowered recidivism rates in the experimental period but raised them in the baseline period. It is hard to imagine how delayed data collection could explain that result.

3. Distorted memory could have biased the victim interview data. Baseline victims had to recall events that occurred 2 to 4 years before the follow-up interviews; experimental victims were interviewed between one and almost 3 years after the initial incident. Reliance on memory is particularly problematic in this study because victims from the baseline period had to recall behaviors that occurred, on the average, twice as long ago as victims from the experimental period.

Sample/population sampled.   Research was based on domestic violence cases in the official records of Lincoln/Lancaster County, Nebraska. Cases for the experimental period included data on the "first case in which every male offender was involved" after the implementation of the DVC on June 1, 1986. From July 1987 to May 1989, data were collected one year after the initial incident occurred. For the baseline period, official records were used to review all police reports for a 12-month period (between 6/1/85 and 5/31/86) and data were collected on those cases that the researcher believed involved battering. The final sample size depended on the number of victims that participated in follow-up interviews. The experimental period included data on 275 cases (of 974 victims, 322 were located, 275 of whom were interviewed and 47 of whom refused to participate). The baseline period included data on 63 cases (of 262 victims, 91 were located, and 28 refused to participate in the follow-up). Interviews with baseline victims began in the spring of 1988.

The author described the Lincoln/Lancaster population as predominantly white and middle class. The sample of domestic violence cases was disproportionately minority (27% in experimental period, 32% in baseline period), and most incidents occurred in low-income areas (76% experimental, 78% baseline). The author appropriately noted that the findings may not generalize to "more socioeconomically and racially heterogeneous communities."

Sampling biases.   The method of data collection from archival records was subject to bias. Cases for the baseline period were identified by an officer "working in her spare time" who reviewed all police reports during the 12-month baseline period (June 1, 1985 to May 31, 1986). She collected data on "cases she believed involved battering." Her selection of cases may have biased the results, especially if she knew the research hypothesis. However, she could not have known about the victim reports when she selected the cases, so this source of bias does not provide a clear alternative explanation for the results.

Failure to locate most victims at follow-up is another possible source of bias. Researchers were able to interview only 28% of victims from the experimental period and 24% of the victims from the baseline period. It is unknown, therefore, if those who were located are representative of domestic violence victims in Lincoln/Lancaster County, Nebraska. The author mentioned that locating victims was difficult because of the transient nature of low-income and minority residential and employment histories, their relative inability to pay for telephone service that was necessary for follow-up, and the long wait between initial incident and follow-up.

The author noted that the actual number of baseline cases in which officers took no formal action was unknown (they did not have to file written reports) and was probably underestimated in the analysis. We cannot assume that the offenders for whom information was available are representative of all offenders in no formal action cases—especially during the baseline period.

The key question for internal validity is this: Could this sampling bias explain the results of the study? The practice of not filing written reports effectively decreased the number of offenders in one of the six treatment groups: those from the baseline period against whom no formal action was taken. If data had been available on these missing individuals, the results from the experimental period, which showed a deterrent effect of arrest, would have been unaffected. But the findings from the baseline period—namely, that formal police action increased recidivism—might be invalidated if most of the missing offenders in fact became repeat offenders. Although there is no way to be sure about the missing cases, what seems most likely is that the cases that received no formal action and no written report were probably cases that involved less violence or more cooperative suspects. It seems unlikely that this group would have a higher-than-average proportion of repeat offenders. So, although this sampling bias weakens the study, it does not provide a convincing alternative explanation of the results.

Interactions.   The study hypothesized an interaction between police action (formal and informal) and other criminal justice interventions. Tables 7 and 8 show that Steinman also examined the interaction between the DVC program and the status of the offender and victim as either "dating" or "married or cohabiting." No significant interaction was reported. However, an interaction between the offenders' prior criminal record and the DVC program was found—in the experimental period, recidivism was lower among men without criminal records or histories of battering.

Conclusions. Formal police action, when coordinated with other criminal justice interventions, reduces repeat domestic violence. Uncoordinated formal police action (arrest and citation) increases subsequent violence. The author concludes that arrest policies and government intervention in domestic violence cases should not be abandoned.

You now have some detailed notes on a group of articles. Your next job, before writing a review, is to try to make sense out of the results of all the studies. Although there is no foolproof procedure that will guide you through a tangle of research to a clear view, there is a procedure that can be of some help. Try to proceed in this way:

1. Look at your notes on the FINDINGS of the studies.

If the relationship between the variables you are interested in is always the same, you are almost home free. Go to Step 5.

This rarely happens. Usually some results will point in one direction and others will either point the other way, or find no relationship, or conclude that the relationship depends on other variables (interaction effects). You could decide the point by "majority vote" (the most common result "wins"), but that isn't a very satisfactory way to proceed because it doesn't explain why some results don't fit. Besides, the unusual result often points the way to deeper knowledge. So, if the results do not agree, go to Step 2.

2. Look at your notes on INTERACTIONS.

See if any of the studies you read discovers a third variable that influences the relationship between the ones you have chosen to study. If you do find an interaction, look back at the other studies to see if they measured the third variable. If they did, was the same interaction present? (If there was no interaction effect, you have another problem to solve: Why isn't the interaction universal?) If other studies did find the interaction, or if no other studies measured the third variable, look at the other research in terms of the third variable.

In our group of studies of domestic violence, Steinman (1991) proposed an interaction effect that might explain what was found in other studies. He concluded that police action by itself has little effect on domestic violence recidivism, but that the interaction of police action and the level of coordination between police and prosecutors in their responses to domestic violence accounts for the effects of arrest: when there is good coordination, arrest deters batterers, but when arrests do not lead to prosecution or other serious consequences, arrest may even increase the likelihood of repeat offenses. The reports from Minneapolis and Omaha do not, unfortunately, provide information on the ways prosecutors handled domestic violence in those cities, so it is not possible by reading Sherman and Berk (1984) and Dunford et al. (1990) to tell whether Steinman's hypothesis explains the discrepancy between those two studies. It might be possible, however, to go to Minneapolis and Omaha and, by a combination of interviews with police and prosecutors and an examination of prosecutors' records, make an independent judgment of how well the police efforts to arrest batterers were coordinated with the actions of prosecutors. If that effort found much better coordination in Minneapolis than in Omaha, Steinman's hypothesis would receive additional confirmation.

If you are able to find a third variable that makes sense out of some of the discrepancies in the research, you have one possible way to make sense of all the literature you have found. But whether you have found such an explanation or not, go on to Step 3.

3. Look at each of the ALTERNATIVE EXPLANATIONS you have suggested for each study reviewed.

Can any of these explain the results of more than one study? If so, you have something worth noting, especially if you are able to use an alternative explanation to explain the results of studies that seem, on the surface, to contradict each other.

Are there studies that provide evidence against an alternative explanation you have suggested for a different study? If so, you can think about ruling out that explanation. (If you find this, you might briefly mention it in your review.)

For example, we noted that the latitude allowed officers in the Minneapolis experiment might explain away the observed deterrent effect of arrest. But it would not explain Steinman's (1991) results. Steinman gives no information on how the choice was made to arrest, cite, or take no formal action. We must presume that the choice was left entirely to the officers' discretion. Yet Steinman reported results like those of Dunford et al. (1990) in the baseline period and like those of Sherman and Berk (1984) in the experimental period. So officer discretion may make a difference, but it does not fully explain why arrest deters battering under some conditions but not others.

This is the general line of thinking. Until you have a sense of which alternative explanations look the most promising, it might pay to look through them all, methodically, trying to see if any of them helps you make sense out of several different studies. After you have done this, you will have some idea of which studies seem to make sense together (on the basis of the same assumptions), and which ones you still feel are unexplained. Then go on to Step 4.

4. Compare the studies in terms of
OPERATIONAL DEFINITIONS OF INDEPENDENT VARIABLES
OPERATIONAL DEFINITIONS OF DEPENDENT VARIABLES
POPULATIONS SAMPLED
SETTINGS USED IN GATHERING DATA

The task is to try to find some consistency between one of these four things and the results reported. Sometimes the results you get depend on the way you measure the variables, or the subjects you use, or the place and time you choose to gather data. When two studies get different results, the difference might be explained by a difference in any of these areas. When two studies get the same results, one is tempted to conclude that differences between them in these four areas are unimportant in terms of the variables being studied. A good way to begin is to *take two studies that seem most inconsistent with each other* and look for differences between them in terms of operational definitions, populations sampled, and/or settings. Use any difference you find as a hypothesis, and test it using the evidence of the other studies.

Table 3 of the article by Dunford et al. (1990) provides us with a quick way to compare the populations, settings, and operational definitions from the Minneapolis and Omaha studies, which yielded discrepant results. Any difference between the columns in the table may suggest a way to reconcile the studies' results. For example, 60% of the suspects in Minneapolis were unemployed, compared to only 31% in Omaha. This comparison suggests the hypothesis that arrest may be a more potent deterrent for the unemployed than the employed. The hypothesis makes sense of the two studies that generated it; the study in Lincoln does not report unemployment rates for the batterers, so we do not know if the hypothesis can make sense of those results. (In fact, this hypothesis is not supported by recent research on police intervention in domestic violence in other U.S. cities, as we discuss at the end of this chapter.)

The goal of this step in your thinking is to find one or more consistent relationships between some detail of the studies and the results they report. If you can find a detail that is consistently correlated with a particular result, you have something worth mentioning, because it may help explain why different researchers get different results. This is the way reviews of empirical literature can be useful in extending knowledge. Armed with a hypothesis about what makes the results turn out different, a reviewer like you can suggest further research to test the new hypothesis.

With this groundwork done, you can proceed closer to writing.

5. Decide on a logical order in which to present your articles (or other scientific evidence).

You might present articles in the chronological order in which they were written. This organization makes good sense when the authors were aware of each other's work, as is the case with these articles on police intervention (Dunford et al. cite Sherman and Berk and Steinman cites both Sherman and Berk and Dunford et al.). When each article reviews the older ones, chronological order makes good sense because the studies follow logically as well.

Another form of organization is topical. You might group laboratory studies together and field research together, or you might divide the research according to the population sampled or according to the ways the variables were operationalized, and so on. With topical organization, you should use a category system that will make sense in terms of your ultimate conclusion. If, for example, you decide that Steinman's results differed from those of Dunford et al. because Steinman compared naturally occurring groups (a quasi-experiment), it makes sense to separate studies that use natural manipulation from controlled experiments. You could then summarize the controlled studies, summarize the uncontrolled studies, and compare the two summaries. Your point would be strongly made.

You could also organize your review like a detective story. You would start with a problem and present articles to piece together an answer. Begin with a general or preliminary piece of research that still leaves open several possibilities, and then present other pieces of research that slowly eliminate alternative explanations, or else suggest new ones. Again, the order of presentation depends on the final point you want to make. In social science, many of the mysteries are unsolved, and it is often interesting to see how what everybody thought was true turned out to be false.

With a logical organization, you are ready to write.

6. WRITE.

In preparing a review for a professional journal, space is at a premium and you are writing for an audience of experts in the field. Thus, in such reviews it is unnecessary or undesirable to include a great deal of detail about each study you review. For a beginner, however, some detail is desirable. If you are not used to writing reviews of research articles, or if your audience is nonexpert, you should write with a fair amount of detail about each study you are evaluating. You can learn a lot about how to do this concisely by reading the abstracts that appear at the head of many articles in the professional journals. Here is an outline of what you should probably tell your reader about each article:

What was the general question?
What was the hypothesis?
What method was used to collect the data?
What population was sampled?
What were the variables important to your review?
How were these operationalized (briefly)?
What results were found?
What was the author's conclusion?

This is a good approximate order in which to present the information, and it is the order most frequently used in abstracts. Once you have said all this, the reader is "with you"—he or she knows what the study was all about. You may then go on with your critique (alternative explanations due to uncontrolled extraneous variables, sampling bias, etc.) and discuss other articles, in the order you have planned.

Unfortunately, there is no rule concerning how much criticism of an article is appropriate while you are first summarizing it. It is a matter of judgment whether to put your commentary after each article or to save it for the end. The most crucial point is not to lose the reader in details.

These suggestions should help you organize your thinking and writing about a group of scientific articles. The following student review of the three articles on arrest and domestic assault may also help.

The Effect of Police Intervention on Domestic Violence: A Literature Review

Peter Collings
State University of New York, Plattsburgh

What is the most effective police response to domestic violence? The widespread occurrence of domestic assault has generated considerable research into how police action might deter future violence. For example, women's rights advocates have traditionally supported a strong police response to domestic disputes, arguing that arresting the offender would best ensure the safety of the victim and reduce future violence. This is a review of three studies that examined the effect of police intervention in reducing repeat incidence of domestic assault. Two of the studies (Sherman & Berk, 1984; Steinman, 1991) found that arrest, when combined with either temporary incarceration or other criminal justice interventions, reduced recidivism. However, the third study (Dunford, Huizinga, & Elliott, 1990) found no effect of police intervention on subsequent violence.

Sherman and Berk (1984) discussed two opposing theories of the effects of police intervention in domestic violence. According to the deterrence theory, the pain of punishment for criminal actions acts as an effective means to deter repeat offenses. Recent research has uncovered an antithetic theory which proposes that "punishment often makes individuals more likely to commit crimes because of altered interactional structures, foreclosed legal opportunities and secondary deviance" (Sherman & Berk, 1984, pg. 181–182). To test the hypothesis that arrest has deterrent effects in domestic assault cases, the researchers conducted a between-subjects experiment.

The sample for this experiment was 314 cases of domestic assault that occurred in two high domestic violence crime precincts in Minneapolis, Minnesota, between March 1981 and August 1982. The experiment included all cases of misdemeanor domestic assault in which the police were authorized (but not required) to make an arrest, there was probable cause that the suspect had assaulted a partner or spouse, and both the suspect and the victim were present when the police arrived. Sherman and Berk's sample included a large number of unem-ployed, unmarried, poorly educated minority couples in which the suspects had violent histories and high rates of prior arrests (29% of the suspects had a prior arrest for an alcohol offense).

Police officers assigned to the experimental areas (the areas in the city with the highest reports of domestic violence) were provided with color-coded report pads indicating which of the three police interventions was to be used for that particular case: arrest (and incarceration for a minimum of 8 hours), separation (ordering the offender from the premises for 8 hours), or advice (a wide-ranging option which included anything from mediation to doing nothing at the officer's discretion). When responding to a domestic violence call which fit the experimental criteria, the officers were to follow the intervention designated by the color-coded report pad.

Recidivism was measured over a 6-month period through official police records and victim self-reports. The police records were official reports of repeat offenses. The victim reports of recidivism were gathered through personal interviews, followed by telephone interviews conducted every other week for a total of six months (with every fourth interview conducted in person). Victims reported on whether there had been any further victimization by the same offender in the form of an actual assault, threatened assault, or property damage.

This experiment found that certain police intervention strategies influenced repeat incidence of domestic assault. The police data indicated that arrest produced the lowest recidivism, separation produced the highest, and advice was "indistinguishable from the other two effects" (Sherman & Berk, 1984, p. 190). Victim follow-up data also showed that when offenders were arrested, there were fewer repeat incidents of assault, threatened assault, or property damage, but advising offenders produced the highest rate of recidivism. The authors concluded that arrest and temporary incarceration acts as a deterrent in misdemeanor domestic assault cases, and police should operate under a presumption-of-arrest policy.

The between-subjects experiment conducted by Dunford et al. (1990) was designed as a replication of the Sherman and Berk study. The focus of this experiment was to see if Sherman and Berk's findings would hold in a different setting at a different time period. Their study was guided by the same research hypothesis as the original experiment: police intervention in domestic violence cases has an influence on repeat assault. However, this replication found that police action had no influence on recidivism.

The subjects for this experiment were all 330 cases of simple misdemeanor domestic violence reported to the police between 4 p.m. and midnight throughout the city of Omaha, Nebraska, over an 18-month period beginning in February 1986. Similar to the Sherman and Berk study, cases were included in the experiment if both victim and suspect were present when the police arrived and if there was probable cause for a misdemeanor assault arrest. Eligible cases in Omaha also had to involve a "clearly identifiable victim and suspect," individuals that were at least 18 years of age who had lived together sometime during the year prior to the assault, and individuals that were not under warrant for arrest. Felony cases were excluded from the study. Like Sherman and Berk's sample, a large number of the couples in the Omaha experiment were minority, unmarried, poorly educated, with violent histories and high prior arrest rates for the suspects. There was much less unemployment in the Omaha sample than in the Minneapolis sample; among the

Omaha suspects, 31% were unemployed, compared to 60% in Minneapolis.

As in the earlier experiment, there were three different types of police intervention which could be assigned to each case: arrest (no specified minimum time in jail), separation (asking the suspect or victim to leave the premises for at least 8 hours), and mediation (a range of actions including advising victims to leave, legal advice and referrals, and most often simply the restoration of order). All of the offenders were randomly assigned to one of the three interventions. Unlike the Sherman and Berk study, however, officers received their assignment instructions from a computer after determining that a particular case fit the experimental design. The authors report the results of the analysis of the assigned interventions, regardless of the intervention actually delivered at the scene.

Domestic assault recidivism was based on 5 outcome measures which were obtained from official police records and victim reports over a 6-month follow-up period. Official records included new arrests and complaints for any crimes in which the original offender victimized the original victim (repeat cases of misdemeanor assault were considered repeat arrests). Victim-reported outcome data were collected in two personal interviews over the 6-month follow-up period and were based on the number of times a victim felt endangered, was actually pushed or hit, or was physically injured after the initial assault.

The Omaha experiment found that police intervention strategy (as randomly assigned) had no influence on repeat incidence of domestic assault. Official records and victim reports indicated no significant difference in the prevalence of repeat violence across the three types of police intervention, although there was a tendency for victims in the arrest group to report fewer incidents of repeat violence. Police intervention also had no statistically significant effect on recidivism when the data were reanalyzed using formal (arrest) and informal (separation and mediation) police action. The authors concluded that an arrest policy for misdemeanor domestic assault "may not, by itself, have any impact on the likelihood of repeated violent acts" (Dunford et al., 1990, p. 215).

In an attempt to reconcile the discrepant results in the above two studies, Michael Steinman (1991) devised a between-subjects experiment using a nonequivalent group design to assess whether police action combined with other criminal justice interventions deters subsequent domestic violence. Drawing on the argument that "complex strategies are needed to treat complex problems" (Steinman, 1991, p. 217), this study postulated that police response coordinated with other criminal justice interventions would reduce repeat assaults.

Two groups of subjects were compared on the basis of whether they offended before (baseline) or after (experimental) the local adoption of arrest policies and aggressive prosecution for domestic violence (the Domestic Violence Coalition, or DVC, program) in Lincoln/Lancaster County, Nebraska. Researchers collected archival data on domestic violence cases from official police and county records and data on post-incident violence from victims in follow-up telephone interviews. Data for the experimental period were collected on the first incident in which a male offender was involved after the implementation of the DVC in June 1986. The sampling period for the experimental data ran from July 1987 to May 31, 1989 and included 275 cases. For the baseline period, official records between June 1, 1985 and May 31, 1986 were reviewed, and all

cases that a volunteer researcher believed involved battering were included in the sample. The baseline period included 63 cases. Compared to the mostly white, middle-class population of Lincoln/Lancaster, Nebraska, the cases in both experimental and baseline periods were disproportionately minority and low-income.

At both the baseline and experimental periods, officers responding to domestic disputes could intervene formally or informally. Formal police action included arrest (offenders were booked, no minimum jail time) and citation. Informal police action included responding to a call, but taking no official action. During the experimental period, police action was combined with arrest policies that included the expectation that police will arrest offenders whenever probable cause exists, aggressive prosecution for domestic violence, offender treatment programs, officer training about domestic violence issues, arrest policies, and some victim advocacy. Officers were required to file reports in all cases, including cases in which they took no formal action.

Victim reports of subsequent battering were collected in telephone interviews during a 12 to 48 month period after the original incident. Subsequent abuse was measured using a modified version of a conflict tactics scale that assessed whether the victim had experienced 13 different types of physical battering since the original police intervention.

The results of Steinman's experiment supported his hypothesis that formal police response coordinated with other interventions would reduce recidivism. In the experimental period, arrest significantly reduced repeat violence. There was also some evidence that citation coordinated with other interventions decreases recidivism. In the baseline period, formal police action (arrest and citation) increased repeat violence. Steinman concluded that formal police action, specifically arrest, coordinated with other criminal justice interventions, reduces repeat violence, while uncoordinated formal action increases repeat violence.

Alternative explanations can be suggested for each of the studies described above. In the Sherman and Berk experiment, assignment to treatment was accomplished in a nonrandom way when officers decided to make arrests in certain cases that were assigned to receive separation or advice treatments. Five variables determined whether a case was upgraded to arrest: the suspect was rude, the suspect tried to assault one or both of the officers, weapons were involved, the victim demanded an arrest, there was a violation of a restraining order. This may have caused the arrest group to have more of what the authors referred to as "bad guys" than either the separation or mediation treatments. Thus, upgrading could have had an impact on the deterrent effects of arrest found in Sherman and Berk's study. To be more specific, rude and uncooperative offenders may be more likely to be deterred by arrest. A possible explanation for this seemingly illogical conclusion may be a result of offenders' initial reaction to the police intervention. For example, if the officers initially attempted to separate or mediate the parties involved, the offender may have realized that an arrest was not imminent. Therefore, the offender may have become difficult and uncooperative, believing that the officers would not make an arrest. However, when the officers changed their treatment and arrested the offender, this may have had a significant impact on the offender's assessment of the situation, resulting in a more deterrent effect of the arrest treatment.

Dunford et al. ignored violations of the experimental design and analyzed the data based on the initial random assignment even if different than the intervention delivered. In addition, their sample included only domestic assault cases which occurred between 4 p.m. and midnight. It is quite possible that those involved in domestic disputes between 4 p.m. and midnight may be different from those involved after midnight. For example, alcohol-related incidents are likely to be more common during the early morning after the bars close. Thus, by sampling only during the evening shift, this study may have overlooked certain types of offenders that would have been deterred by arrest.

Finally, to assess the effect of police action coordinated with other interventions, Steinman compared domestic violence cases that occurred before the introduction of a community program to combat domestic violence with those that occurred after the initiation of the program. While some important extraneous variables were statistically controlled (e.g., prior history of abuse, marital status), the comparison of nonequivalent groups from different time periods is reason to view with caution Steinman's finding that formal police action when coordinated with other criminal justice interventions reduces repeat violence. Any number of variables may have changed between the two time periods. If they were not statistically controlled this could have biased the results. For example, economic conditions may have improved after the initiation of the DVC program, which might tend to decrease repeat domestic violence. Another speculation might be that a change in the local political structure introduced new attitudes toward domestic violence. Therefore, the observed deterrent effect of arrest may not have been the result of arrest and vigilant prosecution, but instead the result of improving economic conditions or a change in political structure.

The inconsistent findings from these experiments may be due in part to how the experimental interventions were carried out. In both the Sherman and Berk and the Steinman studies, officers were directly involved in determining which of the police interventions was used in each case. In the Sherman and Berk study, this resulted in the upgrading of certain cases from separation and citation interventions to arrest. Such officer discretion may have also played a part in Steinman's study since police officers were directly involved in the selection of the "intervention." In the Dunford et al. experiment, however, the results are based on computer assignment of intervention strategy, and the results they report are based on the computer assigned intervention. Therefore, the upgrading of interventions in Sherman and Berk and officer discretion in Steinman may have caused a skewing of results which was not evident in the Dunford et al. study. The upgrading of certain offenders to the arrest condition resulted in nonrandomization of subjects to treatment groups. Thus, people in the arrest condition in Sherman and Berk and in Steinman may have been significantly different than those individuals in the arrest condition in the Dunford et al. study. It is reasonable to speculate, therefore, that certain kinds of offenders (those likely to be arrested based on the officer's discretion) are more likely to be deterred by arrest. This deterrent effect is fairly clear in Sherman and Berk; it is less clear in the Steinman study.

The operational definition of arrest in each of the three studies may have also caused the different experimental results. In Sherman and Berk's study, the arrest condition included a mandatory incarceration period, and Steinman studied the impact of a strict arrest policy with the introduction of the DVC program. The Dunford et al. experiment, however, lacked this interaction of arrest and mandatory jail time or arrest and aggressive prosecution. While some offenders were incarcerated, there was no specified minimum jail time in the Dunford et al. study. In addition, Dunford et al. relied on victim reports to determine the content of the arrest treatment, and they noted that some victims did not know what happened after the arrest was made. It is therefore likely that an arrest policy combined with incarceration (as in Sherman and Berk) or aggressive prosecution (as in Steinman) reduces repeat incidents of violence, while arrest without a strictly enforced follow-up policy has no effect on subsequent assault (as in Dunford et al.).

Another possibility that might reconcile the differences in these studies involves the victim reports. In Sherman and Berk, both victim reports and official police records found that arrest reduced subsequent domestic violence. Steinman based his entire research on victim self-reports and found that arrest coordinated with other criminal justice interventions reduced recidivism. Dunford et al., however, reported that while official police records showed no effect of arrest on recidivism rates, the victim reports tended to show that arrest decreased subsequent violence. Further, the researchers noted that time spent in jail tended to decrease recidivism according to the victim reports. Although these findings were not statistically significant, they do concur with the deterrent effects of arrest reported by Sherman and Berk and of arrest coordinated with other interventions reported by Steinman. Perhaps victim reports may be more reliable indicators of repeat violence than official police records. It should also be noted that domestic violence cases are notorious for not being reported to the police. More research is warranted in this area.

Any of the above explanations might explain the discrepancies in the three domestic violence experiments reviewed here. While the Dunford et al. experiment might be regarded as the least problematic methodologically, it still had several vital flaws. Primary among these drawbacks were the limited time period for data collection, a general dismissal of the tendency for victim reports to show different experimental results than the official measures, and the analysis based on treatments as assigned rather than as ultimately delivered. Although the Sherman and Berk and Steinman studies were not as flawless in design as Dunford et al., their results seem to be more credible. Both of these studies found that arrest, along with a strict follow-up procedure (incarceration or prosecution), reduced subsequent domestic violence. This finding is also supported by the victim reports in Dunford et al. which showed that both arrest and time in jail tended to reduce repeat offenses, although the relationships were not statistically significant.

In conclusion, the studies reviewed here seem to provide evidence that supports deterrence theory in cases of misdemeanor domestic assault: arresting offenders, particularly when arrest is coordinated with other criminal justice efforts, deters future violence. However, the domestic violence research is far from perfect and requires expansion. In the continued search for the most effective social response to the problem of domestic violence, future research should strengthen the measurement of victim-reported outcomes and disentangle how formal police action interacts with mandatory incarceration and/or other criminal justice interventions in reducing repeat violence.

REFERENCES

Dunford, F. W., Huizinga, D., & Elliott, D. S. (1990). The role of arrest in domestic assault: The Omaha police experiment. *Criminology, 28,* 183–206.

Sherman, L. W., & Berk, R. A. (1984). The specific deterrent effects of arrest for domestic assault. *American Sociological Review, 49,* 261–272.

Steinman, M. (1991). Coordinated criminal justice interventions and recidivism among batterers. In M. Steinman (Ed.), *Woman battering: Policy responses* (pp. 221–236). Cincinnati, Ohio: Anderson Publishing.

The preceding paper was written by a student who has learned how to critically review the scientific literature. While it is not a perfect paper, it is a good example of how to review a set of articles bearing on a general question, and it could be used as a model for your own literature review.

Certain features of the paper are important in preparing a scholarly review article. These features are discussed below:

Style: The paper is written using the standard style of professional work in psychology. The citations and references follow the guidelines set forth in the *Publication Manual of the American Psychological Association* (3rd ed., 1983). In addition, the reviewer is careful to give credit to the original authors in the citation of direct quotes, with the relevant page numbers in the text. Most students in the social sciences may use these guidelines as a stylistic model in preparing their own papers.

Organization: The paper can be divided into four major sections:

1. *Introduction.* The first paragraph provides a description of what the paper is about, including the general question, the specific focus of the studies in the review

(usually stated as a hypothesis), and the findings of each study. This introduction should give the reader a clear sense of what the paper is about.

2. *Description of the studies.* The studies are described one at a time, in chronological order, with the 1984 Minneapolis experiment discussed first, then the 1990 Omaha experiment, followed by the 1991 Lincoln study. For each study, the reviewer describes the research design, the hypothesis, the sample, how cases were assigned to treatment groups, how independent and dependent variables were operationalized, the results, and the authors' conclusions. This generally follows the outline we suggest for what should be included in a review article. You will note that considerable detail has been given concerning case eligibility, the method of assignment to interventions, and operational definitions of independent and dependent variables. Some of this detail may be omitted (but do not omit the operational definitions), but this reviewer considered the detail important enough to include in the review. We will see why later.

3. *Comparison of the studies.* After the descriptions, the reviewer critiques each experiment and suggests some alternative explanations for the findings (devoting one paragraph to each study to cover what he considers the major weaknesses), and then discusses the three studies together. Here we see some of the reviewer's thinking. He has shown us where he has found possible explanations of the findings of all three studies together. He points out some differences (and similarities) in the studies in terms of the procedures used (particularly the assignment of interventions), possible interaction effects, and the operational definitions of arrest and of recidivism (police records or victim reports). This is a good way to organize your comparison, since it makes your thinking clear to the reader.

4. *Conclusions and suggestions for research.* The last paragraph of the paper gives the reviewer's conclusions. Based on his review of the three studies, he concludes that arresting domestic violence offenders will deter subsequent violence when arrest is combined with other interventions. Finally, he makes some specific suggestions for future research. It is best to try to resolve contradictory research results, or come up with a formulation that at least might make sense of the findings, as this reviewer did. It is not uncommon, however, to have some doubts about which conclusions follow from a body of literature, particularly if the studies are numerous and complex.

Content: Let's look at selected parts of the paper.

1. *Method of gathering data.* The reviewer describes the research method for each study, how the independent variables were manipulated, and how random assignment was achieved in Minneapolis and in Omaha. He names the research method for each study. We consider this acceptable in a review, but this detail is not always necessary. What is necessary is to give the reader enough information to tell what method was used. For example, in describing the way suspects were assigned to treatment conditions in Minneapolis, the reviewer tells the reader enough to determine that the study was a between-subjects experiment, equivalent-groups design.

2. *Alternative explanations/comparison of the studies.* By design, the Minneapolis and Omaha studies controlled for some organismic variables. But because of violations of random assignment, certainly in Minneapolis, and perhaps also in Omaha, the treatment groups were in fact not equivalent. In Omaha, the group equivalency

was maintained, but the final treatment of suspects in the groups is unknown, and the non-arrest groups actually included offenders who were arrested. The reviewer discussed this issue as it affected alternative explanations for individual experiments and as a way to reconcile the findings of different studies. He discussed the tendency for officers to upgrade certain cases to arrest in Minneapolis and speculates that the arrest group ended up with more cases likely to be deterred by police intervention. He criticized the Omaha study for not reporting the effect of the police action as ultimately delivered, and for bias caused by the time of day for data collection. He questioned the Lincoln study because it compares nonequivalent groups from different time periods. The reviewer could have addressed a number of other alternative explanations. For example, characteristics of the sample (other than those that generated upgrading to arrest) that might explain the results were not discussed—60% of the Minneapolis suspects were unemployed, compared to only 31% in Omaha. Perhaps unemployed suspects are more readily deterred by arrest (read on for further evidence both for and against this explanation). Try to follow the general rule of discussing in this part of the review only those aspects of the studies that you feel may truly explain the results. Don't burden yourself and the reader by discussing alternative explanations that you will later identify as useless.

The reviewer speculates that the inconsistent findings between Omaha and Minneapolis could be the result of the different outcomes associated with two different treatments—treatment as assigned and treatment as ultimately delivered. He suggests that when officers are involved in the treatment decision, as in Minneapolis, arrest is more likely to have a deterrent effect. In Minneapolis, officers violated the experimental design and upgraded certain cases to arrest even when they were supposed to deliver a non-arrest treatment. The Minneapolis analysis was based on treatment as ultimately delivered, and arrest had a deterrent effect. In Omaha, there was no deterrent effect of arrest, but the analysis was based on treatment as assigned, not as actually delivered. Unfortunately, as the reviewer notes, the Lincoln results do not fit this explanation. While officer discretion was certainly used in Lincoln, arrest increased repeat assault during the baseline period, but had a deterrent effect in the experimental period.

The reviewer also suggests that the interaction of arrest and other interventions (incarceration in Minneapolis and the DVC program in Lincoln) may have a deterrent effect. He argues that the arrest in the Omaha experiment did not include mandatory jail time or aggressive prosecution, and thus arrest had no influence on subsequent violence. We agree that this explanation is plausible and deserves further study.

Finally, the reviewer discusses the issue of using victim reports to measure repeat violence. He states that the Omaha victims reported fewer incidents of subsequent violence when the suspects were arrested, and he adds that time spent in jail tended to decrease repeat violence according to the victim reports. He argues that none of these findings were corroborated with the official police records of recidivism. However, since the findings were not statistically significant at conventional levels, we must consider this argument weak. The reviewer speculates that deterrent effects of arrest are more likely to be observed if research uses victim report data as the outcome measure. Given the general knowledge that many domestic assaults are not reported officially, this explanation is a plausible one. Indeed, it has been estimated that only 52% of all domestic violence incidents are officially reported (Langan &

Innes, 1986), and even this figure may be too high. Sherman (1992) estimates that only 20% to 40% of the 18 million assaults a year are reported to police. So it may indeed be true that victim reports are a more sensitive measure of recidivism than police records.

Obviously, there are other possible explanations that aren't mentioned in this review, yet this does not detract from the paper.

3. *Conclusions.* The reviewer concludes that arrest, when coordinated with other interventions, can be a deterrent in domestic violence cases, and he makes some suggestions for future research. This is a respectable literature review: the writer has successfully described the studies, pointed to the contradictions and inconsistencies, and suggested some possible meanings of the whole body of information. Other reviewers may not agree with his conclusion, but the reasoning is spelled out, and the argument is strong enough to take seriously.

We should note that the experiments reviewed in this paper have recently been replicated in other cities (see, for example, Hirschel & Hutchison, 1992; Pate & Hamilton, 1992; Sherman & Smith, 1992). These studies have found that the effect of arrest is conditional on characteristics of individuals. In other words, arrest works differently for different kinds of people, particularly as a function of an individual's "stake in conformity" (Sherman, 1992). Thus, while arrest had a deterrent effect among employed suspects (Pate & Hamilton, 1992), it increased repeat assault for the unemployed (Pate & Hamilton, 1992; Sherman & Smith, 1992). Further, both of these studies reported an interaction between arrest and composite measures that included both employment and marital status, suggesting that those who are deterred are those who have something to lose because of their "commitment" or "stake in conformity."

And the controversy continues. Berk and his colleagues (1992) pooled the results of four replication experiments and reported some confusing findings. The effect of marriage on recidivism was in the opposite direction from the effect of employment. The interaction effects they estimated were not consistent with each other. And the data showed that for suspects who were not arrested, those who were employed were more likely to engage in new violence. Berk and his colleagues (1992) argue that their pooled analysis demonstrates how "the impact of arrest can vary widely depending on the implied model specification" (p. 704). So far, the more this particular question has been studied, the less clear the answer has become. This frustrating situation is all too common in social science; sometimes, additional research and analysis will clear up what has been confusing researchers, but sometimes frustration continues for a long time.

Policy Implications of Social Science Knowledge

We cannot conclude this discussion without addressing the policy implications of the research. All these studies were done to help inform very practical decisions on how to treat suspects in domestic violence cases, and the authors were not bashful about making recommendations to police departments based on their findings. Did they recommend wisely, based on the evidence?

It is particularly interesting to look at the writings of Richard Berk, coauthor of the Minneapolis experiment and the 1992 review article. On the basis of the single experiment in Minneapolis, Sherman and Berk (1984) wrote, "We favor a presumption of arrest; an arrest should be made unless there are good, clear reasons why an arrest would be counterproductive" (p. 194). Many urban police departments followed this advice, possibly because of the well-publicized study or because of a change in public attitudes about domestic violence. Eight years passed, and several replications demonstrated that the Minneapolis results were unreliable. What conclusion follows for policy?

Berk and his colleagues (1992) concluded that there is some evidence that arrest works better for employed suspects than for unemployed suspects, and thus "deterrence may be effective for a substantial segment of the offender population" (p. 706). They argued that even though the evidence is "hardly overwhelming, and its meaning unclear . . . the findings do not provide a sound rationale for abandoning arrest, even presumptory arrest, as a policy *option*" (p. 706). But if Berk favored arresting domestic violence suspects on the basis of the 1984 study, shouldn't he change his mind when the study is called into question? For that matter, should he have advocated a change of policy in the first place on the basis of a single study that had not yet been replicated?

These questions are very important for understanding how to draw inferences—especially practical ones—from social science research. With the help of hindsight, we are inclined to say two things. First, the 1984 study provided only weak evidence in favor of an arrest policy. The results fit the tenor of the times, which probably explains the great attention they received. But the evidence of one study, even a between-subjects experiment with equivalent-groups design, still needs replication before it can be represented as solid knowledge.

Second, the confusing research picture as of 1992 does not imply that the arrest policy should be reversed. Why? Because the policy question and the research question are very different. The policy question is this: Should suspects in domestic violence cases be arrested? The research question is much narrower: Does arresting domestic violence suspects decrease their likelihood of becoming repeat offenders? There is not necessarily any inconsistency if the answer to the policy question is "yes" and the answer to the research question is "we don't know yet." Suppose an arrest policy deters people from becoming first offenders? Suppose it teaches citizens that domestic violence is a serious crime and not something to be brushed aside and forgotten? Many people would support an arrest policy for those reasons alone, regardless of what effect it had on people who had already become offenders. In fact, many would support the policy simply because they believe it is right for society to take a strong stand against domestic violence.

The point is that the group of studies we have examined looked at only one of the many issues concerning arrest policies for domestic violence. Not surprisingly, they looked at one that it is possible to study with rigorous methods. It is not possible to experiment with an arrest policy on people who have not yet committed any violence, and nonexperimental methods of answering the question about deterring first offenders, such as looking for changes in overall domestic violence rates in a city, are plagued by numerous alternative explanations for any possible finding. So, as with very many other policy questions, social science research can provide useful information for making a judgment, but it cannot provide all the information one might desire. As readers of social science research, we are wise to check back from time to time to see how well the available knowledge matches the questions we would like it to answer.

META-ANALYSIS: A QUANTITATIVE METHOD FOR REVIEWING BODIES OF LITERATURE

This chapter describes and demonstrates what has traditionally been the only method available for making sense of bodies of literature that consist of numerous studies that measure the same independent and dependent variables. It is basically a method of careful and organized critical thinking. In the past two decades, however, researchers have developed a statistical technique, called meta-analysis, that is designed to make sense of conflicting scientific studies by synthesizing their data quantitatively (for sourcebooks, see Cook et al., 1992; Light & Pillemer, 1984; Rosenthal, 1984; Wachter & Straf, 1990).

In essence, meta-analysis treats each study as if it were a subject in a study of studies. The results of each study are summarized by a measure of "effect size," which is treated as the dependent variable in the meta-analysis. Meta-analysis asks two questions: Is the effect size for the group of studies greater than zero? And what characteristics of the studies are associated with larger or smaller observed effects? It is easy to see how quantitative analysis of the second kind of question might help make sense of a body of literature such as the one on the effects of arresting batterers, in which the studies differ in many ways that might help explain the results.

Meta-analyses combine the results of all the available studies of the same question, taking into account the size of the samples in each study. The technique is much more sophisticated than a simple "vote" of studies, in which the most common finding is taken to be the truth. Some researchers see meta-analysis as the wave of the future in social science—as not only replacing traditional narrative reviews like the student review in this chapter, but also as the best way to gain understanding of complex social phenomena (Schmidt, 1992). Meta-analyses are becoming more common in some social science literatures, so you should be aware of how they can help make sense of bodies of literature. You should also be aware of their limitations, because they do not eliminate the need for critical thinking.

One advantage of meta-analysis is that it combines the results of many small studies to yield a much larger sample than is used in any single study. This makes it possible to reveal relationships that cannot be found in small studies. Small effect sizes in small studies may not be statistically significant, but if they are consistent across studies, a meta-analysis can uncover a statistically significant relationship. A very important advantage of meta-analysis is that it makes possible quantitative tests of hypotheses about why different studies yield different results. For example, some of the recent studies of domestic violence suggest the hypothesis that men who batter their wives are more likely to change their behavior after arrest if they have a high "stake in conformity"—that is, if they are married and employed. A meta-analysis of all the studies of police response to domestic violence could test this hypothesis by constructing an index of "stake in conformity" for the offenders in each study and treating it as the independent variable in a hypothesis, with the "effect size" of the effect of arrest on recidivism as the dependent variable. If arrest had the greatest effect in the cities where the men had the highest stake in conformity, the meta-analysis would make a very convincing case that stake in conformity explains the discrepancy among the studies.

A good example of the value of meta-analysis is a 1984 review of 18 experiments on experimenter expectancy effects—specifically, studies that gave schoolteachers expectancies about their pupils' future performance and used IQ measures as the dependent variable. A number of studies had attempted to replicate the groundbreaking work of Rosenthal and Jacobson (1968/1989) on "Pygmalion effects" (discussed in Chapter 3), with inconsistent results. Raudenbush (1984) hypothesized that "the better the teachers know their pupils at the time of expectancy induction, the smaller the treatment effect would be" (p. 85), and the 18 studies in fact showed that pattern. They also showed that effect size was not related to the type of IQ test used or to whether or not the test administrator was blind to details of the research, and that expectancy effects were larger with first and second graders than in grades 3–6. It would have been very difficult to arrive at these findings in any single study or to convincingly support them with only a qualitative, narrative-style review.

Meta-analysis, despite its potential as a research tool, has some important limitations. The most obvious one is that there are not always enough studies to analyze quantitatively, so that meta-analysis is not possible in fields that are in the early stages of research. Sometimes the studies in a field are so different from each other as to be very difficult to compare quantitatively, and meta-analyses are not done. A second limitation is that journals tend not to publish studies that find statistically nonsignificant results (the study by Dunford et al. [1990] is an exception to the rule). As a result, meta-analyses may be biased toward finding significant effects because they review a biased sample of all the studies done.

A third limitation concerns the fact that studies are not equally rigorous. Some question the appropriateness of combining data from different studies that vary widely in their internal validity. Researchers who do meta-analyses address this problem in two main ways: they either exclude studies that fail to meet some stated criterion of rigor (e.g., they may exclude all retrospective studies or all but experiments) or they rate the internal validity of each study and use the rating as a variable in the meta-analysis to test the hypothesis that the better the study, the stronger (or the weaker) the observed effect. The problem with both of these ways of dealing with differences in quality is that researcher bias can enter into the judgments, just as it does in observations of actual behavior—biased judgment may lead the researcher to see what he or she wants to see.

Also, the studies to be analyzed may differ so much in the samples studied or the operational definitions of the key variables that it makes little sense to combine them as if they were all measuring the same things under equivalent conditions. This can be a limitation of meta-analysis, but it can also be an advantage. Researchers deal with this issue in much the same way they handle differences in quality. They may restrict the studies reviewed (e.g., only those using IQ scores as the dependent variable), or they may use the characteristics on which the studies differ as independent variables in the meta-analysis, classifying or rating them and examining whether they are related to effect size. The need for judgments and the problem of researcher bias again arise, but it is possible to address this problem in the ways researchers normally do—for example, by having someone blind to the hypotheses of the meta-analysis make the judgments.

In sum, meta-analysis is a potentially valuable tool for making sense of bodies of social science literature, but the reader must evaluate each meta-analysis critically, as with any other type of research. In evaluating a meta-analysis, it helps to think of it as a correlational study in which each of the studies under review is a single subject, effect size is the dependent variable, and every other aspect of a study (its research method, operational definitions, sample size, and so forth) is an organismic variable that the study carries with it into the meta-analysis. When the meta-analytic researcher classifies studies—for example, by rating each one on its quality—the researcher is providing an operational definition of that organismic variable that may or may not be reliable and valid.

If you have followed and understood what you have read and practiced to this point, you should be ready to try to do what Peter Collings did, with other material. No examples are provided because it is time for you to go out on your own. If you must find research on your own before writing your review, use the Appendix as a reference, and be sure that all the evidence you have is really about the same general question. Be sure the studies you choose deal with the same variables, or closely related ones. If they do, the procedures suggested in this chapter, together with what you know, should guide you to a competent critical review.

This is the payoff from all your work so far. By now, you should be able to draw your own conclusions and be fairly certain of your opinions in an area you care about—even if you must decide that you aren't sure. We hope that you continue to use your skills to evaluate evidence, and that you use them responsibly.

APPENDIX

ASKING ANSWERABLE QUESTIONS AND FINDING SCIENTIFIC EVIDENCE

This Appendix is designed to help you transform an interest of yours into a question that is answerable by appeal to scientific evidence. This is a necessary process before you can evaluate the available facts pertaining to your question.

If you have completed Chapter 2, there should be little new vocabulary to learn here because you will mainly be applying what you have learned as well as practicing some library skills. However, the term *answerable question* should be defined before we go further. According to Doherty and Shemberg, "in order for a question to be answered scientifically, it must be asked so that *repeatable, controlled observations of all significant items* in the question can be made" (1970, p. 6, emphasis added).

The crucial point is that whether a question is answerable by appeal to evidence *depends on how it is asked*. This seems obvious. However, the implication is that whether a question can have a scientific answer does *not* depend on how important it is, or whether you feel you have a good idea of what you want to know; you can get an answer *only* if you frame the question properly. Let's look back at the definition.

"So that repeatable . . . observations can be made." This means that abstractions must be concretized well enough for independent observers to agree on what is what.

"So that . . . controlled observations . . . can be made." Essentially, this means you must be able to rule out alternative explanations for what you observe. It may not always be possible to tell before you ask the question whether fully controlled observations are feasible. We may not have the technology needed to measure what you want to observe, or it may be unethical to control the conditions of observation, or, if you are studying real life events, such as the functioning of governments, control is impossible. The goal of ruling out alternatives is still desirable, no matter how hard it may be to attain control in practice.

"So that . . . observations of all significant items . . . can be made." The "significant items" are *variables*. This means that you must identify the relevant variables, concretize them, and observe them.

Thus, to have an answerable question, you must identify variables and concretize them, so that they may be observed under conditions that rule out possible effects of other events ("extraneous variables"). An example may make this clearer. To use the one given by Doherty and Shemberg (1970), you may begin with a general question:

"Why does one's personality change when under stress?" The significant items here are personality, change, and stress. Personality and stress are variables, and the fact that they change is what makes them variables. Since the variables are unconcretized, the question is unanswerable. "Personality" can be concretized in many ways. If we use, for example, scores on the CPI (California Personality Inventory, a standard personality test), we can now look, concretely, for different scores depending on whether the person is under "stress." "Stress" can also be concretized in many ways (e.g., deprivation of sleep for 96 hours, or incarceration in a concentration camp, or immersion in ice water, etc.). Once the variables are concretized (in any way you choose), the question becomes answerable. You need only to make the necessary observations.

You probably cannot help noticing the difference between measuring the effect of sleep deprivation on CPI scores (for example) and understanding why personality changes with stress. When you concretize the variables, you know only about a certain kind of stress and its effects on those aspects of personality the CPI measures. In short, you have evidence on only part of the original question. Worse yet, even if you find out that changes occur, and even if you know *which* changes occur, you still don't know *why*, which was the question.

(You will usually find that in the process of making questions answerable, "why" questions tend to be transformed into "under what conditions," because, given evidence, independent observers can rarely agree about "why" something happened. It is much easier to agree on what conditions surrounded the event. One way is to get clear evidence of how CPI scores change under conditions of 96 hours' sleep deprivation. If we find that similar changes occur under other conditions, we can conclude that these conditions have something in common, and identifying the common element gets us closer to a satisfying answer to "why?")

Let's try to relate this to your own interests. If your background in your field is limited, you may well not be able to ask a question even as specific as "Why does one's personality change when under stress?" This is a fairly common position for students to be in since many don't yet know their subjects well enough to ask a question that is phrased in variables, let alone concretized ones. Thus, the purposes of this Appendix are:

To assist you in using bibliographic resources to focus your interests
To help you to ask a question in answerable terms
To aid you in finding a bibliography of the evidence relevant to your question.

There is a more or less logical progression that people take in accomplishing these goals:

1. Identify an area you are interested in.
2. Gather general information, noting whether scientific evidence exists.
3. Identify a variable you are interested in, and about which evidence exists.
4. Get information about the variable. What other variables are related to it?
5. If you can, choose a second variable that has been related to the first by some scientific evidence.
6. Make a bibliography of evidence about the relationship of the variables.
7. Assess the amount of evidence available, and redefine the variables so that it is possible to evaluate all evidence within your time limits.

Let us slowly go through these steps, with an example, and comment on some problems you may run into along the way. You may use the following as a guide when you have to assemble a bibliography of scientific evidence on a question that interests you.

STEP 1. IDENTIFY AN AREA YOU ARE INTERESTED IN

You should be able to do this without help. It's all right to start with something very general. For example, we'll start with the topic of "body language," sometimes also called "nonverbal communication."

STEP 2. GATHER GENERAL INFORMATION, NOTING WHETHER SCIENTIFIC EVIDENCE EXISTS

Use as resources textbooks in your area of interest, the library card catalog, and handbooks. We do not advise that you use computerized bibliographic search programs until at least Step 4. Until then, you may not know which terms or keywords to use in your search.

Textbooks

These can be very useful for beginning a search. If you look through several recent ones in your area of interest, you will quickly get an idea of whether there is much research on the question you are interested in. There may be no way to predict (without knowledge of the field) whether there are hundreds of good studies on a topic, or a few, or nothing but a lot of unsupported conjecture. A look at several books will give you a feel for this. Textbooks will also help you identify the key terms used in connection with your topic. Knowing these, you can look them up when you are ready to use sources of more detailed information.

We're interested in "body language." Not being sure, we might seek textbooks on introductory psychology, language, communication, sociology, and social psychology. Look in the index under anything that might be relevant (e.g., body language, nonverbal, language, communication). See how much coverage is given to what you are interested in. Keep in mind that some topics will get coverage in one textbook but not in another, even though both texts are on the same subject. Look in several similar books before you give up. This won't take too long: textbooks on the same subject are usually on the same library shelf.

In our search for material on "body language," let's suppose we don't get much from textbooks (this could easily happen). The linguistics books use a lot of fancy language but don't seem to provide scientific observations, and most of the psychology and sociology books have little coverage. This may be what you would find in a search on this topic; if so, go to another source.

Card Catalog

The library card catalog, or its electronic replacement, is an easy source to consult, and you are probably familiar with it. For most topics it will not be fruitful, because few questions in the social sciences have had whole books written about them. Still, if you *do* find a recent book on your subject, you may save yourself a lot of searching.

The topic of "body language" is one that you will find in the card catalog. (Don't forget to use both title and subject headings.) Some of the books are popularized, and contain mostly unsupported assertions. Others seem more scholarly, and contain a mixture of scientific evidence, casual observation, and speculation. By looking through these books, you find that there seem to be many kinds of body language or nonverbal communication: posture, gestures, tone of voice, eye contact, facial expression, and proxemics (the use of interpersonal space), to name the most prominent ones. You also find that there is a fair amount of scientific evidence that seems to be available about at least some of these. If your topic is "body language," you are ready to go on to the next step. You know that there is enough evidence available to continue.

If you still haven't found out whether there is scientific evidence on your topic, you might look for some useful *handbooks*.

Handbooks

Handbooks are reference works in specialized fields. They often contain reviews of research and theory on particular subjects related to the topic of the handbook (e.g., *Handbook of organizations, Handbook of sociology, Handbook of psychotherapy and behavior change*). Articles are written by experts, and are usually valuable for some years after the publication date. If you can find a relevant article, it will be useful at all steps of the process of preparing your question. The articles may, however, presume more technical knowledge than you have at the beginning of your search. Handbooks may be found either in the reference section or with ordinary books and you may locate them through the card catalog or by asking an instructor or reference librarian.

At this stage, you are mainly interested in finding out whether there is a body of scientific evidence on your topic. If you can find a handbook article that seems to cover your subject, look at the references cited in the article that are in your area of interest. If there are several, and if they seem to involve scientific observation, you are safe to go on to the next step. If you don't think you can understand the article, make a note of it and return to it when you have read a bit more.

STEP 3. IDENTIFY A VARIABLE YOU ARE INTERESTED IN, ABOUT WHICH EVIDENCE EXISTS

This step involves thinking. When you found that "body language" includes posture, gesture, tone of voice, eye contact, and so on, you found a list of variables that might be of interest. You may realize that some of them are more complex than others. For example, there are many ways that facial expressions can differ, but few ways that eye contact can vary (mainly, contact is made or it isn't). At this stage, this difference will not matter much. You can feel free to pursue any of the types of body language you are interested in, as long as you are sure there is scientific evidence about it. Your main task is to narrow your focus from the broad topic (body language) to a variable (say, interpersonal space).

STEP 4. GET INFORMATION ABOUT THE VARIABLE, AND FIND OUT WHAT OTHER VARIABLES ARE RELATED TO IT

Ideally, what you want to find now is a "review article" about your variable. Review articles are articles summarizing what has been written (both theory and factual evidence) on a subject.

Resources for review articles include: textbooks, card catalog, handbooks, and serials. A computerized literature search may also lead you to review articles. Sometimes, the term "review" even appears in the output of the search.

Textbooks

Look back at the useful texts you may have found to see if there is a chapter or a subchapter section on your variable. If there is, make a list of the variables that are supposedly related to it, noting whether this relationship is merely speculative or is based on casual or scientific observation.

Card Catalog

Treat any useful books you may have found in the card catalog as textbooks, and look for sections on your variable. You may also want to look again at the card catalog, under the name of your variable. If it is a variable such as personal space, you may find a book on the subject.

Handbooks

If you found a handbook article covering your topic, look now for a subsection on the variable you are interested in. Get the same information you would get from a book.

Serials

A serial is a periodical, published usually once a year or so (regularly or irregularly), that contains articles of current interest in a particular field. Like handbooks, serials often contain articles reviewing research and theory on specific topics. A particularly useful serial is the *Annual Reviews* series, which is published for psychology, sociology, anthropology, and other disciplines. These contain *only* reviews of recent work in areas in which progress is being made. If you can find a recent review of this type, which covers your variable, much of your work is done. The author will have carefully searched for all the latest published work in the field, and you will have not only a good overview, but a valuable source of bibliography.

If you can find a review article in any of the above sources, or even a discussion of several pages' length about your variable, you can begin to identify other variables related to it. Compile a list of other variables, and note the kind of evidence that seems to link each to the variable you are interested in. If there appears to be scientific evidence, about how much is there?

Judging from the books you find, personal space seems to be related to the individual's personality, to attraction between people, to stress, to whether people are same-sex or opposite-sex, to eye contact, to cultural differences, and to the setting in which the people meet. These relationships are in some cases supported by casual observation, and in other cases, there seem to be scientific studies (one or more) that relate the variable to interpersonal space. Do not attempt to judge whether personal space is, in fact, related to personal attraction for example. All you want to do is note that there is some evidence bearing on the question of whether the variables are related. You can decide whether there is a relationship only after you have evaluated the evidence.

STEP 5. IF YOU CAN, CHOOSE A SECOND VARIABLE THAT HAS BEEN RELATED TO THE FIRST BY SOME SCIENTIFIC EVIDENCE

After you have finished Step 4, you can perform Step 5 from your notes.

It's possible that you can find nothing but unsupported assertions and casual observations about your variable. If this seems to be happening, it's a good time to look for help from an instructor or an advanced student who might have more experience with the area your question deals with. Such a person may be able to direct you to a source that mentions scientific evidence, or may confirm your suspicion that there just *isn't* much scientific evidence in the field. If the latter occurs, you would be wasting your time trying to review the scientific literature on the subject. (This does not mean your interest was not a good one. Many important questions lack evidence because nobody has shown the interest or because no one has figured out how to collect scientific evidence on them that would be relevant.)

You may find that there is scientific evidence relating your variable to each of several other variables. This is what would probably happen in researching interpersonal space. Suppose you have found only one or two scientific studies relating interpersonal space to each of the other variables mentioned. Since two studies are not enough to review, you might try to define a variable yourself; for example, you might relate interpersonal space to *social comfort*. You could assume that both stress and lack of interpersonal attraction make people socially uncomfortable and should have the same effects. In this way, it would make sense to look at studies on stress and personal space together with studies on attraction and personal space. (If both stress and lack of attraction make people stand farther apart, the evidence would support your assumption that there is such a thing as "social comfort" that involves both stress and attraction.) You should understand that inventing a variable of your own is a little risky, but if several of the "other variables" seem to you to form a cluster, you can study them all, as long as you make your assumptions explicit when you review the research. You are in better shape if one of the "second variables" is related to the first variable in several scientific articles. In this case, you do not have to go out on a limb by inventing variables.

For interpersonal space, let's say we have found several scientific studies relating it to interpersonal attraction, and also several relating it to eye contact. We have a choice of which relationship to explore. Before going on to the next step, we should look carefully at the kind of relationship between the two variables. For example, are we conceiving of one as the independent variable and the other as the dependent variable? With personal space and attraction, the relationship might go either way. Attraction may determine the amount of space people keep between each other, or— at least with people meeting for the first time—the space they keep between them may determine attraction. There are at least two different questions concerning the relationship between attraction and personal space, and *evidence relevant to one question may be irrelevant to the other.*

Before you go on, frame a tentative question about the relationship between the two variables you plan to study. Be sure you understand whether you are assuming a causal relationship between the variables and, if so, be clear about the direction of causality. Your choice may be dictated by the practical consideration of available evidence. You may be more interested in how personal space influences attraction, but most of the evidence may be on how attraction influences personal space. If this happens, you may choose to look at the less interesting question, to examine both questions but discuss them separately, or you may decide to select a different variable.

When you have a second variable, and a tentative question relating your variables, go to the next step. Let's decide to ask "How does attraction influence people's use of interpersonal space?"

STEP 6. MAKE A BIBLIOGRAPHY OF EVIDENCE ABOUT THE RELATIONSHIP OF THE VARIABLES

Use as resources review articles in books, handbooks, or serials, recent journals, abstracts, indexes, and computerized searches.

Review Articles in Books, Handbooks, or Serials

If you have found one of these, look through it for the sources it cites relating your two variables. Put these in your bibliography. Also, be alert for review articles on your *second* variable in the same way you looked for articles on the first. An article on interpersonal attraction may include some useful references. What you find in review articles is usually current to within a year or two of the publication date. Check the dates of the references. For newer work, you will have to look elsewhere.

Recent Journals

This might be a good place to begin your search, especially if textbooks or other information suggest that research is currently going on. Journals are the most up-to-date source of evidence you can find, and a *single* recent article will lead you, through its bibliography, to other related research. You also may discover that in tracing the bibliographies of journal articles, you come upon a fairly recent review article, which will give you more bibliography.

If you don't know which recent journals to look at, you might start with current issues of the journals that published the older articles in your bibliography.

Abstracts and Indexes

Indexes are reference works that give author, title, and source for articles of theory and research. They are most useful if you know what terms to look up (look for the names of your variables), or if you know the name(s) of author(s) who have done work in the field. One way to get more recent information is to look up the names of the authors of older articles you have found to see if they are still doing work. The most recent work will probably cite what has been done in the interim.

Abstracts resemble indexes, but also include brief summaries of all works indexed. These are highly useful in making bibliographies because the summaries can save you the effort of tracking down articles that have interesting titles but that turn out, on inspection, to be irrelevant.

Abstracts and indexes usually exist for whole disciplines: *Psychological Abstracts, Social Science and Humanities Index, Crime and Delinquency Abstracts,* and *Sociological Abstracts* are some examples. The larger ones run to thousands of pages annually. It is therefore useful to have a fairly specific idea of what you are looking for so that you are not bogged down in masses of irrelevant material. A good method is to look up the variable that has *fewer* scientific articles on it. Since abstracts and indexes are generally cross-referenced by subject, this will give you the articles that relate your two variables with the least time spent attending to irrelevant articles on only one variable. You will quickly find that there are many more studies done on attraction than on personal space and consequently you will save time by looking up personal space.

Computerized Searches

Many of the key abstracts and indexes are now searchable by computer. The logic of searching remains the same, but the speed increases. It may also be possible to do a much more up-to-date search by computer than by hand. Ask your reference librarian how to search in your field of interest and how up-to-date the entries are. Some computer searches now give you access to titles and abstracts almost as fast as your library gets the actual journal, so that you may not need to look first at recent journals in the library.

Other Resources

There may be *specialized bibliographies* in some area that includes your question. Your instructor may know if there is such a source, and a reference librarian may also be helpful. Specialized bibliographies are coming out all the time, and even professors may not be aware of the newest ones unless they are working in the particular specialized field.

Ask for help. This is a good general rule if you are having trouble finding material. Instructors, librarians, and sometimes advanced students may be able to suggest a source that you can use.

The following are some general notes on preparing a bibliography:

1. It will save time to begin by looking for very recent work in the field. The bibliography of a recent study will cite older sources, but the reverse never occurs. In using abstracts, indexes, serials, and recent journals, always begin with the most recent and work backwards.

2. Your bibliographic sources usually give you only the title of an article or source. You should try to determine whether the article is a report of scientific evidence, a review article, a theoretical article, or a statement of opinion. Without prior experience, it will often be impossible to do this from the title alone. But reviews often leave the word "review" in the title, and titles that include mention of your variables by name and are very specific and technical-sounding are generally articles containing scientific evidence. Very general titles for very short articles (e.g., a five-page article called "personal space") will usually contain speculation or an oversimplified review of the literature, often without bibliography. In your notes, keep the reports of scientific evidence separate from review and theoretical articles.

3. If you are working with a deadline, check to see if the articles you need are available in your library. When you are working in a carefully defined research area, you may find some references that cannot be instantly located. Ask about inter-library loan services in your library, and request material early so you will have it when you are ready to read it.

4. In gathering your bibliography, make a note of all the standard information (title and author, place of publication, date, and volume number and pages, if applicable). It is usually helpful to also make a note summarizing the nature of the reference, if the title does not make it obvious. This can save you many trips back to a journal because you couldn't remember exactly what an article was about.

STEP 7. ASSESS THE AMOUNT OF EVIDENCE AVAILABLE, AND REDEFINE THE VARIABLES SO THAT IT IS POSSIBLE TO EVALUATE ALL THE EVIDENCE WITHIN YOUR TIME LIMITS

After doing Step 6, you can do this step by careful thinking.

To know how much evidence is available, you must first have some idea whether you have found it all. The easiest way to determine this is to look at the references listed in each new source you find. When all the interesting references you find are already in your own bibliography, you can get ready to stop. If other people working in the same subject area can't find more references than you can, you have probably found almost all of them.

At this point, you have a practical decision to make. You want to do a complete job yet you don't have unlimited time to do it. The skills involved in reviewing and evaluating a body of scientific literature are difficult and take quite a bit of practice. Assuming that you haven't done this sort of review before, and assuming that you have not read many scientific papers before, you can count on a lot of rereading and a good investment of time for each article you try to review carefully. For a typical term paper, a careful review of, say, five to ten scientific articles should be quite a bit. (You may decide that you can handle more, but don't commit yourself to doing so until you have tried writing a review, as in Chapter 5.)

With your bibliography fairly well complete, you should have an idea if the number of scientifically acceptable sources is only a few, or a few dozen, or a few hundred. If your bibliography is about the size you want, after you have completed a fairly exhaustive search for the evidence, you are lucky, and are ready to go ahead. If not, one of two things has happened:

(a) You *do not have enough references* to satisfy your needs. The following are some possible solutions:

Seek help. There may be sources of evidence you haven't found yet.

Redefine one of your variables to make it broader (including stress and attraction in a common category of "social comfort" is an example of this strategy).

Loosen the criteria of evidence to include some casual observations. This is a risky option, since you are including poor evidence that may lead to weakly supported conclusions, or otherwise cause confusion. Casual observations are hard to interpret, and are especially open to bias. It is best to avoid casual observations entirely, unless you feel that the question is of such importance that it must be discussed even in the absence of a good body of acceptable evidence or that a particular piece of casual observation reveals something that is missing in the scientific studies. If you decide to include casual observations in your review, justify this decision early in the paper, and carefully note the limitations of the evidence.

Eliminate one of your variables, and switch to another one (that is, go back to Step 5).

Give up the whole thing (go back to Step 3 or Step 1). Of course, this is not recommended if you are genuinely interested in your question. It *is* done, unfortunately, by students who are mainly concerned with getting a paper in on time.

(b) You have *too many references* to do an adequate job on them all. Here are some possible solutions:

Redefine one of your variables to make it narrower. We might narrow "personal space" by considering only studies measuring the face-to-face distance between people, and ignoring studies of how close they sit on benches or how much they touch each other.

Narrow the range of evidence you will consider while keeping the same variables. For example, you might choose to consider only evidence about use of personal space by children or same-sex pairs of people.

Restrict yourself to certain research methods. You might, for example, consider only research based on observation of the actual behavior of people, and reject studies measuring personal space by the placement of cardboard models or other symbols of people. With some questions, you might choose to evaluate only experimental evidence, and not to consider correlational studies.

The general rule is to narrow your topic in some way that makes conceptual sense and keeps the focus on what you think is most interesting or important. It is always good to make your decisions to narrow explicit at the start of your written review. This shows your reader that you have done your homework, and that your choice of a subject and of which research to discuss was rational, rather than arbitrary. It is much better to do a complete job of reviewing carefully selected research than to do a superficial review of a large number of loosely related studies.

SUMMARY

When you have completed these steps, you may have arrived at a question that seems far removed from your original interest in the topic. "Body language," for example, is very much different from (and broader than) the results of a set of studies of the effect of the distance between two people talking to each other or the degree of interpersonal attraction between them. Usually, the question that you ask as a result of going through these steps is much narrower than your original interest. The transformation of the question often indicates progress in your thinking: you have refined your original topic to squeeze out the ambiguity and confusion that might have been in your original idea and made it possible to get a definitive answer. It may also reflect the fact that research on the topic has shown it to be much more complex and varied than you originally thought—so much so that you can only hope to understand a small piece of the topic in the time you have available.

But the transformation of your topic may also mean some less satisfying things. It may be that the aspects of the topic that interest you most have simply not been studied. Researchers in the field may not have shared your particular interests, or the relevant academic disciplines may have focused on different questions, or research funds may not have been available to study the part of the issue that interests you most. Sometimes these events are not accidental. Gaps in science sometimes result from widely shared intellectual prejudices or other biases in the society. For example, there was relatively little research interest in gender differences before the 1970s; the women's movement changed that by raising a number of research questions that had previously been ignored. If, in transforming your area of interest into a research question that can be addressed by a body of published scientific research, you are left with the unsatisfied feeling that the scientific community has somehow bypassed an important research issue, take that possibility seriously. What is left out of a body of scientific knowledge can be as important as what is included. Of course, you cannot review the scientific studies that have not been done, but you can raise questions about the ones that have. What is missing from the research literature may direct your thinking toward a source of alternative explanations for the research that has been done, or give you reasons to question how far the findings generalize beyond the settings in which they were collected.

After you have defined your question and compiled your bibliography, there remains one objective of this Appendix: to ask a question in answerable terms. We have said that an answerable question is one asked in terms of variables, in such a way that reliable observations of the variables can be made. If you were gathering your own data, you would be responsible for concretizing the variables. To review research, you need only be sure that different studies are in fact dealing with the same variable. (This sounds easy enough, but as you begin to read research, you will see that a major reason why similar studies get different results is that they do not concretize the same variable in the same way. In effect, they are studying different variables without knowing it beforehand.)

If your question is asked in terms of variables that can be concretized, you will have an answerable question for the purpose of reviewing the literature. You could try to concretize your variables as an exercise, but you may find that no published research has concretized them in the way you would choose.

No formal exercises or problems are offered to test your ability to reach the objectives of this Appendix. The obvious exercise is to pursue an interest of yours as far as you can in the direction of preparing a complete bibliography on a carefully asked question. You can evaluate your success by your ability to proceed through the steps. If you aren't sure whether you are proceeding in the most efficient way, or if you would like comments on what you have done, you can have your work (reformulated questions, bibliography, etc.) evaluated by an instructor or other well-informed person. If you are not making good progress, don't get discouraged; it takes experience to know where to look for material. Ask someone with the experience—this is one purpose of a teacher.

REFERENCES

Abbey, A. (1987). Misperceptions of friendly behavior as sexual interest: A survey of naturally occurring incidents. *Psychology of Women Quarterly, 11,* 173–194.

Achen, C. H. (1986). *The statistical analysis of quasi-experiments.* Berkeley, CA: University of California Press.

Adair, J. G. (1984). The Hawthorne effect. A reconsideration of the methodological artifact. *Journal of Applied Psychology, 69,* 334–345.

Adair, J. G., Sharpe, D., & Huynh, C. (1989). Hawthorne control procedures in educational experiments: A reconsideration of their use and effectiveness. *Review of Educational Research, 59,* 215–228.

Agnew, N., & Pyke, S. (1969). *The science game.* Englewood Cliffs, N.J.: Prentice-Hall.

Altman, I., Taylor, D. A., and Wheeler, L. (1971). Ecological aspects of group behavior in social isolation. *Journal of Applied Social Psychology, 1,* 76–100.

American Psychological Association. (1983). *Publication manual of the American Psychological Association.* (3rd ed.) Washington, D.C.

American Psychological Association, Committee for the Protection of Human Participants in Research. (1982). *Ethical principles in the conduct of research with human participants.* Washington, D.C.

Anderson, C. A., & Anderson, D. C. (1984). Ambient temperature and violent crime: Tests of the linear and curvilinear hypotheses. *Journal of Personality and Social Psychology, 46,* 91–97.

Antunes, G., & Gaitz, M. (1975). Ethnicity and participation: A study of Mexican-Americans, blacks, and whites. *American Journal of Sociology, 80,* 1192–1211.

Bardwick, J. (1973). Psychological factors in the acceptance and use of oral contraceptives. In J. T. Fawcett (Ed.), *Psychological perspectives on population.* New York: Basic Books.

Baron, L., & Straus, M. A. (1988). Cultural and economic sources of homicide in the United States. *The Sociological Quarterly, 29,* 371–390.

Baum, A., & Valins, S. (1977). *Architecture and social behavior: Psychological studies of social density.* Hillsdale, N.J.: Lawrence Erlbaum Associates.

Beckham, B. (Ed.). (1984). *The black students' guide to colleges.* (2nd ed.) Providence, RI: Beckham House Publishers.

Bell, J. E. (1974). *Critical evaluation in psychology.* Columbia, Md.: Howard Community College.

Berk, R. A., Campbell, A., Klap, R., & Western, B. (1992). The deterrent effect of arrest in incidents of domestic violence: A Bayesian analysis of four field experiments. *American Sociological Review, 57,* 698–708.

Brady, J. V. (1958). Ulcers in executive monkeys. *Scientific American, 199*(3), 95–104.

Braginsky, B., and Braginsky, D. (1967). Schizophrenic patients in the psychiatric interview: An experimental study of their effectiveness at manipulation. *Journal of Consulting Psychology, 21,* 543–547.

Cameron, J., Livson, N., & Bayley, N. (1967). Infant vocalizations and their relationship to mature intelligence. *Science, 157,* 331–333.

Campbell, D. T., & Stanley, J. C. (1963). *Experimental and quasi-experimental designs for research.* Chicago: Rand-McNally.

Chambliss, W. (1975). On the paucity of original research on organized crime. *American Sociologist, 10,* 36–39.

Code, L. (1991). *What can she know? Feminist theory and the construction of knowledge.* Ithaca, NY: Cornell University Press.

Cook, T. D., & Campbell, D. T. (1979). *Quasi-experimentation.* Chicago: Rand McNally.

Cook, T. D., Cooper, H., Cordray, D., Hartmann, H., Hedges, L., Light, R., Louis, T., & Mosteller, F. (Eds.) (1992). *Meta-analysis for explanation: A casebook.* New York: Russell Sage Foundation.

Cox, D. E., & Supprelle, C. N. (1971). Coercion in participation as a research subject. *American Psychologist, 26,* 726–728.

Dalmiya, V., & Alcoff, L. (1993). Are "old wives' tales" justified? In L. Alcoff & E. Potter (Eds.), *Feminist epistemologies* (pp. 217–244). New York: Routledge.

Den Hollander, A. J. N. (1967). Social description: Problems of reliability and validity. In D. G. Jongmans & P. C. W. Gutkind (Eds.), *Anthropologists in the field.* Assen, Netherlands: Van Gorcum.

Dietz, T., Kalof, L., & Frey, R. S. (1991). On the utility of robust and resampling procedures. *Rural Sociology, 56,* 461–474.

Doherty, M. E., & Shemberg, K. M. (1970). *Asking questions about behavior.* Glenview, Ill.: Scott, Foresman.

Doob, A. N., & Gross, A. E. (1968). Status of frustrator as an inhibitor of horn-honking responses. *Journal of Social Psychology, 76,* 213–218.

Duncan, S., Rosenberg, M. J., & Finkelstein, J. (1969). The paralanguage of experimenter bias. *Sociometry, 32,* 207–219.

Duncan, S., & Rosenthal, R. (1968). Vocal emphasis in experimenters' instruction reading as unintended determinant of subjects' responses. *Language and Speech, 11,* 20–26.

Dunford, F. W., Huizinga, D., & Elliott, D. S. (1990). The role of arrest in domestic assault: The Omaha police experiment. *Criminology, 28,* 183–206.

Eder, D., & Parker, S. (1987). The cultural production and reproduction of gender: The effect of extracurricular activities on peer-group culture. *Sociology of Education, 60,* 200–213.

Ehrenreich, B., & English, D. (1973). *Witches, midwives, and nurses: A history of women healers.* Old Westbury, NY: The Feminist Press.

Epstein, Y. M., & Baum, A. (1978). Crowding: Methods of study. In A. Baum & Y. M. Epstein (Eds.), *Human response to crowding.* Hillsdale, N.J.: Lawrence Erlbaum Associates.

Fanon, F. (1966). *The wretched of the earth.* New York: Grove Press.

Festinger, L., Riecken, H., & Schachter, S. (1956). *When prophecy fails.* Minneapolis: University of Minnesota Press.

Freedman, J. L. (1973). The effects of population density on humans. In J. T. Fawcett (Ed.), *Psychological perspectives on population.* New York: Basic Books.

Freedman, J. L. (1975). *Crowding and behavior.* San Francisco: Freeman.

Freedman, J. L., Levy, A., Buchanan, R. W., & Price, J. (1972). Crowding and human aggressiveness. *Journal of Experimental Social Psychology, 8,* 528–548.

Friedman, H. (1972). *Introduction to statistics.* New York: Random House.

Gaertner, S., & Bickman, L. (1972). A non-reactive indicator of racial discrimination: The wrong number technique. In L. Bickman & T. Henchy (Eds.), *Beyond the laboratory: Field research in social psychology.* New York: McGraw-Hill.

Gamsky, N. (1970). Team teaching, student achievement, and attitudes. *Journal of Experimental Education, 39*(1), 42–45.

Geller, E. S., Wylie, R. C., and Farris, J. C. An attempt at applying prompting and reinforcement toward pollution control. (1971). *Proceedings of the 79th Annual Convention of the American Psychological Association, 6,* 701–702.

Glaser, D. (1964). *The effectiveness of a prison and parole system.* Indianapolis: Bobbs-Merrill.

Glock, C. Y., Ringer, B. B., & Babbie, E. R. (1967). *To comfort and to challenge.* Berkeley: University of California Press.

Goffman, E. (1959). *The presentation of self in everyday life.* New York: Doubleday.

Goodman, N., & Ofshe, R. (1968). Empathy, communication efficiency, and marital status. *Journal of Marriage and the Family, 30,* 597–603.

Gottman, J. M., McFall, R. M., & Barnett, J. T. (1969). Design and analysis of research using time series. *Psychological Bulletin, 72,* 299–306.

Guagnano, G., Stern, P. C., & Dietz, T. (1995). Influences on attitude-behavior relationships: A natural experiment with curbside recycling. *Environment and Behavior, 27,* 699–718.

Hammersley, M., & Atkinson, P. (1983). *Ethnography: Principles in practice.* London: Routledge.

Hansen, E. C. (1977). *Rural Catalonia under the Franco regime.* London: Cambridge University Press.

Harries, K. D., & Stadler, S. J. (1983). Determinism revisited: Assault and heat stress in Dallas, 1980. *Environment and Behavior, 15,* 235–256.

Hays, W. L. (1963). *Statistics for psychologists.* New York: Holt, Rinehart, and Winston.

Heise, D. R. (1969). Problems in path analysis and causal inference. In E. F. Borgatta & G. W. Bohrnstedt (Eds.), *Sociological methodology.* San Francisco: Jossey-Bass.

Hirschel, J. D., & Hutchison, I. W. (1992). Female spouse abuse and the police response: The Charlotte, North Carolina experiment. *Journal of Criminal Law & Criminology, 83,* 73–119.

Holdaway, S. (1982). An inside job: A case study of covert research on the police. In M. Bulmer (Ed.), *Social research ethics: An examination of the merits of covert participant observation.* London: Macmillan.

Janis, I. L., & Mann, L. (1965). Effectiveness of emotional role-playing in modifying smoking habits and attitudes. *Journal of Experimental Research in Personality, 1,* 84–90.

Johnson, D. W. (Ed.) (1973). *Contemporary social psychology.* Philadelphia: Lippincott.

Jones, S. R. (1992). Was there a Hawthorne effect? *American Journal of Sociology, 98,* 451–468.

Jourard, S. (1971). *Self-disclosure: Experimental investigations of the transparent self.* New York: Van Nostrand Reinhold.

Kerlinger, F. N. *Foundations of behavioral research.* (2nd ed.) New York: Holt, Rinehart, and Winston, 1973.

Koss, M. (1985). The hidden rape victim: Personality, attitudinal, and situational characteristics. *Psychology of Women Quarterly, 9,* 193–212.

Kratochwill, T. R., & Levin, J. R. (Eds.) (1992). *Single-case research design and analysis: New directions for psychology and education.* Hillsdale, NJ: Lawrence Erlbaum Associates.

Kytle, R. (1969). *Clear thinking for composition.* New York: Random House.

Land, K. C. (1969). Principles of path analysis. In E. F. Borgatta & G. W. Bohrnstedt (Eds.), *Sociological methodology.* San Francisco: Jossey-Bass.

Langan, P. A., & Innes, C. A. (1986). *Preventing domestic violence against women.* Washington, D.C.: U.S. Bureau of Justice Statistics.

Lawick-Goodall, J. van. (1971). *In the shadow of man.* Boston: Houghton-Mifflin.

Lieberman, L. R. (1973). Untitled letter, *Science, 180,* 369.

Light, R. J., & Pillemer, D. B. (1984). *Summing up: The science of reviewing research.* Cambridge, MA: Harvard University Press.

Lofland, J., & Lofland, L. H. (1984). *Analyzing social settings: A guide to qualitative observation and analysis.* (2nd ed.) Belmont, CA: Wadsworth Publishing Company.

Lorenz, K. (1966). *On aggression.* New York: Harcourt Brace Jovanovich.

Malamuth, N. M., & Check, J. V. P. (1981). The effects of mass media exposure on acceptance of violence against women: A field experiment. *Journal of Research in Personality, 15,* 436–446.

McAfee, J. K. (1987). Classroom density and the aggressive behavior of handicapped children. *Education and Treatment of Children, 10,* 134–145.

McCroskey, J. C., Larson, C. E., & Knapp, M. L. (1971). *Introduction to interpersonal communication.* Englewood Cliffs, N.J.: Prentice-Hall.

Mitchell, R. E. (1971). Some social implications of high-density housing. *American Sociological Review, 36,* 18–29.

Muehlenhard, C. L. (1988). Misinterpreted dating behaviors and the risk of date rape. *Journal of Social and Clinical Psychology, 6,* 20–37.

National Advisory Commission on Civil Disorders. (1968). *Report of the National Advisory Commission on Civil Disorders.* New York: Bantam Books.

Orne, M. T. (1962). On the social psychology of the psychological experiment: With particular reference to demand characteristics and their implications. *American Psychologist, 17,* 776–783.

Pate, A. M., & Hamilton, E. E. (1992). Formal and informal deterrents to domestic violence: The Dade County spouse assault experiment. *American Sociological Review, 57,* 691–697.

Rabin, A. I. (1965). Motivation for parenthood. *Journal of Projective Techniques and Personality Assessment, 29,* 405–411.

Ransford, H. E. (1968). Isolation, powerlessness, and violence: A study of attitudes and participation in the Watts riot. *American Journal of Sociology, 73,* 581–591.

Raudenbush, S. W. (1984). Magnitude of teacher expectancy effects on pupil IQ as a function of the credibility of expectancy induction: A synthesis of findings from 18 experiments. *Journal of Educational Psychology, 76,* 85–97.

Roethlisberger, F. J., & Dickson, W. J. (1939). *Management and the worker.* Cambridge, Mass.: Harvard University Press.

Rogers, Carl R. (1970). *Carl Rogers on encounter groups.* New York: Harper and Row.

Rose, S., & Frieze, I. H. (1989). Young singles' scripts for a first date. *Gender & Society, 3,* 258–268.

Rosenberg, M. J. (1965). When dissonance fails: On eliminating evaluation apprehension from attitude measurement. *Journal of Personality and Social Psychology, 1,* 18–42.

Rosenberg, M. J. (1969). The conditions and consequences of evaluation apprehension. In R. Rosenthal & R. L. Rosnow (Eds.), *Artifact in behavioral research.* New York: Academic Press.

Rosenhan, D. L. (1973). On being sane in insane places. *Science, 179,* 250–258.

Rosenthal, R. (1966). *Experimenter effects in behavioral research.* New York: Appleton-Century-Crofts.

Rosenthal, R. (1984). *Meta-analytical procedures for social research.* Beverly Hills, CA: Sage.

Rosenthal, R., & Jacobson, L. (1968/1989). *Pygmalion in the classroom: Teacher expecta-*

tions and pupils' intellectual development. (Enlarged ed.) New York: Irvington Publications.

Schachter, S. (1959). *The psychology of affiliation.* Stanford: Stanford University Press.

Schaefer, V. H. (1976). Teaching the concept of interaction and sensitizing students to its implications. *Teaching of Psychology, 3,* 103–114.

Schein, E. H. (1960). Interpersonal communication, group solidarity, and social influence. *Sociometry, 23,* 148–161.

Schmidt, F. L. (1992). What do data really mean? Research findings, meta-analysis, and cumulative knowledge in psychology. *American Psychologist, 47,* 1173–1181.

Scott, J. P. (1945). Social behavior, organization, and leadership in a small flock of domestic sheep. *Comparative Psychology Monographs, 18* (Whole No. 4).

Seyfrit, C. L., & Martin, J. P. (1985). Status and social distance in the faculty office: A replication. *West Georgia College Review, 17,* 21–27.

Sherman, L. W. (1992). *Policing domestic violence: Experiments and dilemmas.* New York: The Free Press.

Sherman, L. W., & Berk, R. A. (1984). The specific deterrent effects of arrest for domestic assault. *American Sociological Review, 49,* 261–272.

Sherman, L. W., & Smith, D. A. (1992). Crime, punishment, and stake in conformity: Legal and informal control of domestic violence. *American Sociological Review, 57,* 680–690.

Shoham, S. G., Rahav, G., Markowski, R., Chard, F., Neuman, F., Ben-Haim, M., Baruch, L., Esformes, Y., Schwarzman, Z., Rubin, R., Mednick, S., & Buickhuisen, W. (1987). Family parameters of violent prisoners. *The Journal of Social Psychology, 127,* 83–91.

Small Families are smarter, IQ boom ahead, Zajonc birth order study predicts. *Intercom,* June, 1976, pp. 2–3.

Stack, S. & Gundlach, J. (1992). The effect of country music on suicide. *Social Forces, 71,* 211–218.

Steinman, M. (1991). Coordinated criminal justice interventions and recidivism among batterers. In M. Steinman (Ed.), *Woman battering: Policy responses* (pp. 221–236). Cincinnati, Ohio: Anderson Publishing.

Stern, P. C., Dietz, T., & Kalof, L. (1993). Value orientations, gender, and environmental concern. *Environment and Behavior, 25,* 322–348.

Stern, S. (1994). *Social science from below: Grassroots knowledge for science and emancipation.* Unpublished dissertation, Department of Sociology, City University of New York Graduate Center.

St. Lawrence, J. S., & Joyner, D. J. (1991). The effects of sexually violent rock music on males' acceptance of violence against women. *Psychology of Women Quarterly, 15,* 49–63.

Strodtbeck, F. L., & Hook, L. H. (1961). The social dimensions of a twelve man jury table. *Sociometry, 24,* 307–415.

Taylor, D. A., Wheeler, L. and Altman, I. (1968). Stress relations in socially isolated groups. *Journal of Personality and Social Psychology, 9,* 369–376.

Tryon, R. C. (1940). Genetic differences in maze learning in rats. In *National Society for the Study of Education, the thirty-ninth yearbook.* Bloomington, Ill.: Public School Publishing.

Wachter, K. W., & Straf, M. L. (Eds.) (1990). *The future of meta-analysis.* New York: Russell Sage Foundation.

Watson, G., & Johnson, D. W. (1972). *Social psychology: Issues and insights.* (2nd ed.) Philadelphia: Lippincott.

Webb, E. J., Campbell, D. T., Schwartz, R., & Sechrest, L. (1966). *Unobtrusive measures: Nonreactive research in the social sciences.* Chicago: Rand McNally.

Winer, B. J. (1962). *Statistical principles in experimental design.* New York: McGraw-Hill.

Wolfenstein, M. (1951). Fun morality: An analysis of recent American child-training literature. *Journal of Social Issues, 7*(4), 15–25.

Wrightsman, L. S. (1969). Wallace supporters and adherence to "law and order." *Journal of
Personality and Social Psychology, 13,* 17–22.

Zimbardo, P. G., Haney, C., Banks, W. C., & Jaffe, D. (1974). The psychology of imprison-
ment: Privation, power, and pathology. In Z Rubin (Ed.), *Doing unto others.* Englewood
Cliffs, NJ: Prentice-Hall.

Zucker, R., Manosevitz, M., & Lanyon, R. (1968). Birth order, anxiety, and affiliation during
a crisis. *Journal of Personality and Social Psychology, 8,* 354–359.

Index

Page references in *italics* indicate definitions of indexed terms.